The Limits of Freedom of Contract

MICHAEL J. TREBILCOCK

The Limits of Freedom of Contract

HARVARD UNIVERSITY PRESS
Cambridge, Massachusetts, and London, England 1993

Library of Congress Cataloging-in-Publication Data

Trebilcock, M. J.
  The limits of freedom of contract / Michael J. Trebilcock.
      p.   cm.
  Includes index.
  ISBN 0-674-53429-8 (acid-free paper)
  1. Contracts. 2. Contracts—Economic aspects. I. Title.
K840. T74 1993
346'.02—dc20
[342.62]   93-18706
CIP

Preface

I am a law and economics scholar by trade. Over the course of an academic career spanning thirty years, I have focussed most of my energies on what might loosely be called commercial law: contract law, commercial transactions, debtor-creditor law, corporate law, international trade law, anti-trust law, and government regulation. At the heart of all these subject areas lies a central legal institution—the law of contracts. Behind the law of contracts lies a much broader set of economic, social, and political values that define the role of markets in our lives. In writing this book, I have been motivated by several considerations: a concern that much law and economic scholarship is far too unself-critical in assuming that particular normative values are or ought to be vindicated by the law of contracts and the underlying economic institution of private markets; a sense that the law of contracts often continues to be presented to law students as a body of largely technical, desiccated legal doctrines, without due acknowledgement of the centrality of both the law of contracts and the institution of markets in our lives and the momentous value choices and conflicts that underlie both these institutions; a sense that as the countries of Eastern Europe and the former Soviet Union and an increasing number of developing countries commit themselves to capitalist institutions in their economies, and democratic institutions in their collective governance, these value choices and conflicts need to be thought about much more self-consciously, both in these countries and in ours; and a sense that the complacency, and often exhilaration, that the collapse of communism has engendered in many in the Western world—that the end of history has arrived and economic and political liberalism have triumphed—are, in large part, unwarranted. I hope that this book will contribute, in some small measure, to a more imaginative and self-critical examination of the role of the law of contracts in a market economy.

. . .

In writing this book, I have incurred a number of substantial debts of gratitude. Two research assistants, Rosemin Keshvani and Lisa Freeman, played major roles in researching a number of topics in the book and assumed a special responsibility for educating me about the insights of feminist theory as it bears on some of these topics. A number of colleagues and friends have been enormously generous with their time in commenting on and criticizing drafts of various chapters: David Beatty, Maureen Brunt, Frank Buckley, Bruce Chapman, Richard Craswell, Ron Daniels, Tony Duggan, Fran Hanks, Robert Howse, Jason Johnston, John Keeler, Brian Langille, Timothy Muris, Iain Ramsay, Sam Rea, George Triantis, Catherine Valcke, Stephen Waddams, Wanda Wiegers, Alan Wertheimer, Philip Williams, and Toni Williams. My debt to Richard Craswell for searching comments on the entire manuscript is especially great. I am also grateful to participants who provided comments and criticisms at workshops or seminars where I presented early drafts of many of the chapters: the University of Toronto Law School, the University of Western Ontario Department of Economics, McGill Law School, the University of Alberta Law School, the University of Manitoba Law School, the University of California Law School, the University of Chicago Law School, Georgetown Law Center, Harvard Law School, Rutgers Law School, the American Association of Law Schools Annual Conference (January 1992), Northwestern Law School, the University of Adelaide Law School, the University of Melbourne Law School, and the University of Hong Kong Law School. I would like especially to thank my students at the University of Toronto, where I have presented much of the material that follows in upper year seminars over the past several years, and where they have subjected the arguments to persistent and perceptive scrutiny, enlightening me on various topics through the essays they have written in these courses. I would also like to thank my friends who have participated in informal Friday night seminars at the Idler Pub, where many of the issues canvassed in this book have been debated with great vigour and conviviality, and periodic clarity. Debra Forman, the International Business and Trade Law librarian at the University of Toronto, has been wonderfully helpful in tracking down unlikely bibliographic sources for me. Barbara Hendrickson meticulously checked and reformatted all notes. Michael Aronson and Christine Thorsteinsson of Harvard University Press shepherded the book with great competence through the publication process.

I owe a special debt of gratitude to my secretary, Margot Hall, who typed and retyped numerous drafts of the manuscript with great skill and cheerfulness and persistently and vigorously challenged me on many points of the analysis. I, of course, remain wholly responsible for whatever shortcomings the book still exhibits, despite the best efforts of all of the above to rescue me from the shoals of egregious error.

• • •

I wish to acknowledge permission to reproduce the following material: Figures 1, 2, 4, and 5 from my essay "Economic Analysis of Law," in Richard Devlin, ed., *Canadian Perspectives on Legal Theory* (Toronto: Edmond Montgomery Publications, 1991), and portions of the text therefrom that appear in Chapter 1; Figure 3 from R. D. Luce and Howard Raiffa, *Games and Decisions* (New York: Dover Publications, 1957); Figure 6 from George Triantis, "Contractual Allocations of Unknown Risks: A Critique of the Doctrine of Commercial Impracticability," 42 *University of Toronto Law Journal* 450 (1992), p. 465; Figure 7 from Jagdish Bhagwati, *Protectionism* (Cambridge, Mass.: MIT Press, 1989), p. 46; Table 1, adapted from Joel Feinberg, *Harm to Self* (New York: Oxford University Press, 1986), p. 115; and portions of the text in Chapter 2 from M. J. Trebilcock and Rosemin Keshvani, "The Role of Private Ordering in Family Law," 41 *University of Toronto Law Journal* 553 (1991).

Contents

CHAPTER ONE

The Private Ordering Paradigm and Its Critics

Modes of Economic Organization

The "End of History"[1] has recently been proclaimed. With the transformation of Eastern Europe and the Soviet Union and the subsequent dismantling of centrally planned economies, Fukuyama has claimed "an unabashed victory of [classical] economic and political liberalism," which he considers to herald the end of history in the sense that the decisive struggle between collectivist and liberal rights and market systems is now over, at least at the level of ideas or ideologies. Fukuyama has a somewhat mixed reaction to this prospect, foreshadowing a blandness, homogeneity, and materialism in lifestyles and values that he associates with the absence of fundamental debate about alternative political and economic paradigms. In many respects, this book challenges this sombre conclusion. Even if Fukuyama's prediction proves true, and even if a society commits itself, at a general level, to economic liberalism and a market economy, many troubling and potentially divisive normative issues remain. This book addresses a number of these issues.

Heilbroner, in *The Making of Economic Society*,[2] argues that beyond conditions of basic subsistence or survival, a fundamental economic challenge confronting every society is to devise social institutions that will mobilize human energy for productive purposes. He identifies three basic modes of social organization: tradition, command, and market. In the case of communities or societies whose productive activities are organized around tradition, conventions become imbedded that assign to individuals particular tasks or activities, thus solving the production problem, while other conventions govern the distribution of productive output. Such societies tend to place a high premium on very stable social and economic relationships, although at the expense of large-scale, rapid social and economic change and growth. Moreover, the importance of status in such societies often consigns certain members of the society to subordinate or oppressed roles, women being one example. Communities or societies which organize their productive activities on the basis of a command system may avoid the problems of resistance to change or innovation associated with traditional societies. However, the economic commander-in-chief, whether a despot or a democratically elected government, faces immense information problems in determining what should be produced by whom and what should be consumed by whom; and then immense coordination problems of inducing the desired production and consumption once these decisions have been made, the effectuation of which typically depends on various forms of direct or indirect coercion, rather than social conventions or individual incentives.[3] In the case of a market economy, production and consumption decisions are decentralized and depend on the myriad decisions of individual producers and consumers, acting in furtherance of individual preferences and incentives, thus minimizing the role played by social conventions or status in traditional societies and centralized information gathering and processing and coercion in command economies. Market economies also possess the potential for dramatic shifts in consumption and production in response to shifts in preferences, changes in costs or technology, or major innovations, which at the same time have a far-reaching capacity to destabilize personal, social, and community relationships and networks, of which traditional societies are more protective.[4] A market system cannot generally guarantee that any given level of needs or wants of every member of the community will be met. Indeed, market economies depend on significant degrees of inequality to give effective reign to individual incentives, upon which their efficient functioning is critically dependent, and thus may generate higher degrees of inequality than traditional or command economies.[5] In the transition we are currently witnessing from command economies to market economies, the need to inculcate a culture of emulation and ambition, rather than the prevailing culture of envy and distrust, has emerged as a major challenge.[6] Of course, all societies invoke some combination of all three modes of social organization, though the degree of emphasis on each has varied dramatically from one society to another throughout history and, indeed, in the contemporary world. In this book, I assume a society which, in terms of relative emphasis, has opted for a market economy.

The Private Ordering Paradigm

The Economic Perspective

The central preoccupation of economics is the question of choice under conditions of scarcity. Given scarcity, economics assumes that individuals and communities will (or should) attempt to maximize their desired ends (which may be of infinite variety) by doing the best they can with the limited resources (means) at their disposal. To the extent that means (or resources) can be made relatively less scarce, or stretched further, more ends or goals of individuals or communities can be realized. Obviously the legal system, in important ways, structures the choices available to individuals and groups in a broad range of settings. In analyzing issues of choice under conditions of scarcity and subject to other constraints, including those imposed by the legal system, neo-classical economics employs two conceptually different kinds of analysis.[7] The first is conventionally referred to as positive analysis, meaning descriptive or predictive analysis. The second is normative analysis, meaning prescriptive or judgmental analysis. The first kind of analysis tends to be much less controversial than the second.

POSITIVE ECONOMICS

An analyst adopting a positive economic perspective tends to ask the following kind of question: If this (legal) policy is adopted, what predictions can we make as to the probable economic impacts, allocative (the pattern of economic activities) and distributive (winners and losers), of the policy, given the ways in which people are likely to respond to the particular incentives or disincentives created by the policy? In predicting these behavioural responses, the positive analyst will assume that most individuals are motivated by rational self-interest, in the sense of maximizing their individual utilities, subject to whatever constraints are imposed on the choices open to them. Utility functions may be infinitely varied. Mother Teresa may be motivated out of pure altruism to buy rice on the best possible terms from rice dealers to feed starving children in the streets of Calcutta. Another person may be motivated out of a desire to sustain a decadent lifestyle to buy narcotics for dealing to drug addicts, causing enormous human suffering as a result. In conventional supply and demand analysis, it is assumed that in most contexts more goods or services will be supplied at higher than lower prices and that fewer goods or services will be demanded at higher prices than lower prices—supply curves slope up to the right, demand curves slope down to the right. Even the supply of altruism is likely to be inversely related to its cost; for example, more blood (a renewable resource) is likely to be supplied altruistically than are steak and potatoes. Thus, positive economic analysis is individualistic and subjective in its behavioural premises. A positive analyst of legal issues back in the 1920s might have asked, what behavioural responses on both the supply and demand sides can be predicted in reaction to Prohibition laws? Similar questions might be asked today about various features of the war on drugs. Or the analyst might ask, what kind of first- and second-order behavioural responses might one predict to rent control laws, or agricultural supply management regimes that impose price floors and production quotas on producers, or minimum wage laws, or cost-plus regulation of public utilities, or exclusive dealing contracts, or the adoption of strict products liability over negligence? and so on. Understanding the incentives effects of these various regimes is a necessary prelude to formulating normative judgments as to the merits of the regime under analysis relative to different policies that might be employed to pursue the same or alternative social goals.

Two examples from this list will help to illuminate the predictive implications of the basic relationship between demand and supply functions. First, let us take the case of rent controls. Assume that out of concern for affordability, the government imposes controls on rental accommodations to force rents down below the rate that would otherwise prevail in an unregulated market. The impact of the intervention might be graphed as shown in Figure 1.

At the competitive price (P^C), quantity Q^C will be demanded and supplied. At the regulated price (P^R), D^R will be demanded but only S^R will be supplied, yielding a shortage of rental accommodation of $D^R - S^R$. With this initial disequilibrium in the market, economists would predict the following behavioural responses on the demand side. Prospective tenants will offer key money to obtain accommodation. Incumbent tenants will charge

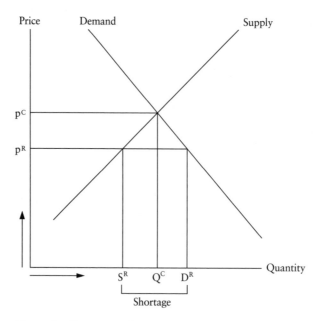

Figure 1. Rent controls.

premiums on sub-letting, and they will be less mobile in labour markets, given the costs of leaving a rent-controlled apartment and the prospects of extensive search costs and queues in finding alternative accommodation in new work locations. Some incumbent tenants will benefit from the controls even though they may be well endowed—perhaps better endowed than some landlords. On the supply side, economists would predict that some land-lords will attempt to extract key money from prospective tenants, reduce investments in maintenance, impose "adult only" conditions in leases to reduce wear and tear costs, perhaps indulge a taste for racial discrimination in clearing queues of prospective tenants (economics *is* sensitive to the existence of non-pecuniary sources of utility), or even withdraw units from rental markets, or convert to condominiums or co-operatives. Some of these effects can be partly contained by additional regulation, but they are un-likely to be entirely eliminated. Generally, realigning incentives is easier than applying constraints on behaviour.

Let us now take the case of agricultural supply management schemes that set minimum price floors and maximum production quotas for agricultural products (for example, eggs) and that are introduced ostensibly to enhance the welfare of small family farmers. The initial impact of the intervention can be graphed as shown in Figure 2.

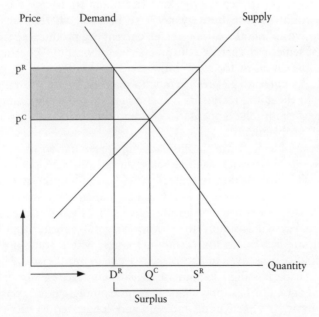

Figure 2. Agricultural supply management.

At the competitive price (P^C), quantity Q^C will be demanded and supplied. At the regulated price (P^R), S^R will be supplied but only D^R will be demanded, yielding a surplus of $S^R - D^R$. The function of maximum production quotas is to ensure that producers produce only D^R so that the market clears. On the demand side, an obvious prediction is that consumers will buy fewer eggs and that those who continue to buy eggs will pay more for them, including people of modest means, for whom eggs are a staple. On the supply side, assuming that production quotas are initially allocated on a historical basis (producers with an established presence in the market), the initial quota recipients will obtain supra-competitive returns, measured by the hatched rectangle, at the expense of consumers who remain in the market. Because some of these initial quota recipients are relatively less efficient egg producers, resources devoted to producing D^R of eggs will be greater than necessary. Quotas might, on that account, be made tradeable to allow more efficient (lower-cost) egg producers to produce the eggs demanded at P^R. Prices paid for the quotas will probably reflect the capitalized value of the future stream of supra-competitive prices (the hatched rectangle). Thus, after paying quota prices, the second generation of egg producers are likely to be making a normal, competitive rate of return on their combined investment in egg production resources and quotas. The end result, it could be predicted, would be an allocatively inefficient industry (too few eggs—D^R—are produced), but a productively efficient industry (the low-cost producers service the market after quota transfers); the outcome, arguably, would be distributively perverse because whereas small family farmers receive an initial wealth transfer, current egg producers gain nothing from the scheme and current consumers, including poor consumers, pay more than they need to for eggs. Moreover, the scheme may be politically irreversible, as current egg producers who may have paid substantial sums for quotas to the initial recipients will strenuously resist any termination of the scheme without full compensation (often referred to as "the transitional gains trap" problem).[8]

These examples illustrate the fundamental presumption of neo-classical economics: that economic agents, in all their various activities, *respond to incentives*. This proposition is central to understanding the functioning of any pricing system, whether it involves explicit (grocery store) prices, or implicit (penalties for different crimes) prices. To the neo-classical economist, the legal system is simply an institutional arrangement for prescribing, and setting implicit prices for, certain activities, within some over-arching consequentialist objective. In the case of legal or regulatory regimes that constrain the permissible domain of private contracting (as in the rent control and agricultural supply management examples above), positive economic analysis, by uncovering indirect and longer-term effects of these constraints, will raise normative questions as to the wisdom of the constraints.

NORMATIVE ECONOMICS

The orientation of normative economic analysis, like positive analysis, is individualistic and subjective. This style of analysis—conventionally referred to as welfare economics—would tend to ask the question, is it likely that this particular transaction, or this particular proposed policy or legal change, will make individuals affected by it better off in terms of how they perceive their own welfare (not how some external party might judge individuals' welfare)? In this context, two concepts of efficiency are of central importance: *Pareto efficiency* and *Kaldor-Hicks efficiency*. Pareto efficiency would ask of any transaction or policy or legal change, will this transaction or change make somebody better off while making no one worse off? Kaldor-Hicks efficiency, in contrast, would ask the question, would this collective decision (for example, a change in legal rules) generate sufficient gains to the beneficiaries of the change that they could, *hypothetically*, compensate the losers from the change so as to render the latter fully indifferent to it but still have gains left over for themselves? This second approach is effectively a form of cost-benefit analysis. Let me elaborate a little on these two concepts of efficiency.[9]

Neo-classical economists in general attach strong normative value to regimes of private exchange and private ordering and often bring some degree of scepticism to bear on the capacity of collective decision-makers, including legislatures, regulators, bureaucrats, or indeed courts, to adopt policies or laws that will unambiguously increase net social welfare. This predilection for private ordering over collective decision-making is based on a simple (perhaps simple-minded) premise: if two parties are to be observed entering into a voluntary private exchange, the presumption must be that both feel the exchange is likely to make them better off, otherwise they would not have entered into it. Thus, in most exchanges, the economic presumption is that they make all the parties thereto better off, that is, they are Pareto superior. This presumption is rebuttable by reference to a fairly conventional list of forms of market failure or, in a transaction-specific context, contracting failure, which neo-classical economists recognize as inconsistent with this presumption, for example, monopoly, externalities, information failures. Or, as Milton Friedman puts the presumption in *Capitalism and Freedom*: "The possibility of coordination through voluntary cooperation rests on the elementary—yet frequently denied—proposition that both parties to an economic transaction benefit from it, *provided the transaction is bilaterally voluntary and informed*."[10]

Collective decisions which are not the result of voluntary agreement among all affected parties may technically be able to satisfy the Pareto criterion (making some better off and none worse off), but typically such decisions will generate both winners and losers. The question for the economist then becomes whether the net effect of these decisions is an increase in social welfare as judged by all affected individuals in terms of the impact of such decisions on their levels of present or prospective utility. The central difficulty here is that these impacts on individuals' utility functions are not directly observable by collective decision-makers and there is no ready way of ensuring accurate revelation by individuals of their evaluation of these impacts, thus rendering the utilities and disutilities associated with such a decision largely unmeasurable and incommensurable. For example, suppose that it were proposed that a major new multi-lane highway be constructed through an urban area, generating gains in utility for commuters from more distant areas but losses in utility to inner-city residents immediately adjacent to the throughway. How can decision-makers be confident that the net effect on social welfare of a decision to proceed with construction of the through-way will be positive? Similar questions arise with respect to changes in legal regimes which are imposed on affected parties by collective decision and which make some individuals better off and others worse off. How does one go about determining whether the gains in utility to one group exceed the losses in utility to the other? Thus, economists feel much more confident making welfare judgements about the impact of private exchanges on the parties thereto than the impact of collective decisions on all parties affected by them.

The Political Perspective

In addition to *economic* justifications for the primacy of private ordering, a closely related *political* justification is also often offered by classical liberals or libertarians. As articulated by earlier scholars such as Mill,[11] and contemporary scholars such as Hayek,[12] Friedman,[13] Nozick,[14] and Fried,[15] individual autonomy is seen as a paramount social value and a central precondition to individual freedom. Private ordering is most compatible with this value because it minimizes the extent to which individuals are subjected to externally imposed forms of coercion or socially ordained forms of status. Private ordering is the quintessential form of government with the consent of the governed. Or, to quote from Fried: "The law of contracts, just because it is rooted in promise and so in right and wrong, is a ramifying system of moral judgments working out the entailments of a few primitive principles—primitive principles that determine the terms on which free men and women may stand apart from or combine with each other. These are indeed the laws of freedom."[16]

Liberal political theories that assign substantial weight to individual autonomy, in contrast to welfare economics and its utilitarian analogues, tend to a deontological or non-consequentialist justification of freedom of contract—autonomy is a good itself, and autonomous choices should be respected because they are the legitimate exercise of the right of self-government or self-determination, regardless of what outside observers may feel about the individual or social virtues of those choices. Individuals have a right to pursue their own conception of the good without interference from others or the imposition of alternative conceptions of the good by others, at least where the interests of the latter are not harmed or jeopardized by the actions or choices of the individual concerned. Classical liberal theories of individual rights or autonomy have thus tended to stress negative liberties: freedom from external intrusions on the domain of self-determination. Some liberal theories also emphasize a more expansive conception of individual liberty that has both negative and positive dimensions[17]—the latter focusing on some base-line conception of equality of access to opportunities and resources that make the pursuit of non-demeaning, self-fulfilling, and meaningfully autonomous life plans or choices a realistic prospect. This second, more expansive conception of liberty stresses with welfare economics a concern with outcomes or end-states that emerge from whatever economic or political system we should choose. These end-states, of course, are not necessarily or likely to be the same in these two normative frameworks. Welfare economics is concerned with ensuring the adoption of economic and legal regimes that maximize social welfare, with the inevitable utilitarian connotations this carries. Proponents of a positive or affirmative theory of liberty are concerned less with general aggregate measures of welfare or utility than with the fairness of distribution of that welfare or utility.

An even more expansive conception of liberal ideals would emphasize not only liberty and equality, but also fraternity (community).[18] Communitarianism raises important and difficult questions as to whether the individualistic orientation of both neo-classical economics and classical liberalism can be reconciled with the essentially social nature of people.

Throughout this book, as I explore various problematic issues in the law of contracts, I will be centrally concerned with congruences and conflicts between the normative implications of welfare economics, negative and positive theories of individual liberty or autonomy, and theories of community.

The Economic Role of Property Rights

Defining and specifying property rights is primarily the function of the law of property and, to a lesser extent, the law of torts (nuisance). The protection of property rights is principally the function of both tort law (nuisance, trespass, conversion, detinue) and criminal law. Providing for the transferability of property rights is principally the function of the law of contracts. A market system necessarily assumes a large domain for exclusive private property rights upon which the private exchange process can operate. Similarly, a political system that assigns substantial weight to the value of individual autonomy will also assign substantial weight to private property rights and freedom of contract.[19] In the contemporary transition from command to market economies, the establishment of a stable, durable, and credible regime of private property rights is proving to be one of the most daunting, yet critically important, challenges.[20]

In defining and specifying property rights, an economic perspective would seek definitions and specifications that internalize as fully as possible to a property rights holder all the costs and benefits associated with utilization of the property rights in question. Failure to internalize costs may create negative externalities, leading to over-utilization of the resources in question from a social perspective. For example, a widget factory that pollutes the surrounding neighbourhood treats clean air as a free resource even though people in the neighbourhood place a positive value on it. By not including this social cost in the costs of production of widgets, the price of widgets does not reflect their true social costs; hence, too many are demanded by consumers, too many are produced, and too much pollution is created. Failure to internalize benefits may create positive externalities, leading to under-utilization of the resource in question from a social perspective. For example, if I plant corn on my farm but other people are allowed to help themselves to it when it is ripe, there is little or no incentive for me to utilize the land in this way. Similarly, if I spend considerable resources inventing a new product but others are allowed to copy my idea without making any such investments and without reimbursing me, I have little incentive to use my innovative talents in this fashion. Optimal resource allocation and utilization requires that divergences between private costs and social costs be minimized and that divergences between private benefits and social benefits also be minimized. Hence, arguments for exclusivity in the definition of property rights. Assuming that property rights have been defined and specified in ways that internalize costs and benefits from utilization of a resource as fully as possible, the economic perspective on property rights would then focus on the importance of facilitating the transferability of these property rights to ensure that they end up in their highest-valued social uses.[21] This is principally the function of the law of contracts and the exchange process, to which I will turn shortly.

The Prisoner's Dilemma and the Tragedy of Commons are two related and important paradigms that address the problems of cooperation described above.

The Prisoner's Dilemma

In tracing out the implications in various contexts of the economic perspective on property rights, a central conceptual building block is an understanding of the Prisoner's Dilemma paradigm.[22] In the dilemma's original formulation, game theorists postulated the following kind of example. Two suspects are taken into custody and separated in different rooms, where they cannot communicate with each other. The prosecutor is certain that they are guilty of a specific crime, say, armed robbery, but he does not have adequate evidence to ensure their conviction at trial. He points out to each prisoner in turn that he has two alternatives: to confess to the crime that the police are sure the two have committed, or not to confess. If they both do not confess, then the prosecutor states that he will charge them with a minor offense, such as illegal possession of a firearm, and they both will receive a minor sentence, for example, one year's imprisonment. If they both confess to the major charge, they will be prosecuted, but the prosecutor will recommend less than the most severe sentence, and he expects they will receive approximately eight years' imprisonment each. However, if one confesses, that is, turns State's evidence, and the other does not, then the confessor will receive lenient treatment, maybe three months in prison, whereas the latter will receive the most severe sanction provided by the law—ten years in prison. The pay-off matrix is depicted in Figure 3.

Obviously, the *joint welfare maximizing* solution available to the two prisoners is for neither to confess and each to receive one year in prison. However, each faces the temptation to confess in order to receive the lightest sentence (three months in prison) for turning State's evidence. If each reasons in this way, both may end up confessing and receiving eight years in prison, which is the *joint welfare minimizing* outcome among the various alternatives. In a range of contexts, game theorists predict that, though not inevitable, there will be strong tendencies for this outcome to be the one that emerges.

In the original formulation of the Prisoner's Dilemma, the parties whose welfare is directly at stake are not permitted to communicate with each other. However, even in settings where communication is possible, there is still a significant risk that defection rather than cooperation strategies may dominate. In a property rights context,[23] let us consider the example outlined in Figure 4.

Let us assume that in this pre-legal society, where individuals and groups

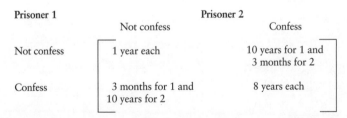

Figure 3. The prisoner's dilemma.

exist in a so-called state of nature, Tribe A grows corn in one valley and in a neighbouring valley Tribe B produces beef. Let us assume further that Tribe A's land is unsuitable for producing anything other than corn and that Tribe B's land is unsuitable for producing anything other than beef. Suppose that members of Tribe A would prefer to vary their diet from time to time by eating beef as well as corn and that, similarly, members of Tribe B would prefer some corn as well as beef. Thus, the question arises as to how transfers of corn from Tribe A to Tribe B and transfers of beef from Tribe B to Tribe A can be achieved. The two basic options are trade or theft. A cooperative strategy would clearly dictate trade; a defection strategy would entail theft. The question is, will a cooperative outcome emerge? Obviously, in the short-run, members of each tribe face substantial incentives to engage in theft rather than trade because theft entails lower costs for the recipient than trade, where something has to be given up as a quid pro quo. However, if members of both tribes reason similarly, the limiting outcome may entail each tribe's engaging in predatory strategies, with members of the other tribe engaging in defensive strategies, the result being that no corn or beef is any longer produced, as all the energies of both tribes become absorbed in predatory and counter-predatory activities. This exemplifies the application of the Prisoner's Dilemma to a property rights conflict, where there is some significant risk that the *joint welfare minimizing* outcome may emerge.

To reduce the likelihood that this outcome will emerge, members of each of the two tribes would first need to recognize the exclusive property rights held by the other tribe in its land and the produce therefrom. Even in a state of nature, given that parties often face the prospect of repeated interactions with each other, the Prisoner's Dilemma problem may solve itself, with the eventual recognition that cooperation rather than defection is the *joint welfare maximizing* strategy (although long-standing, mutually destructive religious factionalism in countries such as Northern Ireland raises important questions as to why cooperative outcomes have not evolved over time). However, in contemporary societies involving much larger numbers of people, and more impersonal and transient relations, solving the Prisoner's Dilemma problem may prove more daunting in many contexts, and the

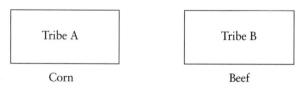

Figure 4. Property rights in a state of nature.

formal legal system may need to play a much more central role in preventing the externalization of costs or benefits from resource ownership and utilization.[24]

The Tragedy of the Commons

In many villages of medieval England, individual villagers or families traditionally had access to a commons for grazing their livestock. Historical evidence apparently suggests that these commons in some cases were over-utilized and permanently grazed-out.[25] Let us imagine the situation depicted in Figure 5.

An economic perspective on property rights would ask the following question: If each villager, for example, A, has unrestricted access to the commons, how will he decide how many cattle to graze? The individual welfare maximizing calculus would be to equate marginal private benefits and marginal private costs (MPB = MPC). The marginal private benefits are presumably the milk or beef derived from grazing an additional cow. The marginal costs of raising another cow presumably are principally the pasture consumed, but here the marginal private costs are less than the marginal social costs, because villager A bears only one-sixteenth of the cost of the additional pasture consumed, and hence there is a wedge between marginal private costs and marginal social costs, that is, MPC < MSC.

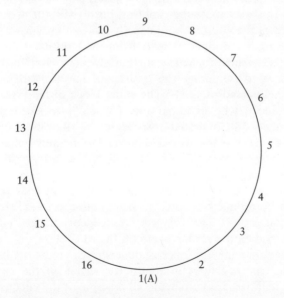

Figure 5. The tragedy of the commons.

Obviously if each villager reasoned the same way as A, substantial over-grazing would result and again the *joint welfare minimizing* outcome may emerge. If only one person owned the entire commons, this wedge between marginal private costs and marginal social costs would cease to exist, because the single owner would derive all the benefits from grazing the land but also would bear all the costs.

The problem of common property resources or common pools is pervasive in contemporary society. For example, most problems pertaining to the environment can be thought of as common pool problems, as can urban or highway congestion, or over-utilization of beaches or parks, or crowding out of broadcast frequencies on the airways.

An interesting institutional exercise is to contemplate the range of possible solutions to the Tragedy of the Commons as originally formulated. These options might include the following: (1) The Commons could be divided up into smaller and equal entitlements, for example, pie-shaped slices, with each villager entitled to a slice. This would internalize costs and benefits associated with ownership of the divided resource but is likely to engender significant diseconomies of small scale, such as duplication of milking sheds, implements, fencing, and so forth. It also treats efficient and inefficient farmers equally and is unlikely to maximize total economic benefits from the land. Some of these inefficiencies could be minimized if the subsequent sale of initial entitlements were to be permitted. (2) A variant of the above would be to allocate to each villager a cow quota, say, four cows each, which would reflect the long-term sustainable grazing burden on the land. Again, this may mute the problem, but it will not necessarily be the case that each of the villagers is an equally efficient farmer, so that maximization of the total economic benefits from the land may not be achieved. Again, as in (1), subsequent sale of initial quota entitlements might be permitted so as to encourage the transfer of initial entitlements into the hands of higher-valued users. (3) The entire block of land could be sold to the highest bidder, who as noted above would face incentives to equate marginal benefits and marginal costs from the utilization of the land in choosing how many cattle to graze on it. The highest bidder could then employ the other villagers. An objection to this solution may be that it is non-egalitarian and hierarchical and, moreover, will raise incentive problems in terms of whether villagers under employment contracts will be as motivated to be productive as when their returns derive directly from the effort they put in. (4) The villagers could incorporate a company or a co-operative to own the resource, elect a board of directors, which in turn would appoint a manager to operate the resource on their collective behalf, buying cattle from villagers in return for shares in the corporation or co-operative and perhaps employing all or some of the villagers. This solution, at first sight, is attractive because the resource will be managed as a single entity, and hopefully marginal social benefits and marginal social costs will be fully equated. Also, it has more of an egalitarian and communitarian appeal than a sale of the whole resource to the single highest bidder. However, questions would arise as to what incentives the manager would have to maximize total economic benefits from the resource as opposed to total personal perquisites or simply shirking on the job. This is the classic agency cost problem confronted in many principal and agent settings,[26] and it may pose significant difficulties in specifying and monitoring contractual arrangements with the agent. There is also the further serious problem of whether a majority of shareholders (assuming majority rule) will always face incentives—in electing a board and adopting collective policies—to maximize total economic benefits from the resource. There may well be a temptation to appropriate wealth from the minority for their own benefit, such as through biased dividend policies. But attempting to solve these problems by a voting rule of unanimity may substitute tyranny of the minority for tyranny of the majority, where individual villagers face incentives to "hold-out" for a disproportionate share of the benefits from collective resource management.[27] It should be noted that these problems would also have to be addressed in collectively choosing and operationalizing options (1), (2), and (3). Again, as with the Prisoner's Dilemma problem in the primitive society, informal social conventions or sanctions may develop to discourage either over-grazing or shirking (depending on the property rights regime chosen). Indeed, evidence suggests that these social conventions have worked reasonably well in many cases.[28] In more transitory, larger, and less closely knit societies, these conventions are unlikely to prove as effective.

In these problems of collective governance in modern settings, there is a clear analogy to democratic politics more generally. In choosing voting regimes, and accountability mechanisms to contain agency cost problems, the original Prisoner's Dilemma and Tragedy of the Commons problems are unlikely to be perfectly solved with incentives for what economists call "rent seeking" (political largesse) by coalitions of voters or interest groups, and incentives for agents of the voters—politicians or bureaucrats—to maximize the personal returns from office rather than collective returns.[29] Thus, many features of corporate law in the private sector and constitutional and administrative law in the public sector can be seen as attempts to address these collective action problems.

The Economic Functions of Contract Law

As noted above, neo-classical economists have a predilection for resource allocation through voluntary exchanges as opposed to collective decisions because they believe that one can have a higher degree of confidence in the welfare implications of private exchanges, where both parties stand to benefit, than in collective decisions, where typically there are both winners and losers and it is difficult to net out gains against losses. However, this predilection for the private exchange or market process in the allocation of resources does not speak to the economic role of contract *law*. From an economic perspective, we can identify several major functions of contract law.[30]

Containing Opportunism in Non-Simultaneous Exchanges

Let us return to the earlier example of Tribe A's producing corn and Tribe B's producing beef. Even if a stable regime of property rights is established so that members of Tribe A and members of Tribe B agree to respect each other's property rights, this in itself does not ensure that mutual gains from trade will be realized. In other words, we have ruled out theft, but we have not yet facilitated exchange. Suppose that Tribe A's corn is ripe now and must be eaten within a few days and that Tribe A is prepared to trade a quantity of this corn for a calf from Tribe B, but that the calf will not be ready for delivery for another six weeks. If Tribe A delivers the corn today against the promise of delivery of the calf in six weeks' time, there is a serious risk of defection by Tribe B when it comes time to meet its delivery obligations. Tribe A, perceiving this risk, may be disinclined to deliver the corn. In this event, the potential for a Pareto superior exchange would not be realized. This is a variant of the Prisoner's Dilemma. Whereas in traditional societies conventions may develop that mitigate the problem, in contemporary societies the law of contracts—by providing remedies in the event of breach of contractual promises—provides an essential check on opportunism in non-simultaneous exchanges by ensuring that the first mover, in terms of performance, does not run the risk of defection, rather than cooperation, by the second mover.[31]

Reducing Transaction Costs

A second economic function of the law of contracts is to supply parties to given categories of exchanges with standard sets of implied terms, which in most cases save the parties the transaction costs entailed in fully specifying a complete contingent claims contract, but typically leave them free to contract out of these rules if they find them inappropriate to their particular transaction.[32] In addition to various aspects of the common law of contracts, many statutes dealing with sales law and partnership law, and perhaps certain aspects of corporation statutes, can be thought of in these terms.

Filling Gaps in Incomplete Contracts

A related function of the law of contracts is to provide a set of default or background rules where the explicit terms of a contract are incomplete, not because the parties consciously adverted to the default or background rules and accepted them as appropriate to their transaction, but typically because particular contingencies were not consciously adverted to by one or the other party (or both) at all. Here, an economic framework of analysis would tend to ask, what rule would maximize the parties' joint welfare, on the assumption that this rule would generally be the rule that rational parties would have agreed to *ex ante*?[33]

Distinguishing Welfare-Enhancing and Welfare-Reducing Exchanges

A central economic role of contract law is to formulate a set of excuses for contract performance that permits the enforcement of efficient exchanges but discourages the enforcement of inefficient exchanges. Individual exchanges might be evaluated from a Paretian perspective, where one would ask whether it is reasonable to infer that such exchanges are welfare-enhancing in the sense of making somebody better off and somebody worse off. Lack of voluntariness, imperfect information, and externalities are likely to provide the principal economic bases for declining to draw such an inference, whatever the legal forms that excuses reflecting these factors might take. Alternatively, one could employ a Kaldor-Hicks criterion of efficiency, asking whether society on net would be better off by permitting the class of transaction of which the instant transaction is representative or if, in contrast, society would be better off on net by imposing certain legal rules or constraints on the class of transaction in question. As we shall see in later chapters, economists are not always precise about which of these two concepts of efficiency should be employed and when.

Thus, neo-classical economists' predilection for private ordering turns centrally on legal regimes of well-defined and exclusive private property rights and a regime of contract law that facilitates the voluntary exchange of those rights. Liberal political theories of individual autonomy generally reflect a similar predilection, though not necessarily for the same reasons or with the same normative entailments.

Critiques of the Private Ordering Paradigm

Critiques of the private ordering model, at least in its most austere form, can be organized under several major categories.

Limits on the Domain of Markets: The Issue of Commodification

The claim as to the centrality of individual autonomy as a social value has been strongly contested by many scholars who see the autonomous individual self of neo-classical economies and classical liberal theory as reflecting an impoverished, pre-social conception of human life. Rather, it is claimed, it is constitutive attachments to particular families, communities, groups, and institutions that make human life rich and formative of true human identities.[34] Adam Smith, conversely, claimed that man possesses an innate "propensity to barter, truck and exchange one thing for another."[35] This observation in time led to the conception of Homo Economicus, or the Economic Man. Economic historians such as Karl Polanyi, in contrast, claim that most societies throughout history have placed social relationships and institutions above economic relations and institutions; markets, over the great sweep of human history, have played an incidental role.[36] In most pre-market societies, Polanyi claims, the values of reciprocity and redistribution rather than individual maximizing behaviour have predominated. With the advent of the industrial revolution at the beginning of the nineteenth century and the emergence of economic and political liberalism, Polanyi argues, the market paradigm revealed itself as completely insensitive to the social costs to communities and individuals of traumatic economic change and dislocation. He sees the mass movement of people from rural communities to the "dark satanic mills" of the new industrial cities that burgeoned during the industrial revolution as the most dramatic example of this insensitivity. Moreover, he maintains that the market paradigm commodifies aspects of human and physical nature that are essentially non-economic and which in pre-market societies have been treated as non-economic, for example, land, which Polanyi equates with physical nature, and labour, which he equates with human nature itself. In pre-market societies the rights of individuals to dispose of or otherwise deal with either land or labour were heavily constrained by convention, custom, or centrally or collectively imposed formal legal constraints.

Polanyi's attack on the market paradigm raises a number of questions. First, one must ask whether Polanyi unduly romanticizes the characteristics of pre-market societies. Here, one should recall the characteristics of societies that have organized their economies on the basis of tradition as described by Heilbroner. Second, even if Polanyi's historical interpretation of pre-market societies is correct (and other authors, such as Posner, have contested this in attempting to explain features of these societies as having an economic rationality, given the inherent natural constraints within which they functioned),[37] it is not clear what normative implications this interpretation has for the choice of contemporary or future forms of economic organization—presumably not a return to hunter-gatherer societies or forms of feudalism. Third, the essence of his commodification objections, particularly in the case of land and labour, are not well specified, and it is far from clear why he considers it inappropriate for markets to develop with respect to either. Fourth, even when considering his claim about the costs of social and economic dislocation wrought by the industrial revolution, it is not clear that the empirical evidence is as unambiguous as he assumes. An economist would naturally ask why people moved to the cities if they thought they were likely to be worse off there. Moreover, Hayek[38] cites evidence on trends in real incomes, health levels, and infant mortality during the industrial revolution which suggests that all these social indicators were substantially enhanced even in the short-run. Finally, Polanyi's claim that economic liberalism and the rise of the market paradigm led to the separation of economic and political spheres of life also is contentious because conterminously with the emergence of market economies in the nineteenth century emerged the concept of democratic government. This seems far from coincidental, since the value of individual autonomy underlying both economic and political liberalism provides a major normative basis for decentralized markets and representative forms of government. Indeed, the chief proponents of both were often, during the nineteenth century, the same people—Bentham, his followers, and the two Mills (father and son).

Despite these questions, the kind of critique mounted by Polanyi continues to find significant currency today.[39] For example, would permitting the sale of votes or public offices, the sale of blood or body organs, commercial surrogacy contracts, prostitution contracts or pornography undermine values of human self-fulfilment or human flourishing? Would permitting these kinds of exchange activities undermine broader social values of sharing, caring, altruism, and community conceptions of the public good?

The central theme that emerges from this line of critique of the private ordering model is that even if a society commits itself, in general, to political and economic liberalism, there is still substantial room for debate about the scope of the market. In particular, what kinds of things should be permitted to be commodified, either completely, or subject only to various legal constraints?

The Indeterminacy of the Paretian and Kaldor-Hicks Conditions

A frequent objection to the concept of Pareto efficiency, even in its own terms, is that the concepts of voluntariness, complete information, and absence of externalities upon which it is conventionally predicated are extraordinarily vague, subjective, and to an important extent indeterminate.[40] For example, the concept of voluntariness, which any theory of contract that rests on notions of individual autonomy and consent must accept as a central condition, is extraordinarily difficult to define, given the pervasiveness of scarcity and therefore the pervasiveness of choices under the constraints of scarcity. A radical view is that markets are inherently coercive, because few individuals have the choice of engaging in exchange activities or not, especially with respect to the sale of their labour.[41] Similarly, the concept of an informed choice is extremely difficult to define with precision, since in the real world almost no choices are made with perfect information about present facts or possible courses of future events. And in the concept of externalities, few transactions have no tangible or intangible impacts on third parties[42]—in some cases if only because third parties take offense at the exchange activities of others. Determining which of these impacts, if negative, are to count in constraining the ability of parties to contract with each other poses major conceptual problems.

When an economic framework of analysis moves away from the application of the Paretian principle to particular transactions and asks instead what set of legal rules is likely to enhance social welfare on net, that is, is Kaldor-Hicks efficient, with respect to a particular class of transactions or with respect to a particular type of contracting behaviour, then actual consent of the parties becomes irrelevant, and many of the same welfare indeterminacies that economists commonly ascribe to collective resource allocations are likely to arise. Even if the social maximand is empirically discoverable, it is argued that Kaldor-Hicks efficiency is a normatively incoherent concept because to maximize average utility or wealth is to reify an abstraction: welfare counts only at the level of the individual, and at the level of the individual it is impossible to avoid distributional judgements and interpersonal comparisons of welfare or well-being.[43]

The Issue of Distributive Justice

Whereas it might be argued that the private ordering paradigm liberates individuals from the burden of despotic or majoritarian coercion or the oppressive incidents of caste, class, or status, critics claim that it often subjects individuals to a new form of oppression. Although they emphasize equality of opportunity rather than equality of outcome, proponents of the private ordering paradigm disregard the fact that individuals do not start out equal, if only because of the effects of the genetic lottery or early family circumstances, which are morally arbitrary.[44] Thus, the argument is that the concept of Pareto efficiency is wholly insensitive to the justice or injustice of the prior distribution of endowments and property rights. Similarly, the value of individual autonomy can be rendered meaningful only by reasonably equal access to opportunities and resources. On this view, the State is justified in adopting policies designed to redistribute private resources in accordance with some collectively or communally determined concept of distributive justice, and there may be a role for contract law or contract regulation in furthering this objective by attempting to redistribute or constrain the gains from trade.[45]

The Primacy of Preferences

A conventional ethical critique[46] of the concept of Pareto efficiency is that it takes existing preferences, of whatever kind, as givens and provides no ethical criteria for disqualifying morally offensive, self-destructive, or irrational preferences as unworthy of recognition. This is a standard objection to any form of utilitarianism. Because proponents of a regime of private ordering are compelled to acknowledge, as they must—at least in extreme cases such as those involving minors and mental incompetents—that not all preferences should be recognized, some theory of paternalism is required, the contours of which are not readily suggested by the private ordering paradigm itself.

Moreover, it is claimed that many preferences are socially constructed, and their existence and validity should not be viewed as prior or exogenous to the choices of social, economic, and legal systems which help shape them.[47] Again, the issue is raised as to whether preferences ordain the modes of social and economic organization that should be put in place to validate them, or whether the choice of these institutions is prior to discussions of which preferences to accord validity to.

It is argued further that some preferences are simply "bad" in that they are inconsistent with notions of the individual good, human self-fulfilment, or civic virtue and ought to be disregarded on that account—all preferences or autonomous choices should not be treated as equally valid and deserving of equal respect.[48]

• • •

A common theme runs through these critiques of the private ordering model. It is that collective or community values are unavoidable and central to a determination of the scope of the domain of the market and of the ground rules which will constrain its operation even within its proper domain, and that an "internal" theory of exchange or contract which is premised on vindication of private preferences or individual autonomy and consent is likely to be a seriously incomplete account of the normative bases of the law of contracts. These are the issues that I take up in the ensuing chapters of this book. In exploring these issues, two major themes unify the discussion. First, I focus on the relationship between autonomy values or welfare (end-state) values (efficiency, utility, equality, community) in constructing a normative theory of the law of contracts. In this respect, the claim made by writers from Adam Smith (and his theory of the "invisible hand") to Milton Friedman on behalf of the private ordering paradigm—

that it simultaneously promotes individual autonomy and advances social welfare—requires close scrutiny. If true, this convergence claim would be a powerful vindication of markets and freedom of contract. A central focus of this book entails an evaluation of the robustness of this convergence claim. Second, I focus on the more pragmatic question of the appropriate choice of instrument or institution for vindicating more broadly the values claimed to be implicated by the private ordering paradigm. That is, what values can the common law of contracts as judicially applied in two-party disputes (contracting failures) appropriately vindicate? What values can legislative or regulatory controls on generic classes of exchange activity (market failure) appropriately vindicate? And after contracting and market failures are appropriately addressed, what set of values are likely to be systematically unaddressed or under-addressed in the common law of contracts and contract regulation that require other forms of collective intervention for their vindication?

CHAPTER TWO

Commodification

The Nature of the Conceptual Problem

Even if one shares the neo-classical economist's predilection for private exchanges over collective resource allocation mechanisms, this does not address the question of the limits on the domain of the private exchange process. As Arrow has pointed out, a private property–private exchange system depends, for its stability, on the system's being non-universal.[1] For example, if political, bureaucratic, regulatory, judicial, or law enforcement offices were auctioned off to the highest bidder, or police officers, prosecutors, bureaucrats, regulators, or judges could be freely bribed in individual cases, or votes could be freely bought and sold, a system of private property and private exchange would be massively destabilized.[2] However, one cannot assume that all these public officials will be saints and give endlessly of their time, energy, and wisdom without some attention being given to appropriate remuneration and other incentive arrangements. The extent to which a healthy private sector presupposes the existence of a public sector, and the design of incentive structures in the public sector that are complementary to the existence of a healthy private sector, has not been sufficiently explored in much of the standard economics literature. I will return to some of these issues in my concluding chapter.

A second dimension of the commodification issue is whether certain human attributes or resources should lie wholly or partly beyond the exchange process, because to allow full commodification would be inconsistent with theories of personhood or human flourishing. John Stuart Mill in his famous essay *On Liberty*, in a much-debated passage, argued against the validity of voluntary contracts of enslavement—individuals should not have the freedom to decide not to be free.[3] Margaret Jane Radin[4] has recently developed an extensive critique of economic liberalism, which she claims (despite Mill) implies universal commodification, which in turn "means that anything some people are willing to sell and others are willing to buy, in principle, can and should be the subject of free market exchange." As we have seen from the previous chapter, objections to commodification have a long intellectual genesis. Radical objections, deriving from Marx, espouse an ideal of universal non-commodification, where it is claimed that relationships between people are disguised as relationships between commodities which appear to be governed by abstract market forces; such relationships permit individuals to be used as means to the ends of others. Individuals become as fungible as the goods or services they produce or sell, leading to what Marx called "commodity fetishism." According to Marx, "false objectification—false separateness from [ourselves]—in the way we conceive of our social activities and environment reflects and creates dehumanization, powerlessness," and alienation. Although Radin does not necessarily espouse this radical critique of commodification, at least in the non-ideal world that she sees us living in, she believes that appropriately rich theories of personhood and human flourishing would identify some resources and attributes that should not be subject to commodification at all, or at least not to unconstrained commodification. She is critical of attempts by liberal theorists to establish these boundaries. For example, German theorists, such as Kant and Hegel, attempted to draw that boundary by reliance on a subject-object dichotomy. This dichotomy asserts that any object separate from the self is suitable for alienation. However, this poses the problem of distinguishing things internal from things external to the person. For Kant, personhood is the subject side of the dichotomy, but "Kantian persons [noumenal selves] are essentially abstract fungible units with identical capacity for moral reasoning and no concrete individuating characteristics." Radin claims that this Kantian conception of personhood makes us all interchangeable and facilitates conceiving of concrete personal attributes as commodifiable objects. Similarly, in the case of Hegel, who sought to distinguish things external by nature from those internal by nature, she claims that his distinction between subject and object is quite arbitrary and, in many cases, purely conclusory. For example, his claim that wage labour is "external" to personality is merely asserted rather than derived from his foundational conceptual distinction.

Radin, for her part, rejects a purely negative definition of liberty as freedom from constraints on individual autonomy; rather, she adopts a positive conception of liberty that includes proper self-development as necessary for freedom, in which case inalienabilities needed to foster that development can be seen as freedom-enhancing rather than unwanted constraints on individual freedom. She develops an ideal of human flourishing that turns on three concepts: freedom, identity, and contextuality. Whereas freedom focuses on will and on the power to choose for one's self, "the identity aspect of personhood focuses on the integrity and continuity of the self required for individuation." "To have a unique individual identity, we must have selves that are integrated and continuous over time. The contextuality aspect of personhood focuses on the necessity of self-constitution in relation to the environment of things and other people." To be differentiated human persons—unique individuals—we must have relationships with the social and the natural world. The relationship between personhood and context requires a positive commitment to act so as to create and maintain particular contexts of environment and community. Recognition of the need for such a commitment turns towards a positive view of freedom, in which the self-development of the individual is linked to the pursuit of proper social development and in which proper self-development, as a requirement of personhood, could in principle sometimes take precedence over one's momentary desires or preferences. Radin claims that "universal commodification undermines personal identity by conceiving of personal attributes, relationships, and philosophical and moral commitments as monetizable and alienable from the self. A better view of personhood [she holds] should understand many kinds of particulars, including one's politics, work, religion, family, love, sexuality, friendships, altruism, experiences, wisdom, moral commitments, character, and personal attributes, as integral to the self."[5]

Her theory of personhood leads Radin to raise serious questions as to whether, for example, a market for newborns should replace the adoption system, whether prostitution should be permitted, whether commercial surrogacy contracts should be allowed, whether the employment relationship should be tightly regulated, or whether residential tenancy agreements should similarly be subject to regulation. In deciding whether to prohibit commodification or exchange altogether in some of these contexts, or instead to permit commodification or exchange subject only to substantial legal constraints, Radin worries about the problem of transition in moving from our present non-ideal world (in her terms) to her ideal world (which arguably is universal non-commodification or some undefined third alternative). The problem of transition raises in turn the problem of what she calls the "double bind." The problem of the double bind arises because in many contexts prohibiting commodification or exchange may make the plight of the individual whose welfare is central to the commodification objection actually worse. For example, banning prostitution or commercial surrogacy contracts, as morally offensive as these may be to many people, may eliminate one of the few income-earning options available to poor women and thus exacerbate their plight and that of their families. Conversely, counterbalancing the double-bind effect may be the domino effect. By this Radin means that permitting transactions such as these, along with the market rhetoric and manifestations that accompany them, may change and pervert the terms of discourse in which members of the community engage with one another about their personal or social relations.[6] For example, if permitting prostitution without any legal constraints led to billboards, mail-order catalogues, television advertising, and so forth, this overt commercialization of sexuality might over time lead members of the community generally to perceive their sexual relations in these detached, non-affective, non-sharing terms. This argument is analogous to the "social disintegration" version of legal moralism espoused most prominently by Lord Devlin[7] in his opposition to legalizing homosexuality, and it is discussed at greater length in Chapter 3. In many of the cases with which Radin is concerned, she seeks to balance the double-bind effect against the domino effect.

Radin's attempt to conceptualize the unarticulated moral intuitions that many of us feel about many of the examples she uses is both ambitious and provocative. However, at a general level, several concerns might be noted. First, while she is critical of Hegel for his arbitrary and conclusory assignments of human attributes to the external and internal dichotomy, her own position on this is confusing and unpersuasive. She argues that "there is no algorithm or abstract formula to tell us which items are (justifiably) personal. A moral judgment is required in each case. We have seen that Hegel's answer to a similar problem was to fall back on the intuition that some things are 'external' and some are 'internal.' This answer is unsatisfactory because the categories 'external' and 'internal' should be the conclusion of a moral evaluation and cannot be taken as obvious premises forming its basis."[8] She concludes, however, by "suggesting that we relinquish the subject-object dichotomy and rely instead on our best moral judgement in the light of the best conception of personhood as we now understand it." This seems inevitably to lead to equally arbitrary and conclusory judgements on a case-by-case basis. For example, weighing both the double-bind effect and the domino effect, she concludes that on balance prostitution should not be totally banned, but should be permitted only without all the market paraphernalia of advertising or intermediaries like pimps; in other words, it should be discreet and non-public. With respect to pre-adoption contracts, she favours complete prohibition. With respect to commercial surrogacy contracts, in general she favours complete prohibition but would permit voluntary surrogacy arrangements. With respect to residential tenancy arrangements, out of a concern to preserve family integrity and community ties, she favours rent controls, habitability requirements, and security of tenure protections. Similarly, with respect to employment contracts, she apparently favours minimum wage laws and job security protections.[9] Although each of these proposals may arguably be defensible in its own right, it is unclear how Radin's general theory of personhood assists in making such judgements in these cases, while in other cases it permits relatively unconstrained commodification.

A second problem with Radin's approach is that, once situated in the non-ideal world within which she accepts she must apply her theory, the strength of the double-bind and domino effects entails essentially empirical observations about the world. Here, in sorting out cases where full com- modification should be permitted, where no commodification at all should be permitted, or where incomplete (constrained) commodification should be permitted, she is entirely casual in her empirical judgements of the strength of these effects from case to case.[10] This difficulty is exemplified in the well-known debate between Titmuss and Arrow on the provision of blood for transfusions. Titmuss, in his book *The Gift Relationship: From Human Blood to Social Policy,*[11] argued that Britain, which has traditionally de- pended on a system of voluntary donations, in contrast to the United States, which has traditionally relied on commercial payments for blood transfu- sions, has out-performed the United States in a number of dimensions: the quantity and quality of blood supplied, the avoidance of severe shortages or surpluses, and the fostering of a sense of altruism, reciprocity, and commu- nity—important non-economic values that he claimed the donation system reinforces and which the commercial system undermines. One of Titmuss' claims is that the two systems cannot co-exist. Like Gresham's law about money, or like Radin's belief about the domino effect, Titmuss' theory holds that the bad system will drive out the good. If potential donors of blood observe other people receiving money for their blood, this will undermine their altruistic motivations. Arrow questions what theory or evidence leads Titmuss to this conclusion. Applying the standard economic paradigm, Arrow[12] conjectures that adding a commercial regime onto a scheme of voluntary donations would simply increase the supply of blood, drawing more providers into the system. Arrow, on the level of empirical evidence, poses the possibility that the commercial regime in the United States may have been a response to the inadequacies of a voluntary regime. In other words, on the evidence presented by Titmuss, it is not clear which way the cause-and-effect relationships run.

A third concern, related to the previous two, is the generalizability of the implications from the Titmuss thesis. Titmuss, while focusing on the blood transfusion phenomenon, obviously sought, in Arrow's terms, to illuminate a much broader landscape: the limits of economic analysis, the rival uses of exchange and gift as modes of allocation, the collective or communitarian possibilities in society versus the tendencies towards individualism. But in this broader context, where does the blood example take us? For example, could we equally depend, should we so determine, on farmers to provide us with steak and potatoes out of a sense of altruism? If not, is there something peculiar about blood? Even in the case of blood, according to Arrow only 5 percent of eligible donors give blood in Britain—yielding in his terms the idea of an "aristocracy of saints." Economists' standard reaction would be that blood donation is a relatively low-cost form of altruism (but apparently not costless), entailing the donation of a renewable resource,[13] but like other things in society, the supply of altruism is inversely related to its cost. Or to take Radin's example of extensive regulation of residential tenancies, why not extend this thinking to detailed zoning of residential neighbourhoods to preserve the existing or established character of the neighbourhood, no matter what the exclusionary effects on individuals who are not currently members of the local community? Or if preserving employment relationships and the direct and indirect set of personal and social networks that surround them is important and thus justifies detailed regulation, why not extend this thinking to small businesses or family farms and adopt regulatory or other policies designed to perpetuate their existence in the interests of preserving stable communities? Indeed, why not argue for trade protectionism across the board in the interest of preserving existing job patterns, social relations, and community structures?

Fourth, as Mack[14] has pointed out, with reference to the philosophical tradition that distinguishes things or attributes that are internally valued— that is, valued for their own sake—and those that are valued for external or instrumental reasons, there is a tendency to draw false correlations between internal values and altruism and between external values and selfishness. However, many internal (non-commodified) values may imply all kinds of oppression, hierarchy, and domination, as exemplified in many traditional family structures. Conversely, many externally valued activities may be motivated purely by altruism. For example, taking on additional paid labour or a second job in order to contribute to third world aid or, less dramatically, in the case of recent immigrant parents, working hard as joint income earners to provide children and extended family members with a better standard of living and better life chances would seem clear examples of altruistically motivated market behaviour. Indeed, these examples illustrate a deeper ambiguity. Often analysts who stress the values of altruism, reciprocity, and community recognize the nature of the social contract entailed where apparent acts of altruism are forthcoming on the generalized understanding that they will be reciprocated in appropriate circumstances. Thus, as the term "social contract" implies, there is an indirect and generalized sense in which an element of exchange is entailed. Similarly, claiming that individuals who are engaged in market activities are acting as individual, rational, self-interest maximizers does not address at all the underlying motivations or utility functions the market activity is designed to advance.[15] Thus, this false juxtaposition of internally valued activities and externally valued activities on the one hand, and altruism and selfishness on the other, provides a tenuous foundation for the domino or Gresham's law argument that one regime is likely to drive out the other if both are permitted initially to co-exist.

A final concern with the Titmuss argument is that if values of altruism, reciprocity, and community are likely to be suppressed or undermined by the operation of "external" market forces, it is not clear why this argument should not also apply to coercive forms of redistribution through the tax and transfer system that are central to the modern welfare state, of which Titmuss himself was a passionate defender. How can we any more readily justify externalizing these values through the state than externalizing similar values through the market?

Thus, it is not clear how Radin's theory of personhood or human flourishing or Titmuss' concepts of reciprocity, altruism, and community provide us with much real purchase on what attributes or resources should be permitted to be commodified; and what should not be, or what should be, commodified only when subject to substantial legal constraints. Given, as must be emphasized, that we are contemplating prohibitions or constraints on exchange relationships that the parties thereto would, in the absence of such prohibitions or constraints, apparently wish to enter into, ultimately some justification is required for this form of paternalism. Although I discuss theories of paternalism in more detail in Chapter 7, it is not clear that to this point we have a theoretical justification for paternalism in the contexts where anti-commodification objections have been invoked, let alone what the content of that theory is.

In my view, Radin too quickly dismisses, as a strategy for structuring our moral intuitions about commodification, a more richly textured theory of contracting or market failure than that which she attributes to traditional economic liberalism. I believe that many of these intuitions ultimately rest on notions of contracting or market failure, in particular, on externalities, coercion, and information failures. Although these concepts themselves are highly problematic, as I elaborate in later chapters, at least they direct our inquiry at particular sources of potential infirmities in the classes of transactions where the commodification concern is commonly raised. In this respect, I follow Gauthier: "Morality arises from market failures. The first step in making this claim good is to show that the perfect market, were it realized, would constitute a morally free zone, a zone within which the constraints of morality would have no place."[16] I now turn to a discussion of a number of problematic cases that exemplify, on the one hand, the anti-commodification theorists' approach and, on the other hand, a contracting or market failure approach.

Some Problematic Cases

Scarce Lifesaving Technology

The scenario envisaged here is one where, in the early period of some new lifesaving technology, say, dialysis machines, many fewer units of the technology are available than can meet existing demand.[17] For example, let us assume that immediately after the invention of the dialysis machine, in any given jurisdiction there are ten machines available and one hundred patients with serious kidney problems who face shortened life expectancy if they do not obtain access to a machine. Because supply is assumed initially to be fixed and the consequences so serious for those who do not obtain access to the scarce resource, Calabresi and Bobbitt characterize this type of case as a "tragic choice."[18] The possible modes of allocation and the strengths and weaknesses of each can be briefly summarized.

MARKETS

Here, as with other resources in a market economy, we could allocate the scarce resources to the highest bidders. Conventional economic analysis would assume that they place the highest value on them. Of course, the obvious objection to this regime is that people who may derive a disproportionately enhanced life expectancy from access to the technology or who may value the resources very highly but cannot substantiate their valuations with personal resources will not be able to bid successfully, including people who may claim that their past or prospective social contributions render them especially meritorious. Posner, however, would argue that wealth maximization is an attractive ethical norm, precisely because it validates only those preferences supportable by resources, which in most cases have been obtained by providing goods or services to others that have presumably enhanced the welfare of the latter.[19] This claim has proven highly contentious and, for many critics, unpersuasive, in part because the capacity to sell goods or services that others value is at least in part a function of fortuities, such as the genetic lottery and early family and social circumstances, which do not comport well with a defensible theory of desert. An alternative line of defence of the market regime in this context is that if there is a concern about the justice of prior endowments, it should be rectified separately and generally and not through attempts to redress distributive justice concerns through the manipulation of the allocation of this particular scarce resource. For example, if prior endowments have been generally redistributed to comport with some defensible theory of distributive justice, would it any longer follow that a market form of allocation here would be objectionable on distributive justice grounds? In any event, the question why this particular scarce resource should be viewed differently from a host of other scarce resources such as automobiles, housing, food, and clothing would have to be faced. What specifically makes the allocation of this particular scarce resource more "tragic" than the others? If the answer is that this allocation decision bears on issues of life and death, it might equally be argued that access to less rather than more risky occupations, to better rather than worse quality housing and food, and so on, also bears on the matter of life expectancy. Finally, in defence of the market, it may plausibly be argued that it is the one mechanism, of all those to be reviewed, where the incentives created on the supply side from a bidding mechanism are likely to increase supply of the scarce resources over time as the initial scarcity rents engender further innovation and new entry into the production of the scarce resource or close substitutes for it. In other words, this mode of distribution of the scarce resource in itself will affect the future allocation of resources to its production (unlike the distribution mechanisms that follow).

LOTTERIES

We could allocate the ten dialysis machines in the above example by putting the names of the one hundred patients into a hat and providing machines to the first ten people whose names are drawn out of the hat. This regime would have the virtue of being a randomized form of allocation which is wealth neutral. It is also presumably very cheap to administer. However, it will be insensitive to various claims of merit or desert that the one hundred patients may wish to make in establishing priorities for themselves. There would also be the question of whether a secondary market should be permitted after the initial lottery, whereby winners in the lottery would be permitted to auction off their entitlements to the highest bidders. One might well argue that such a secondary market should be permitted, in that if a holder of an initial entitlement values expenditures on other purposes more than some extension of life expectancy through access to the machine, society should not interfere with that preference.

QUEUING: FIRST COME FIRST SERVED

Like a lottery, a queue is likely to be wealth neutral and, depending on how it is organized, may even favour those with low opportunity costs who can afford to invest a good deal of their time establishing and maintaining a high position in the queue. However, as with lotteries, this method of allocation will be insensitive to various claims of merit or desert that patients in the pool may feel should influence priorities in the allocation of the machines. The question would again arise whether a secondary market should be permitted.

VOTING REGIMES: DEMOCRATIC ALLOCATION

Although many variants of a voting regime might be devised, one could imagine a regime where the one hundred claimants to the machine constitute themselves a political assembly and decide the allocation collectively through democratic means. However, this assembly could not proceed directly to a vote, because each person would simply vote for herself and there would be no collective decision. First, the assembly would have to decide (unanimously?) on a constitution that would govern how decisions would be made. Perhaps the decision-rule adopted might entail each claimant's presenting the merits of her claim to other members of the assembly, and then each claimant would vote for ten claimants (perhaps excluding herself). The top ten vote getters would receive the machines. A number of questions would be raised by such a regime. How would ties be resolved? Would side-payments for votes be permitted (allowing wealth effects to intrude)? Could groups (parties) form to run slates? How stable would these coalitions be? In the light of Arrow's well-known impossibility theorem,[20] would collective outcomes reflect any coherent aggregation or ranking of individual preferences? In other words, would the collective outcomes reflect *anybody's* preferences? Would any set of rankings command stable majority support or simply engender voting cycles?[21] Even if individual preferences are rejected as the basic reference point in favour of some communitarian theory of the good, such a theory must identify and justify both a substantive theory of the good and some person or institution empowered to apply that theory and make the requisite allocations. Both tasks present formidable difficulties,[22] as exemplified in the discussion of merit allocation mechanisms that follows.

ADMINISTRATIVE (MERIT) ALLOCATION

Various merit-based criteria could plausibly be chosen for application in an administrative allocation regime. These criteria are likely to have different implications for the institutional design of the regime. For example, the criterion chosen might be a quantitative one of simply maximizing Patient Life Years (P.L.Y.). Here one assumes that a group of medical experts are best able to decide which of the ten patients in the pool of one hundred are likely to increase their life expectancies most through access to the dialysis machines. However, it may be objected that this criterion may pick up patients whose past or prospective social contributions are minimal or negative, such as habitual criminals, rapists, or child abusers. To address this problem, one could choose instead a criterion of merit that focuses on future social contributions. Which ten patients in the pool of one hundred are likely, in various ways, to most enhance the quality of life of the society of which they are members? Here, the problem will obviously be that these contributions will be of very different kinds and will not be readily commensurable, once one has rejected, as one would have done if the market form of allocation has been rejected, a metric of future social contributions that simply reflects what society is prepared to pay different people for different kinds of contributions. When we consider institutional design, it seems obvious that medical experts have no particular comparative advantage in making these social valuations, but now the composition of the committee or agency which is to make the choices would become critically important. What would be the criteria for membership on such a committee or agency, and who would make the appointments? Or, alternatively, would one simply randomize the composition of the committee or agency by picking, say, the names of twelve citizens out of a hat to constitute the adjudicative body (by analogy to a jury)? In terms of process, what kinds of information or submissions would the agency solicit from the one hundred claimants, and against what criteria would the information be evaluated? How would the veracity of the information be tested? Should wealth differentials be neutralized in terms of resources employed in making representations? Should invasion of privacy be a concern? Would a reasoned set of decisions be required? Would these decisions be subject to judicial review, and against what criteria? Or should we adopt a completely non-rationalistic ("black box") rather than a rationalistic decision-making process?

An alternative criterion to future social contributions would be past social contributions. That is, despite the fact that a claimant may be elderly and therefore likely to derive limited enhanced life-expectancy from access to a dialysis machine, and may be able to make only a minimal claim in terms of future social contributions, to the extent that this person has been a particularly valuable past contributor to the welfare of society, should this claim not be admitted (although, as in the case of future social contributions, difficulties of both substance and process would arise as to what would constitute a more rather than a less important past social contribution)?

Again, as with lotteries and queuing, under any system of administrative allocation the issue would arise of whether a secondary market should be permitted once initial entitlements have been determined. Moreover, the more general question would have to be faced: If we feel so confident of the robustness of the criteria for evaluating either prospective or past social contributions in this context and for rejecting market valuations of either, why would we not wish to extend these criteria to all allocational decisions, including automobiles, housing, food, clothing, and so forth?

When we consider scarce lifesaving resources such as dialysis machines, we tend to focus on the ethical dilemmas regarding modes of allocation. While raising many of these same concerns, the practice or potential of organ transplantation generates debate surrounding the ethics of the commodification of human body parts. Whereas in the dialysis example, the production of the machine is largely unproblematic, the harvesting of organs leads to as many difficulties as does their allocation.

The Sale of Human Organs and Foetal Tissue

In the past twenty years, organ transplantation technology, including the use of foetal tissue, has become so sophisticated that widespread transplantation is close to a reality. Currently, the demand for organs is greater than the supply.[23] The Manitoba Law Reform Commission reported that in 1984, there were 1000 people on the waiting list for kidney transplants in Canada and that by 1986, there were 2500 people waiting.[24] The best organs come from young, healthy people who have been killed in accidents. Anywhere from 12,000 to 27,000 such people die each year in the United States, yet only 2000 of them donate their organs.[25] Most provinces in Canada and many states in the U.S. now provide drivers with an opportunity to register for organ donation every time they receive or renew their driver's license. A sticker or card on the back of the driver's license usually signifies a donor. In the prairie provinces of Canada, 23 percent of the population have signed donor cards (either on their drivers' license or independently).[26] However, over 70 percent of Americans[27] and 60 percent of Canadians surveyed have expressed a willingness to donate.[28]

Three main reasons have been identified for the discrepancy between the number of actual donors and the number of people who claim willingness to donate. First, altruism is much easier to exhibit in theory than in reality; people might like to think they would donate their organs, but when they actually have to commit themselves to doing so, they refrain. Second, people have expressed fears of over-eager doctors harvesting their organs before they are actually dead. Finally, signing an organ donor card forces a person to confront her own mortality, something which most people are hesitant to do.[29] Obstacles to donation are also created by physicians. Even if a person has signed a donor's card or a driver's license, doctors often feel morally obligated to request the family's permission prior to extracting the organs. If the person has neither objected nor consented, some physicians feel especially uncomfortable requesting the organs from a family that has just lost a loved one in a tragic accident.[30] *Inter vivos* donation presents a separate set of concerns from those posed by cadaveric donations. The main non-regenerative organ used in *inter vivos* donations is the kidney, and the main regenerative body parts used are bone marrow, skin (for grafts), semen, and blood. One proposed solution to the problem of organ scarcity is the creation of a futures market in organs.

MARKETS IN HUMAN ORGANS

The position of both the Australian[31] and the Manitoba Law Reform Commissions[32] on a market for cadaveric and *inter vivos* organ transfers is representative of the main arguments against such a market. Organs are considered by both commissions to be something which cannot justifiably be commodified in a humane society. Examples of contracts which the justice system generally does not enforce are those made under duress, those which are contrary to public policy, and those which involve sales of basic rights.[33] The Manitoba Commission contends that commerce in human organs potentially falls into all three categories and that "[c]ommerce in human tissue would likely encourage blackmail, coercion, or duress; cause deterioration in standards of testing; increase the possibility of donors lying or concealing health defects, thus increasing the danger to recipients, as well as wrongly encourage donations from the poor."[34]

One concern with respect to legal sanctioning of *inter vivos* organ sales is that people will begin to view their organs entirely as commodities. The moral spectrum ranges from altruistic donations—a parent donates a kidney to her child who is sick—to sales reflecting personal indulgence—a person has lost money through gambling and sells her kidney to recoup the loss.[35] Some foresee a situation whereby "a man with a $50,000 kidney, like a man with $50,000 in the bank, would not qualify for welfare."[36] The primary concern with respect to *inter vivos* selling of organs, however, seems to be that indigent people will, for lack of a wider range of options, sell kidneys for the benefit of the rich. The resulting suggestion of a prohibition has been viewed by others as a perverse kind of paternalism. Henry Hansmann argues that "if society is not willing to give the poor sufficient assets so that they are not inclined to sell a kidney, then society should not refuse to let them sell one of the few assets they have."[37] Moreover, there is arguably little difference between selling a kidney and working in a meat packing plant; both are dangerous, and both reflect a limited range of choices.[38] However, Hansmann recognizes the need for legislative controls to avoid the situation of opportunistic buyers inducing mentally incompetent, inebriated, or desperate people to sell their kidneys for $50.00. With this in mind, he suggests age limits on selling *inter vivos* organs, as well as a six-month waiting period between the signing of the contract and the harvesting of the organ.[39]

Clearly, the market system has its merits. The average cost of a heart transplant is $100,000–$110,000.[40] In 1985 the United States government spent $284,700,000 for 7073 kidney transplants, amounting to over $40,000 per transplant.[41] The estimates for U.S. government expenditures on heart transplants for 1990 range from $20,000,000 to $47,000,000 per year.[42] This does not include expenditures of state governments or organizations such as the Veterans Administration.[43] Although arguably everyone should have an equal right to life, regardless of wealth, at $25,000 to $238,000 per transplant,[44] government-subsidized organ transplantations are very expensive. The saving of lives through organ transplantation takes away from the quality of all our lives. To contain the public costs, Peter Schuck proposes a modified market wherein children and low-income people receive government-subsidized transplants, while the economically advantaged must buy them.[45]

Lloyd Cohen suggests a futures market in cadaveric organs, whereby healthy people contract out their organs to others, and if the seller dies, his estate receives the money for the organs used.[46] Cohen argues that this is ethical because it involves cadaveric donation only, so poor people will not be exploited, and, since people will be selling their own organs, "their next of kin will not be required to traffic in the decedents' remains."[47] In response to the argument that a market for organs will actively discourage altruism, Cohen points out that "[i]t is hardly an act of great generosity to donate that which you cannot use and may not sell."[48] Unfortunately, Cohen fails to indicate how a futures market would actually work. It is clear that an intermediary is necessary, because if someone is in need of an organ, he cannot wait until the person with whom he has contracted dies—he must have access to an immediately available organ, which means that the donor is dead and could not possibly have contracted with him.

To deal with this problem, Hansmann outlines a scheme for a futures market in cadaveric organs involving insurance companies. Its advantages are that the seller gains an immediate benefit and that it is ethically more acceptable than straight cash for organs. Hansmann suggests that people who buy health insurance be given the option on the insurance forms of being an organ donor. In return, the donor receives a reduction in insurance premiums based on the expected profit of the insurer (the market price of the organ multiplied by the chance that this person will die with harvestable organs).[49] A national registry would exist containing the name of each donor. Every time a person renews her insurance, she has the choice of retracting or renewing her commitment to donate. If the donor dies, her organs are sold to the recipient and are paid for by the recipient himself, or by his insurance company. Hence, simply by committing to donate, one receives a financial benefit, even if one dies a natural death at age eighty and one's organs are never used. The price of organs would be determined by the health insurance market, which, as Hansmann points out, in the United States is very competitive.[50] To those who find this scheme unethical, Hansmann retorts that it is much more ethical than approaching a family hours after a tragic death in an attempt to solicit organs.[51] He contends that this scheme will increase the supply of organ donations because the money is an incentive for incurring the psychic transaction costs entailed in making a pre-commitment.[52] A modest alternative to Hansmann's scheme would be for the government to waive annual drivers license or motor vehicle registration fees in return for drivers' signing a donor's card. This would create a quasi-market on the supply side but would leave to be independently resolved how organs should be allocated on the demand side, which would implicate the same set of issues that were noted above with respect to scarce lifesaving technology (dialysis machines).

MARKETS IN FOETAL TISSUE

A market system for *inter vivos* and cadaveric organs may increase the supply of human tissue, both by providing people with an economic incentive to overcome the psychic costs of confronting their own mortality and by providing doctors with a clear indication that the deceased has actually consented to the removal of her organs. However, a market in foetal tissue raises very different concerns. Research in the field of medical uses for foetal tissue is progressing rapidly. Foetal brain cells and tissue can now be used to treat Parkinson's disease and diabetes and, in the near future, may be used to treat Alzheimer's, Huntington's, epilepsy, brain injuries, and perhaps even AIDS.[53] In addition, newborns with defective organs are in need of foetal organs, since those of adult donors are obviously too large.[54] As with the sale of human organs, commodification of human body parts is an element of the ethical debate surrounding the sale of foetal tissue. However, the focus of the foetal controversy is the intimate connection between abortion and the use of foetal tissue.

The crux of the debate is the use of foetuses born alive but not viable.[55] According to U.S. law, the harvesting of foetal tissue may be conducted only once the foetus is dead.[56] The problem with this law is that the organs of a dead foetus are often unharvestable because of the lack of necessary oxygen.[57] The law exists ostensibly to "protect the rights of the aborted fetus when its parts are to be used for transplantation."[58] However, given the alternative to transplantation, which is disposal of the foetus, it is difficult to understand why the "rights" of the aborted foetus need be shown particular respect. Berger, however, points out that there is a slippery slope involved in labelling foetuses as non-persons, since this could lead to similar labelling of anencephalic babies,[59] which could eventuate in the killing of imperfect babies to save the lives of perfect babies.[60] Thus, she opposes the practice of artificially maintaining the anencephalic infant so that his organs can be harvested to save another baby.[61]

The principal opponents of the harvesting or sale of foetal tissue tend to be those who are opposed to abortion. John A. Robertson identifies two objections to the use of foetal tissue, both of which he rejects. The first is the so-called complicity argument. People who oppose abortion think that to use foetal tissue is to be a retroactive accomplice to the sin of abortion.[62] Robertson rejects this objection by suggesting that even if abortion is unethical, the consequences exist and should be used for a good end, rather than being discarded.[63] The second objection is that using foetal tissue will legitimize abortion and hence encourage it.[64] Robertson responds that by parity of argument the use of cadaveric organs could encourage such activities as homicide, suicide, and drunk driving, but that the connection is too tenuous to be plausible.[65]

One widely held fear regarding the sale of foetal tissue is that women may be induced to jeopardize their health by deferring abortions to later stages in their pregnancies, when foetal organs are more fully developed, or by agreeing to more invasive forms of abortion. This is a very real concern because the most common method of aborting a foetus is dilation and evacuation, or scraping. The foetus emerges dismembered, and thus the tissue is more difficult to use. A caesarean section would result in a whole foetus, which would be optimal for tissue or organ transplantation, but this entails greater health risks for the woman.[66] Another fear is that selling foetal tissue will result in women conceiving merely to abort and hence to profit from the tissue.[67] Robertson claims that a market is unlikely to develop, because there are 1.5 million abortions performed each year in the United States and therefore no shortage of supply. Histocompatibility[68] between foetal tissue and recipients is not necessary, so the supply is harvestable.[69] Nicolas Terry, however, disagrees. He notes that in the United States there are 10 million people with diabetes, 2.5 million people with Alzheimer's, and .5 million people with Parkinson's.[70] He also points out that the more widely birth control is used, and the more uses researchers find for foetal tissue, the greater the chance of a market developing.[71] Bauer suggests that a market in foetal tissue be not prohibited, but regulated. The most significant regulation he proposes is that the donation or sale of foetal tissue to a specific person be prohibited. This would prevent women from conceiving specifically to abort and sell the foetal tissue, but it would allow women who had abortions for other reasons to receive compensation for the tissue.[72]

Currently in Canada and the United States, the sale of all non-regenerative and most regenerative organs is illegal. This reflects the commonly held notion that body parts are among those things which ought not to be bought and sold, because they are intrinsic to our personhood. However, given the high demand for organs and foetal tissue, a futures market in cadaveric organs such as Hansmann proposes, and regulated markets in *inter vivos* organs and foetal tissue, may well alleviate the supply shortages where the donation system has failed. The saving of people's lives seems a defensible justification for the commodification of human body parts.

Sexual services are also often placed in the category of those things which ought not to be bought and sold. Unlike the selling of organs, prostitution does not supply a commodity on which human life is dependent. The following discussion will examine arguments against the commodification of sexual services and will then consider the merits of the three most common solutions to the difficulties posed by prostitution: increased criminal sanctions for prostitution; legalization; and decriminalization.

Prostitution

THE COMMODIFICATION OBJECTION

Margaret Jane Radin argues that the commodification of sexual services is inconsistent with an affirmative notion of human flourishing.[73] Radin's concept of human flourishing is based on a notion of humans' relating to each other as unique beings, valued for their intellectual, emotional, and social strengths and contributions. In a market society, it is maintained that this concept of human flourishing is frustrated, because people are valued for their monetary worth rather than for their human worth.[74] Radin asserts that "[w]e feel discomfort or even insult, and we feel degradation or even loss of the value involved, when bodily integrity is conceived of as a fungible object."[75] As discussed earlier, Radin modifies Marxist theories of alienation with what she terms the "domino theory." Applied to prostitution, the domino theory implies that if sexual services are freely commodified in our society, non-commodified sex may decrease.[76] Although Radin advocates decriminalization of the exchange of money for sex, she would support a ban on procuring and advertising, because "[t]he open market might render subconscious valuation of women (and perhaps everyone) in sexual dollar value impossible to avoid."[77]

Moreover, most prostitutes are women and are viewed by many feminists as victims of male exploitation.[78] Carole Pateman sees prostitution as "part of the exercise of the law of male sex rights, one of the ways in which men are ensured access to women's bodies."[79] Catharine MacKinnon views prostitution as "the fundamental condition of women."[80] MacKinnon argues that sexuality is a social construct by men, of women, and for men; that inherent in this social construct of female sexuality is a notion of women as needing, enjoying, or deserving pain, rape, abuse, and humiliation;[81] and that the fundamental force of this sexuality is the reduction of a person to a sub-human object.[82] According to MacKinnon, prostitution perpetuates this construction of sexuality, because it allows men access to women simply by paying for it, thereby endorsing a non-mutual, unequal set of relations between the sexes.

CRIMINALIZATION

Currently in the United States, the act of commercializing sex is prohibited in forty-six states.[83] In Canada, the actual act of payment for sex is legal, but the surrounding activities—solicitation,[84] procuring,[85] keeping a common bawdy house,[86] and living off the avails of prostitution[87]—are criminal offenses. This effectively criminalizes prostitution, as it is virtually impossible to sell one's services if one is prohibited from "communicat[ing] with any person for the purpose of engaging in prostitution or of obtaining the sexual services of a prostitute."[88] Although in Canada and the United States, women who work the street are the most visible prostitutes, they constitute only 10–20 percent of the prostitute population.[89] According to United States data however, 85–90 percent of all prostitutes arrested are those working the street, 55 percent of those arrested are women of colour, as are 85 percent of prostitutes receiving jail sentences.[90] The vast majority of women working on the streets in Regina, Saskatchewan, are Native.[91] Findings from various studies indicate that anywhere from 50 to 75 percent of prostitutes were the victims of sexual abuse as children.[92] The prevalence of child sexual abuse in the female population overall is reported to range from 15 to 62 percent.[93] Due to the lack of consistent data, it is not possible to reach a reliable conclusion as to the correlation between the incidence of childhood sexual abuse and entrance into the sex trade. Even if child sexual abuse could be identified as a strong influencing factor in the decision of a woman to become a prostitute, it might be argued that this is all the more reason not to victimize prostitutes further through harsh criminal sanctions. However, this still leaves open the question of whether pimps, bawdy house keepers, and particularly customers of prostitutes ("johns"), who are mostly men and who exploit the vulnerabilities and dependencies of these women, should be the target of criminal sanctions.

The majority of the 80–90 percent of prostitutes who do not work the streets were not physically coerced into prostitution, but are making an informed, albeit limited, economic choice.[94] In North America, where most women are functionally literate and have other job options, those entering into prostitution are often motivated by remunerative rewards but are not always poverty-stricken; a number of prostitutes are university graduates.[95] Belinda Cheney cites data indicating that 44 percent of the prostitutes surveyed in New South Wales, Australia, were mothers who were attracted to the sex trade because of the flexible hours.[96] Moira Griffin states that many prostitutes view sex as a power game, one in which they are in control.[97] Many have claimed that they are not merely sellers of sex, but therapists, social workers, and companions as well.[98] In short, these advocates of prostitutes' rights consider the feminist view of themselves—as victims of male domination unable to make choices or express true consent—to be patronizing, presumptuous, and arrogant.[99]

LEGALIZATION

In several European countries, and in two counties in Nevada, prostitution is legalized but regulated by the state. Generally this involves restricting the areas within which prostitutes can work, legislating mandatory medical checks, and issuing licenses. One feminist objection to regulation, espoused by Belinda Cheney, is that it legitimates and sanctions prostitution.[100] Following MacKinnon and the Fraser Committee, Cheney maintains that prostitution is a reflection of a sexist society which allows men to use women as sexual objects.[101] Hence, while opposing criminalization, Cheney views regulation as sanctioning the objectification of women. Regulation eradicates the dignity of the prostitute by expropriating her sexuality and assigning control over it to the state.

A lesson can be learned from Nevada, the only state in the United States which, in two counties, does not criminalize either the exchange of sex for money, or secondary activities such as soliciting, procuring, and so forth. The women are prohibited from entering the casinos and bars; they are allowed out of licensed brothels only during certain hours; they are forbidden from being seen alone with a man in public; and, if they cease to sell sex, they must wait three months before they can seek alternative employment in the same county.[102] These women are virtually sexual prisoners of the state. The Nevada model is extreme, but it presents some of the realities entailed in regulation.

DECRIMINALIZATION

Criminalizing prostitution turns the state against the prostitutes so that they are unable to avail themselves of the protection of the authorities with respect to violence perpetrated against them by customers, pimps, and police officers.[103] Moreover, prohibition is ineffective, as prostitution thrives throughout North America, where it is generally prohibited. In addition, the average cost of arresting and jailing a prostitute for two weeks in New York City in 1977 was $3000.00;[104] in 1988, the City of Toronto spent over $6.3 million controlling prostitution.[105] Most feminists and virtually all prostitutes support the decriminalization of prostitution. Decriminalization can be modified or absolute.

Modified decriminalization would abolish any laws which criminalize the activity of prostitutes themselves, but it would continue to penalize pimps and possibly clients. The Fraser Report recommends that both the acts of soliciting one's sexual services and purchasing the sexual services of another be removed from the Criminal Code[106] but that procurement and living off the avails, when physical or psychic coercion is involved, remain in the Criminal Code.[107] In addition, the Report suggests that the current statute prohibiting the existence of a "common bawdy house" be replaced by a prohibition of prostitution establishments. Up to two prostitutes would be allowed to live and work out of their residence without its being considered a prostitution establishment.[108] The Fraser Report posits prostitution as an institution which reflects the sexism of society; it therefore envisions social as well as legal solutions. Some of these are affirmative action programmes, better enforcement of employment standards legislation, improved child care facilities, retraining programmes, and changes to social benefits legislation. These measures would enable women to gain economic power so that prostitution would be less financially necessary or attractive.[109]

The Canadian Organization for the Rights of Prostitutes argues that modified decriminalization is undesirable because it may continue to restrict the freedom of prostitutes. For example, if the actual exchange of sex for money is decriminalized, but living in a bawdy house or living off the avails of prostitution is still a criminal act, prostitutes will be restricted in terms of where and with whom they live. Absolute decriminalization confers three benefits on prostitutes: it allows them the freedom to work indoors and arrange their business as they wish; it reduces the potential for abuse by customers, police, and pimps; and it gives them a greater sense of dignity and self-worth.[110]

When the issue of prostitution is placed in a private law contractual setting, obviously issues of coercion, contractual incapacity, and information failures (dealt with in later chapters) provide relevant bases for not enforcing prostitution contracts. Assuming that none of these factors is present, consider the following example (by way of embroidery of the facts of the recent popular movie *Pretty Woman*). An out-of-town businessman hires the sexual and escort services of a prostitute for the week he is in town, agreeing to pay $5,000. Suppose she provides the services and he reneges on the promised payment, opportunistically and without valid reasons, at the end of the week. Should she be allowed to sue for the agreed fee? Or what if, conversely, he pays the fee at the beginning of the assignation, and she opportunistically reneges on her side of the deal. Should he be allowed to sue for restitution of the fee on the grounds of unjust enrichment?[111]

There appear to be persuasive arguments for complete decriminalization of prostitution and for encouraging the activity to move off the streets and to evolve as a small-scale "cottage industry." Equally, in a private law setting it is not clear why the law should refuse to recognize all contractual claims arising out of prostitution arrangements on the grounds that they are contrary to public policy.

According to Moira Griffin, in patriarchy the wife and the prostitute share much in common: both provide sexual services in return for compensation. The only differences are that the prostitute is not tied to one man, is not expected to perform domestic tasks, is more independent, and is usually better paid.[112] Historically, wives shared the legal status of slaves, being considered the property of their husbands.[113] Until 1884, in Britain a woman could be imprisoned for refusing to honour her husband's conjugal rights.[114] Even today, women who work at home are often treated as servants (if not slaves), in that compensation is not commensurate with the value of their labour, but rather is weakly substituted by some measure of economic security.[115] Although it is cogently argued that most women suffer from living in patriarchy, I reject Griffin's analogy between wives and prostitutes. The analogy is particularly inadequate in the context of the status of dependent spouses upon marriage breakup. A prostitute is paid for her sexual services, but many feminists and myself advocate compensation to dependent spouses on marriage breakup for the opportunity costs incurred as a result of specialization in household production, rather than for sexual services rendered throughout the marriage. A discussion of the validity of separation agreements illuminates the importance of establishing an appropriate set of background compensatory entitlements.

Separation Agreements and the Economically Dependent Spouse

THE EVOLVING CONCEPT OF MARRIAGE

Unlike the traditional common law structuring of the husband-wife relationship, modern family law reforms reflect the growing attitude that men and women should receive equal treatment before and under the law.[116] Contemporary attitudes regarding the role of women in society and the diversity of views on the purpose of marriage and family, together with a general shift towards serial marriages, have resulted in numerous reforms of the laws governing divorce, alimony and support, divorce and separation agreements, and child support and custody. To draw on Nitya Duclos,[117] the institution of marriage no longer has its basis in a "partnership for life" model, but instead focuses on a union favouring equality of the partners and individual responsibility, "allowing men and women to define their own roles within marriage"[118] and the consequences of marriage breakdown.

The basic underlying model is that of two equal partners, voluntarily contributing to a joint venture, in which the division of functions—financial provision, household management, and child care—is the result of mutual agreement between the partners.[119] The goal of reform has been to affirm in women the ability to operate as fully autonomous and self-determining agents, free to bargain and enjoy all the rights and freedoms previously held only by men. Current laws providing for "no-fault divorce" and governing the division of marital assets, support, and alimony payments are reflective of this new model of a joint venture. Not only does Ontario law provide for the equal distribution of property upon divorce[120] but, contrary to the norms underlying the partnership for life model, the purpose of alimony and support is the promotion of economic self-sufficiency and self-reliance.[121] The law's goal is to restore parties as quickly as possible to their status as autonomous individuals for the purpose of terminating all relations between the two partners, including that of economic interdependence.[122] In this regard, marriage is a neutral factor which does not automatically create a support entitlement.

THE VALIDITY OF SEPARATION AGREEMENTS

In the context of separation agreements (and, for that matter, ante-nuptial agreements that provide for the contingency of marriage breakdown), it is not difficult to identify the major advantages of private ordering.[123] First, private ordering acknowledges the unique aspects of each relationship and allows parties to fashion separation agreements which best suit their particular preferences and life plans. Categoric rules laid down by legislatures or courts are unlikely to fulfil this function. Second, agreements which are negotiated by the parties involved are more likely to be abided by than those imposed by a third party, such as a court. In the latter case, one party will often perceive himself as the undeserved loser and may be more inclined to be delinquent in his obligations under the agreement. Third, negotiated separation agreements conserve on various kinds of costs that may be loosely grouped under the rubric of transaction costs. These include the risks, uncertainties, delays, financial costs, invasive public scrutiny, and emotional trauma of litigation. Fourth, separation agreements, if binding, provide the parties with a sense of finality and security with respect to arrangements they have made. This in turn encourages the parties to fashion new life plans, build new relationships, and undertake new commitments.

Although these are powerful advantages favouring private ordering in the context of marital breakup, separation agreements are contracts, and the law of contracts at large recognizes a rich array of defences and excuses in contract enforcement. Moreover, even economists who strongly favour the contractual paradigm recognize that issues such as coercion, imperfect information, and externalities may generate contracting failures in not yielding Pareto superior bargains. However, an even more fundamental issue is the adequacy of the background legal entitlements (or default rules), against which parties negotiate separation agreements.

Neither markets nor contractual exchanges function in a vacuum; every contract occurs against a regime of rights recognized and protected by the state. Thus, to use Mnookin and Kornhauser's memorable phrase,[124] bargaining, in most contexts, is bargaining in the shadow of the law. In a matrimonial context, a critical threshold question that must be addressed is whether the background entitlements of the parties have been appropriately defined by the legal system, because in the absence of agreement the background or default rules, to which either party can have recourse, will govern. Even if private ordering of separation agreements were banned and replaced by court-imposed outcomes, many of the same results would obtain under the existing legal framework. An important example of the inadequacy of the current law in remedying private ordering failures, resulting from unsatisfactory background entitlements, is the lack of attention paid to a major class of family assets: human capital.

Although courts in many jurisdictions have begun to grapple with such problems as valuing professional degrees, there is much inconsistency and uncertainty associated with judicial policy on intangible assets more generally. As a prelude to her analysis of this issue, Katherine Baker notes:

> Divorce is an economic disaster for women. The latest census figures reveal that only 15 percent of divorced women in this country [the United States] are awarded any alimony or maintenance payments. Of that 15 percent only a small percentage receive any of the awarded money, the mean alimony awarded in 1986 being only $3,733. A recent California study found that the standard of living for men increases 42 percent after divorce, while the standard of living for women decreases by 73 percent.[125]

The impact of marriage on the value of human capital is one of the major unresolved issues on the family law reform agenda.

Feminist concerns in this area generally reflect a good deal of ambivalence, indeed moral anguish, over what Martha Minow has eloquently called the "dilemma of difference."[126] On the one hand, the concern is that recognizing the state of economic dependency in which wives in more traditional marriage relationships find themselves, through more generous property division or support rules, risks legitimating and reinforcing the subordinate roles of women in our society. On the other hand, failure to recognize the differences that actually exist in the current roles of men and women in many relationships risks discriminating against women who find themselves in this state of dependency. As reflected in recent decisions of the Supreme Court of Canada,[127] current background legal entitlements regarding support obligations of husbands to wives stress need and rehabilitation as central criteria, as well as the importance of finality in the termination of a relationship and the rapid attainment of economic self-sufficiency by both former spouses. However, as feminist critics of this line of thinking rightly argue, support payments predicated on these notions of equal individual autonomy and responsibility unfairly ignore the realities facing a former wife who, in a traditional marriage relationship, has specialized in household production while her former husband has specialized in market production.[128] In the course of this division of labour, she may have suffered a substantial depreciation of her human capital with respect to market opportunities and thus, on marriage breakdown, confronts the prospect of limited employment opportunities and modest income-generating potential, while his earning potential is unaffected and indeed may well have been enhanced by the marriage.

One approach to the valuation issue, espoused by Nitya Duclos,[129] is to focus on the opportunity costs incurred by a woman in an economically dependent relationship in forgone career opportunities that translate into reduced earning capacity on marriage breakdown relative to the earning capacity the wife would probably have enjoyed had her career not been interrupted by marriage, and attempt to compensate for this reduced earning capacity in the future (perhaps discounted by the probability of re-marriage). This focus on the opportunity costs of marriage is consistent with the approach advocated by law and economics scholars, for example, in valuing the loss of a housewife's services in fatal accident litigation.[130] My concern is that while this proposal would generate significant additional financial awards to many women on marriage breakup, it would still substantially under-compensate women who have specialized in household production for extended periods of time, thus forgoing income-generating opportunities during marriage. In recognition of the need to compensate for these past opportunity costs, Baker[131] would award wives who have specialized in household production to various degrees prescribed percentages of a husband's income over the course of the marriage. But even these two measures of compensation for investment in household production may be less than fully compensatory. In many economically dependent relationships, the wife, by investing in household production in the early period of the relationship, may reasonably expect to realize returns on these investments in later periods of the relationship, when the husband's income will provide economic security for herself and the family. One of the purposes of contract law is to discourage opportunism, where the first mover risks appropriation of her performance under the contract by the second mover, who faces strong incentives to take the first mover's performance and run. This scenario of opportunistic breach may well provide insight into the circumstances surrounding many marriage breakdowns involving economically dependent relationships.[132]

In designing a default rule that would apply unless the parties have validly contracted away from it by ante-nuptial or separation agreement, we may find it useful conceptually to construct a hypothetical contract at the time that marriage is entered into, when the parties decide on a specialization of functions involving one partner's devoting time to market production and the other to household production. If we assume that the wife is more risk averse than the husband, given the differential impact of divorce on the economic welfare of men and women reflected in the data cited above, the wife may rationally demand an "insurance policy" from the husband to the effect that if there is no marriage dissolution, she will share in the economic returns to the husband over her life, and if there is marriage dissolution, she should be no worse off than had she not married, which would seem to require a focus on the opportunity costs to her of the marriage and some combination of the Duclos and Baker approaches. One drawback of the opportunity cost approach is, of course, that it will reflect enduring differentials in opportunities in the labour market for men and women. For example, a waitress who marries at the age of nineteen may conceivably have suffered no opportunity costs during marriage or after divorce, but should her husband enjoy prospects of enhanced earning capacity in the future, she will be denied the benefits. Here a difficult issue must be confronted. In constructing the hypothetical contract at the time of marriage, would the two parties agree that the wife should share in the husband's economic returns, both where there is no marriage dissolution and where there is? No insurer would write such a policy because the wife may well be rendered largely indifferent to sustaining or terminating the marriage, given the assumption that under no-fault divorce laws her entitlements on divorce are not contingent on proof of absence of fault on her part for the marriage dissolution.[133] This is the standard problem of moral hazard in insurance markets (where once a person is fully insured there is no incentive to take precautions to minimize the risk of the insured contingency materializing) or, in the present context, reciprocal opportunism. Such a policy would be analogous to a fire insurance policy on a widget factory that provided coverage not only for the replacement costs of the factory in the event of fire, but also the present value of all expected future widget sales. Such coverage means that incentives on the part of the insured to preserve and protect the insured asset are highly attenuated.

Thus, if the opportunity cost measure of compensation (essentially, a reliance interest measure) for household production on divorce reflected in the Duclos-Baker approach generates a value of x, and an income or profit-sharing measure of compensation (essentially, an expectation interest measure) generates a higher value of y, optimal insurance for the two parties—to make it rational for her to invest exclusively in household production and containing the reciprocal opportunism problem—may fall between these lower- and upper-bound values. To the extent that one moves beyond the x value towards the y value, it will become increasingly important to calibrate the additional compensation to the length of time the wife invests in household production[134]—a factor automatically impounded in the opportunity cost calculation.

I realize that this approach risks resurrecting the partnership for life conception of marriage which the recent thrust of family law reform measures has sought to exorcise and which many feminists, recognizing one horn of the dilemma of difference, also generally reject, at least in cases of subordinate or dependent relationships. The alternative and more powerful argument, however, is that by making economically dependent relationships much more expensive for men (and indeed, more reflective of actual relative investments) in the event of their termination, one may discourage many relationships driven by considerations of exploitation or subordination, rather than by genuine considerations of mutual advantage. I also do not seek to minimize the methodological problems entailed in developing a rigorous and operational valuation methodology for compensating for investments in non-market time, even if this approach has merit. However, these difficult valuation problems confront the courts daily in other contexts, such as personal injury and fatal accident litigation, and I am confident that if the legal system ordained a requirement of compensation, reasonably robust valuation techniques would in due course emerge.

In constructing an appropriate background or default rule, I would, of course, allow parties to displace it by agreement if they so wished. However, here we must be sensitive to various forms of transaction-specific failures that parties may be particularly vulnerable to in times of extreme stress, guilt, remorse, and emotional turmoil. I can readily see a case for legal requirements where, in entering into a separation agreement, the parties should be independently legally advised, that the agreement should be subject to a cooling-off period (say, 60 days), and that any agreement that *prima facia* confers on one of the parties substantially inferior net benefits than would have accrued to that party under the default rules raises a presumption of unconscionability that the other party bears the burden of rebutting.

In the context of separation agreements and entitlements on marriage breakdown, many feminists view remuneration for household production, child bearing, and child rearing as essential to women's equality. Lack of compensation for this type of labour is considered a clear statement to women involved in household production that their work is not significant enough to merit remuneration. Hence, feminist theorists invoke market ideology and advocate the commodification of these services in the name of equality and dignity. In the context of surrogacy, however, the commodification of a woman's child bearing capacity is often viewed by feminists to be an erosion of a woman's dignity and a debasement of an intrinsic element of her personhood. The following discussion will examine these issues and present a proposal for a framework of background entitlements against which a private ordering regime for surrogacy might defensibly operate.

Surrogacy Agreements

The practice of surrogacy was recorded as early as biblical times and probably existed long before. However, recent advances in reproductive technology have dramatically increased the types of possible surrogacy arrangements. The moral and legal implications of these various new forms of artificial reproduction have sparked substantial public controversy, numerous public inquiries, and diverse legislative responses and proposed responses. Many of the implications of surrogacy contracts were cast into sharp public relief by the widely publicized *Baby M*[135] case in New Jersey, in which commercial surrogacy contracts were held illegal and unenforceable in that state as being contrary to public policy.

I confine my attention to surrogacy situations in which a married couple desiring a child consist of a fertile male and an infertile female. They arrange for a fertile female to be impregnated artificially with the sperm of the would-be father, to carry the foetus to term, and to relinquish it to them for adoption. This arrangement may involve payment of compensation to the birth mother or may be entirely voluntary.

THE ADVANTAGES OF SURROGACY CONTRACTS
Adopting a law and economics perspective on these contracts, I ask the standard question, do they provide scope for mutual gains from exchange? In answering this question, one must examine both the demand side and the

supply side of such an arrangement. On the demand side, the childless couple, in many cases, presumably see themselves as being denied one of the most cherished sources of joy and pride in life—procreating and raising a family. Although adoption is, of course, an obvious alternative, in many jurisdictions today waiting lists of adoptive parents for newborns entail many years of delay. Although children with special needs may be more readily available, not every couple may feel that they have the capacity to meet the special demands of such children.[136] Moreover, for many parents, the wish to procreate is partly motivated by the desire to perpetuate the genetic lineage. In the *Baby M*[137] case, the natural father was, following the death of his mother, the only remaining member of his lineage, the others having all been killed in the Holocaust. Wives of infertile men often seem equally to feel these concerns, as evidenced by the growth of artificial insemination by third-party donors (AID). On the supply side, a surrogacy contract presumably holds out the potential for gains to the birth mother. These gains may be partly non-pecuniary—for example, an altruistic desire to give the gift of life to a childless couple—and partly pecuniary. Pecuniary motivations might well include a desire to use the monetary returns from the surrogacy contract to substantially enhance the quality of life of the other children of the birth mother and her spouse or partner. In other words, surrogacy contracts at least seem to possess the potential for making all parties to them better off.[138] Is this potential in fact likely to be realized? In answering this question, I now turn to the principal objections to surrogacy contracts.

OBJECTIONS TO SURROGACY CONTRACTS
One objection to surrogacy contracts is that they entail violations of traditional conceptions of the family.[139] This line of objection often is embedded in broader religious conceptions of the role of sex, procreation, and marriage. The most conservative position on these issues, perhaps exemplified most prominently by official views taken by the Catholic Church,[140] is that sex outside of marriage is immoral, that sex within marriage should not be separated from the act of procreation, and that marriage is a sacred union for life that the parties should not be free to terminate. Thus, this position leads to opposition to pre-marital sex, to contraception, to abortion, and to divorce. Although one can question any view that derives its legitimacy from a static conception of "nature,"[141] perhaps the most radical critique of this position comes from the many feminist critics[142] who have argued that the traditional "status-based" biological conception of the family provides the justification for a patriarchal regime motivated by the male's drive to maintain his lineage and to gain control over the uncertainty of paternity through mastery of women's reproductive labour by separating women from one another, confining them to the level of oppressed, unpaid domestic labourers

who enjoy little contact with the outside world, and, finally, reinforcing this regime through the power of self-serving legal norms such as adultery,[143] illegitimate reproduction, private property, the private/public dichotomy,[144] and the patrilineal family. This line of feminist critique is highly seditious of the traditional family, and though not everyone may subscribe to its interpretation of patriarchal family organization, it is clear that evolving norms of individual autonomy and freedom have caused many members of society to reject at least some of the norms underlying the traditional family and to question seriously any absolute declarations of authority regarding the correct nature, purpose, and structure of familial relations. Obviously, individuals are entitled to hold, and act upon, traditional or religiously based values in their own lives, but it is not nearly so clear why their values or preferences should be imposed on others who do not share them.

The second objection to surrogacy contracts is that payment for the birth mother's role in the arrangement commodifies and debases an intrinsic element of her personhood, in this case, her reproductive faculties.[145] An alternative way of formulating this objection is to say that surrogate motherhood embraces an offensive form of utilitarianism insofar as it involves the use of one person as a means to the ends of others.[146] Critics who object to surrogacy contracts on commodification grounds portray such contracts as reinforcing negative and oppressive gender roles.[147] Scenarios are constructed where surrogacy fees would vary depending on the physical and mental attributes of a birth mother akin to different breeding fees associated with the rearing of pedigree livestock.[148]

This argument has a powerful emotive force. Those who subscribe to this view would, at most, permit voluntary surrogacy arrangements among relatives and friends and even permit the birth mother to renounce the arrangement on the birth of the child.[149] On this view, what appears to be the central objection to surrogacy contracts is the payment of money to the birth mother for her role in the arrangement.[150] Nevertheless, the issues are not as straightforward on this score as the critics imply. First, the objection that surrogacy entails the birth mother's being used as a means to the end of others is an objection that can be directed to all contractual arrangements, where each party is being used as a means to the ends of the other.[151] However, this relationship is reciprocal. This is simply another way of saying that both parties benefit from an exchange.

Second, as to whether payment in the surrogacy context (the "cash nexus") diminishes the personhood of the birth mother, banning payment may entail other objections. Now—reinforcing traditional gender stereotypes—the birth mother is expected to perform her role as child-bearer without any compensation at all—an objection I developed in the previous section of this chapter with respect to failure to compensate for investments in household production on marriage breakdown. Surrogacy has the potential to transform the confining stereotype of "womanhood as motherhood" by removing the activity of reproductive labour from the private sphere, where it is largely an uncompensated and assumed duty borne by women, thereby allowing women the benefits of economic recognition of their labour. Essentially, the "dilemma of difference" must be confronted in the case of reproductive labour—should reproductive labour continue to be market exempt to protect against the exploitation of uneducated and financially disadvantaged women,[152] or is it possible that by denying women the opportunity to profit from reproductive/gestational labour, this form of labour will continue to be under-valued by society? One feminist scholar has argued that the failure to compensate women for reproductive labour is itself a form of "moralized" exploitation. "It seems clear that the imposition of 'wages for reproduction' as a universal norm would upset the present system of monetary economy . . . Are we all getting richer from the surplus value of the free labour of childbearing women? If so, is not the prohibition of payment for 'surrogate' reproductive services tantamount to moralized slavery?"[153] Moreover, the potential for coercion, exploitation, and domination in allegedly voluntary surrogacy arrangements among relatives seems seriously underestimated by the proponents of this regime.

Third, given that many feminists and others strenuously argue that women should have full dominion and autonomy over their bodies in deciding whether to abort a foetus or not, it is not clear on what principle those who take this view would hold that women should not have the same freedom to decide whether to enter into a surrogacy contract.[154] To assume or assert that women should not be free to exercise such a right if they wish is to imply a degree of paternalism that is rejected vehemently as invidiously patronizing in the abortion context, where at least on one view, life is being terminated, when in the case where life is being created, such a right is denied.[155] Moreover, the decision to abort is often confronted by women in desperate circumstances who lack full information of the psychic trauma that may be subsequently entailed, but these considerations are rarely recognized as invalidating their right to make this decision.

Finally, the differential fees for differential attributes objection to commercial surrogacy contracts ignores the fact that financial differentials for different physical, intellectual, and other attributes routinely obtain in labour markets generally, and unless one objects to their existence in this broader context, it is not clear why they are any more objectionable in the surrogacy context.

A different aspect of the commodification objection to surrogacy contracts focuses not on the birth mother but on the prospective child. The concern in this context is that in allowing the pricing of parental rights and duties within a commercial surrogacy arrangement, the arrangement not only offends our conception of life as a pearl beyond price,[156] but similarly, it may result in adverse consequences for the welfare of the child, who may not see himself or be perceived by his parents as intrinsically valuable. However, I believe that this objection is misconceived and overly alarmist. First, it must be recognized that the birth mother is providing a service involving considerable labour and time, a dramatic change of lifestyle, and additional responsibilities towards a potential human being. In any other context the failure to remunerate would likely be considered unconscionable. Second, in a provocative article, philosopher Eric Mack has argued that despite the fact of commodification there is a core of internally valued activities which persistently escape the market's pricing mechanisms:

> Typically, one can know the price of something yet not identify the value of that something with its monetary price because the two somethings are not identical . . . *What is paid for when one "buys" a child is the opportunity to become parent to that child* (the child it will become through one's parentage of it); one does not buy that developing child and one's relation to it. The costs incurred for such an opportunity can hardly be identified with the value (even the discounted value!) one enjoys in the child.[157]

Although carrying a child to term may mark the beginning of becoming a parent, the real task of child rearing begins with the birth of the child. The care, love, and nurturing demanded by children involves substantial resources, many years of a parent's life, endless degrees of energy, patience, and understanding, and ongoing financial commitments. That money is required in the raising of children, whether it be to pay for day-care, education, health care, or other amenities of life, does not seem to have destroyed the love most parents feel for their children, and it is difficult to believe that allowing commercial surrogacy contracts is antithetical to this love.

Just as in the context of separation agreements, where various forms of contracting failure may warrant upsetting a transaction, in the surrogacy contract context similar factors may be present. There may be fraud, misrepresentation, material non-disclosure, coercion, and so forth on the part of the commissioning parents or the agent acting on their behalf in negotiations with the birth mother. More specifically, some sub-set of birth mothers may systematically and seriously underestimate the emotional costs and psychological damage that they may incur from the time when they must give up the child to the commissioning parents.[158] In these cases, various forms of information failure may render a surrogacy contract objectionable. Apart from information failure, problems may also arise relating to the voluntariness of the transaction. To the extent that a birth mother faces both severely constrained alternative choices as to income generation and immediate, pressing, subsistence financial needs, there is a clear danger of the commissioning parents or their agent opportunistically exploiting these circumstances and, in effect, coercing the birth mother into entering into an arrangement that in less constrained circumstances she would not have considered. Alternatively, there is the possibility of their exacting unfair terms from her, especially with respect to the level of remuneration.[159] Finally, contracting failures may relate to a failure to address externalities created by the contract, especially concerning the future welfare of the prospective child.[160] These latter issues seem similar to those noted under the previous heading, although specific forms of negative externalities may arise in cases where the commissioning parents, perhaps because of intervening pregnancy or separation, or because the child has been born disabled, renounce the child, who the birth mother is also either unable or unwilling to support.

These concerns all seem to be legitimate, but they argue for a legal framework that constrains such agreements rather than for a prohibition altogether of commercial surrogacy arrangements, at least if one accepts that in some significant range of cases they carry the potential for substantial mutual benefits to all affected parties. Those advocating complete prohibition on grounds of the pervasiveness of contracting failures risk infantilizing women and reinforcing perverse gender stereotypes. Moreover, those advocating complete prohibition must also address various second-order or substitution effects that such a prohibition is likely to engender on both the demand and supply sides. On the demand side, childless couples may be induced to engage in fertility treatments that pose significant health risks to both mother and prospective children; or alternatively, the couple may separate in the face of unfulfilled aspirations. On the supply side, birth mothers may be driven into a state of impoverishment or into genuinely demeaning or degrading alternative activities (what Radin refers to as the "double bind").[161] Surrogacy arrangements may even be driven underground, where the birth mother is deprived of any basic legal protections at all.[162]

I will now sketch what I believe is an optimal legal framework that, on the one hand, preserves the potential benefits of commercial surrogacy contracts and, on the other hand, constrains the various forms of transaction-specific failures that I have identified.

THE CHOICE OF OPTIMAL LEGAL FRAMEWORK FOR REGULATING SURROGACY CONTRACTS

One approach that might be proposed is simply to leave the choice of appropriate legal response to the various forms of transaction-specific concerns to be dealt with within the standard range of contract defences and excuses, for example, fraud, misrepresentation, material non-disclosure, inequality of bargaining power, unconscionability, and so on. I reject this approach. Issues of transaction-specific unfairness in the surrogacy context present many novel issues and therefore high levels of uncertainty in their resolution. An unstructured legal framework is likely to invite litigation risks, causing psychological damage both to adopting parents and to birth mothers and, most important, to children born under such arrangements, who as the focal point of high profile litigation may become bizarre public celebrities for life, with all of the negative psychological and developmental connotations that could be associated with being involuntarily cast in this role. Thus, a firmer form of regulation seems required that specifies the rights and obligations of the various parties with a fairly high degree of precision.[163] An approach proposed by Martha Field in its broad terms seems appealing. She would not subject the biological parents to *ex ante* judicial scrutiny for fitness, as recently proposed by the Ontario Law Reform Commission,[164] but, by analogy with adoption laws, would instead provide a short period after birth for the biological mother to repudiate the contract and keep the child (subject to an unfitness caveat as defined in current social welfare laws).[165] This general approach is appealing for several reasons. First, it seems to minimize the degree of coercion and information failure involved in the arrangement by allowing birth mothers an opportunity to re-assess their judgement of the implications of the arrangement for them in the light of evolving feelings and information. Second, it creates self-enforcing incentives for commissioning parents and their agents to screen prospective birth mothers with a great deal of care to ensure that they fully appreciate the implications of the arrangement and possess the necessary emotional strength and stability to go through with it. Third, Field's proposal creates a clear presumption as to custody rights in the event of a birth mother's repudiating the contract. Presumptively, the baby remains with her in the absence of proof of unfitness to parent, on the basis that at the date of birth the mother and baby will be bonded much more closely than will the father and baby. This avoids the uncertainty and psychological trauma for the parties to the agreement of custody litigation and particularly the damaging publicity and uncertainty that may impair the future well-being of the child. It is also important to acknowledge, however, that this arrangement is likely to come at a cost to both birth mothers and commissioning parents.[166] Commissioning parents are now bearing a risk that they would not bear in the absence of a right of repudiation and are likely to discount the surrogacy fee offered accordingly. They are also likely to re-apportion payments from the pre-delivery period to the delivery juncture to induce waivers of the right of repudiation; as the Coase theorem in law and economics would predict,[167] in many contexts parties will attempt to bargain around constraints the legal system imposes on them. However, making the two sides of the exchange more simultaneous arguably confronts the birth mother with a more reasoned choice.

It might, of course, be argued that if a birth mother wishes to waive any right to opt out of the initial contract and bear the risk of subsequent regret in return for higher remuneration, the law should not proscribe this option. After all, we allow individuals to make far-reaching decisions on education and career choices, often without prior experience of the choices entailed, without providing mandatory opt-out rights. The arguments for a mandatory opt-out right in the surrogacy context (like the long-standing right to revoke a consent to an adoption for a limited period of time) must ultimately rest on empirical evidence that when entering into surrogacy contracts women in a high proportion of cases underestimate the strength of gestational bonding that is likely to occur and the psychic costs of disrupting these bonds. An *ex ante* decision to waive the opt-out right may simply reflect an under-appreciation of these costs.

Field is motivated to propose the opt-out regime as a second-best solution to prohibiting or rendering unenforceable all surrogacy arrangements, partly in recognition of the deeply held and diverse views on the subject that seem for the moment to permit only of a compromise solution. Her first-best solution would apparently reflect her view that "on balance surrogacy is not a socially beneficial policy."[168] Perhaps ironically, I arrive at a similar position to hers from the opposite presumption. I also do not accept her characterization of the proposal that she advances, which she describes as rendering surrogacy contracts unenforceable under contract law.[169] In fact, once the surrogate mother has allowed the period for repudiation to lapse and has handed over the child, the contract is fully enforceable and her rights with respect to the child are presumably fully terminated. This regime is analogous to that familiar in some consumer protection settings (such as door-to-door sales) attended by high levels of *ex post* regret by consumers, where a short cooling-off period is often provided by legislation.

Formulating a complete legal regime for regulating surrogacy contracts would require the resolution of a number of other issues. First, may a birth mother undergo an abortion during her pregnancy without the consent of the natural father? The answer would seem to be that since natural mothers in other relationships now have such a right,[170] the position should be no different in the case of surrogate motherhood. Second, if the adoptive parents should change their minds about the arrangement during pregnancy or before transfer of the child, for example, because the adoptive wife has become unexpectedly pregnant, or the adoptive parents have separated, or the child is born disabled or is in some other way unacceptable to the adoptive parents, should they be able to renounce the child? The answer would seem clearly that they should not have such a right. The contract contemplated from the outset that they would assume responsibility for the child after birth, and as in the case of natural parents in a traditional marriage, they must take the risks of conceiving or helping conceive a child in circumstances different from those which obtain subsequently or of conceiving a child that is disabled. Third, if the birth mother repudiates the contract and keeps the child, should she be entitled to support payments from the biological father, and should he in turn be entitled to visitation rights? I am inclined to think that in principle, she should not be entitled to support payments from the biological father in cases where she chooses to repudiate the contract. Indeed, there would seem to be a persuasive case for requiring her to make restitution of any payment received to that point for medical or living expenses, so as to discourage opportunistic behaviour on her part. However, should the biological father desire visitation rights and apply and receive such rights from the court, it may well be appropriate that as a quid pro quo he should accept some support obligations. Where the biological father has not had a pre-existing relationship with the child, it is not clear that visitation rights should be available at all:[171] they compromise the birth mother's right of repudiation, create the potential for litigation and damaging uncertainty in the lives of the birth mother and the commissioning parents and particularly in the life of the child. Finally, there is the question of what agencies should be permitted to act as intermediaries in surrogacy arrangements. In Ontario, the Children's Aid Society routinely vets adopting parents for suitability for parenthood and counsels natural mothers in reaching a decision on whether to give a child up for adoption. There may well be a case for confining the intermediation role in this kind of jurisdiction to such a quasi-public agency. In other jurisdictions, where private adoption agencies or more specialized private surrogacy agencies exist, a serious agency cost problem arises because the intermediaries are commissioned and paid by the adoptive parents and are therefore unlikely to be equally attentive to the interests of the birth mother. This may indicate the need for a legal requirement of independent legal advice and other counselling for a surrogacy contract to be valid.

With these background legal rules in place, I am optimistic that most surrogacy contracts entered into would generate mutual gains for all concerned. Bargaining parameters have been constrained in the light of potential contracting failures, leaving room for bargaining principally on the choice of birth mother and the surrogacy fee.

. . .

In this chapter, in five difficult and controversial contexts—the allocation of scarce lifesaving resources, organ transplantation, prostitution, separation agreements, and surrogacy contracts—I have demonstrated the substantial advantages of a significant role for private ordering. In a secular and increasingly pluralistic society, private ordering holds out the possibility for individuals to fashion life plans for themselves and those with whom they share relationships that meet their aspirations in a way that no across-the-board legal norms or expansive ad hoc judicial discretion exercised by others who are not privy to those life plans or aspirations are likely to achieve. I do acknowledge, however, the central importance both of formulating an appropriate set of background legal entitlements, in the shadow of which a private ordering regime must necessarily operate, and of sensitivity to various forms of transaction-specific failures which may require legal responses. As noted in Chapter 1, economics conventionally takes prior endowments and entitlements as givens in evaluating the potential for bargains to generate mutual gains from exchanges. In this respect, economics has limited insights to offer on the crucial question of fashioning an appropriate set of background legal entitlements. However, I have shown that economics can suggest worthwhile ways of fashioning legal rules for ordering the classes of agreements discussed in this chapter. Thus, I claim only partial insight or wisdom for the law and economics perspective and emphatically eschew any Panglossian or imperialistic claims for the perspective. However, starting from very different premises, I have shown how a law and economics perspective and some feminist perspectives might quite closely converge with respect to some of the issues examined in this chapter.

More generally, as I argue in greater detail in the final chapter of this book, I contend that we need to be much more alert to the possibilities of adopting public policies that broaden (rather than restrict) access to market opportunities for members of the community who either historically as classes, or as individuals through more specific sources of misfortune or disadvantage, would be denied these opportunities. These policies are more worthy of our attention than preoccupation with marginal market activities such as prostitution and surrogacy, which are likely to be further marginalized if we can identify and implement a successful set of market access-broadening strategies. In this sense, the market, precisely because of the preeminent weight it accords to individual merit and autonomy, holds out the prospect of the liberation of traditional victims of status, oppression and subjugation, rather than reinforcing these conditions, as is commonly and, in my view, mistakenly contended by its critics.[172] In other words, the focus should be on autonomy–enhancing public policies, rather than on public policies that reflect new forms of paternalism and that further restrict choices that are already too meagre. Neither autonomy nor welfare is likely to be promoted simply by proscribing altogether, without more, these choices, though legal regulation may be required to minimize the dangers of defective choices. Only an affirmative notion of liberty, effectuated by positive government policies and programmes outside the domain of contract law, can expand the domain of autonomous choices and promote enhanced equality of opportunity.

CHAPTER THREE

Externalities

The Nature of the Conceptual Problem

Even if both parties to a particular exchange benefit from it, the exchange may entail the imposition of costs on non-consenting third parties. From both a welfare and an individual autonomy perspective, such exchanges are problematic. From a welfare perspective, the Pareto criterion will not be met if an exchange has made some better off while making others worse off. In terms of Kaldor-Hicks efficiency, the welfare implications of the exchange would entail balancing the costs to third parties against the gains to the immediate parties to the exchange. While the individual autonomy of the parties to the exchange may be enhanced by permitting them to exercise their autonomy in this way, that of third parties may well be violated by external impacts of the exchange. The problem of third-party effects from exchange relationships is pervasive and not aberrational. Almost every transaction one can conceive of is likely to impose costs on third parties. If I agree to sell a rare stamp or painting to you, we are likely to be depriving some third party of a good he might otherwise have obtained. If I open a pizza shop close to yours on the same street, compete all your customers away and drive you out of business, the transactions between my customers and me generate a negative externality for you. If I decide to buy a car (not currently owning one), my purchase may marginally increase pollution in the environment, to the detriment of other members of the community. If I buy garish clothing that offends your sense of taste, or engage in unconventional private sexual practices with a partner that offend your sense of decency, the transactions or interactions involved generate negative externalities. If all these, and similar externalities, should count in prohibiting the exchange process or in justifying constraints upon it, freedom of contract would largely be at an end.[1] The crucial questions then become (1) what should count as an externality in welfare terms, or what should count as a harm to others in liberal terms? and (2) what should count as an externality or a harm which one may justifiably impose on others? As we will see, the concept of externalities is one of the least satisfactory concepts in welfare economics, and the concept of harm to others is one of the least satisfactory and most indeterminate concepts in liberal political theory.

The Economic Concept of Externalities

With respect to economists' notions of externalities, Dahlman in a well-known essay[2] identifies two basic models that have dominated the literature, though they carry very different policy implications. The first approach to externalities (which Dahlman calls the "Walrasian general equilibrium approach") is to assume any given initial endowment of resources and appropriate production and utility functions and then infer a Pareto optimal allocation of resources, that is, a competitive equilibrium that would be likely to result from a "Walrasian auction," with the Walrasian auctioneer grinding out prices and soliciting bids in a transaction-cost-free world. If the real world allocation of resources diverges from the allocation implied by this model it is because of external benefits or disbenefits that have not been captured in real world exchanges and that may accordingly justify government intervention to correct these market failures. On this view, it is assumed that the government can always or often take social costs and benefits into account better than the market can; that is, when there are externalities, the market does not work, but the government does.

A second approach to externalities reflected in the economic literature is to view externalities as a function of transaction costs—in particular, search and information costs, bargaining and decision costs, and policing and enforcement costs, all of which prevent Pareto superior deals being struck—but nevertheless to view transaction costs like any other production cost, such as transportation costs, and therefore as inherent in the nature of the allocational process. On this view, Pareto-relevant externalities exist only if they reflect deviations from an *attainable* optimum, which is a transaction-cost constrained optimum.[3] This view leads to a very restrictive notion of Pareto-relevant externalities and of the role of the government in correcting for externalities, because the assumption is that third parties affected by these externalities place a lower value on their removal than the resource (transactions) costs associated with negotiating their reduction or removal. Thus, the status quo presumptively reflects the attainable optimum. Legal intervention would be justified only if it could be demonstrated that the government, in some fashion, could either reduce the transaction costs that inhibit exchanges or, if that is not possible, employ taxes or some other form of regulatory intervention to achieve the preferred allocation of resources. Here, however, it is assumed that governments are unlikely to be able, in most cases, to deal with transaction costs better than market actors. Dahlman concludes:

> It may then be seen that *any* kind of transaction cost is capable of generating an "externality." If some transactions do not occur because of a proportional transaction cost, an externality may exist—*if* we can show that the government knows a better way of internalizing the side-effect than private parties do. Or if there is a setup cost that prevents internalization, there may be an externality—*if* the government can find a better way than markets. Or if uncertainty and imperfect information prevent certain transactions from occurring, the side-effect may be there—*if* we can assume that the government knows better. However, if we cannot assume that the government knows better, then there is no externality.
>
> The conclusion is rather startling: transaction costs *per se* have nothing to do with externalities. What is involved is a value judgment: if you believe that markets internalize everything, you will believe that externalities do not exist; on the other hand, if you believe that markets do not internalize side-effects, you will believe in the persistence of externalities as deviations from an attainable optimum. This is not science; it is metaphysics: value judgments and political goals will enter into the determination of whether externalities occur in our world.[4]

At best, we seem drawn into a comparative systems approach, which explicitly attempts to ascertain the economic consequences of alternative ways of organizing the allocation of resources (as Coase[5] and Demsetz[6] have argued). The question then ultimately becomes, according to Dahlman, how can the economic organization be improved upon by endogenous institutional arrangements?

A final complication must be noted in contrasting an economic approach to externalities with a liberal or libertarian approach. An economic approach is concerned with efficient resource allocation, whereas a liberal approach is concerned with protecting and promoting individual autonomy. As Mishan[7] has pointed out, efficient resource allocation, at least in Kaldor-Hicks terms, may well be consistent with some externalities, for example, certain levels of pollution. However, increasing product offerings where some of these offerings entail bads along with goods (say, environmental or health hazards) may improve resource allocation, but individual choice may be restricted in that consumers face "involuntary" packages, where they must take the goods with the bads. For example, in a strict application of the harm principle, pollution might not be permitted unless everyone affected by it voluntarily consented to its imposition in a series of discrete transactions. But if this requirement were to be insisted upon, it would dramatically curtail much market activity, presumably with substantial negative effects on aggregate social welfare. This would be tantamount to protecting all third-party interests by what Calabresi and Melamed[8] have called "property rule protection" (injunctive relief) on a discrete case-by-case basis, rather than by (at best) liability rule protection (compensation or damages). Thus two difficult issues arise in any given case: first, is an externality involved?; second, if so, how should third-party rights be protected?

Liberal Theories of Harm

In a classic formulation of the so-called harm principle, John Stuart Mill in his essay *On Liberty* stated:

> The object of this essay is to assert one very simple principle, as entitled to govern absolutely the dealings of society with the individual in the way of compulsion and control, whether the means used be physical force in the form of legal penalties, or the moral coercion of public opinion. That principle is, that the sole end for which mankind are warranted, individually or collectively, in interfering with the liberty of action of any of their number, is self protection. That the only purpose for which power can be rightfully exercised over any member of a civilized community, against his will, is to prevent harm to others.[9]

Mill seems to have been largely oblivious to the unavoidably moralized nature of the harm principle, assuming that relatively mechanistic application of it was possible.[10] However, as Joel Feinberg acknowledges in the introduction to his four-volume work[11] on the moral limits of the criminal law, in which he attempts to elaborate and refine Mill's harm principle:

> The harm principle must be made sufficiently precise to permit the formulation of a criterion of "seriousness," and also, if possible, some way of grading types of harms in terms of their seriousness. Without these further specifications, the harm principle may be taken to invite state interference without limits, for virtually every kind of human conduct can affect the interests of others for better and worse to *some* degree, and thus would properly be the state's business.[12]

Feinberg's starting point is the assertion that it is legitimate for the state, through criminal laws, to prohibit conduct that causes serious private harm, or the unreasonable risk of such harm, or harm to important public institutions and practices. To contain liberty-limiting principles, Feinberg develops an elaborate analytical structure designed to assign narrowly circumscribed roles to what he calls the "offense principle"—the prevention of hurt or offense (as opposed to injury or harm) to others; the "legal paternalism principle"—the prevention of physical, economic, or moral harm to the person prohibited from acting, as opposed to others; and the "legal moralism principle"—the prevention of inherently immoral conduct, whether or not such conduct is harmful or offensive to anyone, or the prevention of conduct which is currently viewed by most members of society as immoral and the occurrence of which may, in their view, lead to social disintegration. The appropriate scope of each of these three liberty-limiting principles is highly controversial and contestable and engages a great deal of Feinberg's attention over the course of his four volumes.

Setting aside the issue of legal paternalism, which I will deal with in Chapter 7, I will consider both the offense principle and the legal moralism principle, which warrant further comment. Feinberg uses the word "offense" to cover the whole miscellany of universally disliked mental states (disgust, shame, hurt, anxiety, and so on).[13] The offense principle recognizes a case for preventing some people from wrongfully offending others. However, Mill himself pointed out:

> There are many who consider as an injury to themselves any conduct which they have a distaste for, and resent it as an outrage to their feelings: as a religious bigot, when charged with disregarding the religious feelings of others, has been known to retort that they disregard his feelings by persisting in their abominable worship or creed. But there is no parity between the feeling of a person for his own opinion and the feeling of another who is offended at his holding it; no more than between the desire of a thief to take a purse and the desire of the right owner to keep it. And a person's taste is as much his own peculiar concern as his opinion or his purse.[14]

To illustrate the potential scope of an offense principle, Feinberg constructs an imaginative set of scenarios that occur on a bus, which scenarios a passenger at the back of the bus is required involuntarily to witness.[15] Such scenes include a group of passengers eating a picnic lunch consisting of live insects and the pickled sex organs of animals; a female passenger changing her sanitary napkin and dropping the old one into the aisle; a heterosexual couple copulating or masturbating on the bus; a homosexual or lesbian couple engaging in similar activities; a counter-demonstrator leaving a feminist rally to enter the bus carrying a placard "Keep the bitches barefoot and pregnant"; a passenger entering the bus with a sign bearing a scurrilous anti-Jewish or anti-black caption, and so on.

Feinberg concedes that though activities of this kind do not cause harm to the passenger in any tangible sense, they are likely to cause extreme offense in many cases. The problem then becomes how to respond to this form of offense without succumbing to the attitude of the religious bigot. To resolve this dilemma, Feinberg constructs an elaborate balancing test,[16] partly by way of analogy with the law of torts on public and private nuisances. He would weigh the seriousness of the offense involved by reference to the following standards:

1. The magnitude of the offense, which is a function of its intensity, duration, and extent. The more intense a typical offense taken at the type of conduct in question, the more serious is an actual instance of

such an offense. The more widespread the susceptibility to a given kind of offense, the more serious is a given instance of that kind of offense.

2. The standard of reasonable avoidability. The more difficult it is to avoid a given offense without serious inconvenience to one's self, the more serious is that offense.

3. The *volenti* maxim. Offended states that were voluntarily incurred, or the risk of which is voluntarily assumed by the person who experienced them, should not count as offenses.

4. The discounting of abnormal susceptibilities. Insofar as offended states occur because of a person's abnormal susceptibility to offense, their seriousness is to be discounted.

Against the seriousness of the offense is to be balanced the reasonableness of the offending conduct. In weighing this, the following principles are to apply:

1. Personal importance. The more important the offending conduct is to the actor, as measured by his own preferences and the vitality of those of the actor's own interests that it is meant to advance, the more reasonable that conduct is.

2. The social value. The greater the social utility of the kind of conduct of which the actor's is an instance, the more reasonable is the actor's conduct.

3. Free expression. Expressions of opinion must be presumed to have the highest social importance in virtue of the great social utility of free expression and discussion generally, although the offensiveness of the manner of expression may be a countervailing factor.

4. Alternative opportunities. The greater the availability of alternative times or places that would be equally satisfactory for the actor and his partners (if any) but inoffensive to others, the less reasonable his conduct in circumstances that render it offensive to others.

5. Malice and spite. Offensive conduct is unreasonable to the extent that its compelling motive is spiteful or malicious.

6. Nature of the locality. Offensive conduct performed in neighbourhoods where it is common, and widely known to be common, is less unreasonable that it would be in neighbourhoods where it is rare and unexpected.

The balancing exercise entailed in this formulation of the offense principle is obviously far from straightforward, and it belies any notion that either an independent offense principle or offense as a sub-set of the harm principle is self-defining and uncontentious in its application. Feinberg goes on to consider an extreme version of the offense principle—what he calls "profound offense"[17]—where the conduct in question is not witnessed by the offended party, but the "bare knowledge" of its occurrence is deeply offensive, for instance, desecration of religious symbols in private; desecration of corpses in private; secret meetings of the Klu Klux Klan or Nazi groups; private screenings of violent pornographic movies. Feinberg is sceptical that these bare knowledge offenses should constitute a wrongful offense, unless they serve no other function but to affront, insult, or threaten targeted sub-groups of the population, or entail external manifestations, such as public advertising, that third parties cannot readily avoid.

Feinberg rejects the legal moralism principle as inconsistent with the principle of individual autonomy.[18] There are several versions of the legal moralism principle. In its strict form, it is argued that there are certain inherent moral principles, dictated by religious or natural law precepts, that are violated by conduct, irrespective of whether it causes harm to others, that is, "free-floating" evils; in another version, made famous by Lord Devlin,[19] even if the moral principles generally subscribed to by members of a community at any given time cannot be justified as inherently right and immutable, to allow wholesale disregard of these is likely to cause social disintegration, and society would lose the "moral cement" that defines it as a society. On this view, the state has the right to step in and prevent personal immorality where it clearly offends the sense of propriety and decency of the majority of the community, or in the oft-cited phrase of H. L. A. Hart in his critique of Lord Devlin, "For him [Lord Devlin] a practice is immoral if the thought of it makes the man on the Clapham omnibus sick."[20]

Feinberg himself has been persuasively criticized for presenting his offense principle as a liberal principle, when it is in fact a disguised form of legal moralism. The requirement that parties engaging in certain conduct may do so only in private in order not to offend others who might otherwise be unable to easily avoid confronting that which they find offensive itself employs a moral judgement about the quality of the conduct.[21]

The Complexities Exemplified: The Problem of Pornography

The complexities identified above at a general level with the concept of externalities in welfare economics and the concept of harm in liberal political theories are well exemplified in debates over the prohibition or regulation of pornography (defined as commercially produced and disseminated films, video, or literature depicting various forms of sexual activity designed to induce sexual arousal). The U.S. Attorney General's Commission on Pornography in 1986 sub-categorized pornographic material as follows: The first category comprised material which depicts sexually violent behaviour by men towards women. A second category of pornographic material includes that which depicts not overt violence towards women, but conduct involving the degradation, domination, subordination, or humiliation of women. A third category of pornographic material identified by the Commission encompasses non-violent and non-degrading sexual depictions. These are materials in which the participants appear to be fully consenting individuals occupying substantially equal roles in settings devoid of actual or apparent violence, degradation, domination, or humiliation. Such material, however, sometimes depicts unconventional sexual practices, including oral sex, or promiscuous sexual activities taking place outside of the context of marriage, love, commitment, or affection, that is, uncommitted sexuality. A final category of pornography includes simple cases of nudity or sexual activity between married couples in apparently equal relationships, where it might be argued that the very publicness of the depiction of sexuality is in itself objectionable since it violates moral conventions about sex and privacy. A similar categorization of pornography has recently been adopted by the Supreme Court of Canada in R. v. Butler.[22] How might the various conceptual approaches outlined above confront these categories of pornographic material?

Externalities and Pornography

Applying Model I, as outlined in Dahlman's analysis, one might conjecture that in a world without transaction costs, women and sympathetic men would get together and "bribe" producers of pornographic material to terminate their activities. That is, the value to women and sympathetic men of being rid of this influence in their community might be conjectured to exceed whatever value is derived from this activity by the producers and consumers thereof. Given the collective action problems faced by such a large and diffuse group, one might reasonably argue that the government can properly act as an agent on their behalf in internalizing the social costs of these activities to the participants therein through prohibition or regulation. In contrast, adopting Model II, depending critically on how the initial entitlements are assigned, in a transaction-cost-constrained world, one might infer that women and sympathetic men do not feel that the value of suppressing this material is worth the cost to them, and therefore whatever level of pornographic activity is occurring reflects the attainable optimum. However, this inference is reversed if the initial entitlements are assigned to women, and pornographers have to "bribe" all women to consent to the dissemination of pornographic material, yielding the likely conclusion that a world without pornography reflects the transaction-cost-constrained attainable optimum. Alternatively, one could engage in some kind of comparative institutional exercise and ask whether there is any basis for believing that the government can reduce the transaction costs that inhibit cost-internalizing bargains between pornographers and aggrieved third parties (which seems highly unlikely) or otherwise internalize the costs more cheaply than the parties themselves, which in this case seems likely to be true, *if one assumes* that the government will act as a faithful agent effectuating the views of its aggrieved constituents.

Another option would be for one to attempt to mimic transactions in a transaction-costless world (a hypothetical contract) and assign the initial entitlements to whomever values them most highly (a common prescription by law and economics scholars in high transaction-cost situations), but this is largely sleight of hand in that in the absence of revealed preferences in actual transactions, there is no reliable way of knowing who values the entitlements most highly.[23] Similarly, one can simply engage in a balancing exercise in which the costs to third parties are weighed against the benefits to the participants in pornographic activities, a Kaldor-Hicks efficiency test, and suppress or regulate pornographic activities that do not generate net social benefits. However, this cost-benefit test largely replicates the hypothetical contract impasse and is simply a cruder version of the more sophisticated balancing exercise proposed by Feinberg with respect to the offense principle and has little to offer independently. In short, it is not clear to me that conventional economic theories of externalities have much, if anything, to offer on the problem of pornography.

Liberal Theories of Harm and Pornography

Feinberg, applying the framework of analysis that he develops for the offense principle and for the sub-set of cases involving profound offense, argues that in the case of pornographic material of a sexually violent kind, if there is robust evidence that the dissemination of this material leads to a significant increase in the incidence of violent acts towards women by men who have been exposed to it, then this clearly violates the harm principle.[24] The U.S. Attorney General's Commission on Pornography[25] was satisfied that social science research has adequately demonstrated that exposure to such materials does increase aggressive male behaviour towards women and that in a sub-set of cases, it increases the level of sexual violence directed at women. Feinberg, in contrast, suggests a measure of caution in evaluating such claims. He points out that in several Scandinavian countries, where pornographic material is freely available, there are fewer acts of sexual violence against women than in many countries, including the United States, where pornography is more tightly regulated. Moreover, he claims that the causal connection between depiction of sexual violence and violent acts by viewers is not sufficiently made out if the impact of the material on viewers is mostly incidental to some predetermined macho cultural values (and may induce some off-setting measure of sublimation), any more than one would accept the case for banning rebukes by workplace supervisors of errant employees, on the grounds that this sometimes leads to violence in the family. He argues that suppressing pornographic material will have little impact on these established macho cultural values, which require much more attention through the education system and broader socialization processes. Indeed, a fair reading of the social science literature suggests a high degree of inconclusiveness in establishing a solid causal connection between exposure to violent forms of pornography and the commission of acts of violence.[26] However, on the issue of principle, there is no doubt that liberal theorists committed to the harm principle would accept the case for criminalization or regulation of pornography where there is evidence of a systematic causal linkage between violent pornographic materials and sexually violent behaviour by those exposed to them.

As to the second category of pornographic material identified by the Commission—non-explicitly violent material depicting degradation, domination, subordination, or humiliation of women—the U.S. Commission had little difficulty in agreeing that the activities depicted an objectionable form of harm in that women are represented as existing solely for the sexual satisfaction of men or as engaging in sexual practices that to most people would be considered humiliating. As to whether the dissemination of such material causes an increase in the kind of harm depicted, the Commission considered that the social science research findings were somewhat more ambiguous, but it was satisfied that, on balance, exposure to such material again increases male aggressiveness in relations with women and probably increases the incidence of sexual violence, sexual coercion, or unwanted sexual impositions, as well as reinforces negative gender stereotypes such as the rape myth, that is, that the woman who says "no" really means "yes" and that the victims of rape and other forms of sexual assault or violence are significantly more responsible and offenders significantly less responsible for the violation. Feinberg is deeply sceptical of the case for criminalizing or regulating pornographic material of this kind. He views the physical harms alleged as speculative and treats this as a case of offense, or even profound offense, sustained by a large group of the population on the strength of the bare knowledge that this material is in private circulation. While the material is clearly offensive to many women and men, he views it as an avoidable offense—one does not have to view it if one does not want to. He sees the intangible harm allegedly associated with it (reinforcement of negative gender stereotypes) as no more strongly associated with this kind of material than many soap operas, much commercial advertising, or indeed many classic and not so classic novels (for example, Harlequin Romances). Presumably he would take the same view, *a fortiori,* with respect to depictions of uncommitted sexuality, nudity, or sexuality per se. The U.S. Commission was divided on these latter forms of pornography.

In R. v. Butler,[27] the accused had been convicted under the obscenity provisions of the Canadian Criminal Code (s. 163) for video material that was offered for sale and rent in his store in Winnipeg. The key provision in s. 163 for the purposes of this case was s. 163(8), which provides that "any publication a dominant characteristic of which is the undue exploitation of sex, or of sex and any one or more of the following subjects, namely crime, horror, cruelty and violence, shall be deemed to be obscene." The accused argued that this provision violated his freedom of expression rights under s. 2(b) of the Canadian Charter of Rights and Freedoms and that it was not demonstrably justified under s. 1 of the Charter as a reasonable limit prescribed by law. The Supreme Court of Canada (Sopinka J.) upheld the validity of these provisions. According to Sopinka J., the portrayal of sex coupled with violence will almost always constitute the undue exploitation of sex. Explicit sex that is degrading or dehumanizing may be undue if the risk of harm is substantial. Finally, explicit sex that is not violent and neither degrading nor dehumanizing is generally tolerated in our society and will not qualify as the undue exploitation of sex unless it employs children in its production. Sopinka J. accepted that to impose a certain standard of public and sexual morality, solely because it reflects the conventions of a given community, is inimical to the exercise and enjoyment of individual freedoms, which form the basis of social contract. In Sopinka's view, however, the overriding objective of s. 163 is not moral disapprobation, but the avoidance of harm to society. With respect to social science evidence on the negative effects of exposure to pornography, Sopinka J. held that though a direct link between obscenity and harm to society may be difficult, if not impossible, to establish, it is reasonable to presume that exposure to images bears a causal relationship to changes in attitudes and beliefs. In the face of inconclusive social evidence, it is sufficient for Parliament to have a reasonable basis for concluding that harm will result, and this requirement does not demand actual proof of harm.

Legal Moralism

Just as Lord Devlin took the view, in response to the Wolfenden Report, that prevailing social mores found offensive the notion of consenting homosexual or lesbian sexual acts in private, moral conservatives or strict legal moralists may well take the position that all of the various sub-categories of pornography are morally offensive and should be criminalized. However, depending on which variant of legal moralism one espouses, one might take stronger objections to depictions of untraditional sexual relationships or sexual acts, or uncommitted sexuality. This form of collective prescription and enforcement of community moral standards (moral majoritarianism) would be anathema to liberals to whom individual autonomy is a paramount value and who maintain a fundamental commitment to the ideal of state neutrality in regard to different conceptions of "the good life." It would also, in some contexts, be anathema to many feminists,[28] who recognize that communal values, legislatively enforced or otherwise, have in the past been a major source of the problem of gender inequality, rather than its solution. There are many examples in the contemporary world of traditional societies or societies where religious fundamentalism dominates and where communal values are often officially imposed and enforced which relegate women to highly suppressed and subordinate roles, as well as highly constraining individual freedom of choice in personal relations more generally. Simply counting noses on fundamental moral issues and imposing the view of the majority, even a substantial majority, on all individual members of a given community, or asking whether particular kinds of conduct are likely to make the representative member of the community on the Clapham omnibus sick, is sharply antithetical to fundamental liberal values, as well as to many feminist values. Although Sopinka J. in R. v. Butler rejected moral majoritarianism as a legitimate justification for the pornography provisions in the Canadian Criminal Code, his willingness to accept, without convincing proof, a causal connection between exposure to pornography and adverse actions or negative attitudinal changes towards third parties (especially women)—on the grounds that Parliament was entitled to maintain "a reasoned apprehension of harm"[29]—in fact comes perilously close to collapsing the distinction between the harm principle and moral majoritarianism.

Feminism

From a feminist perspective, our society is seen as built around a sexual class system, which frustrates the legitimate aspirations of half the population for economic, social, and sexual freedom.[30] Pornography is seen as especially odious because it reinforces the system by instilling and perpetuating notions about women's inferiority and limited role within society. It sets women apart as different and inferior and characterizes them as the legitimate objects of not only male sexual pleasure but male frustration and violence. Feminist theorists differ in their views as to the appropriate response to these concerns. Those of a Marxist orientation incline to the view that the answer to sexism lies in the removal of the capitalist values and structures they see as making it possible. Others see little value in the use of legal expedients to reform society, believing that education and other socialization processes are likely to be much more successful in the long-run.

However, a third and substantial group favours the vigorous use of legal as well as political and social strategies to combat and eliminate sexism. According to this group of feminist theorists, the liberal tends to characterize rights issues in terms of infringement by the state on the rights of an individual. Little or no attention is paid to the fact that rights issues often develop out of what is, at base, a conflict in the exercise of rights by individuals. In this case, the legal system is called upon not only to protect rights, but to choose which right is entitled to greater protection.

Feminists who would seek to criminalize or regulate pornography attack two central tenets of liberal theory: freedom of expression and privacy. The classic dilemma surrounding freedom of expression is that too much of it inevitably infringes on the rights of others. Almost everybody can agree that the prohibition on gratuitously shouting "Fire!" in a crowded movie theatre is an acceptable limit on freedom of expression. However, the consensus stops there. While some view pornography as harmful, they accord priority to freedom of speech over women's equality. Others view pornography as so harmful that they are willing to infringe on the pornographer's freedom of expression in order to ensure women's equality. MacKinnon,[31] Dworkin,[32] and Jacobs[33] attack the myth on which freedom of expression is premised—that everyone has an equal voice in the marketplace of ideas. They argue that the status quo is the silence of women and that to protect the speech of pornographers is to ensure and maintain women's silence.

Catharine MacKinnon distinguishes between pornography and obscenity by arguing that the former is a political act, while the latter is a moral idea.[34] More forcefully, MacKinnon states that "[p]ornography is not an idea any more than segregation or lynching are ideas, although both institutionalize the idea of the inferiority of one group to another."[35] MacKinnon argues that when people view pornography as an idea and not an act, they conceptualize it under the rubric of freedom of expression. In so doing, they defend pornography on the basis of freedom of speech, in a way that they would not defend rape, lynching, or child abuse.[36]

MacKinnon attacks freedom of expression absolutism by claiming that "the marketplace of ideas is literal: those with the most money can buy the most speech, and women are poor."[37] Jacobs supports this argument by categorizing freedom of expression as essentially a negative liberty, so that those who can afford to exercise it will, while those who are economically disadvantaged will not. Hence, absolute freedom of expression enables pornographers to flood society with their speech, while women remain silenced.[38] This is a difficult proposition to refute. Pornography is a multimillion dollar enterprise; the women's movement relies on meagre private donations and government funding. MacKinnon further argues that pornography objectifies women as mindless sex toys, thus stripping them of their credibility, and hence cannot be combatted with more speech.[39]

Andrea Dworkin adds to this a critique of the North American "obsession" with freedom of expression as self-indulgent and naive.[40] She argues that compared with police states such as South Africa and the Soviet Union (the article is from 1985), North Americans are so privileged regarding freedom of expression that to defend pornography on that basis misses the point of the right entirely. Dworkin argues that the regulation of pornography is not censorship, because "pornographers are more like the police in police states than they are like the writers in police states. They are the instruments of terror, not its victims."[41]

A complementary view is advanced by Cass Sunstein. Sunstein agrees that pornography harms women and maintains that at a minimum, pornography increases the aggregate level of violence against women.[42] He thus argues that regulation of pornography is consistent with First Amendment principles. Sunstein classifies pornography as low-value speech, and in this way he justifies its regulation. He outlines several factors to be used in determining whether speech is low-value or high-value.[43] First, the more political speech is, the higher its value; for example, criticism of the government is the highest-value speech. However, this seems to miss MacKinnon's point that pornography is a form of political speech or act, so that its inferior value must rest on other factors. Second, speech can be divided into cognitive and non-cognitive forms. The former appeals to the intellect and is high-value, while the latter appeals to the passions and is low-value. Attempts to communicate messages as opposed to appeals to mere passion are high-value. Finally, some forms of speech are not protected at all, for good reasons, such as private libel and fighting words, and lesser levels of protection are accorded to commercial speech than to political speech.

In short, it seems perverse to deny that there is a tension between a woman's right to equality and a pornographer's right to freedom of expression. Both Sunstein and Pollard suggest that the superior risk-bearer should assume the burden of losing his or her right.[44] Both authors agree that the pornography industry is the superior risk-bearer. Pornographers bear the risk of losing profits and some freedom of expression of limited intrinsic value. Women bear the risk of being brutally raped, abused, mutilated, humiliated, sexually harassed, and generally considered to be less than human.

A second classical liberal tenet is that what a person does in the privacy of his own home is not the business of the state, and thus pornographic videos and magazines, as opposed to public exhibitions of pornography, should be free of regulation. A counter-thesis argues that the sanctification of privacy has served to conceal and obscure violence against women.

MacKinnon contends that judges and jurists, in common with liberal theorists (such as Feinberg), are fixated on causation and require proof that pornography causes violence against women—in the way that smoking cigarettes causes lung cancer—before they are prepared to regulate it.[45] MacKinnon maintains that this emphasis on causality draws pornography out of the public sphere and hence privatizes it. This serves to insulate the whole industry from the threat of gender equality.[46] Lack of proof of causation means no regulation, which in turn means freedom for pornographers to objectify women while hiding behind the rubric of privacy.[47] An alternative approach to the myth of privacy is offered by Christina Spaulding in her critique of deontological liberalism. Spaulding attacks liberal notions of human beings as atomistic, self-interested units, disengaged from community.[48] She claims to show how this approach is detrimental to women in that it prevents them from associating as a group and claiming injuries which have been suffered precisely because they fit into the category of woman. For the status of women to improve, women must be viewed as a group which has traditionally been denied equality and respect as human beings.[49] Spaulding maintains that women have traditionally earned their living through commodifying their sexuality—be it as wives, mistresses, or hookers. Pornography in turn is harmful because it perpetuates this construction of heterosexuality.[50] Deontological liberalism cannot address these issues, because it does not recognize women as members of an oppressed group, or male dominance as the current socio-political form of hegemony.[51] Although all women are dehumanized by pornography, it is argued further that women of colour are especially dehumanized, since they are often portrayed as animals,[52] and lesbians are portrayed in ways designed merely to satisfy male fantasies.[53]

This view is supported from an egalitarian liberal perspective by Dyzenhaus,[54] who argues that autonomy is realized only when individuals can exercise their choice about how to live under conditions of fundamental social equality. If social practices are of the kind that dominate and subordinate individuals just because they are born into an identifiable group, these individuals cannot be said to have a free choice. Thus, standards of substantive equality and individual autonomy are both fundamental in that individual autonomy is a practicable ideal only when there are conditions of equality such that one's membership in an identifiable group is not an obstacle to forming and exploring one's own conception of the good life. This view, though still liberal in the value it attaches to individual autonomy, abandons any notion of individuals as discrete atomistic entities abstracted from their social contexts.[55]

In developing this opinion,[56] Dyzenhaus interestingly relies on an essay by John Stuart Mill, *The Subjection of Women*, where he argues that women's subordination results from a status quo of inequality, which is made manifest in the private realm and which is made to look natural by a false appearance of consent. In effect, Mill invokes an idea of false consciousness or adaptive preferences. On this view, pornography—*especially non-violent pornography*—is pernicious because the appearance of consent is given to a deeply coercive relationship. This argument for censorship or prohibition of pornography rests on a broad conception of harm, one which

embraces harm to fundamental interests, such as the interest in an autonomous life of the kind that is achievable only under conditions of equality.

Dyzenhaus' egalitarian liberal perspective provides a normative basis for
abandoning any requirement of a causal linkage between exposure to pornographic material and violent or oppressive acts towards women by those
so exposed. Indeed, women themselves may often be the target audience.
This is less obviously so with conventional forms of pornography. Indeed,
in creating the false consciousness to which Dyzenhaus refers, soap operas,
commercial advertising (for example, of fashions, cosmetics, and lifestyles),
classic novels depicting women in traditional roles and Harlequin Romances
(mainly read by women) may be more pernicious than conventionally understood forms of pornography, because their influence is more ubiquitous,
subtle, and insidious. But now the argument for censorship potentially cuts
a vastly wider swath than pornography and rests as much on a theory of
legal paternalism as on any theory of offense or externalities, often because
women will *not* be offended by exposure to many such materials, but would
be, it is conjectured, if they could form autonomous choices in conditions
of equality, freed from the influence of historical socialization processes that
have inculcated a sense of subordination and submission.

Although many feminists converge in their criticisms of the primacy of
freedom of expression and privacy with respect to pornography, there is
more disagreement over the appropriate legal responses. Some, such as
Marianna Valverde and Lorna Weir,[57] take the view that criminal censorship
merely serves to put control of women's sexuality into the hands of male-
dominated courts, governments, and police forces, with the alleged consequence that the material most frequently targeted for censorship is non-violent gay and lesbian publications. Others, such as Catharine MacKinnon
and Andrea Dworkin,[58] have proposed a kind of civil rights ordinance for
women,[59] which would allow civil suits by women for injunctive or compensatory relief, with pornography being defined as the subordination of
women in sexual images, including sex coupled with violence, degradation,
abuse, and subordination. A woman would be able to bring suit under such
legislation (1) where she has been coerced, manipulated, or tricked into
acting or modelling for a pornographic enterprise; (2) if she is forced to see
pornography at her workplace, school, home, or any location where she has
not consented to see it; (3) if a woman is raped or otherwise sexually
assaulted and can prove on a balance of probabilities that the man or men
who assaulted her were provoked by specific pornographic magazines or
videos; and (4) any woman would be permitted to sue a pornographer for
trafficking—production, sale, exhibition, or distribution—in pornography
as defined above. The merit of legislation of this kind is claimed to be that
it defines pornography as that which harms women in these specific ways,
rather than that which is obscene in some undefined way. In this sense, it

avoids the anti-liberal implications of the legal moralism principle, while preserving some expanded notion of harm. Of course, the problem remains that such a statute would still be interpreted and enforced by male-dominated courts.

The problem of pornography underscores how difficult it is for any theory of contract that is based on either individual autonomy or welfare (efficiency) to generate a coherent concept of externalities. However, there would seem to be broad agreement that pornography that depicts and promotes violence towards women would offend any such principle (the U.S. Commission's first category) if empirical evidence were to demonstrate a causal connection between exposure to such materials and an increased propensity to engage in violent behaviour, and that pornography that merely depicts uncommitted sexuality, public sexuality, or nudity (the U.S. Commission's third and fourth categories) probably does not, unless one subscribes to a broad theory of legal moralism that any liberal theory must reject. The U.S. Commission's second category—pornography that depicts women as subordinated sex objects who exist to service the pleasures of men—clearly is the most contentious category and requires an affirmative theory of liberty (or equality), as propounded by Dyzenhaus and others, to justify proscription. Because such a theory focuses on the conduct of some that perpetuates or reinforces the historical inequality or subordination of others, it is more circumscribed in its scope than legal moralism and thus avoids some of its dangers, although in turn it courts many of the difficulties associated with theories of legal paternalism (discussed in Chapter 7), including in this context the risk of infantilizing women by not taking their preferences seriously.

In the end, I am not persuaded that the case for criminalizing or regulating pornography (beyond protection of children and against involuntary exposure of adults) is especially compelling, in part because the empirical evidence does not strongly suggest any significant causal relationship between exposure to pornography and an increased propensity to engage in violent acts or to adopt negative attitudinal changes towards women—indeed the causal relationship may run the other way—and in part because any theory of egalitarian liberalism that dispenses with the harm principle seems to entail censorship of a vast array of material other than pornography premised on a highly patronizing assumption of false consciousness or false preferences.

•   •   •

Some externalities cases are clear-cut. If A enters into a contract with B to act as a hitman in killing or maiming an enemy or rival of A's (C), we would have little difficulty in viewing this exchange as failing to meet the criteria for Pareto superiority as well as violating the liberal harm principle. In reaching this judgement, we would not be particularly concerned with balancing the costs imposed on the third party against the gains to A and B, simply because C's rights, or autonomy, have been non-consensually violated. However, beyond cases such as this, the issue of externalities becomes much more problematic. Even in the standard pollution case, where A manufactures and sells widgets to B, and in the process of manufacture inflicts pollution on a range of third parties in the neighbourhood, the contract between A and B is not, strictly speaking, Pareto superior, given the costs imposed on the third parties (A and B are made better off, but the third parties are made worse off). Nevertheless, we may still want to balance the costs to the third parties against the gains to A and B or, alternatively, the relative avoidance or abatement costs confronting the third parties on the one hand and A or B on the other (essentially a cost-benefit, utilitarian, or Kaldor-Hicks efficiency calculus that is not consistent with either the Paretian test or a strict liberal harm test).

Similar externality issues arise in other contexts. For example, is it appropriate to require motorcyclists to wear helmets or motorists to wear seatbelts, paternalistic justifications aside (I will address these in Chapter 7), on the grounds that risk-taking behaviour imposes costs on dependents, the social welfare system, and the public health care system? or, similarly, in the case of smoking, with the health effects of second-hand smoke an additional third-party cost? Again, should mood-altering narcotics such as alcohol, heroin, and cocaine be banned on the grounds that at least in some cases their mood-altering properties increase the incidence of violence towards others, may induce physical assaults on others or property crimes in order for the user to obtain the resources to service his addiction, lead to neglect of dependents, loss of productivity on the job, or increased costs to the social welfare or public health care systems? Once one moves beyond rather tangible harms to third parties, however, many activities might be viewed as generating some of these third-party effects, including inadequate dietary or exercise regimens, excessively stressful work habits, risky leisure activities (hang-gliding, skiing, motor-racing, or white water rafting), or risky business investments, thus inviting wholesale social controls on all kinds of activities.[60] In some of these cases, it is difficult to know whether abnormal negative externalities are actually involved. For example, though smokers impose higher than average costs on the health system while alive, they also die sooner on average than non-smokers and save the health care and social welfare systems the costs entailed in servicing the health and related needs of the elderly.[61] Even where externalities are entailed, internalizing costs to the individuals in question through additional taxes or financial contributions rather than invoking prohibitory sanctions (liability rule rather than property rule protection in Calabresi and Melamed's terms)[62] may reflect a more appropriate balancing of costs and benefits,[63] at least in cases where the socially optimal level of an activity is not zero.

Yet other cases are even more problematic. In a recent Supreme Court of Canada decision, the Prostitution Reference,[64] the majority of the court held that provisions in the Criminal Code (s. 319) that prohibit soliciting for purposes of prostitution in a public place, while violating section 2(b) of the Charter of Rights and Freedoms (freedom of expression) were justified under s. 1 as a reasonable limitation on such freedom in a free and democratic society, largely relying on the public nuisance and public offense features of public solicitation activities. In contrast, the minority would have struck down the provisions as disproportionate to the legitimate objectives of the legislation, in that this prohibition extended to solicitation activities in little frequented public places, such as remote corners of public parks or back-alleys, where members of the public are unlikely to be harmed or offended by the activity. In another recent decision of the Supreme Court of Canada, R. v. Keegstra,[65] provisions in the Criminal Code that prohibit the dissemination (other than by private conversation) of literature that wilfully promotes hatred against any identifiable group (a section of the public distinguished by colour, race, religion, or ethnic origin) were upheld by the majority of the court under section 1 of the Charter as a reasonable limitation on freedom of expression, on the grounds that such literature is deeply hurtful and offensive to minorities and prejudicial to harmonious social relations. The minority would have struck down the legislation as a disproportionate response to a legitimate legislative objective, because the legislation was over-broad (it could be invoked to suppress legitimate forms of personal expression, such as native leaders' decrying white intransigence in redressing historical grievances, scientific research that bears on differences between ethnic groups, Salman Rushdie's *Satanic Verses,* or Shakespeare's portrayal of Shylock in *The Merchant of Venice*); was likely to have a "chilling effect" on legitimate forms of expression and vigorous public debate; and might well be counter-productive in providing accuseds with mass publicity in criminal trials. Whereas in the minority's view, violent forms of expression, threats of violence, or incitement to violence would not warrant section 2(b) protection or would justify restrictions thereon under s. 1, the Criminal Code provisions were not so limited and the conduct of the accused in the case at hand (systematic and abusive denigration of Jews by the accused as a teacher in his school classes) did not entail this.[66]

Dyzenhaus argues[67] that only by invoking a substantive theory of equality can one develop a coherent understanding of the normative issues implicated in these two cases. With respect to the Prostitution Reference, he argues that the law impugned violates notions of equality by further victimizing members of a class who historically have been victims of generalized inequality, and hence, it should have been struck down. R. v. Keegstra, however, involved legislation designed to protect members of classes who historically have been victims of inequality and therefore it should be upheld. In both cases the harm principle receives a definition that entitles individuals to protection against intrusion by the state or private actors, which jeopardizes their interests in an autonomous life that is achievable only under conditions of equality. However, Dyzenhaus does not explain why the theory of false consciousness or legal paternalism that he would invoke in the case of pornography would not also justify a prohibition of prostitution, at least to the extent of criminalizing the activities of customers ("johns") who exploit the false consciousness of women.

Even though liberal theories of contract reject as anathema legal moralism theories that would proscribe bare knowledge forms of offense, can we avoid legal moralism altogether? Suppose I feel harmed, offended, or diminished by the mere thought that Bengal tigers or a rare species of whale are being hunted into extinction, or that a rare environmental or scenic treasure in a remote, inaccessible location is being despoliated. Even though I never intend to visit the locale of the Bengal tigers, the whales, or the scenic treasure, should my preferences count for nothing?

In the face of the complexities that all these examples pose, one might, of course, be tempted simply to throw up one's hands and accept that these matters must be remitted to the political domain for collective determination, reflecting as best our political processes can our prevailing community norms. However, the serious risks entailed by this option are that all morality is then simply reduced to counting noses and imposing a set of collective norms on all individuals in the community, whether they share them or not (unconstrained legal moralism). To avoid these risks, courts, in bringing a sober second judgement to bear on collective norms, are unlikely to avoid some form of balancing test of the kind proposed by Feinberg, as recent Canadian Charter cases exemplify, although divisions in the Supreme Court of Canada also suggest that no such test will yield a high level of determinacy and objectivity. Moreover, in balancing competing liberties ("freedom to . . ."; "freedom from . . ."), we are driven to a realization that, at least in the context of externalities, rights-based theories of individual autonomy and utilitarian or welfare-based theories of the public good are not nearly as sharply divergent as many of their respective proponents sometimes claim.

CHAPTER FOUR

Coercion

The Nature of the Conceptual Problem

For any theory of contract law based on individual autonomy and consent or Paretian concepts of welfare, the question of what constitutes voluntary consent to a transaction is of crucial importance. For the purposes of this chapter, I am not, for the most part, addressing questions of information failure or cognitive defects, but assume that in the kinds of exchanges I am concerned with, there is full information about the contract subject matter and no cognitive deficiencies in processing that information. I am also assuming that the contract is complete in the sense that all relevant obligations are embodied in clear, express terms, so that the courts are not facing the task of designing interpretative or default rules or hypothetical bargains for the parties. Rather, the question is whether the constrained choices facing one of the contracting parties renders her consent to the express contract in question involuntary so as to vitiate that consent. This question typically arises in the context of legal doctrines such as duress, unconscionability, or inequality of bargaining power.

As Scanlon has pointed out,[1] a problematic issue arises at the outset in the adoption of market institutions themselves. This choice—presumably the product of prior history and prior collective choices—undoubtedly does not reflect the actual individual unanimous consent of all members of market economies. Scanlon notes that in choosing between non-market institutions and market institutions, they face a choice between institutions that restrict the liberty of some people and institutions that restrict the liberty of others. Thus, assuming that each generation will include some representatives of each group, no matter how we frame our institutions some people will be faced, without their consent, with institutions that in an obvious sense they would not have chosen. However, setting aside the issue of coercion at this systemic level, and proceeding on the assumption that, for better or worse, we have adopted market institutions and a regime of contract law designed to complement those institutions, I want to focus in this chapter on the preconditions to voluntary consent in the case of a particular transaction. This issue is deeply problematic, if only because of the pervasiveness of scarcity, which renders all choices constrained choices. Most individuals do not enjoy the luxury of being able to pursue any career they wish, or to be employed by any employer they wish, or to buy any house they wish, and so on. Most exchanges are entered into under constraints as to either available trading partners or, even more commonly, the terms of trade. More fundamentally, scarcity often explains the need to contract in the first place. If everybody possessed all the endowments he needed to pursue any life plan he wished, contracting would be unnecessary. In this sense, all contracts can (unhelpfully) be viewed as "coerced."[2] When do the constraints on contractual choices become so severe or assume such a character that it is appropriate to infer an absence of voluntariness with respect to the decision to enter into such an exchange?

The concept of individual autonomy or individual liberty, standing alone, provides very little purchase on this problem. If consent is defined simply as a decision that is the product of a rational, deliberate choice, assuming away informational and cognitive deficiencies, almost every exchange can be viewed as voluntary. Only in the extreme limiting case of somebody's seizing my hand and forcing me to sign a contract, or torturing me or psychologically traumatizing me, or inducing a hypnotic trance and in the course of the trance inducing me to sign a contract would there be an absence of rational, deliberate choice. These cases can all be thought of as involving non-volitional acts that do not reflect my real will or preferences. However, these limiting cases are of little analytical interest and do not reflect the bulk of contract cases where issues of coercion arise, which might (in Wertheimer's terms)[3] be viewed as cases of "constrained volition." In addressing these cases, two broad normative approaches have emerged in the literature: rights theories and welfare theories. Although there are many important differences of viewpoint among scholars within each of these two schools, the basic approaches can be briefly sketched. Rights theorists, of whom Nozick,[4] Fried,[5] Feinberg,[6] and Wertheimer[7] might be viewed as representative, draw a basic distinction between threats and offers. Threats reduce the possibilities open to the recipient of a proposal, whereas offers expand them. Threats are thus coercive, while offers are not. This distinction has a strong intuitive appeal to it and, in some sub-set of cases, involves a relatively straightforward factual inquiry. However, in many other cases, substantial normative difficulties arise in specifying the offeree's (B's) base-line, against which A's proposal is to be measured. Although this base-line obviously refers to B's expectations about the future, different kinds of expectations can be identified. Wertheimer identifies three: the statistical, the phenomenological, and the moral.[8] The statistical base-line is what B might reasonably expect the future to hold on an objectively calculated balance of probabilities. The phenomenological base-line is what B in fact, from her own viewpoint, expects the future to bring. This may or may not be the same as her statistical base-line. Finally, there is B's moral base-line. This is what B is morally entitled to expect in her future. Again, the moral base-line may or may not coincide with the statistical and the phenomenological.

An example used by Nozick[9] clarifies these three notions of a base-line: A is a slave-owner who beats his slave every morning for no apparent reason. The night of the preceding day A tells B that if B does X, A will not beat B in the morning. Is A's proposal a threat or an offer? If the statistical base-line is the relevant base-line, then A's proposal is an offer. Almost certainly from B's phenomenological base-line it is also an offer, unless he expects a miracle. However, if B's moral base-line excludes slavery, then this base-line includes not a beating each morning but freedom from slavery. A's proposal is a threat on this account. Fried gives a rather different example to illustrate the same point.[10] A student pianist who has given free annual recitals in the village church for several years announces that henceforth he will require a fee. Is the status quo that which obtained just before the day the annual concert arrived, so that his offer to give the concert for a fee would be an improvement? Or is the status quo defined as including a free annual concert? Thus, as Fried concedes, the success of this criterion of coercion, that is, the distinction between threats and offers, depends on whether it is possible to fix a conception of what is right and what is wrong, of what rights people have in contractual relations independent of whether their contracts should be enforced. He concludes that a promise procured by a threat to do wrong to the promisor, a threat to violate her rights, is without moral force.[11]

The obvious objection to, or limitation of, this rights-based approach is that while it is possible to determine whether A's proposal is coercive once B's moral base-line has been set, once B's moral base-line has been set all the interesting theoretical work will already have been done: according to Zimmerman, "The only real issue would be over the prior rights and wrongs."[12] Presumably, any general normative theory of rights is likely to be highly contestable, at least any theory that goes beyond proposals by A that entail committing torts or crimes, as currently defined, against B, as the extensive philosophical debates over the base-line in the threat-offer distinction (and intermediate categories of "throffers") clearly attest.[13] The vigorous academic debates over the morality of blackmail are an example of these difficulties.[14] Even where A's behaviour entails committing a crime or a tort, as currently defined, A may wish to argue that the existing law is unjust. Moreover, the prior determination of B's rights takes issues of coercion outside the domain of contract law. In other words, contract law cannot itself generate a coherent theory of coercion.

A different rights-based approach that bears on issues of coercion has been developed by Benson[15] from a Hegelian perspective and by Gordley[16] from an Aristotelian corrective justice perspective. For Benson, following Hegel, the conception of individual autonomy must begin with the concept of abstract will, which is constituted by the single moral power of having a capacity to choose that is entirely independent of determination by inclination. Abstract will, or personality, becomes actualized through ownership of property, including one's own personal attributes, either by physical possession of unowned property or through acquisition. In the case of ownership by acquisition (contract), the common will evidenced by the two parties to the contract and reflecting the free and equal moral personality to which each is entitled simply by virtue of being human leads to an inference that only equivalence in exchange fully respects their equal individual autonomy (cases of gifts or voluntary assumptions of risk aside). Gordley reaches a similar conclusion from different premises. As more fully elaborated in Chapter 5, drawing on the principle of commutative or corrective justice as originally articulated by Aristotle, which is designed to maintain the pre-existing distribution of wealth, Gordley argues for an ethical principle of equality in exchange such that inequalities in the value of performances exchanged should be grounds for contractual invalidation or revision. He argues that a party to an arms-length exchange does not intend to make a gift to the other party, which is implied by selling for less than the market price or buying at more than the market price. Benson and Gordley, in measuring the equivalences of goods exchanged, propose that prices in reasonably competitive markets be used as the basic reference point.

From the perspective of the first group of rights theories, an objection to theories of equivalence or equality in exchange of the kind proposed by Benson and Gordley is that they are result-oriented and pay no attention to the circumstances of the interaction between the contracting parties. That is, they are theories of substantive, not procedural, fairness.[17] For example, it is not clear on what basis either Benson or Gordley could object to an exchange coerced at gunpoint if the values exchanged were equivalent in terms of market values. Thus, a farmer coerced into selling his farm at the going market price, when for personal reasons he would prefer not to sell it, would seem to have no basis for objection to the coerced agreement. Moreover, from a rights perspective it seems incongruous to adopt a welfare standard—market prices reflecting aggregations of preferences—as the criterion for identifying violations. From a law and economics perspective, the objection to the Benson-Gordley approach is that it is entirely static and ignores long-run or dynamic incentive effects. For example, there would seem to be little or no incentive for parties to search out under-valued assets with a view to moving them to higher-valued uses as reflected in prevailing or evolving market prices.

In response to some of these concerns raised by rights theories (in particular the first of the two sets of rights theories), Kronman[18] has proposed instead that any coherent concept of consent must entail a theory of distributive justice that determines which of the many forms of advantage-taking that are possible in exchange relations render an agreement involuntary. Kronman claims that according to the liberty principle, advantage-taking by one party should be permitted unless it violates the rights or liberty of the other party. However, he points out that this principle presupposes that we already know what constitutes an individual's rights or liberty, and in this respect he regards the liberty principle as vacuous or at best unhelpful. He accepts, however, that the liberty or autonomy principle has both egalitarian and individualistic elements which should be respected, and to this end he proposes what he calls a "modified Paretian principle" to determine which forms of advantage-taking should be permitted.

Kronman uses the concept of advantage-taking in a non-pejorative form, because in routine exchanges, mutual advantage-taking is entailed, which is what we mean when we describe such exchanges as mutually beneficial. However, in other cases, one party may possess an advantage over the other in terms of superior information, intellect, judgement, or in the monopoly he enjoys with regard to a particular resource, or in his possession of a powerful instrument of violence or a gift for deception. In each of these cases, Kronman argues that the fundamental question is whether A should be permitted to exploit such advantages to the detriment of B, or whether permitting him to do so will deprive the other party of the freedom necessary to make her promise truly voluntary and therefore binding. Whereas Kronman includes in the forms of advantage-taking that may bear on the existence of voluntary consent various informational and cognitive advantages, I prefer to address these separately (see Chapter 6). However, even when the domain of inquiry is restricted in this way, many problematic cases arise. Kronman would resolve these and the more expanded domain of cases in which he is interested by reference to a modified Paretian principle, where one would ask whether the welfare of most people who are taken advantage of in a particular way is likely, in the long-run, to be increased by permitting the kind of advantage-taking in question in the particular case.

Kronman sees his modified Paretian principle as respecting the same values as the liberty or autonomy principle, but as providing more purchase on what specific forms of advantage-taking should or should not be permitted, as well as avoiding the consequentialism of a general utilitarian or welfare approach, where the interests of particular contracting parties could be sacrificed as means to some greater social end.

Benson, in an insightful critique of Kronman,[19] points out that Kronman's principle is in fact highly consequentialist and therefore akin to general utilitarian or welfare perspectives, in that whether A is to be permitted to take advantage of B in a particular transaction turns on whether B or parties similarly situated will be rendered better off in the long-run in a series of transactions involving other parties unconnected with the transaction under scrutiny. For example, Kronman argues that a prospector, A, should be able to take advantage of superior information about possible oil deposits in buying a farmer's, B's, land at agricultural prices, without disclosing this information, because his buying the land is likely to reduce energy costs in the future for farmers as a class. In other words, the validity of the contract between A and B turns not on the nature of the interaction between A and B, but rather on a series of hypothetical or putative interactions between B or parties like B with a variety of subsequent unidentified parties. Thus, the issue of the voluntariness of the interaction between A and B is largely, if not entirely, irrelevant. Moreover, Benson argues that Kronman's principle is not faithful to liberty values, because it implies an affirmative duty on the part of the A's of this world to use their assets in ways that benefit the B's and thus ignores the fundamental distinction between malfeasance and nonfeasance. Also, Benson argues, by conferring veto power on the B's of this world over how the A's can use their assets, Kronman's principle also violates the value of equality.

More general welfare- or efficiency-based tests of substantive contractual unfairness have recently been proposed by Buckley.[20] He argues that incentive theories may justify anti-duress rules in various contexts, in order to discourage parties from taking excessive and wasteful precautions against being subjected to extortionate contractual terms. Similarly, he argues that cooperation theories designed to discourage strategic behaviour in contractual negotiations, for example, bilateral monopolies, may reduce transaction costs and thus increase the number of mutually beneficial bargains that are actually struck.

The fundamental dilemma posed by both Kronman's efficiency-*cum*-distributional approach and Buckley's more conventional efficiency approach to issues of coercion is, as I suggested in Chapter 1, that the conventional predilection of neo-classical economists for voluntary exchanges over other forms of resource allocation, particularly collective forms of resource allocation, is largely based on the proposition that welfare inferences can be more confidently drawn from the fact of parties voluntarily entering into agreements with each other. In other words, it is assumed that a transaction enhances their joint welfare if both parties voluntarily (and with full information) enter into the transaction. However, both Kronman's and Buckley's approaches invert this line of reasoning. The welfare implications of a transaction, judged in accordance with either Kronman's modified Paretian principle or Buckley's efficiency (in effect Kaldor-Hicks) principle, provide the basis on which the voluntariness of a transaction is inferred. But, as Barnett points out,[21] if we are so confident about our ability to make either these Paretian or Kaldor-Hicks judgements as to optimal legal regimes, it would seem to follow that we no longer have a strong reason for doubting our ability to make collective resource allocations more generally by reference to the same principles. In short, the normative primacy of a regime of private ordering is placed in doubt once we move from theories of actual consent to theories of hypothetical consent, at least in cases of complete contracts.[22] Or, as Brennan describes it, "Trade is not good because it is voluntary, but voluntary because it is good."[23] In other words, theories of hypothetical consent add nothing to the basic welfare judgements.[24]

For a law and economics scholar, the only way out of this dilemma would seem to be to retreat to a literal Paretian principle and ask the following kind of question of any particular exchange transaction: Does this transaction render both parties to it better off, in terms of their subjective assessment of their own welfare, relative to how they would have perceived their welfare had they not encountered each other? This reduces the base-line with which the transaction is to be compared to an essentially factual or phenomenological base-line that abstracts from questions of moral base-lines, except perhaps where the proposal entails a crime or a tort. Although this approach has the virtues of relative ease of administration, the concept of coercion that it entails would have a very meagre, indeed impoverished, content; it would for the most part apply only to non-volitional contracts, and most contracts entered into in circumstances of constrained volition would be enforceable. Each of the examples that follows presents its own distinctive structure in that it differs from other examples in at least one arguably important normative dimension.

Cases of Constrained Choice

Creation and Exploitation of Life-Threatening Risks: The Highwayman Case

In the classic case of the highwayman or mugger holding-up a passerby and confronting her with the proposition: "Your money or your life," the passerby's decision to hand over the money may be perfectly rational, deliberate, and fully informed, but it would seem to violate all of the above theories as to what constitutes a voluntary decision. On the approach proposed by Nozick and others, any commitment to hand over the money was procured by a threat to do illegal physical violence to the passerby and thus violated her rights.[25] Put another way, the proposal from A constituted a threat that reduced the possibilities open to B, rather than an offer. Presumably, on the Benson-Gordley approach, this would also be a straightforward case, in that no equivalence or equality in exchange was involved. From Kronman's perspective, it would be impossible to argue that passersby as a class would find their welfare in the long-run enhanced by permitting this kind of advantage-taking. From Buckley's point of view, to permit this kind of transaction would be to encourage wasteful investments by both highway-men and passersby in offensive and defensive activities that have no social value. From a literal Paretian perspective, it is obvious that the highway-man's activities render the passerby worse off relative to her subjectively perceived state of welfare prior to their encounter.

Suppose, however, that the slave in the earlier example from Nozick holds up his owner at gunpoint one night and demands his freedom, to which his owner agrees. Should we enforce this agreement? Even though the slave may be violating the existing law in committing a tort and crime, he can argue that it is an unjust law in this context and that he has not violated the slave-owner's moral base-line. In this case, we might well wish to enforce the agreement.

Exploitation But Not Creation of Life-Threatening Risks: The Tug and Foundering Ship Case

To vary the facts of the highwayman example, suppose that a third party (C) encounters the highwayman and the passerby before the transaction is consummated and offers to rescue B for all her money, less one dollar. C is arguably exploiting B's situation but is not responsible for creating it. Or, to take another classic case, a solitary tug takes a foundering ship and its crew in tow in return for an agreed but extortionate salvage fee that vastly exceeds the competitive value of the services entailed and the risks incurred. Here, it seems to me that all of the above theoretical approaches pose some problems. With respect to the Nozickian rights-based approach, the distinction between threats and offers appears to justify enforcement of the contract, since the tug captain's (A's) proposal increases the possibilities open to the captain (B) and crew of the foundering ship relative to the pre-existing alternatives and, in this respect, is in important contrast to the highwayman or mugger example. Moreover, on the assumption that foundering ships have no moral or legal right to call on other vessels to rescue them, it is not clear that B's moral base-line has been violated by A's proposal.[26] However, in discussing a similar example, Fried suggests that in the absence of a functioning social system, which random events have taken the two parties outside, no systemic provision could be made for the contingency in question and the tug should not be permitted to exploit the absence of a functioning social system directed to such contingencies.[27] But this argument proceeds simply by way of assertion rather than by derivation of the rights of B from predetermined legal norms or more general moral entitlements. According to the Benson-Gordley theories of equivalence or equality in exchange, measured by reference to market prices, the transaction presumably should be viewed as coerced. However, as noted above, this conclusion dismisses as irrelevant any inquiry into possible incentive effects of the transaction in question, in terms of inducing more tugs out in storms in the future, which would presumably both lower salvage fees through greater competition and increase the probability of rescue (or alternatively, as Landes and Posner claim,[28] of inducing a socially excessive amount of investment in rescue activities).

It is not clear from Kronman's approach whether permitting this form of advantage-taking in the long-run reduces the welfare of the captains and crews of foundering ships. On the one hand, we would need to investigate incentive effects on the supply side, as suggested above, and compare these with incentive effects on the demand side, in terms of whether permitting such transactions might induce wasteful avoidance precautions on the part of shipowners, for example, not venturing out in doubtful weather or installing double-thickness hulls. These issues essentially entail estimating elasticities of supply and demand, which are hard to derive in any industry (as the antitrust and industrial organization literature attests), and would require calculation in every context to which a party sought to apply the concept of coercion—a daunting task for both contract disputants and the courts. On Buckley's approach, these incentive (and elasticity) issues would also have to be canvassed. In addition, applying his cooperation theories, one might ask whether in a situation like this, which entails a time-constrained bilateral monopoly, some set of superimposed terms might reduce transaction costs for the parties and the potential for mutual opportunism, thus increasing the likelihood that more salvage contracts in such situations will be entered into. Similar arguments can be made in some contract modification cases. For example, in Alaska Packers Assn. v. Domenico,[29] sailors threatened to mutiny when their fishing boat had reached remote waters unless the captain agreed to pay additional wages. His promise to do so was held unenforceable, because of lack of voluntariness.[30]

The welfare issues raised in many of these examples do not seem to me to permit of easy resolution. From the perspective of the literal Paretian test, the contract in the case of the foundering ship should clearly be enforced, in that the welfare of the captain and the crew of the ship is enhanced relative to what it would have been had the two parties not encountered each other (unlike the highwayman case). From a Kaldor-Hicks perspective, the analysis is much less determinate.

Exploitation But Not Creation of Life-Threatening Risks with One Supplier and Many Bidders: The Dry Wells Case

Suppose there are a number of ships with crews aboard foundering in a storm. A solitary tug on the scene has the capacity to rescue the crew from only one of them and puts its services up for auction by radio-telephone. Here, whatever the allocation mechanism used (markets, lotteries, queues, or administrative (merit) allocation as reviewed in Chapter 2), the inherent scarcity of available rescuing capacity means that some crews cannot be rescued, and an auction has the virtue of allocating this capacity to the highest-value users, while arguably creating efficient longer-run incentives for more tugs to enter the rescue industry. If the crew successful in the auction accept a market allocation, why should they subsequently be able to challenge the price? Or to take a similar example, suppose that all the wells except mine in a remote rural area dry up in a drought and I auction off drinking water to desperate inhabitants for large percentages of their wealth.[31] Is an auction objectionable, even though I have not created the life-threatening situation but am, in some sense, exploiting it? Is this case different from that canvassed in Chapter 2 of putting up for auction scarce lifesaving technology (dialysis machines) where demand exceeds supply? Hayek, for example, would apparently treat a monopolist's threat to withhold the supply of a resource that is crucial to another person's existence or preservation as coercive.[32]

Exploitation But Not Creation of Non-Life-Threatening Situations: The Penny Black Case

Let me take another example, this one from Fried.[33] Suppose that A happens to come across a rare stamp, say, a Penny Black, in her recently deceased great aunt's attic. A stamp collector (B) needs the stamp desperately to complete a particular collection for competition in an up-coming international stamp collectors' convention. In one scenario, A exploits B's very intense, albeit idiosyncratic, preferences for the stamp. Here, as in the tug case, we are dealing with a bilateral monopoly with a very wide bargaining range. Let us assume that the price negotiated is in the high end of this range. In another scenario, the stamp is auctioned off at Sotheby's to the highest bidder (B). In either case, is it objectionable for A to demand a very high price for this scarce resource? Similar examples might entail rare books, paintings, artifacts, homes with unique views, and so on.

Similar questions might also be posed with respect to, for example, an exceptionally talented sports or movie star, such as Michael Jordan or Jack Nicholson, exploiting his rare talents by indirectly charging fans very large fees for his services. One might assume that these fees vastly exceed the opportunity costs of the star in question, that is, the likely returns in the next best form of available employment, so that the fees cannot be justified on the basis of inducing supply of the desired services, because they would have been supplied at a substantially lower price.

On a Nozickian rights-based approach, A's proposal in the Penny Black case would seem properly to be viewed as an offer rather than a threat, in that it increases B's possibilities relative to her position prior to A's interaction with her. Moreover, B's moral base-line would not seem to include any entitlement to the stamp at all, let alone the stamp at any particular price. Fried takes the view that it would be inconceivable to object to this kind of transaction. Hayek also is of the opinion that a monopolist of a resource not indispensable to another's existence or preservation does not act coercively by demanding a very high price for that resource.[34] On the Benson-Gordley approach, the transaction also seems unobjectionable, because, at least in the auction scenario, bidding among stamp collectors for this rare resource presumably generates a market price similar to that which B has agreed to pay. On Kronman's approach, one might argue that permitting a buyer in an individual transaction of this kind to be taken advantage of in this way is likely to increase the welfare of this class of buyer in the long-run by increasing incentives for people to uncover such objects and put them into circulation. From a general efficiency or welfare perspective, it might be argued that there is no alternative rational basis for allocating the scarce resource except by reference to the highest bidder, who is presumably the highest-value user. From a literal Paretian perspective, this transaction clearly makes B better off, in terms of her subjective evaluation of her own welfare, than in the situation that prevailed or would have prevailed in the absence of her interaction with A.

Let us contrast how these various theories come out in the tug case on the one hand, and in the Penny Black case on the other. In the tug case, Fried, at least, among the first class of rights theorists would object to the transaction, as would Benson and Gordley, for different reasons. Kronman's and Buckley's perspectives seem to me to yield a less clear set of implications, although Buckley conjectures that allowing these transactions will have little or no effect on the fortuitous presence of tugs in such circumstances and may encourage wasteful precautions on the part of shipowners. Landes and Posner are concerned that allowing these transactions would induce a socially excessive supply of tug services,[35] although they do not explain why they regard this Kaldor-Hicks calculus as superior to a Paretian test in making welfare judgements in this or other contexts, or even if it is, how they derive the empirical basis for their elasticity conjectures. From a literal Paretian perspective, the transaction is unobjectionable. In the Penny Black case, all theories would apparently regard the transaction as unobjectionable. What are the critical differences between the two situations? An obvious difference is that in the tug case, B confronts a life-threatening situation which A seeks to exploit; we may in this case wish to include in a definition of B's moral base-line the right to protection of physical integrity—thus constituting A's action a fundamental infringement on B's autonomy.

However, courts in salvage cases have not typically distinguished between extortionate salvage proposals involving the saving of life and those involving the saving of cargo. For example, in the famous case of Post v. Jones,[36] the court struck down a salvage arrangement whereby the salvors purchased the cargo of the stricken ship at vastly less than its market value. This follows the general admiralty law rule that in cases involving rescue at sea typically only reasonable salvage fees (risk-adjusted) are permitted.[37] Is salvage of cargo on exorbitant terms conceptually different from the Penny Black case? Suppose that ten ships (oil tankers) are foundering in the storm, and their crews have been helicoptered to safety, but a solitary rescue vessel can take on only one of their cargoes or take one ship in tow. Would an auction of its services yielding a rescue fee close to the value of one of the ship's cargoes be objectionable? Or to take the dry wells case, would an auction of water from the remaining operational well, not for drinking water but for irrigation of neighbouring farmers' crops, be less objectionable? Or in the Penny Black case, suppose that the stamp collector en route by sea to her convention finds herself on a foundering ship (from which she is rescued by helicopter) and a solitary tug offers to rescue her Penny Black (stored in a vault in the captain's cabin) for a fee slightly less than her reservation value for the stamp?

Is what makes the difference in the exploitation but not creation of these non-life-threatening situations that life is not in issue, or rather that demanders in some cases exceed suppliers, so that an auction is an acceptable method of resolving the unavoidable allocational problem? Kahneman, Knetsch, and Thaler[38] report an interesting set of household survey responses to the following hypothetical: "A hardware store has been selling snow shovels for $15. The morning after a large snowstorm, the store raises the price to $20. Please rate this action as Completely Fair, Acceptable, Unfair, Very Unfair." Eighty-two percent of the respondents rated the action as unfair or very unfair. This, of course, arguably involves exploitation of a non-life-threatening situation, where the price mechanism is being invoked to ration goods in temporary short-supply among an excess of demanders. Yet the vast majority of respondents still regarded this as unfair.

For those bothered by transactions such as that in Post v. Jones, or the Penny Black in the captain's vault, life is not in issue and there are no competing demanders for the rescue services. The objection here seems to rest on the fact that unconstrained contracting (or a market) serves no useful direct allocational (rationing) function (and the indirect incentive effects on the future behaviour of rescuers and rescuees are too indeterminate), leaving distributional objections to the division of the gains from unconstrained exchange and the violation of some notion of a "just price," along the lines of the Benson-Gordley theories. But why do these objections not appear to extend to the original Penny Black example, where the seller exploits the buyer's idiosyncratically intense preferences in a bilateral monopoly (non-auction) scenario?

Sexual Favours: The Lecherous Millionaire Case

Let me take three related examples cited by Wertheimer.[39] In the first, the plight of a single mother (B) with a child who has serious medical problems that require expensive treatment she cannot afford comes to the notice of a millionaire (A). She accepts a proposal from him in which he agrees to pay for the treatment in return for her becoming his mistress. Should this agreement be enforced, at least to the extent of requiring restitution of the medical costs if she fails to fulfil her promise? The chairman of a university department offers a permanent academic position to a mediocre young female research assistant on condition that she sleep with him. An employer offers a job to a destitute woman on condition that she sleep with him, or the promotion of a woman lawyer with a large amount of firm-specific human capital within her law firm is made conditional on sexual relations with a senior partner. Or to vary a previous example, suppose that the owner of the Penny Black demands sexual services rather than, or in addition to, money from a stamp collector with very intense preferences for the stamp. Or those with a taste for moral complexity could imagine a situation where the owner of the Penny Black proposes that the captain or crew of the tug put their lives at risk in rescuing the Penny Black from the captain's vault in return for sexual services.

These cases are unlike the highwayman case ("your sexual services or your life") in that B is arguably better off as a result of her encounter with A, but they may be like the tug case. They throw into sharp relief the issue of the moral base-line that is central to many rights-based theories of coercion that turn on the distinction between threats and offers. Assuming that the conduct of the proposer (A) is not illegal in any of the three examples, in the sense of contravening sexual harassment or employment discrimination laws, the question that arises is how we might go about constructing a moral base-line for B that includes her right to be free of these forms of sexual harassment or overtures. Obviously, such a theory of rights would have to be developed, as Fried acknowledges, entirely outside the law of contracts. But if this can be done in an uncontestable way, the question then arises as to whether we could develop a similar kind of moral base-line for the tug and foundering ship example or other extortionate rescue ("bad Samaritan") cases. Of course this means, as Zimmerman points out, that all the normative action with respect to a theory of contractual coercion in these cases occurs outside contract law. On the Benson-Gordley equivalence or equality in exchange approach, it is not clear to me how one would resolve these sexual favours cases. In the case of the Lecherous Millionaire, it is not clear what market prices one would measure the values exchanged against; the situation is similar in the cases of the departmental chairman and the destitute woman who accepts a job on the condition of providing sexual services, unless there are similar jobs available to B's in both cases at a similar wage, without these conditions attached (but then B's would presumably have taken those jobs instead). One might wish to argue that in all these cases, the philanthropist or employer (A) is making a proposal to B that deviates from proposals that A is normally able to make, given more widely prevailing market or philanthropic conditions, and this deviation is explained both by the specific nature of the interaction between A and B and by B's dependency on A, which the latter exploits by demanding supra-normal terms. In this sense, the cases resemble the tug case. Contrastingly, on Kronman's approach one would ask, would permitting these transactions in the long-run make B or parties similarly situated better or worse off? Rendering these transactions unenforceable seems likely to reduce B's opportunity set, thus reducing B's welfare. Both on Buckley's Kaldor-Hicks efficiency approach and on a literal Paretian approach, a similar conclusion would seem to follow.

Here, it seems to me to be difficult to avoid a moral base-line (rights-theory) approach if we are to give effect to the moral intuition that most of us are likely to feel about these cases. The consideration of moral base-lines appears to implicate issues similar to those canvassed in Chapter 2, where to enforce transactions in these circumstances is likely to violate basic notions of human dignity and self-respect.

Contrived Monopolies: The Cartelized Auto Industry Case

To take another example derived from Fried,[40] where he regards the answer as axiomatically obvious, suppose the major automobile manufacturers collude and form a cartel either to fix prices for automobiles or to curtail drastically consumers' rights of action with respect to personal injuries through sweeping disclaimers and warranty terms[41] (the latter is Fried's example, although a monopolist or a cartel will typically not degrade non-price terms of the contract or product quality unless there are information asymmetries; it will instead monopolize the price).[42] Fried takes the view that the collusive behaviour postulated in the example has removed all meaningful choice for consumers and hence they should not be viewed as voluntarily consenting to the reduced rights of action or (I assume) the collusive prices. It is not clear whether Fried would take the same position with respect to a contrived monopoly (through, for example, trade protectionism) of a domestic industry, or whether he would treat it as akin to the Penny Black case. One might also imagine a group of marginal family farmers getting together through a supply management scheme with a view to restricting output and raising the prices of produce consumed by those who on average enjoy larger incomes than they. Or a group of workers may conspire, through a trade union, to raise the price of labour vis-à-vis employers who are financially better endowed, although increased labour costs will, to a greater or lesser extent, be passed along to consumers of the employer's output, and the consumers may or may not be better off on average than the workers.

Clearly, in most of these cases, we are not dealing with life-threatening situations where risks to the physical integrity of individuals are being directly exploited, nor are we dealing with situations arising outside an established social order (as Fried argues to be the case with respect to the tug and the foundering ship). Now, Fried might reasonably argue that some of these kinds of industry arrangements or structures violate antitrust laws, and therefore a contract procured by wrongdoing of this kind violates B's legal rights. Put another way, A's proposal is a threat rather than an offer, once one incorporates into B's base-line the right to be free of collusive or monopolistic conduct.

However, the explanation for antitrust laws from an economic perspective conventionally focuses not on the distributive effects but on the allocative effects of market power and their impact on consumer welfare in terms of consumers who have been *priced out* of the market through reductions in output. But these concerns do not implicate the welfare of immediate contracting parties who *remain in* the market (except arguably if one views the consumer surplus appropriated from them as a proxy for socially wasteful investments in rent-seeking by aspiring monopolists).[43] Fried, however, appears to be concerned about the prospect of these consumers, in effect, being "gouged." This suggests that gouging by cartel members and monopolies both in life-threatening and in non-life-threatening situations, as well as in functioning social systems and outside them, should be viewed as vitiating effective contractual consent. But this then leaves unexplained the original Penny Black case, where Fried would regard it as inconceivable to relieve B of her bargain. One might, of course, argue that in the Penny Black case there are no allocative effects associated with the gouging because there is only one item to allocate, and output cannot be varied by suppliers to inflate the price. In other natural monopolies, for example, rare mineral reserves or local telephone services, output can be varied, and rate-of-return regulation is sometimes invoked to force prices down and output up. But again, it bears emphasizing that these various allocative concerns largely pertain to consumers who are priced out of the market and do not primarily apply to the distributive impact on consumers who remain in the market; the law of contracts, insofar as it is focussing on the issue of voluntary consent, must address itself to the question of the status of contracts entered into by consumers who have remained in the market. In these contrived cartel or monopoly cases, I find Nozickian rights-based theories unhelpful.

In approaching these cases, it is not clear that the other theories of coercion would yield clearer results. Presumably, for Benson and Gordley, if a cartel or a monopoly charges more than competitive prices for its goods or services, this would offend the principle of equivalence or equality in exchange, rendering suspect the automobile cartel, the monopolized domestic industry, the agricultural supply management scheme, and the trade union. Kronman would probably reach a similar conclusion, by reasoning that consumers taken advantage of by these cartels or monopolists are not rendered better off in the long-run by permitting this kind of advantage-taking. On a broader welfare or Kaldor-Hicks efficiency test of the kind espoused by Buckley, objections to these arrangements would focus on an investigation of the allocative effects on consumers priced out of the market, rather than on the distributional impacts on consumers left in the market, which scarcely provides much purchase for anti-duress rules with respect to the latter. A literal Paretian rule would uphold these transactions, on the grounds that consumers apparently perceive themselves as better off entering into these arrangements than not. Thus, on a strict Paretian test, as with almost all the other examples, the contracts would be upheld.

How should we sort out the monopoly problem in terms of the role of a theory of coercion in contract law? I believe that the distinction between situational monopolies and structural monopolies is critical. In a situational monopoly—which the highwayman, tug, perhaps the dry well (if a transitory condition), and sexual favours cases exemplify—it is the relatively fortuitous circumstances surrounding the interaction between the particular parties to the exchange which create the monopoly power that A opportunistically exploits in return for a quid pro quo that has no or negative social value (the highwayman case) or in respect of which B is induced to pay vastly more than the competitive or normal value of the services (the tug case and arguably the sexual services cases). I acknowledge that some complexities are entailed in determining whether opportunistic exploitation has in fact occurred. For example, in the tug case the circumstances really entail a form of bilateral monopoly, so that it is hard to predict where in the bargaining range an agreement is likely to be reached. Moreover, determining the reference point against which this bargain must be compared may be problematic. Ideally, it should be the competitive reference point, where monopoly on both the supply and demand sides is assumed away, that is, there are many tugs and many ships competing with one another over the provision of the service in question (with the price adjusted for risk). This reference point too may not always be easy to discover.

The strongest and easiest case is one where A has violated his own reference price in opportunistically taking advantage of B's temporary dependency. Objections to this case are reflective of the "framing effects" reported in recent experimental literature. As Kahneman, Knetsch, and Thaler state, with respect to transactions such as the snow shovel example cited above:

> A central concept in analyzing the fairness of actions in which a firm sets the terms of future exchanges is the *reference transaction,* a relevant precedent that is characterized by a reference price or wage, and by a positive reference profit to the firm. The treatment is restricted to cases in which the fairness of the reference transaction is not itself in question. The main findings of this research can be summarized by a principle of *dual entitlement,* which governs community standards of fairness. Transactors have an entitlement to the terms of the reference transaction and firms are entitled to their reference profit. A firm is not allowed to increase its profits by arbitrarily violating the entitlement of its transactors to the reference price, rent or wage. When the reference profit of a firm is threatened, however, it may set new terms that protect this profit at transactors' expense. Market prices, posted prices, and the history of previous transactions between a firm and a transactor can serve as reference transactions.[44]

This approach would also explain why most of us do not find the original Penny Black case objectionable—it is a structural, not situational, monopoly, and no reference price is being violated—but why we are likely to find objectionable the later Penny Black example (rescue by the tug of the stamp from the captain's vault for an extravagant salvage fee)—the tug is a situational monopolist violating reference prices that it normally applies to its own services. Other cases are less straightforward. For example, A, a passerby, offers to rescue B, who is drowning in a swimming hole, for one million dollars. A is not normally engaged in rescue activities. Although A does not have a reference price that has been violated, we must remember that the competitive reference price in other situational monopolies serves to establish some reasonable congruence between price and cost, and in this example the lack of this congruence can be independently established. Other cases may be more problematic still. Suppose the case of a structural monopolist who is able to perfectly segregate his customers and exploit those with low elasticities of demand by practising first-degree price discrimination, thus violating his normal (single) monopoly price? Or structural monopolies auctioning off lifesaving resources to the highest bidder—arguably the dry wells drinking water case and the scarce lifesaving (dialysis machines) case?

Generally in the case of structural monopolies—exemplified by the Penny Black case, the automobile manufacturers case, the monopolized domestic industry, the movie or sports star case, the farmers case, and the trade union case—the market power is non-transitory, obtains against all parties in the relevant market, and is exogenous to and precedes the particular circumstances of the interaction between parties to a given exchange, which is arguably the appropriate focus of a theory of coercion in contract law where voluntariness is in issue. In many of these cases, both the allocative and the distributive effects are controversial and contestable. For example, are we dealing with natural monopolies (the stamp case, the mineral deposit case, and the sports or movie star case)? If so, is there any alternative rational basis for allocating the scarce resource or attribute except by reference to the highest bidder, who is presumably the highest-value user? In other words, unlike in the highwayman and the tug cases, here there is competition on the demand side, and some rationing mechanism is required to allocate the resource among competing consumers; also, the price mechanism seems to have some virtues in this context, unless the natural monopoly pertains to a resource whose output can be varied by the monopolist, in which case price regulation may move output out to efficient levels, but again this largely bears on the welfare of consumers otherwise priced out of the market. In the contrived structural cartels and monopolies (the automobile case, the farmer case, and the trade union case), allocating the goods in question on the basis of the price demanded, which reflects prior restrictions on output, will result in a misallocation of resources, which impacts, however, principally on the welfare of consumers who are priced out of the market, rather than on those who remain in the market. For consumers who remain in the market, the distributional implications are not systematic, but rather depend on the characteristics of consumers, on the one hand, and of suppliers, producers (shareholders), or workers, on the other.

Given that we have a complex body of antitrust law directed to problems of structural market power, and in some cases rate-of-return regulation of natural monopolies with variable output, it is not clear that common law courts in two-party contractual disputes would be well advised to attempt to develop a parallel set of legal doctrines relating to coercion as a way of disciplining market power. Nor would courts in two-party litigation seem well advised to address these broader welfare effects as contractual externalities. The distributional and allocative implications of structural market power are sufficiently complex and "polycentric"[45] that other, often more specialized forums, where these implications are a central focus of attention, are better equipped to address them. Conversely, in terms of relative institutional competence, situational monopolies, precisely because they are so time, place, and party specific, are unlikely to attract the attention of institutions concerned with more enduring forms of structural market power.

For private parties who wish to obtain redress from the exercise of structural market power, private antitrust suits may be the appropriate avenue of relief, but it needs to be stressed that the cause of action here turns not on concepts of coercion in exchange, but rather on injury from anti-competitive behaviour. That is, we are dealing with a problem of *market* failure, not contracting failure, and the normative reference point is appropriately a consumer or total welfare standard, not coercion or voluntariness in exchange.

If this approach were to be accepted, our notions of coercion in common law contract disputes would converge around a single principle that is directed at opportunistic exploitation of situational monopolies in particular contractual interactions where parties have egregiously violated their own reference prices or terms or, in their absence, have extracted prices or terms that diverge dramatically from competitive prices or terms or their own costs.

As an alternative to this approach, it may seem tempting to retreat to a kind of Rawlsian social contractarian perspective and ask what rules parties would wish to govern these situations before they know their particular stakes in given transactions. One factor that is perhaps given too little weight in the above theories is that of risk. Assuming risk aversion, one might reasonably argue that individuals would agree to a set of rules that minimizes certain risks to themselves. Permitting the exploitation of situational monopolies increases risk in society, often with few clear, offsetting social benefits. By analogy with the argument made by Polinsky and Shavell[46] as to why it is not socially optimal to reduce to infinitesimal levels the probability of apprehension in regulatory offenses (for example, parking offenses) with correspondingly near-infinite increases in the level of penalties, individuals may prefer a legal regime that does not place at risk their entire wealth in the life-threatening examples, or their fundamental dignity and self-respect in the sexual favours cases, through opportunistic exploitation ("hold-ups") of particularized dependencies that fortuitously beset them.

But in the end this Rawlsian strategy for resolving the theoretical conundrums is unsatisfying. Like the various welfare theories, it does not take the question of *actual* consent to a particular transaction seriously. Instead, it substitutes a notion of *hypothetical* consent to a set of contractual ground rules for a class of transactions or transacting behaviour. That welfare theories can generate such widely divergent and in some cases indeterminate implications suggests that we cannot be sure what ground rules *everybody* would hypothetically consent to. If *actual* consent, upon which the asserted normative primacy of the private ordering paradigm centrally rests, is to be taken seriously, we cannot avoid focussing on the quality of the actual consent to a given transaction.

Non-Monopolized Necessity: The Single Mother on Welfare Case

A range of examples present themselves which share the common characteristic of a person who, because of either a lack of prior endowments or pressing temporal necessity, contracts with another party, who lacks any abnormal market power and is offering terms that are competitive with other contracting parties in the same market but that appear to reflect very low returns to the first party or to entail especially burdensome risks. For example, Sissy Jupes (from Charles Dickens' *Hard Times*), facing starvation in the streets, enters into a long-term contract with a sweatshop operator under the terms of which she receives a dollar a day, which reflects the competitive wage rate among sweatshop operators who, in the face of intense international competition, cannot survive in the industry with a higher wage cost structure. Or, a single mother of six living in an urban ghetto finds that food supplies for the family have run out a week before she is to receive her next welfare cheque, and she approaches a local foodstore operator and asks him to provide her with food on credit until she receives her next cheque. Or a loanshark in a poor neighbourhood, where unemployment rates are high, lends small amounts of money on short terms at very high interest rates, reflecting high risks of default and high costs of collection. Or peddlers sell appliances on credit door-to-door to low-income consumers, charging prices substantially above those that prevail in normal retail outlets, reflecting the high cost of marketing, distribution, default, and collection.

On the assumption that the foodstore operator in the case of the welfare family is not a monopolist but one of several foodstore operators in the area and is charging competitive prices, is it inappropriate for him to enforce this contract against the mother, perhaps by way of seizure of her personal effects, when, through intervening misfortune, she is unable to pay for the food from her next welfare cheque? Or to take an example given by Fried,[47] a small contractor specializing in exterior repairs offers jobs at low wages to young men in a time of high unemployment. He explains that the work is dangerous and that he has limited safety equipment and limited insurance coverage. Each employee signs an undertaking to accept the full risk of the work and under no circumstances to sue for injuries. An employee falls from a shaky ladder, the danger of which he was clearly aware, and is seriously injured. He sues, claiming that the employer was negligent and had not furnished a safe place to work.

Critics of the market paradigm view these transactions as suspect. For example, McPherson[48] criticizes Friedman in *Capitalism and Freedom*[49] for extrapolating from a simple market model to modern market economies. Friedman argues, with respect to the simple market model, that "since the household always has the alternative of producing directly for itself, it need not enter into any exchange unless it benefits from it. Hence no exchange will take place unless both parties benefit from it. Cooperation is thereby achieved without coercion."[50] However, in extrapolating from the simple model to a complex contemporary market economy, Friedman argues that transactions are voluntary if individuals are effectively free to enter or not enter into *any particular exchange*. McPherson claims, however, that for a transaction to be strictly voluntary, it is not freedom not to enter into any particular exchange, but freedom not to enter into any exchange at all that is the requirement that should be met, as in Friedman's simple market model. In a contemporary market economy, McPherson argues, what distinguishes the capitalist economy from the simple exchange economy is the separation of labour and capital, that is, the existence of a labour force without its own sufficient capital and therefore without a choice as to whether to put its labour into the market or not. Thus, McPherson claims that Friedman's attempted demonstration that capitalism coordinates without coercion fails. Furthermore, McPherson argues that Friedman's criticisms of various features of the modern regulatory and welfare state fail to recognize that in many respects they constitute possible forms of mitigation of this pervasive type of coercion.

It is not clear how helpful this critique of the qualities of a market economy is, even if true, in adjudicating issues of voluntary consent and coercion in the context of particular exchange relationships within such an economy. In all of the examples given, there appear to be two powerful reasons that courts should not intervene in particular contractual exchanges because of an alleged inequity flowing from the absence of alternative occupational or consumption choices. On one side of these transactions, there is a clear double-bind or substitution problem of the kind recognized by Radin in her discussion of the problems of commodification.[51] If we restrict the available contract opportunity set even further than the restricted range of opportunities available at present to allegedly disadvantaged parties, in most cases we are likely to make them even worse off.[52] On the other side of the transaction, given the assumption that no market power exists and no supra-competitive returns accrue to the parties in question, it is not clear what defensible ethical basis might be invoked to justify imposing the entire redistributive burden on these parties to transactions, simply because they happen to engage in exchange relationships with poor people. To the extent that there is an obligation to underwrite redistributive policies in favour of such individuals, it would seem much more appropriate that the costs of such policies should be underwritten by the community at large, or at least better-endowed members of the community, through more general programmes of redistribution.

Most theories of coercion would accept this conclusion. Nozickian rights theories would view the proposals made in the examples in this section as offers rather than threats, because they expand the possibilities open to B. Moreover, B's moral base-line typically is not viewed in liberal theories as including unilateral entitlement to the resources of other private individuals on a gratuitous basis. Benson and Gordley would presumably also take the same view provided that the goods being exchanged were exchanged at competitive market prices. A general efficiency or welfare perspective of the kind adopted by Buckley would emphasize the double-bind or substitution effects likely to result from non-enforceability of such contracts. A literal Paretian view would regard the parties as better off in their own estimation as a result of these transactions, otherwise they would not have entered into them.

Kronman,[53] perhaps surprisingly, takes an opposing view on this issue. He points out that libertarians and liberals often converge on the view that contract regulation is an inappropriate vehicle for realizing goals of distributive justice—the libertarian because he views all forms of coerced redistribution as theft, the liberal because he believes that the tax and transfer system is a more appropriate way of realizing distributive justice goals than detailed contractual regulation. Assuming that we accept the validity of distributive justice goals (unlike many libertarians), Kronman is concerned with challenging the liberal view that contract regulation is an inappropriate way to pursue these goals. He takes as examples of contract regulation in the service of distributive justice goals usury laws, minimum wage laws, rent-control laws, habitability laws, and laws prohibiting racial discrimination in employment and the sale of real property. The conventional liberal view, as well exemplified by Rawls,[54] insists on a distinction between what Rawls terms the "basic structure of society" on the one hand, and rules that apply directly to individuals and associations and are to be followed by them in particular transactions on the other hand. In Rawls's view, the function of the basic structure, especially the tax and transfer system, is to establish and maintain a framework of entitlements that satisfies the principles of distributive justice, within which individuals remain free to pursue their own ends through voluntary transactions with others, secure in the knowledge that elsewhere in the social system the necessary corrections to preserve background justice are being made. Rawls thus takes the view that rules governing private exchange between individuals, unlike the tax laws, should not be manipulated to help achieve a fair distribution of wealth among the members of society. On his view, apparently, the law of contracts cannot be used in this way without illegitimately infringing the right of individuals to pursue their own conception of the good, free from excessive governmental interference.

According to Kronman, this view rests on two related premises: First, unlike taxation, contractual regulation discriminates between different pursuits by prohibiting some forms of exchange but not others, and it is therefore inconsistent with the view, central to most liberal theories, that the state should remain neutral between the aims and activities of its citizens, as far as possible. Second, taxation leaves more room for individual freedom than does a system of regulation that attempts to ensure distributive justice by manipulating the rules of private exchange. Kronman contests both these premises.

As to the first premise, Kronman argues that there are no *a priori* reasons for assuming that taxes are more neutral and less discriminatory than contract regulation. Although contract regulation often imposes the full distributive burden on some sub-set of the community, many taxes have the same effect. As to the second premise, the argument that contract regulation is more intrusive on individual liberty than taxation is again challenged empirically. Many taxes, such as sales taxes, apply to individual transactions. Even other taxes, such as income taxes, cast a shadow over all transactions which are likely to generate taxable income, thus creating incentives for individuals to substitute non-taxable activities or transactions. Kronman also disputes the claim that contract regulation is of necessity administratively more costly than tax and transfer policies. Although contract regulation, in most cases, requires continuous administrative oversight and enforcement, taxes also have to be enforced and collected, and, with respect to transfer programmes, for example, subsidy programmes of various kinds, often extensive administrative resources are entailed. Moreover, Kronman argues that contract regulation typically effects its redistributive aims in one step, without the mediation of the state, whereas tax and transfer programmes require that taxes first be collected and then disbursed.

Although I accept Kronman's argument that these claims and counter-claims are essentially empirical at base, as an empirical observation his claims strike me in general as unpersuasive. First, contract regulation, almost by definition, entails imposing disproportionate distributive burdens on some sub-set of society on the relatively fortuitous basis that they happen to be involved in exchange relationships with other members of society who engage our distributive concerns. This seems an ethically perverse basis on which to single them out to bear this burden. Second, with most, but admittedly not all, forms of contract regulation, particularly in the settings in which Kronman and I are interested (which I have characterized as non-monopolized necessity), there will be unavoidable double-bind or substitution effects that make some members of the intended class of beneficiaries worse off as a result of the intervention, thus offending Kronman's own modified Paretian principle. Although I acknowledge that it is possible to devise tax and transfer instruments that replicate these problems, they are much less inherently a characteristic of these instruments than they are of contract regulation. Assuming good collective intentions in choosing policy instruments to effectuate our distributive justice goals, and an absence of political malice or subterfuge, I believe that it would be a serious mistake to assign major weight to contract regulation as a vehicle for achieving our distributive justice goals relative to the tax and transfer system.

. . .

The principal focus of a theory of coercion in the common law of contracts in two-party disputes should be situational monopolies that arise out of the particular circumstances surrounding specific exchanges, where this trans-action-specific market power is exploited opportunistically to extract commitments in return for quid pro quos that have a zero or negative social value, or for quid pro quos, which, while socially positive, cannot in the normal competitive environment surrounding the type of transaction in question justify anything like the commitment extracted for them. I view this as a form of *contracting failure*. In remitting problems of structural monopolies to our antitrust laws, and some natural monopoly problems to rate-of-return regulation, I am, of course, recognizing the essential complementarity between public and private forms of legal ordering. I rely simply on pragmatic considerations of relative institutional competence in suggesting that private law adjudication in two-party contract disputes is not well situated to address issues of *market failure* (as opposed to contracting failure). In remitting problems of non-monopolized necessity in general to the social welfare domain, I again rely on pragmatic considerations of relative institutional competence and efficacy. Even well-functioning markets will systematically fail to vindicate all society's distributive justice values, but regulation of such markets motivated by this objective is rarely likely to advance this end. Thus, in terms of the relative institutional division of labour, the common law of contracts will be principally concerned with *autonomy* issues in evaluating claims of coercion, antitrust and regulatory law issues of *consumer welfare,* and the social welfare system issues of *distributive justice.*

CHAPTER FIVE

Asymmetric Information Imperfections

The Nature of the Conceptual Problem

Even the most committed proponents of free markets and freedom of contract recognize that certain information preconditions must be met for a given exchange to possess Pareto superior qualities. For example, to recall the statement of Milton Friedman: "The possibility of coordination through voluntary cooperation rests on the elementary—yet frequently denied—proposition that both parties to an economic transaction benefit from it, *provided the transaction is bilaterally voluntary and informed.*"[1]

In this chapter, the organizing assumption is that one party to a contract is substantially less well informed about some aspect of the contract subject matter than the other party, and in the light of this assumption, I ask whether in some cases contracts should not be enforced on that account, or enforced on different terms, and why. The relevance of this question to both autonomy and Paretian welfare justifications for private exchanges will be obvious. In autonomy terms, Kim Lane Scheppele argues:

> Information plays a dual role in rational choice theory. On the one hand, it is a precondition of choice. That is, one needs a certain amount of information in order to be able to imagine one's alternatives, to understand enough of their implications to be able to distinguish among them, and to assess which one would best realize one's aims. All of this requires quite a lot of knowledge and, generally speaking, the more the better. On the other hand, knowledge is itself an object of choice; that is, one can choose whether to acquire more information. Whether one decides to acquire more information depends not only on what one already knows but on one's estimates of the chances that more knowledge will improve the decision enough to be worth one's efforts. Generally speaking, in such a situation the less additional knowledge one needs, the better.[2]

Thus, how much information is required for the exercise of autonomous choices presents a complex puzzle: it is difficult to conceive of a choice as autonomous without basic information on its implications, but because information is often costly it may be rational to choose to forgo the acquisition of further information where its expected benefits are less than its expected costs.[3]

The Paretian justification for private exchange assumes that both parties to an exchange are rendered better off by it—in terms of the subjectively perceived impact of the exchange on their respective utility functions—or they would not have entered into it. But if at least one party inaccurately perceives or evaluates the impact of the exchange on her utility, we can no longer be confident that the exchange will in fact render both parties better off. Having said this, we immediately begin to encounter some serious conceptual problems. As with the issue of voluntariness in endemic conditions of scarcity, the issue of imperfect information is pervasive, not exceptional, in the contracting process. Almost no exchanges are entered into with absolutely perfect information by both parties. Even the purchase of the morning newspaper in the local variety store on the assumption that it will contain an interesting film or restaurant review, when this assumption turns out to be false, reflects an exchange entered into with incomplete information. Thus, if we were to insist on a blanket requirement of perfect information, very few contracts would be enforceable. A related conceptual problem also confronts us. This is what I call the "Paretian dilemma." If we adopt an *ex post* Paretian perspective in transactions where one party has committed or is threatening breach—presumably because in most cases the contract does not appear to him to be as advantageous *ex post* as it seemed to be *ex ante*—most contract breaches would be excused. However, if we adopt an *ex ante* Paretian perspective on particular transactions, and both parties feel better off at the time of entering into the contract (and were happy to assume whatever risks might be entailed), then we should enforce all exchanges, even when based on imperfect information. Alternatively, a Kaldor-Hicks efficiency perspective would ask what set of ground rules on information asymmetries is likely to maximize social welfare for contracting parties generally in the long-run, irrespective of the welfare implications for parties to a given transaction.

Categories of Information Failure

Fraud

Recall that in the case of coercion, Kronman has argued[4] that it is impossible to generate a coherent theory of voluntariness that is not at the same time a theory of distributive justice in the sense of some specification of what endowments or advantages particular parties will be permitted to exploit vis-à-vis other parties with whom they have entered into contractual relationships. In the case of coercion, we seek to disqualify the use of superior force. In the case of fraud, we disallow the exploitation of a superior capacity for deception. Conversely, Fried dismisses as "specious" the argument that the contractual prohibition on fraud is a form of redistribution. Although it is true that condemning bargains reached by force or fraud will have distributive effects, it does not follow that redistributive aims lie behind these judgements. Instead, Fried argues[5] that the capacity to form true and rational judgements and to act on them is at the heart of moral personality and is the basis of a person's claim to respect as a moral being. A liar seeks to accomplish his purpose by creating a false belief in his interlocutor, and so he may be said to do harm by touching the mind, as an assailant does harm by laying hands on his victim's body. To enforce a promise induced by fraud is to invoke *against the victim* the very morality of respect and trust that the liar betrayed in eliciting the promise. Although I find Fried's characterization of why we object to fraud and provide relief against contractual undertakings on that account more intuitively appealing than Kronman's, I will shortly address some more problematic cases, where a non-instrumental theory of contractual objection seems to provide much less insight.

In any event, on either Kronman's or Fried's theory there is no dispute as to the end result: a party who enters into a contract with another as a result of a fraudulent representation by the latter is, and should be, entitled to relief. It is also the case that from a literal Paretian welfare perspective, a transaction induced by fraud is unlikely to make both parties better off, although this involves an *ex post* judgement which, as noted above, would also excuse many other contract breaches. From a Kaldor-Hicks welfare perspective, one would ask whether a rule against fraud is likely to increase net social welfare from transactions generally. The case for such a rule would rest on a judgement that investments in fraudulent activity have no positive social value and that the absence of such a rule may induce socially wasteful investments by potential victims in avoidance precautions.

Negligent Misrepresentation

Let us take three cases. In the first, a used-car dealer or private seller turns back the odometer on a car to deceive prospective buyers about the car's mileage. We have no difficulty recognizing this as a case of fraud. In the second case, a perspective buyer asks a seller whether the odometer reading on the car is correct, and the seller represents in good faith that it is, even though he should have known, from the prior history of the car or its documentation, that it was highly unlikely the odometer reading was accurate and that some previous owner had probably tampered with it. Here the seller is not promising, as a contractual term, that the odometer reading is accurate, but his misrepresentation has induced a buyer to enter into a transaction which, *ex post,* is not Pareto superior, that is, the buyer is rendered worse off as a result of the transaction than he would have been had he not entered into it. This kind of case is not addressed by either Kronman or Fried, although it is a very common class of situation in the contract case-law. A third type of case entailing negligent misrepresentation is one where the seller knows all along which propositions are true and false, does not intend to assert any false proposition, but is negligent in his use of language, so that the buyer gets the impression that the seller has asserted some proposition that in fact is not true. Unlike the second case, where the seller should have undertaken a fuller investigation of the facts, in this case, the seller should have been more careful about his choice of language.[6] In the second and third categories of cases, it seems difficult to rely on a non-instrumental or autonomy-based theory of contractual obligation to determine whether the buyer should obtain relief from the contract. Rather, what we have is careless and presumably avoidable conduct on the part of the seller and reasonable reliance on the part of the buyer. This evokes tort-like concepts of fault and reliance, but to the extent we assign liability to the seller, it is not obviously premised on a consensually assumed obligation to the buyer. Although we can justify liability for negligent misrepresentation, at least in some contexts, in efficiency or welfare terms, in order to induce efficient precautions,[7] it is also true that liability for negligence generally in tort law can be justified in autonomy terms—in terms not of consensually assumed obligations but of an obligation to avoid unreasonable conduct that violates the equal autonomy of another.[8]

Innocent Misrepresentation

Let us imagine a slight variation on the previous example. A prospective buyer, responding to a classified ad, telephones a private seller of a car and asks the mileage of the car. The seller reports the current odometer reading, which the seller believes to be accurate when, in fact, it is not, although he has no reason for supposing it to be otherwise. Subsequently, the inquirer purchases the car. Here, we have reliance by the buyer and absence of fault on the part of the seller. One might tentatively argue that the seller should have been more cautious in his response, given his lack of information about what might have happened to the car in the hands of previous owners; one might thus argue that to encourage appropriate circumspection on the part of sellers in claims they make about goods they are selling whose prior histories they are not fully informed of, the law would be justified in providing the buyer with relief. But again, the seller's obligations to the buyer here do not derive from any consensually assumed obligation. Nor is it clear how Kronman's theory of advantage-taking helps us much in the situation, unless one believes that his modified Paretian principle (discussed in Chapter 5) would yield the conclusion that buyers generally and in the long-run would not be rendered better off by permitting this kind of conduct on the part of sellers. But this simply seems an elaborate way of formulating a straightforward least-cost-avoider test of the kind that is conventionally favoured by law and economics scholars in a tort context, invoking Kaldor-Hicks efficiency considerations. A literal Paretian test, at least if applied *ex post* in this context, might yield relief for the buyer, irrespective of relative precaution costs, though for reasons noted, most contract breaches would be excused on this basis.

Material Non-Disclosure

Cases of deliberate non-disclosure are much more problematic than the cases I have been considering and have generated a complex and confusing body of doctrine in both common law and civil law legal systems.[9] First, let me take non-disclosure by sellers. In one case, an owner of a house discovers that he has termites in the attic (after hearing their activities at night or observing their droppings) and that they have done serious damage to the structure of the house. If he sweeps up the droppings to conceal their presence and permits showings of the house only during the daytime, when they cannot be heard, we might want to view this as a species of fraud. Suppose, however, that the seller of the house takes no active steps to conceal the termites but sells the house to an unsuspecting buyer who the seller is aware is seriously misinformed as to the structural damage done by the termites and, therefore, the real value of the house. Kronman would resolve cases such as this by reference to a distinction he develops between casually and deliberately acquired information.[10] The first class of information would be subject to a disclosure rule, but the second would not. According to Kronman, this distinction preserves incentives for efficient information generation. This view seems predicated on general Kaldor-Hicks efficiency considerations, and not a literal Paretian test, which would *ex post* excuse most mistakes. It is also not clear whether Kronman's modified Paretian test, at the level of generality at which he formulates the distinction between casually and deliberately acquired information, entails any considerations different from those in a Kaldor-Hicks perspective.

In the second termites example, the information known to the seller and unavailable to the buyer was not acquired as a result of costly investment in information-gathering activities and therefore, according to Kronman, requiring disclosure of it would not create disincentives to the acquisition of the information. This explanation is not particularly convincing. Suppose the seller had suspected the presence of termites in his attic and had hired experts to investigate this possibility, at some expense to himself. Would we feel any less inclined to require disclosure here than in cases where he came across this information fortuitously?

Fried[11] is strongly critical of Kronman's reliance on instrumental efficiency-*cum*-distributional factors in addressing these problems. He argues instead that efficiency, redistribution, and altruism are among the law's many goals, but that by pursuing these goals according, but only according, to established conventions—including conventions ordained prospectively or gradually by courts—the collectivity acknowledges that individuals have rights and cannot just be sacrificed to collective goals. The recourse to prior conventions permits individuals to plan, consider, and pursue their own ends. However, Fried does not tell us how to go about ascertaining the conventions, which presumably involves appeal to externally determined social norms. Moreover, he acknowledges that many of the conventions that establish the background expectations may also embody efficiency or distributional considerations. This is not particularly helpful in deciding what to do about the particular case in question. An autonomy theorist might alternatively argue that the buyer's choice in this case was not fully autonomous or voluntary, because it was informationally flawed in a crucially important respect. As I discuss at greater length in Chapter 7, autonomy theorists customarily accept this as a rationale for paternalistic legal interventions designed to replicate the choices individuals would have made with full information. However the seller came by his superior information in the termites case (casually or deliberately), in entering into a transaction with a buyer who he knows lacks this information arguably entails a violation of the Kantian imperative of equal concern and respect.

Let me take another case of seller non-disclosure. If I advertise a used car for sale through the classified section of the local newspaper, am I under an obligation to point out every rattle, oil leak, whining noise, or rust spot in or on the car to every prospective purchaser in order for a contract to be binding? What would Fried's "established conventions" tell us about a situation like this? Alternatively, where would Kronman's efficiency-distributional factors, as embodied in the modified Paretian test, lead us in this case? One might, of course, argue that prospective buyers of used cars, simply because the cars are used, assume some level of wear and tear and defect, depending on the age, mileage, and price of the car, and it would generate wasteful transactions costs for all parties to require sellers to disclose defects or blemishes that fall within the range normally or reasonably established by these parameters, that is, to require sellers to inform buyers of what is mostly obvious. Perhaps only major but non-obvious (latent) defects falling outside this range should require disclosure. However, it is clear that this duty is not based on a consensually assumed obligation, although one might again argue that the seller's conduct violates the buyer's autonomy in failing to observe a precept of equal concern and respect.

One might also reasonably argue that requiring disclosure for this range of defects avoids various forms of socially wasteful transaction costs, such as a succession of prospective buyers hiring mechanics to inspect cars before purchase or, in the event of purchase in the absence of accurate information, further transactions that might be entailed in moving the goods to their socially most valuable uses, given the now fully revealed condition of the goods. But this is a purely instrumental argument, and those not attracted by general Kaldor-Hicks efficiency considerations of this sort might prefer instead some distributional argument. Perhaps, on Kronman's modified Paretian test, one would conclude that buyers as a class and over the long-term are not advantaged by permitting this kind of conduct by sellers in any particular transaction. And to the extent that buyers of cars are just as often sellers, this might be seen as a fair rule. It is not clear that in its essence, however, it reflects substantially different considerations from those implied by a general Kaldor-Hicks efficiency perspective.

Now let me take two examples involving non-disclosure by buyers. First, a prospective buyer (a professor of economics) observes a very rare first edition of Adam Smith's *Wealth of Nations,* personally autographed by Adam Smith (in his invisible hand), on sale for fifty cents in a carton of books being sold by the executors of an estate on a neighbourhood front lawn at a garage sale. Is the prospective buyer under an obligation to disclose to the sellers the dramatic undervaluation of the book before buying it at the stipulated price? Here, as in the termite cases, Kronman's distinction between casually and deliberately acquired information seems fragile. Perhaps the buyer can argue that he has invested a large amount of human capital acquiring an expertise in economics and that only as a result of this was he able to recognize the true value of this book. Suppose, however, that buying rare editions of old economics treatises is a hobby and is quite incidental to the activities in which he principally employs his economic expertise. Fried would remit us to unspecified, but apparently established, social conventions which would tell us what is or is not expected of the prospective buyer in this case.

Or to take another case involving buyer non-disclosure, if a prospector, through research of various kinds, including flying over vast expanses of farmland taking magnetic soundings, develops a well-informed hunch that a particular block of farmland may have serious potential as a mineral reserve or an oil-drilling site, is he under an obligation to disclose this fact to the incumbent farmer before purchasing the land at a price that reflects only agricultural uses? In this context Kronman again invokes his distinction between casually and deliberately acquired information.[12] In this case, to require disclosure by the buyer effectively deprives him of any economic return on his investments in acquiring the information and thus removes any incentive for the acquisition of it, thereby attenuating the movement of land from lower-valued to higher-valued uses. Applying his modified Paretian test, Kronman asks whether sellers in this class of situation are likely in general and in the long-run to be better off by permitting this kind of advantage-taking. He concludes that they probably would be better off, reasoning that this would ensure that they gain access to cheaper sources of energy. This strikes me as totally speculative and on its face, quite unpersuasive. Fried, while taking vigorous issue with Kronman's approach to this problem, offers us nothing as a substitute except reference to established conventions, which he feels might possibly require disclosure here, unlike another case in which the buyer is purchasing the land from a natural resource company, where one might assume that the parties have appropriately impounded the risk of the land's containing a valuable oil deposit in the terms of the contract and the seller is engaging in a deliberate and well-considered gamble. But as to why social conventions cut in opposite ways in these two cases, and how we ascertain what these conventions are, is not explained.

Scheppele[13] is critical of Kronman's approach on both normative and positive grounds. On normative grounds, she offers a Rawlsian contractarian alternative which abstracts from particular transactions and parties' stakes therein and asks what rules that individuals behind a veil of ignorance but aware of their cultural and social context would agree to. Thus, the issue of consent is shifted from the transactional context to the legal framework context, that is, from actual to hypothetical consent. She argues that from this perspective individuals would agree to rules that (1) provide relief against catastrophic losses from "secret-keeping" (deliberate withholding of information); (2) require disclosure of "deep secrets," where the target of the secret has no reason for imagining the existence of the information in question; and (3) ensure that when secrets are "shallow" (when the target has reason to suspect the existence of relevant information), both parties to a transaction have equal access to it. In the latter case, for two parties to have equal access to information they must first have equal probabilities of finding the information if they put in the same level of effort; and second, they must be capable of making this equivalent level of effort. On positive grounds, Scheppele claims to demonstrate through extensive analysis of the case-law that her normative framework is more consistent with the pattern of reasoning and outcomes in decided cases than Kronman's.

By way of example, she discusses four leading U.S. cases—two where the buyer knew more than the seller, and two where the seller knew more than the buyer. In Laidlaw v. Organ,[14] Organ, on hearing of the unexpected signing of the Treaty of Ghent that ended the War of 1812 and with it the British blockade of New Orleans, approached Laidlaw before this information became general knowledge and bought a large quantity of tobacco in the expectation of a substantial price increase (which subsequently occurred). In the absence of any positive misrepresentation, the U.S. Supreme Court held that Organ was not obliged to communicate this information to Laidlaw and could maintain the bargain. This was so despite the fact that Organ's information was apparently fortuitously obtained, compelling Kronman to rationalize the decision by arguing that buyers generally obtain information about others' products through deliberate search and that a categoric rule may conserve on transaction—adjudication costs entailed in case-by-case inquiry.

In Strong v. Repide,[15] Repide was the majority shareholder, director, and general administrator of a company that was negotiating the sale of its assets in the Philippines to the U.S. government. Minority shareholders, who were aware of these negotiations, were induced by undisclosed agents of Repide to sell their shares to him at substantially less than they proved to be worth when negotiations with the U.S. government were finally concluded. Here, the U.S. Supreme Court upset the transactions, on the grounds that Repide had withheld critical information about the impending change in value of the shares from the sellers of them. Yet, according to Scheppele, Kronman's analysis would lead to the opposite result, as Repide's information about the unexpectedly high reservation price of the U.S. government had been acquired through investment of effort and expertise in negotiations.

In Dyke v. Zaiser,[16] a city councilman leased out a concession business in an amusement centre without disclosing to the lessee that he had made inquiries of the police chief which revealed an imminent police raid that subsequently closed down the majority of the concessions. Here, the court relieved the lessee of the lease, despite the fact that (according to Scheppele) the lessor's superior information was the result of deliberate investments therein.

In Jappe v. Mandt,[17] the owner of a garbage collection business sold it to the plaintiff without disclosing that a municipality whose garbage collection needs were central to the business was contemplating contracting this activity out to a third party. The court declined to provide relief on the grounds that this decision was merely "in the wind" and public rumours were as accessible to the purchaser as to the vendor. Thus, though the vendor had casually heard of the rumours, he was not required to disclose them to the buyer, contrary to the implications of Kronman's analysis.

Scheppele claims her framework better explains these cases. In Laidlaw v. Organ, both parties had equal access to the relevant information, whereas in Strong v. Repide they did not; the same is true of Dyke v. Zaiser (unequal access) and Jappe v. Mandt (equal access). In other cases, the two frameworks converge. For example, in Fuller v. DePaul University,[18] an apostate priest operating under a change-of-name successfully applied for an academic position with a Catholic university without disclosing his circumstances: the university was released from the contract. In Simmons v. Evans,[19] the vendor of a residential property failed to disclose to the purchaser that the local water authority routinely cut off water to residences from 7 P.M. to 7 A.M. each night—the court released the purchaser from the contract. Kronman would support these results on the grounds that the information in question was casually acquired, Scheppele on the grounds that deep secrets were involved or that there was inequality of access to the information.

Although Scheppele's criticism of Kronman's approach reveals significant limitations in a simple distinction between casually and deliberately acquired information, her own approach is not free from difficulty. Her distinction between deep and shallow secrets is vague. As we shall see more fully in the next chapter, the question of whether one party to a contract has failed to completely apprehend certain contingencies does not admit of an easy answer. Moreover, what losses count as catastrophic and what as moderate? Should unanticipated gains be treated differently from unanticipated losses? What constitutes equal access to information? The imprecisions inherent in Scheppele's tests permit of ad hoc rationalizations of the existing case-law, whereby almost any decision can be reconciled with one or another strand of her various criteria. More important, her approach (unlike Kronman's) largely discounts the dynamic (rather than static) welfare gains to be realized from creating appropriate incentives for the acquisition and utilization of information that facilitate the movement of resources from less to more productive uses.

I believe that a reformulation of an economic (welfare) framework for analyzing cases of material non-disclosure is possible that sheds a clearer light on the relevant welfare considerations than either Kronman's or Scheppele's approaches. It bears noting that these latter two approaches do not start from such divergent premises as Scheppele seems to believe. Both essentially purport to be concerned with the choice of legal rules that maximize social welfare, although in Scheppele's case with a welfare floor, reflecting a Rawlsian maximin principle, in the case of catastrophic losses. Even this qualification may be reconcilable with a welfare analysis if one assumes some degree of risk aversion by the parties. Conversely, if one assumes, as Harsanyi[20] argues in a critique of Rawls, that individuals behind the veil of ignorance will rationally choose rules designed to maximize expected utility (and not the maximin principle), a general utilitarian calculus emerges that is not sharply different from the Kaldor-Hicks considerations which seem to motivate Kronman's analysis of mistake. Common to both approaches is an emphasis on hypothetical *ex ante* consent to a set of legal ground rules, with the quality of the *actual* consent of parties to a given transaction entailing asymmetric information relegated to a secondary role.

If the efficiency objective in this context is defined as the adoption of legal rules that facilitate the movement of assets to their most productive uses with as few transaction costs as possible, then it would seem to follow that there should be a general presumption in favour of disclosure of material facts known to one party and unknown to the other. In the absence of such a presumption, the second party and other prospective contracting parties may be induced to invest in wasteful precautions to generate information about the asset that is already possessed by the first party and can be transmitted at trivial marginal social cost. This general presumption, however, entails a static welfare analysis, and Kronman's approach (unlike Scheppele's) properly emphasizes the need also for a dynamic perspective. In other words, will enforced disclosure reduce incentives for parties to generate and utilize the information in the first place? It is here that Kronman's distinction between casually and deliberately acquired information seems seriously inadequate to capture all the relevant incentive effects.

Consider the termites cases. Here, even where the information is deliberately acquired by the seller, if enforced disclosure is unlikely to inhibit its acquisition, disclosure should be required. In many such cases, the information would seem worth acquiring by the owner of the property irrespective of whether he intends to sell the property and irrespective of whether he is required to disclose it on sale. This would also seem true of a case such as Dyke v. Zaiser (the lease of the concessions in the amusement centre). Consider too the used car sale. To require disclosure of information by the seller, even though casually acquired, of every blemish in the car of which he is aware, when these blemishes, either specifically or generically, are well within the range of apprehension of the average used-car buyer ("patent defects"), is to incur needless transaction costs in disclosing what is mostly obvious. Such a rule is also likely to introduce a significant degree of risk into transactions which could opportunistically be rescinded subsequently by buyers who have spotted a better deal (in effect converting the contract into an option) or which could ground a damages claim (in effect revising the agreed purchase price), even though the buyer may already have discounted—if one accepts Akerlof's analysis,[21] perhaps even excessively discounted—the risk of adverse contingencies in the purchase price, thus entailing double recovery.

Take the prospector case. Here, enforced disclosure would almost certainly lead to the non-production of information, leaving the farmer no better off, and the prospector and society at large worse off, as a result of the deferred movement of agricultural land to more productive uses as an oil reserve. This proposition would seem to hold whether the buyer acquired the information casually or deliberately. Suppose a weekend hiker passing through a ravine on the periphery of the farmer's land stumbles across oil seepage from a crevice. Further investigation suggests a strong possibility of an oil deposit on the farmer's land. Here a rule of disclosure may have no effect on the likelihood of *generation* of this information, but such a rule will operate as a major disincentive to its *utilization* in procuring a transaction with the farmer, thus again retarding the movement of resources from lower- to higher-valued uses.

Consider the purchase of *The Wealth of Nations* at gross under-value. Here, even if we assume that the acquisition of expertise in rare first editions of famous economic treatises by the academic economist is quite incidental to his broader investment in expertise in economics, and thus can be viewed as casually acquired in the sense that enforced disclosure is unlikely to diminish significantly his investment in this expertise, there is the further issue of whether enforced disclosure will diminish his incentives to *utilize* this information in the marketplace, thus retarding the movement of resources from lower-valued to higher-valued uses. Clearly, enforced disclosure will have this effect. This would be so even if the buyer quite casually in the course of dinner conversation with a rare book collector acquired information about the true value of a rare book and later fortuitously spotted it for sale at a garage sale at gross under-value. Similarly, in the case of Laidlaw v. Organ, even if one assumes that the information was casually or fortuitously acquired by the buyer, there is still the question of whether enforced disclosure will discourage the *utilization* of the information in transactions that facilitate the movement of resources from lower- to higher-valued uses. Perhaps on the particular facts of Laidlaw v. Organ, when news of the peace treaty and the lifting of the blockade would become general knowledge within hours of the transaction, the resource allocation implications of disclosure or non-disclosure in the transaction in question were minimal, but this will not always be the case. For example, as Kronman himself points out,[22] tobacco farmers may plough under a crop of tobacco in the face of severely depressed prices, rather than incur the costs of picking it, or plant corn instead of tobacco; meanwhile more buyers in the market, acting on undisclosed information, will move the price upwards towards its new equilibrium and thus mute these misallocative tendencies. However, this will be so no matter in what way a buyer acquired the information (casually or deliberately). In the rare book case, if buyers cannot act on undisclosed information, an uninformed buyer may purchase the book for a doorstop or window jam. In other commodity market settings, for example, casually acquired information of a freak hailstorm's destroying the Florida citrus crop, a middleman acting on this information before it becomes general knowledge in the market may arguably serve the socially useful function of shifting supply inter-temporally to future time periods when supply would otherwise be more tightly constricted. In some cases the knowledge in question may be purely redistributive and non-productive, in which case a rule of non-disclosure may create incentives for excessive information generation. For example, in the prospector case, if both the farmer and the prospector know that there is an oil deposit under the farmer's land and the only uncertainty is over its extent, private knowledge on the part of the buyer will go only to the price of the land and not to its use. One might argue that from an efficiency perspective we should not reward the acquisition of such information.[23]

However, it will be clear that the foregoing analysis generally gives buyers much more latitude in exploiting information than it does sellers. On my analysis, sellers will generally have to disclose information they possess of material facts to buyers, whether the information is casually acquired or deliberately acquired, unless disclosure is likely to discourage its acquisition. Material facts might be understood to refer to those facts the ignorance of which is likely to substantially impair the expected value of the transaction to the buyer. A further exception to the disclosure rule would be made in the case of patent defects. In contrast, buyers would generally be under no duty of disclosure, however they acquired the superior information, because we want them not only to acquire the information but to *utilize* it in transactions, if resources are to be moved from less to more productive uses. Where a seller has acquired adverse information about his assets, these (now revalued) assets are a sunk cost for him. What we need to ensure is that they are not further misallocated in ensuing transactions through non-disclosure, subject only to not requiring disclosure where in all likelihood this would discourage the acquisition of the adverse information in the first place or in the case of patent defects. In many contexts, this result may be achieved through implied warranties, which the seller can contract out of by stipulating, for example, that he is selling goods "as is."

This bias favouring buyers over sellers in the material non-disclosure rules that I have proposed can be supported on other grounds. Either by assuming risk aversion generally on the part of contracting parties, or by adopting a related Rawlsian maximin principle (as Scheppele does), the gains forgone by sellers in the event of non-disclosure by buyers (as in Laidlaw v. Organ, or the prospector or rare book examples) probably do not reduce utility as much (assuming the declining marginal utility of wealth) as the reductions in wealth (out-of-pocket losses) sustained by buyers in the event of seller non-disclosure of adverse material facts.[24]

In cases of fiduciary relationships or relationships of public trust of the kind at issue in Strong v. Repide (buyer non-disclosure) and Dyke v. Zaiser (seller/lessor non-disclosure), even if one assumes that the information in question would not have been gathered if disclosure were required (a doubtful proposition in both cases), the buyer of the shares in the first case and the lessor of the premises in the second faced conflicts of interests with respect to their personal interests and those of their constituents, whom they were elected to serve. This is a classic agency cost problem entailing fiduciaries' exploiting their principals by utilizing inside information acquired in the course of performance of their fiduciary duties, for which they are being otherwise compensated. The goal of minimizing agency costs (both monitoring costs and asset diversion) would seem to reinforce the need for a stringent disclosure rule in this context.

I believe that if one keeps centrally in view the over-all efficiency or welfare objective of rules that govern cases of material non-disclosure—facilitating the movement of resources from less to more productive uses with as few transaction costs as possible—and avoid the temptation (to which Kronman succumbs) of attempting to decompose this objective into too crude a set of categoric rules that take on a life of their own, disconnected from this over-riding objective, the material non-disclosure cases are susceptible of principled resolution in welfare terms. Although the nuances in the proposed approach will obviously generate more administrative costs, and perhaps some greater uncertainties, than an austerely categoric rule such as that proposed by Kull[25]—no disclosure should ever be required of any private knowledge pertaining to the value of the contract subject matter—administrative costs cannot be absolutely determinative of contract rules or we would simply ban all actions for breach of contract. Moreover, Kull's distinction between clerical errors that are obvious to the other party (for example, a mistake in pricing a tender or reading a price sticker) and mistakes as to value does not seem to rest on any clear normative principle (other than certainty and ease of administration).

A quite different approach from those of Kronman, Scheppele, and myself to some of these problems has been proposed by Gordley.[26] In contrast to the Paretian principle, which merely requires in order for an exchange to be Pareto superior that both parties gain *something* from the exchange, even if the gains from exchange are unequal, Gordley's proposal holds that both parties should gain equally, in effect postulating a principle of commutative or corrective justice as originally articulated by Aristotle and designed to maintain the pre-existing distribution of wealth. Gordley argues for an ethical principle of equality in exchange such that inequalities in the value of the performances exchanged should be grounds for contractual invalidation or judicial reconstruction of the contract, without examination of the causes of the disparity. He argues that most legal systems from classical Greek and Roman times forward, including the medieval theory of the just price, have recognized some such principle but that in the nineteenth century, courts under the influence of will theories of contract and theories about the subjectivity of value became much less self-conscious in applying the principle, despite similar patterns of judicial outcomes disguised under other principles. Gordley reformulates classical theories of commutative justice and medieval theories of the just price in a modern economic context as requiring contractual relief where parties have contracted for substantially more or substantially less than the market price. For example, A buys from a door-to-door salesman for $1,000 a freezer that commonly sells for $500 at normal retail outlets (holding constant characteristics of consumers in terms of default risk, and so on), or, alternatively, A sells his farm to B for $50,000, when its market value is $100,000. In both cases, it is assumed that A is ignorant of the prevailing market price, and on Gordley's theory we should not be concerned to inquire whether B did or did not deliberately take advantage of his ignorance. In cases where the contract subject matter does not have a readily ascertainable market price, Gordley's theory would apparently be more respectful of the parties' valuation unless there is compelling evidence that the price reflects much more or much less than the seller's costs. The ethical intuition that lies behind Gordley's reformulation of the theory of the just price appears to be that a party to an arms-length exchange does not intend to make a gift to the other party, which is implied by selling for less than the market price or buying for more than the market price.

Although provocative, Gordley's theory raises a number of questions. From an individual autonomy perspective, to take a case outside the fungible goods context, suppose that I am extremely attached to my house for family, sentimental, historical, or locational reasons and would not contemplate selling it for less than a large premium over the going market price for otherwise similar houses. A buyer, perhaps motivated by similar factors to those which weigh with me, agrees to pay me this price. Is this price unjust? From a communitarian perspective of the kind adopted by McPherson,[27] one might imagine a challenge to Gordley's theory along the lines of asking why we should sanctify or even exalt market prices as the dominant indicia of fairness. In terms of the practical implications of Gordley's theory, we need to ask whether a recognition of a reconstituted theory of the just price would yield substantially different results in particular cases from a Paretian test with the conventional conditions attached. In order to violate Gordley's doctrine of equality in exchange, he envisages that the disproportionality between contract and market price must be substantial. Thus, some range of inequalities in values exchanged is still envisaged, and to that extent, Gordley's theory moves closer to a Paretian theory of mutually beneficial exchanges but does not completely elide with it, since, provided that both parties derive *any* gains from the exchange, however they are shared, the Paretian test would be met. Moreover, where the disproportionalities are as large as Gordley apparently envisages in order for the doctrine to be invoked, one would need to ask whether this would be compelling evidence in many settings of a violation of the Paretian conditions, including coercion or fraud or misrepresentation. However, his theory does offer the advantage that one need not investigate the precise source of procedural irregularities or deficiencies in the contract formation process—it is a theory of substantive, not procedural, fairness—and may provide more precision than either Kronman's modified Paretian test or Fried's established conventions test in dealing with cases where, because of asymmetric information, as the facts are subsequently revealed, there is a major disparity between the contract price and the market price for the contract subject matter in the fully revealed state of the facts. It needs to be added, though, that this certainty comes at a price: like Scheppele, Gordley is largely insensitive to the dynamic incentive considerations which motivate Kronman's welfare analysis of mistake (and which I have refined) and emphasize the welfare gains from the acquisition and utilization of information that moves assets from less productive to more productive uses. It needs also to be added that whatever virtues Gordley's theory of equality in exchange might have, the obligations it implies are certainly not consensually based and entail an appeal to external ethical norms, which he presumably believes the community widely endorses.

As with the issues discussed in the chapter on coercion, a deeply troubling issue in cases of asymmetric information imperfections is whether the focus of legal concern should be on the quality of *actual* consent of parties to particular transactions, as autonomy theories should surely regard as central, or on the framing of legal rules to which members of the community might *hypothetically* agree before their stakes in particular transactions are known to them. Fried equivocates on this issue by emphasizing individual autonomy yet appealing to ill-specified social conventions. Kronman's modified Paretianism; Kaldor-Hicks efficiency; Scheppele's Rawlsian regime; and Gordley's theory of equality in exchange all largely ignore the issue of actual consent. Literal Paretianism is unhelpful because, while it conventionally infers welfare effects from consent, it encounters difficulties when *ex post* a transaction does not make both parties better off (thus providing a basis for excusing most contract breaches). This general difficulty is revealed acutely in cases such as that of the prospector. Although welfare considerations seem fairly unambiguously to militate in favour of non-disclosure by the buyer, whether the information was deliberately or casually acquired, the deliberate exploitation by the buyer of the farmer's ignorance of a crucially important fact bearing on the real value of his property seems to involve the taking of advantage of a less than fully autonomous choice by the farmer if one views as pre-conditions for fully autonomous choices, as even Milton Friedman does, lack of coercion and full information. It may be plausible to argue that the buyer's conduct violates the Kantian categorical imperative of equal concern and respect in that if roles were reversed (as in the termite cases), the buyer would not wish his ignorance to be exploited by the seller in this fashion, even though such a precept may come at a cost in terms of long-run community welfare. But the farmer might reasonably ask why his interests should be sacrificed to this greater social end (without his informed consent); that is, why should he be used as a means to the ends of others? One could, of course, argue that the farmer is always free to insist on a condition in the contract that in the event of the buyer's exploiting undisclosed information, the farmer is entitled to rescind the contract. Scheppele's and Fried's ambivalence about this kind of case is understandable, but taking refuge in social conventions or Rawlsian hypothetical social contracts does not make the theoretical problem any more transparent or tractable.

Information Processing Disabilities: Cognitive Deficiencies

Under this category, I include cases where there has been no misrepresentation of information by one contracting party to the other and no non-disclosure of some material fact, but rather where the two parties, while sharing equal access to the relevant body of information about the contract subject matter, have sharply differential capacities to evaluate the implications of that information for their respective welfare—an issue to which I will return in Chapter 8. Eisenberg[28] cites two sub-classes of case, both of which he argues should be addressed by a modern doctrine of unconscionability. The first sub-class he characterizes as "transactional incapacity." The paradigm case he envisages is one where A knows or has reason to know of B's inability to deal with a given complex transaction, because of lack of aptitude, experience, or judgemental ability to make a deliberative and well-informed decision concerning the desirability of entering into the transaction, and exploits that incapacity by inducing B to make a bargain that a person who had the capacity to deal with the transaction probably would not make. He cites as an example a very complex real estate proposal put by a commercial developer to an aging testamentary beneficiary of a commercial building. He also cites the well-known decision of Lord Denning of the English Court of Appeal in Lloyds Bank v. Bundy,[29] where an elderly farmer was induced by his son's bank to sign a guarantee of his son's indebtedness to the bank in circumstances where it was highly unlikely that the farmer was able to evaluate prudentially all the implications of the transaction. The other sub-class of case which Eisenberg identifies is what he calls "unfair persuasion." By this he means the use of bargaining methods that seriously impair the free and competent exercise of judgement and produce a state of acquiescence that the promisee knows or should know is likely to be highly transitory. Examples of such situations which he cites are a creditor's obtaining a promise from a bereaved and distraught widow to pay debts of her husband's business shortly after his death, or a door-to-door salesman's employing importuning and intrusive sales tactics.

I believe that both of Eisenberg's sub-classes of cognitive deficiencies fall within the concerns that in order for contractual promises to be binding, they should in general arise out of the autonomous consent of the parties and reflect base-line conditions of voluntariness and information. Thus, they seem entirely appropriate candidates for a doctrine of unconscionability.

Standard Form Contracts

Standard form contracts[30] have suffered a bad press from both judicial and academic members of the legal fraternity over many years.[31] At least in a consumer setting, the hostility to standard form contracts is based on two principal propositions. First, it is said that the use of standard form contracts is a manifestation of monopoly. Second, it is pointed out that the use of standard form contracts is typically characterized by imperfect information on the part of some of the parties to them. In both cases, the legal implications are much the same: courts should be extremely cautious about enforcing such contracts. These two arguments require evaluation.

The monopoly argument essentially rests on the "take it or leave it" character of most standard form contractual offerings. However, as I have argued elsewhere,[32] the principal justification for standard form contracts is the dramatic reduction in transaction costs that they permit in many contexts. That they may be offered on a take it or leave it basis is as consistent with the benign transaction cost conservation rationale for them as it is with a monopoly or collusion rationale. Simply observing the fact of standard form contracts yields no meaningful implications as to the underlying structure of the market. Indeed, we observe them being used in many settings where manifestly the market is highly competitive, for example, in dry-cleaning stores, hotel registration forms, insurance contracts, and so on. Indeed, even in the absence of standard form contracts, we see many goods being offered on a take it or leave it basis in some of the most competitive retail markets in the economy. For example, corner variety stores (mom and pop stores) typically offer their goods on a take it or leave it basis, presumably to avoid the transaction costs entailed in haggling over price or product offerings.

The imperfect information argument against standard form contracts is clearly more substantial. Almost necessarily implicit in the transaction cost justification for standard form contracts is the assumption that parties will often not read them or, if they do, will not wish to spend significant amounts of time attempting to renegotiate the terms. Thus, to hold parties bound to standard form contracts which they had entered into but which they had not read or understood does not rest comfortably with a theory of contractual obligation premised on individual autonomy and consent. Clearly, in many, perhaps most cases, meaningful consent is absent. Thus, to justify contractual enforcement of these kinds of standard form contracts requires us, once again, to move outside the purely internal, non-instrumental basis for contractual obligation as deriving from the will of the parties and appeal instead to external benchmarks of fairness. In this respect, I have argued first that problems of unfairness resulting from imperfect information are not so severe as they might seem at first sight. To the extent that there is a margin of informed, sophisticated, and aggressive consumers in any given market, who understand the terms of the standard form contracts on offer and who either negotiate over those terms or switch their business readily to competing suppliers offering more favourable terms, they may in effect discipline the entire market, so that inframarginal (less well informed, sophisticated, or mobile) consumers can effectively free-ride on the discipline brought to the market by the marginal consumers,[33] although there is the potential for a collective action problem if every consumer attempts to free-ride on the efforts of others in effective monitoring of contract terms.[34] In addition, where suppliers are able either to term or to performance discriminate between marginal and inframarginal consumers, this generalized discipline will be undermined, and there is a clear risk that the inframarginal consumers will be exploited because of their imperfect knowledge of the contract terms. Here, I have proposed that courts, in evaluating the fairness of standard form contracts in particular cases, should investigate whether a particular consumer seeking relief from the contract or some particular provision in it has received a deal that is significantly inferior, in relation to either the explicit terms of the contract or the performance provided under it, to that realized by marginal consumers in the same market, with the economic as opposed to personal characteristics of consumers in these two classes held constant.[35] In other words, where a supplier has deliberately exploited a consumer's ignorance of terms generally available, in the market for like goods or services, to consumers in an economically similar situation in order to exact terms substantially inferior to these generally prevailing terms, the supplier's actions should be viewed as unconscionable, perhaps again invoking the equal concern and respect basis for protection of individual autonomy. In markets which are so badly disrupted by imperfect information that there is no identifiable margin of informed consumers from which appropriate benchmarks can be derived, then judicial sniping in case-by-case litigation seems less appropriate than legislative or regulatory intervention of the kind that has occurred in many jurisdictions, for example, with respect to various classes of door-to-door sales.[36]

Strategic Behaviour and Game Theory

As noted at the beginning of this chapter, asymmetric information is pervasive in the contracting process. Parties can, of course, explicitly address the possibility of incomplete knowledge through express contractual terms; for example, a purchaser could negotiate for an express warranty from a seller regarding the condition of a house, a car, or other goods that he is selling. However, in many cases, the contract will not expressly allocate the risks associated with information asymmetries, and the courts, or the legal system more broadly, are faced with the task of designing default rules that assign the risks for the parties. This problem is much more general than the specific examples discussed above might suggest.

From an autonomy perspective, a major normative issue that arises is whether, in choosing or designing these default rules, it is possible to remain faithful to a consensual theory of contractual obligations, where consent is understood to reflect the actual consent of the contracting parties, not some hypothetical consent attributed to the particular contracting parties or to contracting parties more generally. Craswell has argued persuasively[37] that consensual theories of contractual obligation cannot explain or justify holding parties bound to default rules to which they had not expressly consented. Barnett in a recent rejoinder[38] argues that a consent theory supports choosing default rules that reflect the common sense expectations of persons in the relevant community of discourse, on the grounds that such rules are likely to reflect their tacit assent. As Barnett acknowledges, however, this view leaves open serious questions as to how the so-called common sense expectations of the parties are to be determined; what exactly is the relevant "community of discourse"? and what if the parties are not members of the same community or are members of more than one?[39] The fact that the parties always have the freedom to contract away explicitly from the prevailing default rule, in Barnett's view, ultimately vindicates autonomy values.

Charny largely rejects this non-instrumental approach to the choice of default rules.[40] He argues that where contracting parties are in a position to bargain around a default rule, the court should design a default rule or an interpretation of a contract by a strictly instrumental calculation; that is, it should choose the default rule or interpretation that will minimize prospective bargaining costs (the interpretation that will induce parties to expend the least effort in bargaining around the rule or interpretation). This position may not be sharply different from that taken by Barnett. However, if future transactors would not bargain around the default rule, either because of the transaction costs so entailed or because of ignorance of the default rule, Charny would allow the courts to take account of considerations such as the distributional impact on the parties of alternative default rules, and whether particular proposed default rules may modify understandings or preferences of contracting parties in a way that the court believes to be socially desirable.

From a welfare perspective, recent game theory literature challenges the consensual approach to the choice of default rules in a more fundamental way. Whether one is speaking of actual consent or hypothetical consent, this literature suggests that choosing default rules on the basis of what the particular parties might have consented to had they addressed the issue, or what contracting parties in general may have consented to had they addressed the issue, may not be welfare enhancing, in the sense of assuring that all mutual gains from trade are realized. Ayres and Gertner[41] refer to such default rules as "majoritarian" default rules or "what the parties would have wanted" default rules, which much of the standard law and economics literature endorses, simply, as Charny argues, on the grounds that this minimizes transaction costs. The authors propose that in particular contexts, penalty default rules may be more efficient than majoritarian default rules. Penalty default rules (either non-enforcement default rules or court-substituted default rules) are designed to give at least one party to the contract, typically the party with superior information, an incentive to contract around the default rule and therefore to choose affirmatively the contract provision both parties would prefer. In contrast to majoritarian default rules, penalty default rules are deliberately set at what the parties "would not want" in order to encourage them to reveal information to each other or to third parties (especially the courts). The authors argue that contracts may be incomplete, not simply because of the transaction costs of fully specifying a contract, but because of strategic considerations. One party may knowingly withhold information that would increase the total gains from contracting in order to increase her private share of such gains. By appropriately designing default rules, lawmakers can reduce the opportunities for this rent-seeking strategic behaviour.

Ayres and Gertner show that different default rules may lead to different degrees of "separating" and "pooling." In separating equilibria, different types of contracting parties, by bearing the costs of contracting around unwanted default rules, separate themselves into distinct contractual relationships. In pooling equilibria, different types of contractual parties fail to contract around the default rules, thus avoiding the transaction costs entailed, but bearing the inefficiencies of the substantive default provisions. According to Ayres and Gertner, lawmakers should select default rules that deter inefficient gaps at the least social cost. In the absence of such rules, the very costs of *ex ante* bargaining may encourage parties to inefficiently shift the process of gap-filling to *ex post* (subsidized) court determinations.

The authors illustrate their approach through an extended analysis of the rule in Hadley v. Baxendale.[42] In this case, a miller contracted with a carrier to have a broken crankshaft transported for repairs. The crankshaft was delayed in transit and the miller sued the carrier for consequential damages in the form of profits lost while the mill was out of operation. The court held that only foreseeable consequential damages could be claimed and rejected a damage award for the miller's full losses. Ayres and Gertner view the holding in *Hadley* as a penalty default rule, which creates incentives for high-risk millers to provide information to carriers about the risks that may be entailed in delays in transport. By not distinguishing themselves, informed parties are able to free-ride on the lower-cost qualities of other parties and thereby contract at a subsidized price. To counteract such strategic behaviour, the courts should choose default rules that are different from what the parties would have wanted. For example, in *Hadley*, fully informed parties may have wanted the carrier to be liable for consequential damage. Yet choosing full liability as the damage default rule may lead carriers to invest sub-optimally in accident prevention because prevention precautions are based on average losses. *Hadley* penalizes high-damage millers for withholding information that would allow carriers to take efficient precautions. Under an unlimited liability rule, high-damage millers would not reveal their true status to carriers because they would be forced to pay more for coverage they already have. High-damage millers fail to distinguish themselves not because of transaction costs, but because they prefer to withhold this information strategically and to receive a subsidized shipping price. High-damage millers do not mind if carriers take inefficiently low levels of precaution with respect to their mill shafts because, like other shippers, high-damage millers are fully insured. According to Ayres and Gertner, low-damage millers bear the costs of this inefficiency but are not hurt enough individually to distinguish themselves contractually.

This analysis is challenged by Johnston[43] in contexts where one can assume market power on the part of someone such as the carrier. Under a limited liability default rule of the kind that Hadley v. Baxendale is conventionally interpreted as espousing, a shipper has no incentive to reveal its true value because if the revelation is credible and fully informs the carrier as to the shipper's value, the carrier would extract all of this value through a higher price. Rather than earning positive informational rents, the shipper would be forced to accept a zero-rent contract. Johnston argues that low-value shippers will have stronger incentives to bargain around an expansive (unlimited liability) default rule. He argues that strategic obstacles to bargaining around a limited liability default rule are more serious than obstacles to bargaining around an unlimited liability default rule. With a limited liability default rule, the message which gets the carrier the contract—a message signalling low breach probability on his part—will, if believed, make the shipper suspicious that the carrier's increased price for an unlimited liability contract is merely an attempt to extract informational rents, in this case because of information asymmetries favouring the carrier with respect to knowledge of breach probabilities. According to Johnston, bargaining around limited liability puts the carrier in a strategic dilemma: if he persuades the shipper that he would be better off with the high-priced–high liability alternative, then he may also persuade the shipper that he is in fact better off not contracting with him at all because the breach probability is too high, no matter what the extent of the carrier's liability.

Ayres and Gertner later[44] claim that Johnston is wrong to conclude or imply that even where contracting around default rule is costless, the choice of default rules may affect the types of contracts made or the social benefits of contracting. They show that in a world without transaction costs, the choice of default rules is irrelevant to the contractual equilibrium, although strategic inefficiencies may remain, whatever the default rule. However, the authors also show that when even slight costs in contracting around a default rule are introduced, the choice of a default rule can affect both the contractual equilibrium and the net social benefits of contracting (efficiency). The introduction of transaction costs produces a proliferation of equilibrium contracts that depend on both the choice of the default rule and a variety of underlying structural variables—such as factual information asymmetries, asymmetrics in knowledge of the default rule, and market power—that may lead to inefficient separation or inefficient pooling. Relatively simple contractual settings can give rise to enormous complexity. While Ayres and Gertner claim they can show that different default rules would be theoretically efficient, they acknowledge that their model suggests that there is small hope that lawmakers will be able to define the efficient rule in practice. They argue that the practical indeterminacy of their model should not be viewed as undermining the appropriateness of either economic modelling[45] or the goal of choosing efficient legal rules. The task of pursuing any other normative theory of social welfare will be just as complex and therefore will encounter similar problems of indeterminacy.

Thus, both autonomy- and welfare-based theories of default rules that purport to respond to problems of asymmetric information in cases of incomplete contracts run into serious difficulties. Although some convergence between the two approaches can be maintained to the extent that contracting parties retain the ultimate ability to contract around whatever default rules the courts or legal system have adopted, even this convergence is challenged by game theoretic or rational bargaining literature which argues that, in some contexts, efficiency requires *mandatory* default rules.

For example, Rea[46] and Aghion and Hermalin[47] argue that mandatory legal restrictions on contracts can in some cases enhance efficiency if one party to a contract has better information than the other. The example that the latter two authors use is an entrepreneur who needs to raise capital to fund a project. She knows how likely it is that her project will succeed, but someone who invests in it does not. Because she can get more generous terms from an investor the more likely he thinks it is that her project will succeed, the entrepreneur has an incentive to signal to the investor that her project is a good project. Because the expected cost of a large payment to be made if the project fails is greater for an entrepreneur with a bad project than it is for an entrepreneur with a good project, one way to signal a good project is to promise a large payment to the investor if the project should fail. The cost of signalling in this manner is that the entrepreneur exposes herself to considerable risk, for example, losing her house if the project fails. Prohibiting signalling may enhance welfare. Because of the additional risk, an entrepreneur with a good project might prefer not to signal if not signalling made it seem that her project was only average. The difficulty is that the investor will interpret not signalling as evidence that the project is bad, and given the choice between looking good and looking bad, an entrepreneur with a good project would prefer to look good. If, however, signalling is restricted, say, by mandatory bankruptcy exemption and discharge rules, then not signalling is no longer informative. Consequently, the investor will treat all entrepreneurs as if they have an average project. Both types of entrepreneurs are better off: an entrepreneur with a bad project now looks average and is partially subsidized by the low-risk entrepreneur, whereas the latter avoids the additional risks imposed by costly signalling. Thus, there exist separating equilibria that yield lower expected utility for the entrepreneur than pooling equilibria. The point of this analysis is to emphasize the possibility that contractual restrictions can improve efficiency because of adverse selection.

Aghion and Hermalin argue that their analysis can be generalized to other cases, such as maternity leave. For example, if an employer voluntarily offers unusually generous maternity leave benefits, such benefits may attract a disproportionately high percentage of pregnant women or women contemplating pregnancy, leading to an escalation in the costs of the benefits and, in some cases, their curtailment or withdrawal. An inefficiently low level of benefits may result. Thus, laws mandating maternity leave benefits for all employers could increase efficiency.

Similar arguments have been made as to the effects of adverse selection on insurance markets. Adverse selection occurs when individuals have different probabilities of loss and insurance companies cannot distinguish between high- and low-risk individuals. The very existence of equilibrium in these markets may be threatened by imperfect information.[48] Mandatory insurance could make both high-risk and low-risk individuals better off in some circumstances, but it will always make high-risk individuals better off. According to Rea,[49] we do not know if the actual conditions in insurance markets, including markets for health care or disability insurance, are such that mandatory insurance would in fact make all groups better off. This conclusion, of course, reflects the indeterminacy acknowledged by Ayres and Gertner in their analysis of optimal default rules in more conventional contractual settings. Bishop[50] makes a similar argument for mandatory terms governing marriage, so as to mark marriage off in a reasonably distinct way from other kinds of relationships. He argues that these terms operate as important signalling devices between potential marriage partners, reflecting the type of relationship they are seeking, and that if the terms are modified by law or can be modified by individual contracting parties so as to elide marriage much more closely with other kinds of relationships, these signals will become muddied and less efficient. In other words, we may end up with inefficient pooling rather than efficient separating equilibria.

The choice of default rules in incomplete contracts, especially in cases of asymmetric information, poses one of the most daunting challenges for theories of contract law, whether based on autonomy or welfare considerations. Choices between mandatory and optional default rules, and between tailored (to the particular parties) and untailored (to classes of transactions or parties more generally) default rules[51] push us to the frontiers of current theorizing on the law of contracts and perhaps reveal, rather starkly, the limits of how far theory can take us. For the moment, "muddling through" may define our aspirational limits.[52]

. . .

I have shown in this chapter that, outside of the case of fraud and cases of cognitive deficiencies, it is difficult, if not impossible, to resolve most problems of information asymmetry within the framework of an internal theory of contract premised on consensually assumed obligations when the contract has not explicitly assigned the risks entailed, that is, it is incomplete. In all the other areas canvassed, analysis of the problems quickly forces us outside this framework and requires an appeal to various external values such as efficiency, distributive justice, or commutative or corrective justice. Thus, once again the notion of contract as exclusively a form of private ordering, at least in the sense proposed by Fried—as legal obligations deriving from the will of the parties—cannot easily be sustained. Having so concluded, I also have acknowledged substantial difficulties in formulating rules for regulating information asymmetries from various external perspectives, including an efficiency perspective. Most of these external perspectives depend, for their legitimacy, on some notion of hypothetical consent to a set of generally acceptable legal ground rules. But what rules individuals hypothetically would rationally consent to is a matter of conjecture and debate, and in any event, such rules lack the legitimacy that is claimed for freedom of contract premised on actual consent. External perspectives, particularly an efficiency or welfare perspective, can sometimes, however, identify a set of relevant and defensible variables in the framing of such rules, recognizing of course that the parties should be free, in most cases, to contract around such rules if they wish by explicit consent, thus preserving ultimate authority in the right of self-governance of the parties.

CHAPTER SIX

Symmetric Information Imperfections

The Nature of the Conceptual Problem

From an efficiency or welfare perspective, if two parties enter into a contract where both are mistaken as to either material facts at the time of contracting or the likely course of future events which may affect the value of the contract, the exchange may not be Pareto superior, in the sense of making one party better off and the other party no worse off, or practically speaking, making both parties better off, than they would have been in the absence of the exchange. However, here one must be careful to distinguish exchanges of the promised performance from exchanges of the contractual rights (including remedies for breach). As noted below, an exchange of contractual rights may be Pareto superior (including agreed risk allocations) even if the subsequent exchange of the promised performance is not. From an autonomy perspective, where choices are made on the basis of critically defective information, at some point such choices presumably cease to satisfy the conditions for an autonomous choice. Or to put the issue differently, in the case of unanticipated risks that fall outside the realm of explicit bargaining, the consensual basis for contractual obligation may be absent. In contract law, this is the domain of contract doctrines relating to frustration, contract modification, and mutual mistake, which share the common characteristic of attempting to define the scope of permissible private or judicial adjustments to contractual relationships in the light of new information on assumed pre-existing states of affairs or assumed future courses of events.

The first troublesome issue that arises is the identification of circumstances which trigger a case for relief from performance obligations under the initial contract owing to such a mistake. If we accept that a major function of contracts is to allocate various types of risks, then the mere materialization of an adverse risk cannot possibly *per se* be a justification for contractual discharge or excuse. For example, on this basis, all insurance policies would be invalid. Thus, the question arises, which adverse risks when they materialize then warrant special treatment? Lawyers often distinguish between foreseeable and unforeseeable risks and assume that contracts have assigned foreseeable but not unforeseeable risks. There is a clear conceptual problem with this dichotomous categorization of risks. Economists, in contrast to lawyers, conventionally conceive of risks as arrayed along a probability distribution, with some carrying lower probabilities than others. The mere fact that a given risk is a low probability risk does not mean that it has not been foreseen or assigned to one or the other party, reflecting an appropriately modest expected cost associated with it. Thus, there is no reason for discharge of a contract *per se* if a remote risk materializes. Again, to take an insurance example, a term life insurance policy on the life of a healthy young person may be insuring a very remote, but nevertheless foreseeable, risk. The remoteness of the risk is reflected in the relatively modest premiums charged to insure it. Triantis argues[1] that individuals (and even more so, commercial entities) are typically aware of the existence of specifically unforeseen contingencies. Although an unknown risk cannot be priced and allocated specifically, it can be priced and allocated as part of the package of a more broadly framed risk. He gives the example of a shipping company that contracts with a coffee merchant to transport coffee beans, for a fixed fee, from the merchant's warehouse in Columbia to consumer markets in California. The usual and cheapest route for the trip is through the Panama Canal and up the west coast of Central America. In determining the appropriate contract price, the shipping company considers the risk that the actual cost will exceed the expected cost of the trip. In Figure 6 Triantis generates a "fault tree" that might be used to organize the various scenarios. Even if the shipping company does not specifically identify and price the narrowest frame of risk (Level 4), these risks will be taken account of in lower level, broader risk frames.

Triantis acknowledges that various judgmental errors and biases which psychologists and decision theorists have identified in empirical or experimental studies of individuals' risk assessments may well lead to inappropriate risk assessments, but he argues that these affect both foreseen and unforeseen risks and, moreover, sometimes lead to over-assessment rather than under-assessment of risk. Doctrines of excuse that focus on the distinction between foreseen and unforeseen risks thus are unlikely to be responsive to concerns over risk misallocation or under-compensation that these biases and errors may induce, and such doctrines may even introduce uncertainties of their own into the contracting process. Even if contracting parties are risk averse, it is not clear that they are advantaged by rules which, in attempting to reduce the costs of risk in contracting, introduce new risks or uncertainties of their own.[2] Given that it is costly to identify

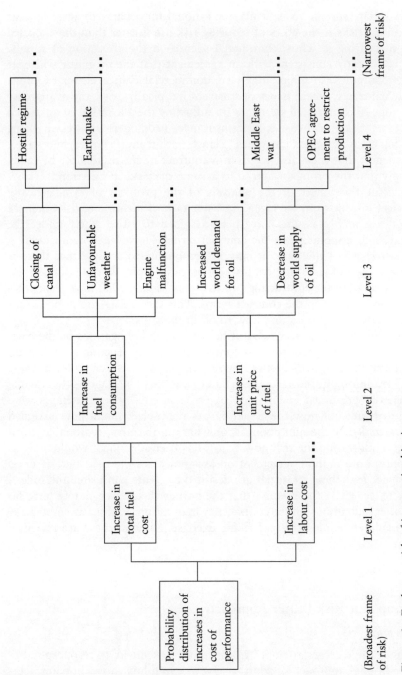

Figure 6. Fault tree: risk of increase in shipping cost.

Hostile regime				
Earthquake				
		Middle East war		
		OPEC agreement to restrict production		
			Level 4	(Narrowest frame of risk)

Closing of canal

Unfavourable weather

Engine malfunction

Increased world demand for oil

Decrease in world supply of oil

Level 3

Increase in fuel consumption

Increase in unit price of fuel

Level 2

Increase in total fuel cost

Increase in labour cost

Level 1

Probability distribution of increases in cost of performance

(Broadest frame of risk)

and negotiate specific risks, it may be rational for a party to agree to bear unspecified risks if the costs of reducing risk are greater than the expected costs of bearing it. Thus, contractual silence on the allocation of specific risks is perfectly consistent with an agreement that the promisor will bear them.[3] Moreover, in major long-term commercial contracts, for example, supply contracts, where issues of frustration typically arise, the availability of a range of contractual strategies for adjusting the allocation of unknown or remote risks, such as explicit insurance, hedging in futures markets, indexing clauses, "gross inequities" clauses, arbitration clauses, and so on, may suggest that their absence from a contract might reasonably be taken to imply that the promisor agreed to assume the risks in question.[4]

Thus, at the outset of the analysis of the problem of symmetrically imperfect information, we face the elusive task of identifying risks that we cannot reasonably assume have been assigned to either party under the contract and impounded in the contract terms. However, notwithstanding the elusiveness of this task, it may be reasonable to assume that there is some sub-class of risks that contracting parties simply did not address their minds to at all in the contracting process, thus leaving what have sometimes been called "gaps" in the contract terms. This then raises the second troublesome conceptual question: how to fill in the gaps?

Classical contract law, which justifies contractual obligations on the basis of an individual's autonomy and consent, has always encountered difficulties in determining a theoretically coherent basis on which to fill in these gaps.[5] Traditionally, resort has been had to a series of stratagems that invoke notions of "presumed intent," or "objective intent," where attempts were made to figure out how the actual parties themselves might have assigned the risk had they thought about it, or what an objective, reasonable, third party, in addressing the risk now that it has been identified, would view as an appropriate mutual agreement on assignment of the risk. But, as Fried acknowledges,[6] these strategies are destined to create confusion and indeed incoherence, given the premise that the parties themselves simply have no convergent intentions on the contingency in question. Various attempts have been made at refining this gap-filling exercise. Some of these are reviewed below.

The Superior Risk-Bearer Approach

Frustration

A sophisticated recent attempt by Posner and Rosenfield[7] to reconceptualize the traditional approach of contract law to gap-filling shows how intractable the difficulties associated with it inherently are. In the context of frustration, they propose that discharge should be allowed where the promisee is the superior risk-bearer; if the promisor is the superior risk-bearer, non-performance should be treated as a breach of contract. They acknowledge that if the parties have expressly assigned the risk to one of them, there is no occasion to inquire who is the superior risk-bearer. They claim that the inquiry is merely "an aid to interpretation." In suggesting this, Posner and Rosenfield are not at all clear about whether it is to be assumed that the parties must have intended to assign the risk to the superior risk-bearer (with appropriate compensation paid for bearing the risk), in which case the two basic questions in this context of whether there is a contractual gap and how to fill it are elided, or whether, irrespective of their intentions, instrumental efficiency considerations are being invoked to impose this rule on the parties in the interest of efficient resource (or risk) allocation in general (and despite the lack of compensation for bearing the risk). In other words, it is not clear whether their approach is based on actual consent to contractual obligations or whether Kaldor-Hicks notions of efficiency are being invoked to assign obligations to the parties. In operationalizing their superior risk-bearer approach, Posner and Rosenfield propose the following framework of analysis:

> It does not necessarily follow from the fact that the promisor could not at any reasonable cost have prevented the risk from materializing that he should be discharged from his contractual obligations. Prevention is only one way of dealing with risk; the other is insurance. The promisor may be the superior insurer. If so, his inability to prevent the risk from materializing should not operate to discharge him from the contract, any more than an insurance company's inability to prevent a fire on the premises of the insured should excuse it from its liability to make good the damage caused by the fire.
>
> The factors relevant to determining which party to the contract is the cheaper insurer are (1) risk-appraisal costs and (2) transaction costs. The former comprise the costs of determining (a) the probability that the risk will materialize and (b) the magnitude of the loss if it does materialize. The amount of risk is the product of the probability of loss and of the magnitude of the loss if it occurs. Both elements—probability and magnitude—must be known in order for the insurer to know how much to ask from the other party to the contract as compensation for bearing the risk in question.
>
> The relevant transaction costs are the costs involved in eliminating or minimizing the risk through pooling it with other uncertain events, that is, diversifying away the risk. This can be done either through self-insurance or through the purchase of an insurance policy (market insurance).[8]

A similar framework of analysis has been proposed by Aivazian, Penny, and myself[9] for the choice of rules governing when contract modifications obtained by one party from another, without fresh consideration, should be enforceable. This problem is particularly germane in settings where there has been a change in the underlying economic environment, or at least in the information available to the parties about that environment. This change may cause at least one of the contracting parties to revise his expectations of the gains from contractual performance relative to the expectations held at the time of contract formation and to induce an un-compensated modification from the other party, typically exploiting a threat of breach, for which the latter's remedies provide, in one respect or another, incomplete protection against the consequences of breach. Although the framework of analysis has not yet been applied in the literature (so far as I am aware) to cases of mutual mistake, its logic seems equally appropriate to cases of mistakes of pre-existing facts (the doctrine of mistake) as to future facts (the doctrine of frustration).

The frustration cases afford a compelling context in which to evaluate the strength of the insurance argument, because in the great majority of such cases the event in question that has disrupted the expectations of the parties is exogenously determined and beyond the control or influence of the contracting parties (for example, the outbreak of war, the closing of the Suez Canal, the formation of oil or uranium cartels).[10] Thus, issues of fault are usually irrelevant to the assignment of liability for losses from such contingencies. Indeed, it is well-established law that "self-induced" (avoidable) alleged frustrating events cannot attract relief under the frustration doctrine.

While Posner and Rosenfield believe that many U.S. frustration cases implicitly reflect the economic logic of the framework of analysis they propose, many of the cases that they discuss seem readily susceptible of analysis within their own framework so as to yield opposing results. For example, they discuss the case of Transatlantic Financing Corp. v. United States,[11] where a shipowner argued (unsuccessfully) that its contract with the U.S. government to transport wheat from the United States to Iran should be discharged by virtue of the closing of the Suez Canal. They cite the following passage from the decision of Judge Wright as support for their framework:

> Transatlantic was no less able than the United States to purchase insurance to cover the contingency's occurrence. If anything, it is more reasonable to expect owner-operators of vessels to insure against the hazards of war. They are in the best position to calculate the cost of performance by alternative routes (and therefore to estimate the amount of insurance required), and are undoubtedly sensitive to international troubles which uniquely affect the demand for and cost of their services.[12]

Posner and Rosenfield comment as follows:

The shipowner is the superior risk bearer because he is better able to estimate the magnitude of the loss (a function of delay, and of the value and nature of the cargo, which are also known to the shipowner) and the probability of the unexpected event. Furthermore, shipowners who own several ships and are engaged in shipping along several different routes can spread the risks of delay on any particular route without purchasing market insurance or forcing their shareholders to diversify their common-stock portfolios. And the shipping company could, if it desired, purchase in a single transaction market insurance covering multiple voyages. Of course, the shipper in the particular case—the United States Government—was well diversified too, but the decision should (and here did) turn on the characteristics of shippers as a class, if an unduly particularistic analysis is to be avoided.[13]

This seems a largely spurious rationalization of the decision. On the particular facts, surely the U.S. government was much better placed than the carrier to appraise the risks of the outbreak of war in the Middle East; better placed than the carrier to evaluate the consequences of delayed arrival of the goods; and better placed than the carrier to self-insure or otherwise diversify away the risk of canal closure.

The objection that these considerations are unduly particularistic seems unconvincing. If the decision should turn on the characteristics of shippers and carriers as classes, what empirical intuitions or generalizations can confidently be offered, or at least are likely to be accessible to a court, as to which class can better determine the probability of given contingencies occurring, can better evaluate the consequences of interrupted or aborted performance should it occur, or as to which class of actors can more cheaply self-insure, market insure, or otherwise diversify away the risks in question? Moreover, why should a court confine its search for the superior risk-bearer to the immediately contracting parties? If one of the contracting parties would have insured the risk with a third party, had the risk been contemplated, why not make the third party liable anyway by judicially constructing a notional, Kaldor-Hicks efficient contract with that party (despite the violence that this would do to the autonomy basis for contractual obligation)?

Similar ambiguities attend another class of case which Posner and Rosenfield discuss—contracts for the supply of agricultural products:

[This group of cases] illustrates how the courts can arrive at an economically efficient result yet disguise it as an apparently meaningless semantic distinction. The cases have similar facts. A supplier contracts to deliver a particular quantity and quality of an agricultural product; an unexpected event such as a flood or an exceptionally severe drought prevents delivery; the buyer seeks damages. The courts generally discharge the contract where the supplier is a grower, but enforce it where the supplier is a wholesaler or large dealer. The result is both consistent and efficient; it places the risk of extreme weather conditions on the superior risk bearer. The purchaser from the grower can reduce the risk of adverse weather by diversifying his purchases geographically; there is empirical evidence to suggest that in some climatic regions geographical separation of only a few miles can dramatically reduce the risk of a large loss. When the seller is a wholesaler or large dealer there is no reason to allow discharge since he can diversify his purchases and thereby eliminate the risk of adverse weather.[14]

Again, this reasoning seems dubious at best. One could just as easily argue that growers are likely to be better able than perhaps distant whole-salers to estimate the probability of a contingency such as adverse climatic conditions or disease interfering with the production of a crop. Buyers, conversely, may be better able to evaluate the consequence of non-perform-ance. As to who can better diversify away the risk, while it may be true that buyers can diversify their purchases geographically, growers can buy crop insurance, diversify their crop production geographically, or, at least in the case of disease, diversify their produce mix, or plant or develop more robust strains of crops. The last possibility raises the risk-incentive trade-off. Pro-viding implicit insurance against the risk of crop failure reduces long-run incentives to avoid the insured contingency, that is, it creates a problem of moral hazard. How should courts weigh this trade-off?[15] Indeed, in Posner and Rosenfield's discussion of the frustration case-law, it is sometimes difficult to be sure whether their analysis turns on least-cost insurer or least-cost avoider considerations. Superior knowledge of the probability of a given contingency materializing, which is presumably relevant to both tests for assignments of liability, is particularly ambiguous in this respect.

Another case that well illustrates these ambiguities is the *Westinghouse*[16] case. Here, Westinghouse entered into long-term contracts to supply ura-nium fuel at agreed prices to twenty-seven public utilities. Commitments under these contracts substantially exceeded uranium supplies in inventory or under contract to Westinghouse. Apparently, a combination of the OPEC-induced oil price shock and the formation of a cartel of major uranium producers drove the price of uranium up to several times Westing-house's price commitments under its contracts with the utilities, generating a potential loss of about two billion dollars, and the company sought discharge of the contracts under s. 2-615 of the Uniform Commercial Code on grounds of "commercial impracticability." On the one hand, it could be argued that Westinghouse was better placed than the utilities to estimate the probability of disruption to the uranium supply market (having closer fa-miliarity with it) and perhaps was also better placed than the utilities to evaluate the magnitude of the price increases that might be associated with such disruption. On the other hand, it might be argued that the utilities were better placed than Westinghouse to diversify away (spread) the risk through their substantial customer, shareholder (many probably institutional), and employee bases, to whom the costs of the price increases could variously have been shifted. However, these factors would need to be compared with Westinghouse's opportunities to have hedged more fully in the upstream uranium market. The litigation was subsequently settled, apparently for about half the claimed losses that full contract enforcement would have entailed.[17] Obviously, the latter option would have been of little value to the utilities if it had forced Westinghouse into bankruptcy.

A similar case is that of Florida Power and Light Co. v. Westinghouse Electric Corp.,[18] where, in a contract between Westinghouse and Florida Power for the sale of a nuclear reactor, Westinghouse agreed to remove and dispose of spent reactor fuel. Changes in government policy after the signing of the contract precluded disposal of the waste as originally contemplated, and Westinghouse, instead of making an anticipated profit of twenty million dollars on reprocessing the waste, now stood to lose eighty million dollars from performance of this obligation. The court relieved Westinghouse of its obligation on grounds of commercial impracticability. But, as Sykes points out,[19] it is difficult to discern any basis for concluding that Florida Power could better bear the burden of waste disposal than Westinghouse.

Even in cases where the contract subject matter is physically destroyed, rendering performance impossible, the analysis is not necessarily any more straightforward. For example, in the classic case of Taylor v. Caldwell,[20] where a music hall which had been rented to a concert group burned down before the scheduled concerts, leading the court to treat the rental contract as frustrated, it may well have been the case (or at least is likely to be in contemporary circumstances) that the hall owner would be insured against the loss of the hall, leaving only the losses sustained by the concert group to be borne by the contracting parties. It is far from clear who of the two parties would be better placed to bear these losses.[21]

Posner and Rosenfield acknowledge that often (I would be inclined to argue, typically) the criteria they propose for identifying the most efficient insurer or risk-bearer will point in opposite directions—one party is better placed to estimate the probability of a given contingency materializing (typically the party whose performance is in issue); the other party, who is to receive the performance in issue, can better evaluate the magnitude of the loss if the contingency does materialize; and either party may be better placed to diversify away or absorb the risk through self-insurance, market insurance, or, more debatably, superior wealth. Uncertainties surrounding these issues are likely to render judicially determined insurance extremely expensive compared with most forms of explicit first-party insurance. Moreover, in contractual settings such as entailed in the frustration cases, at least in the absence of major information asymmetries between the parties, it is not clear that the courts are likely to improve on the risk allocations of the parties by engaging in highly particularistic *ex post* assignments of losses.[22]

A clear, albeit austere, rule of literal contract enforcement in most cases provides the clearest signal to parties to future contractual relationships as to when they might find it mutually advantageous to contract away from the rule.[23] It must be acknowledged, however, that even if one dispensed with or severely circumscribed the scope of the doctrine of frustration, courts would still remain free, and indeed would be unable to avoid, issues of contractual interpretation as to whether given risks fall within the scope of the promised performance. However, following Triantis, a strong presumption to this effect would seem to minimize uncertainties for contracting parties and provide them with incentives to adapt their contractual relationship *ex ante* as they feel appropriate and not cast this burden *ex post* on the publicly subsidized court system. In long-term relationships, where negotiating complete contingent claims contracts may be infeasible, a variety of adaptive mechanisms available to the parties for *ex ante* or ongoing allocations of risks make it presumptively unlikely that *ex post* judicial assignments of losses on a case-by-case basis will achieve a superior risk allocation, at least on insurance grounds.[24] Although the availability of this range of adaptive mechanisms in various transactional settings might suggest that a single categoric presumption (for example, the promisor is presumed in most cases to have assumed the risk) will be ill-adapted to all of the vast range of settings to which it might be applied,[25] Scott persuasively argues that generalized default or interpretative rules and individualized contractual alternatives together reduce the costs and errors of contracting.[26]

Contract Modifications

Similar conceptual problems arise in determining when to enforce contractual modifications. The nature of the apparent analytical paradox presented by contract modifications can be stated briefly: on the one hand, why would any party to a contract agree, by way of modification, to pay more or accept less than originally contracted for, without an appropriate quid pro quo (consideration), unless the other party had obtained bargaining power in the course of the relationship that he did not possess at the time of the contract formation and that he now seeks to exploit?[27] If this explains most modification situations, then it might be argued that the law should attempt to discourage extortionary, coercive, opportunistic, or monopolistic behaviour by refusing to enforce most modifications, perhaps by means of a presumption of invalidity. The traditional legal doctrine that fresh consideration is required to support an enforceable modification might be close to what is socially optimal. On the other hand, especially in commercial contexts, where most litigated modification cases seem to arise, it might be argued that parties would typically not enter into modifications unless they both as a result felt better off relative to the position that would or might have obtained without a modification. Hence, the law should respect the parties' assessment of what course of action best advances their joint welfare and enforce modifications, that is, apply a presumption of validity. This would reflect much contemporary legislative, judicial, and academic thinking. Both propositions, despite being contradictory, have strong axiomatic appeal and hence, the apparent paradox.

Aivazian, Penny, and I have developed an economic framework of analysis that takes as the objective of the legal rules governing contract modifications the minimization of the costs of contracting. In particular, we are concerned with identifying those legal rules that reduce transaction costs, with respect to both initial contract formation and subsequent contract modification, relating to contingencies that may affect the ultimate value of an exchange to the parties. The paradox described above is the product of a tension between two competing sets of efficiency considerations, which in some cases require difficult trade-offs that in part explain the ambivalence and confusion in the evolution of legal doctrine relating to contract modifications. Static efficiency considerations will generally require that contract modifications be enforced on the grounds that the immediate contracting parties perceive mutual gains from recontracting that cannot, at the time modification is proposed, be realized as fully by any alternative strategy. Dynamic efficiency considerations, in contrast, focus on the long-run incentives for contracting parties at large imparted by a set of legal rules. In the modification context, these dynamic efficiency considerations imply an *ex ante* perspective, rather than the *ex post* perspective implicit in static efficiency considerations. On the former perspective, rules that impose no constraints on recontracting may increase the over-all costs of contracting by creating incentives for opportunistic behaviour in cases where "hold-up" possibilities arise during contract performance, most obviously in cases where nothing has changed in the economic environment of the contract except one party's ability to exploit monopolistically the dependency of the other party (for example, where sailors extracted, on threat of mutiny, an increase in wage rates from their captain once their vessel had reached remote waters, where no alternative manpower was available).[28] That is, in Williamson's terms, an *ex ante* large numbers condition becomes transformed by contract into an *ex post* small numbers relationship where competitive alternatives no longer constrain the potential for opportunism.[29]

Even where a genuine change has occurred in the economic environment of the contract between the time of formation and the time of modification such that, in the absence of modification, one party faces an increase in the costs of performance relative to expectations at the time of contract performance, allowing recontracting may facilitate the reallocation of assigned risks that were initially assigned efficiently. This leads to moral hazard problems that may attenuate incentives for efficient risk minimization or risk insurance strategies by the party who subsequently seeks the modification. Thus, what is in the best interests of two particular contracting parties *ex post* contract formation when a modification is proposed and what is in the interests *ex ante* of contracting parties generally in terms of legally ordained incentives and constraints that minimize the over-all costs of contracting may lead to divergent policy perspectives. Our framework of analysis emphasizes the dynamic or long-term incentive effects created by legal rules in the modification context and seeks to identify those rules that will reduce the long-term costs of contracting.

Only where it is not possible to determine the efficient initial allocation of risk or where the risk in question, though initially allocated efficiently, was so remote that the expected costs of bearing it would have minimal incentive effects would we allow the parties to capture the static efficiency gains from recontracting. We argue that in evaluating the efficiency of the initial assignment, least-cost risk avoider and least-cost risk insurer considerations should be relevant. For example, in construction cases, situations sometimes arise where the builder, in the course of contractual performance, encounters, for example, difficult and costly excavation problems because of unusual soil conditions. In the case of a large builder erecting many commercial buildings, it seems obvious that he will typically be the superior risk-bearer relative to the site owner. He can appraise the risks *ex ante* more efficiently and can often diversify them away across a number of similar projects. Some excavation projects will be more difficult, some less difficult, than the norm but these are familiar risks to him and he can be expected to set his contractual terms accordingly. Modifications that reassign the risks to the site owner attenuate the incentive for builders in this situation to act efficiently and should not be enforceable.[30] To enforce modifications in this context is tantamount to turning a fixed-price contract into a cost-plus contract, an arrangement the parties could have negotiated but manifestly did not, presumably for good reason, given the desired allocation of risks.

However, in the case where a small contractor agrees, for a modest sum, to dig a cellar under the other party's house and encounters a hard crust of earth three feet deep under which is a quagmire of wet mud,[31] it is arguable that both qualifications to the superior risk-bearer approach may apply. Determining who is the superior risk-bearer may be difficult: first, these conditions may fall entirely outside the realm of experience of such contractors (making it difficult to know whether he or the homeowner could best appraise the risks or take risk reduction precautions); and second, the builder's ability to diversify across similar projects may be highly circumscribed by virtue of the size or nature of his operations. Even if he is clearly the superior risk-bearer, to deny the possibility of a modification here imposes costs not only on him but on the homeowner, who must search for a substitute contractor and attempt to recover costs of breach in a damage claim against the first contractor that, even if successful, may yield less than full compensation (for example, in the event of the contractor's bankruptcy). Allowing the mutual gains from modification relative to breach to be realized raises the question of whether this significantly attenuates the incentives of contractors in this type of situation to take efficient risk reduction or risk insurance precautions. If the risk in question was highly remote and the *expected* costs associated with bearing the risk so small that no significant changes in behaviour are likely to be induced by shifting it, then permitting a modification seems to enhance the welfare of contracting parties and is efficient.

However, as in the frustration context, we are compelled to acknowledge that the criteria employed to make these judgements will often yield counter-indications. Such a case might arise, for example, where there is a contract to manufacture a machine to the buyer's specifications with a designated delivery date, and a strike in an industry supplying a vital input prevents timely completion. Should a contract modification respecting time of completion be enforceable? The supplier can probably best judge the likelihood of a strike in the input industry, whereas the buyer may best be able to judge the costs to him of delayed delivery. Here, even though the risk may not be an uncommon one, in the absence of a fully specified contract it may be difficult to know where the presumption leads that risks should be treated as initially assigned to the superior risk-bearer and that subsequent reassignments through, for example, frustration or modification should be foreclosed.

Another example of the same ambiguity in the contract modification context is as follows: A enters into a long-term contract to employ B (for example, a baseball player) at a fixed wage. In the course of his contract, B receives an offer of employment from C to work at a higher wage. B proposes modification of his contract with A to offset in whole or in part C's higher wage offer. Should such a modification, if accepted, be enforced? The cost to B of performance under the contract with A has risen since contract formation because his opportunity costs have risen since then. The question would then arise as to whether the contract had clearly assigned this risk—in this case an increase in the market wage rate for B's services—to B or, if not, whether B could be independently identified as the superior risk-bearer. It might be argued that B is the superior risk-bearer because he knows better than anyone else how he is likely to perform in the future, can control the factors influencing his performance better than anyone else, or can perhaps buy a pension or annuity payable on retirement from the sport. However, the team owner, A, may be better able to assess the impact on team performance and spectator appeal of individual performance fluctuations, or be better able to diversify these risks away across players, or, if one believes in the declining marginal utility of wealth and that utility functions are similar and commensurable, be able to absorb the additional cost with less loss of utility than the utility forgone by the player if denied the opportunity to contract with C.

In both examples, judicially induced shifting of initial contractual risk assignments may be a very expensive form of third- or second-party provided insurance, compared with explicit forms of first-party market insurance.

Mutual Mistake

Although cases of mutual mistake have not been analyzed within an insurance framework, such a framework, if compelling in cases of frustration and contract modification, would seem equally compelling in cases of mutual mistake. I am sceptical that it will prove any more tractable in this case than in the other two. Consider the following example. I sell a piece of my farm to you on which you intend to construct a country home. Unknown to either of us, the farm contains an old toxic waste dump that long pre-dates my ownership of the farm and that makes the site hazardous for residential use. After this fact is subsequently discovered in drilling foundations for the home, the market value of the land drops to 10 percent of the purchase price, and you seek to rescind the contract on the grounds of mutual mistake. The seller here may be better placed to evaluate the probability of this contingency arising, having longer access to the history of the land. The buyer may be better placed to evaluate the impact of the consequences for planned land uses if the contingency were to materialize. Neither party is likely to be explicitly insured against such a risk. Can one say which of the two parties is likely to better be able to diversify it away or absorb it? In other words, it is not clear that the superior insurer approach is helpful as a matter of either positive or normative analysis in determining who agreed to bear the risk or who, by way of a default rule, should be obliged to bear the risk.

Take as another example the famous case of Sherwood v. Walker,[32] involving the sale of a cow, Rose 2d of Aberlone. The sellers claimed that they and the buyer both believed that the cow was incapable of breeding and agreed on a price of $80 on that basis. Breeding cows were apparently worth at least $750. Prior to delivery, the seller discovered that the cow was in calf and refused to deliver it on the grounds that the contract was void owing to mutual mistake. The majority of the Michigan Supreme Court set the contract aside on this basis, although the dissenting judge would have upheld the contract on the ground that the buyer agreed to buy the cow only on the chance that she would breed—both parties had made their own estimates of this probability and each had assumed the risk of being wrong. Given that both were professional cattle breeders, on what basis could one identify the superior risk-bearer? Indeed, given the seller's longer acquaintance with the cow, on balance he might arguably have been the superior risk-bearer. In any event, it seems difficult to discern a basis on which to disturb the apparent allocation of risk under the unconditional terms of the contract.[33]

A Sharing Principle

Both Fried and Macneil reject attempts to develop approaches to filling genuine gaps in contracts by reference to any theory of the parties' presumed intent. For example, Macneil argues, especially in the case of ongoing contractual relations, or "relational contracts":

> Somewhere along the line of increasing duration and complexity, trying to force changes into a pattern of original consent becomes both too difficult and too unrewarding to justify the effort, and the contractual relation escapes the bounds of the neo-classical system. That system is replaced by very different adjustment processes of an on-going administrative kind in which discreteness and presentation [the presentation of a transaction involves restricting its expected future effects to those defined in the present, that is, at the inception of the transaction] become merely two of the factors of decision, not the theoretical touchstones. Moreover, the substantive relation of change to the status quo has now altered from what happens in some kind of market external to the contract to what can be achieved through the political and social processes of the relation, internal and external. This includes internal and external dispute-resolution structures. At this point, the relation has become a mini-society with a vast array of norms beyond the norms centred on exchange and its immediate processes.[34]

Macneil further argues that in ongoing contractual relations we find such broad norms as distributive justice, liberty, human dignity, social equality and inequality, domination, and procedural justice. Changes in such contractual relations must accord with at least some of the norms established respecting these matters, just as they do the more traditional contract norms. Changes made ignoring this fact may be very disruptive to long-term contractual relationships.

Macneil's approach, no matter how accurately it describes reality, does not yield determinate legal principles for governing the allocation of unassigned risks. It entails a highly amorphous sociological inquiry that seems well beyond the competence of courts in case-by-case adjudication and seems to exhibit all the vices of other particularistic approaches to designing default rules reviewed above. Moreover, it provides no normative criteria that allow us to move from the "is" to the "ought" and to disqualify some social norms (say, domination) as unworthy of recognition.[35] Fried, in contrast, proposes a somewhat more structured set of principles for filling in contractual gaps.[36] He acknowledges that the gaps cannot be filled by the promise principle, for the simple reason that the parties have no convergent intentions. He notes the two competing residual principles of civil obligation that take over when promise gives out: the tort principle to compensate for harm done (the reliance principle) and the restitution principle for benefits conferred. Each of these principles may have some application to the mistaken assumption cases, but only a limited one. For example, if a contracting party has knowingly concealed or negligently overlooked an eventuality that sharply alters the risks, it may be appropriate for him to bear the resulting loss for that reason. If a party has conferred benefits (built something; paid in advance) under a contract that subsequently fails because of frustration it may be appropriate that the benefit should be paid for or returned. However, in many cases, both parties are harmed, neither is at fault, and neither benefits. Here, Fried argues that a third principle for apportioning losses and gains comes into play: the principle of sharing. In other words, the sharing principle applies where no convergent intentions exist as to the contingency in question, no one in the relationship is at fault, and no one has conferred a benefit. "Sharing applies where there are no rights to respect."[37]

A somewhat analogous argument has recently been made against the theory of efficient breach and in favour of more general availability of specific performance for contract breach.[38] The theory of efficient breach would permit, indeed encourage, unilateral breach where the breaching party has discovered a more profitable opportunity for the resources that would otherwise be dedicated to contract performance, the test of this being whether she is willing and able to compensate the non-breaching party for his full expectancy losses and still be able to realize gains from the new opportunity.[39] In this event breach is argued to be Pareto superior (nobody is worse off as a result of the breach and some are better off). The objection to this theory is first that it encourages uncivil, unilateral, uncooperative attitudes towards contractual relationships ("freedom of contract is never having to say you are sorry"),[40] and second that it deprives the non-breaching party of the possibility of sharing in the gains from the new opportunity presented to the breaching party, which a negotiated release from an entitlement to specific performance would probably engender.

But in the context of mutually mistaken assumptions, in terms of his basic theory of contract as promise, that is, contractual obligations derive from individual autonomy and consent, Fried is on treacherous grounds in proposing a sharing principle. In appealing to this external sharing principle in the case of contractual gaps, he recognizes that he must face the claim that the sharing principle should be more broadly extended so that all life's benefits and burdens are shared. However, as he acknowledges, in such a system the concept of autonomy, which lies behind contract as promise, would be rendered meaningless. He attempts to meet this difficulty by developing a concept of sharing that leaves the person and his liberties intact. The accommodation is sought through the basic division of function in the modern welfare state between private market (contractual) autonomy and general redistributive welfare schemes. Thus, he seeks to recognize only a limited sharing principle in the context of filling gaps in contractual relations. But then, in this context, why not shift the distributional burden of unforeseen risks to the general redistributive welfare schemes that society has adopted or might adopt? Indeed, in commercial contracting contexts, one can view the legal regimes of limited liability and bankruptcy as designed precisely to achieve this form of more generalized loss-spreading.[41] Why confine the sharing of losses to the two parties who happen to find themselves in a contractual relationship with each other?

Fried's response to this difficulty is that those in concrete or personal relations owe each other a greater level of care than those who stand to each other only in the abstract relation of fellow citizens. By this principle, family member and friends are owed and they engross a greater measure of our concern than abstract justice prescribes.[42] Making another person the object of your intention particularizes that person and forms a concrete relation between the two of you. Fried argues that a contractual relation is a good example of a concrete relation that may give rise to a more focused duty to share in others' good or ill-fortune. The relation is, after all, freely chosen. The contractual parties are in a common enterprise—an enterprise they chose to enter. Fried argues that by engaging in a contractual relation, A and B are no longer strangers to each other. They stand closer than those who are merely members of the same political community. They are joined in a common enterprise, and therefore they have some obligation to share unexpected benefits and losses in the case of an accident in the course of that enterprise. In filling the gaps in a contract, he argues, one naturally looks to the agreement itself for some sense of the nature and extent of the common enterprise. Because actual intent is by hypothesis missing, a court respects the autonomy of the parties as much as possible by construing an allocation of burdens and benefits that reasonable persons would have made in this kind of arrangement. This is, as he acknowledges, an inquiry with unavoidably normative elements: "'Reasonable' parties do not merely seek to accomplish rational objectives; they do so constrained by norms of fairness and honesty. Finally, this recourse to principles of sharing to fill the gap does not threaten to overwhelm the promissory principle for the simple reason that the parties are quite free to control the meaning and extent of their relations by the contract itself."[43]

• • •

Fried's arguments are a frank acknowledgment that contract law cannot be a regime that is entirely internal to the parties to the contract.[44] Resort to external principles is unavoidable where the parties lack convergent intentions. In resorting to external principles, we are then in the realm of general normative debate about issues of efficiency, fairness, distributive justice, and community values.[45] The applicability of reliance principles in some contexts, restitutionary principles in others, and the sharing principle in yet others, exemplifies how diverse the relevant external values might be. If one goes further and accepts Macneil's view, then the relevant values appear to be completely at large and mainly reflect whatever the relevant contracting community at any given point in time regards as appropriate normative bases for allocating unexpected burdens and benefits arising from an exchange.

However, I have also acknowledged that appealing to efficiency or welfare considerations as external reference points also fails to yield a set of determinate rules with clear implications for particular cases confronting the courts. It is not clear what other sets of external values are available that are likely to yield a more robust set of implications. For example, a sharing principle (along with any other gap-filling principle) would have to confront the issue raised at the beginning of this chapter of which set of circumstances will trigger its application (when is there a "gap" to be filled?). Even where gaps can be identified, does the principle apply only to adverse risks? What about upside risks (not only "wipeouts" but "windfalls")? For example, I sell my farm to you, and twenty years later you discover that it contains a major gold deposit. If all the unexpected breaks in life—positive and negative—are subject to equalization in this fashion, massive uncertainty would be introduced into the contracting process, and uncertainty generates costs of its own in terms of the welfare of contracting parties.

On this ground, I would propose that in frustration cases, a very austere rule of literal contract enforcement should in most cases obtain, a rule that is reinforced by Triantis' analysis that suggests that most risks, at least in commercial contracts, are at one level or another impounded in the contract, and thus is consistent with autonomy- or consent-based theories of contractual delegation. However, I accept that there are probably limiting cases where this assumption is unwarranted. In these exceptional cases of the materialization of outlandish risks—either a totally unforeseeable contingency or the totally unforeseeable severity of the consequences associated with a foreseeable contingency—an equal sharing rule with respect to totally unforeseeable losses may be the clearest rule that can be devised, probably best operationalized in many cases by allowing the promisee to recover, in effect, only half the normally recoverable damages for contract breach.

Such a rule should be distinguished from several variants of a risk-sharing approach. For example, in the controversial case of Aluminum Co. of America (Alcoa) v. Essex Group, Inc.,[46] the parties entered into a long-term contract in 1967, which Essex could extend to 1983, whereby Alcoa would convert alumina into aluminum and sell it to Essex, which had established a plant near Alcoa for manufacturing a new line of aluminum wire products. The contract contained a complicated cost-plus formula, with certain costs indexed to various indices determined by the eminent economist Alan Greenspan. Beginning in 1973, Alcoa's electricity costs greatly increased as a result of OPEC-induced inflation of oil prices and unanticipated pollution control costs. In June 1979, the cost to Essex of aluminum under the contract was 36.35 cents per pound. Essex bought and resold millions of pounds at 73.313 cents per pound. Alcoa claimed that because of the inadequacy of the cost indices in the contract it stood to lose in excess of $75 million over the balance of the contract. In granting Alcoa relief on grounds of commercial impracticability, the court substituted a complex cost-plus pricing formula of its own, which left Alcoa bearing some losses but shifted a substantial percentage of cost increases to Essex. The decision has not been well received either by subsequent courts or by commentators. The reasons are obvious enough. First, it seems quite implausible to view the risks in question as totally unforeseeable. Second, the risk-sharing rules devised seem totally ad hoc.

Kull[47] has recently proposed a more traditional approach to the problem of unallocated risks in both mutual mistake and frustration cases. He suggests that the rule once widely favoured by English courts in frustration cases should apply—losses should be allowed to remain where they fall in the sense that all obligations that have been executed or have matured before the mistake is discovered or the frustrating event occurs should not be disturbed, but outstanding executory obligations (if any) should be discharged (the so-called windfall principle). Although he acknowledges that the rule is arbitrary in how it distributes losses (depending centrally on issues of timing), Kull claims that it has the virtues of certainty and predictability, and fairness considerations do not clearly militate in favour of any other general rule. This reasoning is not fully persuasive. An equal loss-splitting rule for unallocated risks is as certain and predictable as the windfall principle and has an egalitarian appeal, in the absence of countervailing considerations, that the latter lacks.

A risk-splitting rule also seems preferable, in those rare cases of genuine gaps, to a rule that relieves the promisor entirely of his obligation and casts all the ensuing costs on the promisee, who equally, by hypothesis, has not agreed to bear them. Where there is a genuine gap, to remit the promisor to loss-sharing through bankruptcy or limited liability is to contradict the premise that there is a gap and, in most circumstances, is to inflict larger losses on him than a risk-splitting rule applicable to the immediate contracting parties. Such a rule also seems preferable to a more particularistic set of rules that allocates losses in proportions that reflect the relative degrees of risk aversion of the particular parties.[48] Such rules possess the virtue of being more deferential to the particular preferences of the contracting parties involved in a given transaction, and hence to autonomy values, than an across-the-board rule but, as with the framework proposed by Posner and Rosenfield, would seem hopelessly indeterminate operationally and likely to significantly exacerbate uncertainty, error, and adjudication costs in contracting generally (a welfare cost).

Treating wipe-outs differently from windfalls may be justifiable on the grounds either that risk aversion (and the declining marginal utility of wealth upon which it rests) is more apposite to prospective losses than prospective gains[49] or, on a related Rawlsian difference principle, that people generally would prefer a legal regime that shields them from catastrophic losses. A similar legal regime could be applied to mutual mistakes of fact, in determining when there is a "gap" in the contract and how losses should be shared in the event that a gap is identified. In the case of contract modifications unsupported by fresh consideration, a rule of non-enforceability is clearly appropriate when modifications reflect pure opportunism (that is, no intervening changes in the economic environment of the contract or no new information pertaining thereto). In other contract modification cases unsupported by fresh consideration, enforceability would be the rule only in cases of a genuine gap in the initial contract (applying the same rules of contract interpretation as in the frustration and mutual mistake cases).

CHAPTER SEVEN

Paternalism

The Nature of the Conceptual Problem

The question that will be confronted in this chapter is whether we can always be confident that exchanges which appear to reflect parties' present preferences are really in their own best interests or, even if we believe they are not, whether the collectivity through its legal instrumentalities is entitled to substitute its judgements for those of the individuals involved. In the case of minors and mental incompetents, long-standing legal doctrines of contractual incapacity squarely address this concern, but the question arises of whether the recognition of a broader domain for this concern is warranted.

From a welfare perspective, the conventional neo-classical economic paradigm holds that the primary normative justification for facilitating exchanges is that the welfare of the parties thereto will be enhanced by facilitating the realization of preferences reflecting underlying utility functions. However, neo-classical economics essentially has no theory of how preferences are formed, whether they are good or bad in terms of the welfare of those holding them, or whether some ordering or hierarchy of individuals' preferences is possible or desirable: all preferences are accepted as equally valid. They have thus been viewed as exogenous to the exchange process, which simply facilitates their realization.

From an autonomy perspective, classical liberal theorists have traditionally taken the view that at least for individuals who have the capacity for self-government, the right of self-government is close to absolute and is an end in itself. For example, according to John Stuart Mill:

> His own good, either physical or moral, is not a sufficient warrant [for invading his liberty]. He cannot be rightfully compelled to do or forebear because it will be better for him to do so, because it will make him happier, because in the opinion of others, to do so would be wise . . . these are good reasons for

remonstrating with him, or reasoning with him, or persuading him, or entreating him, but not for compelling him or visiting him with any evil in case he do otherwise.[1]

However, autonomy theorists face the challenge of specifying the pre-conditions for the exercise of autonomous choices. As Feinberg has pointed out, the model of a perfectly voluntary choice is elusive.[2] Aristotle apparently took the position that voluntary actions are those performed neither under compulsion nor by reason of ignorance of the circumstances. But, as depicted in Table 1, adapted from Feinberg, even these two conditions leave open a wide array of circumstances where over-riding an individual's choices may be warranted on the grounds that they were not voluntary.

Table 1.   Voluntary Choices.

A.   *The chooser is "competent":*
Not an animal
Not an infant
Not insane (deluded, disoriented, irrational)
Not severely retarded
Not comatose

B.   *Choice does not result from coercion or duress, including:*
Forced choice of an evil less severe than the one threatened
Forced choice of a lesser evil than one expected from a natural source
Coercive offer
Coercive pressure (e.g., from a hard bargainer in an unequal negotiating position)

C.   *Choice does not result from subtle manipulation, including:*
Subliminal suggestion
Post-hypnotic suggestion
"Sleep-teaching," etc.

D.   *Choice does not result from ignorance or mistaken belief, including:*
Ignorance of factual circumstances
Ignorance of the likely consequences of any alternatives

E.   *Choice does not result from temporarily distorting states or circumstances, including:*
Impulsiveness
Fatigue
Excess nervousness, agitation, or excitation
Powerful passion (e.g., rage, hatred, lust, depression, mania)
Intoxication (alcohol and other drugs)
Pain
Neurotic compulsiveness/obsessiveness
Severe time constraint

However broad the range of circumstances in which coercion and mistake or ignorance may justify legal over-riding of preferences, an individual's existing preferences remain the basic reference point. It is possible to argue, though, that primacy should be accorded to the "good" of the individual rather than to his preferences. This opens up an even broader range of possible interferences with individual preferences. Feinberg identifies four ways of treating the relationship between personal autonomy and personal good.[3] The first, which is especially attractive to the paternalist, is to derive the right of self-determination entirely from its conducibility to a person's own good, usually conceived of as self-fulfilment. The right to self-government is not ultimate, basic, or natural, but entirely derivative and instrumental. On this view, we may exercise a right to self-determination only because, and only insofar as, it promotes our good to do so. Margaret Radin's opinions on commodification, canvassed in Chapter 2, exemplify this view.[4] A second view is that the relationship between a person's right of self-determination and his good of self-fulfilment is not merely a strong instrumental connection but an invariant correspondence. On this view, whatever harm a person might do to his own good by foolishly exercising his free choice would in every case necessarily be out-weighed by the greater harm done by outside interference and direction. A third view is that the right of self-determination is entirely underivative and is as morally basic as the good of self-fulfilment itself. On this view, there is no necessity that the free exercise of a person's autonomy will promote his own good, and even where self-determination is likely, on objective evidence, to lead to the person's own harm, others do not have a right to intervene coercively for his own good. By and large, a person will be better able to achieve his own good by making his own decisions, and even where the opposite is true, others may not intervene, for autonomy is even more important than personal well-being. A fourth view (a compromise view) conceives of autonomy as neither derivative from nor more basic than its possessor's own good or self-fulfilment, but rather as co-ordinate with it. On this view, a person's own good in the vast majority of cases will be most reliably furthered if he is allowed to make his own choices in self-regarding matters, but when self-interest and self-determination do not coincide, one must simply do one's best to balance autonomy against personal well-being and decide between them intuitively, because neither has automatic priority over the other.

Obviously, the first and fourth views are most conducive to paternalistic interventions, whereas the second and particularly the third would be most resistant to such intervention. Feinberg labels the two extreme positions (views one and three) as "hard" and "soft" paternalism respectively.[5] Hard paternalism would countenance legal intervention to protect competent adults, against their will, from harmful consequences of their choices, even if the choices and undertakings are fully voluntary. Soft paternalism, in contrast, holds that the state has the right to prevent self-regarding harmful conduct when, but only when, that conduct is substantially non-voluntary or when temporary intervention is necessary to establish whether it is voluntary. The problems posed by hard paternalism are obvious: once one abandons as the principal reference point an individual's own preferences, the danger of authoritarian imposition of others' preferences (legal moralism, as discussed in Chapter 3) regarding the collective or individual good are relatively unconstrained. Even under soft paternalism, how easy is it likely to be for an outside observer to discover an individual's "true" preferences once he accepts that conduct does not always accurately reveal underlying preferences?

Other second-order distinctions that emerge in the philosophical literature, in large part deriving from a widely cited paper by Gerald Dworkin,[6] distinguish between active and passive paternalism, where the former requires action (say, motorcyclists' wearing helmets) while the latter requires refraining from action (say, swimming at unguarded beaches or using narcotic drugs); and between direct forms of paternalism addressed to the conduct of parties whose welfare or interests are the object of concern and indirect forms of paternalism that are directed to the conduct of others who may interact with the person who is the object of paternalistic concerns or whose cooperation may be elicited by the latter in furthering his choices.

The Scope of a Principle of Legal Paternalism

In contemplating the ambit of a principle of legal paternalism, it seems useful to have in mind several escalating, albeit overlapping, grounds for intervention.

Cognitive Incapacity

In the case of very young children and extreme mental incompetents, it may be that they lack the capacity to form any stable or coherent preference structure at all—their wills are unformed or paralysed[7] (see category A in Table 1). In this event the state has no option but to intervene, through the legal system, to relieve such individuals of the responsibility for their apparent choices. But of course, immaturity and mental incompetence are not discrete states and vary in degrees, which may make some choices much more problematic than others.

The legal categories of minors and mental incompetents are thus quite arbitrary. For example, some individuals who fall within the category of minors presumably are more sophisticated and mature than many adults who fall outside the category, whereas some adults may be no more sophisticated or mature than many minors. Thus the legal category is both over-

and under-inclusive, although it has the virtue of avoiding the transaction costs of pervasive case-by-case judgements with respect to either particular individuals or particular transactions. Kronman explains that the rules on incapacity are premised on the concept of "judgement and moral imagination."[8] He argues that judgement is best thought of as the faculty of moral imagination—the capacity to form an imaginative conception of the moral consequences of a proposed course of action and to anticipate its effect on one's character. A person has good judgement if this faculty is developed and strong, poor judgement if it is not. Failure to exercise good judgement may subsequently lead to paralysing and self-destructive forms of "regret" by undermining a person's confidence in her own judgements, although Kronman has been fairly criticized for ignoring the fact that regret can lead not only to moral anguish but also to moral growth, as individuals learn from their own mistakes.[9] If one sets this objection aside, these qualities of good or bad judgement, defined as the faculty of moral imagination, are distributed very unevenly throughout the entire adult population and would seem to provide a basis for contractual restrictions in many different contexts. Indeed, Kronman rationalizes laws that require prospective marriage partners to wait a prescribed period after the issuance of a marriage licence before marrying and laws that require spouses on marriage break-up to remain separated for a minimum prescribed period of time before divorcing as attempts to mute powerful passions that can cloud judgement and cause subsequent regret. Similarly, cooling-off periods in various kinds of consumer transactions, for example, door-to-door sales, are explained in these terms. The question, of course, is where limits should be drawn on this form of paternalism premised on external judgements of an insufficient faculty of moral imagination on the part of either individuals or classes of individuals. For example, should similar judgements be made about the capacity of women to enter into contracts for the production of pornographic movies or to engage in prostitution? Can similar judgements justify prohibitions on cigarette and alcohol advertising, or perhaps prohibitions on the sale of these products altogether? But if these products, why not fatty or unhealthy foods? Or risky activities like hang-gliding, white water rafting, motorcycle riding, motor-racing, or professional boxing? Or, in the current war on drugs, are our paternalistic concerns with the effects of substance abuse on the users of narcotics more cogent or better able to be effectuated than the concerns that underlay the ban on the production and distribution of alcohol during the Prohibition era?[10]

Choices That Do Not Reflect Underlying Preferences

Here, one is assuming that the actor has a stable and coherent set of preferences, but choices that he makes in particular circumstances are inconsistent with this preference structure. The reasons for this inconsistency may reflect any of the factors listed in categories B, C, D, and E in Table 1. These four categories essentially reduce to two: coercion (B and C); and information failure—in terms of either the availability of information or the ability to process it (categories D and E).

Feinberg argues that requiring that all these conditions be fully satisfied would be to imply an impossibly ideal standard that would rarely be satisfied.[11] Thus, he proposes variable standards for voluntariness whereby, for example, the more risky the conduct the greater the degree of voluntariness that would be required for the conduct to be permitted, and the more irrevocable the risked harm, the greater the degree of voluntariness that would be required for the conduct to be permitted. However, the issues raised by these criteria of voluntariness are not significantly different conceptually from those already addressed in Chapters 4 and 5, and if paternalistic interventions were confined to these circumstances an independent principle of legal paternalism would add little to these two domains of issues. These two classes of factors are clearly easier to administer in specific cases of contracting failure, particularly when the other contracting party is aware of the first contracting party's vulnerable circumstances and might be argued to have taken advantage of them. More problematic issues arise where what is contemplated is not judicial intervention on a contract-specific basis, but legislation or regulation across whole classes of individuals or activities premised on the wide-spread presence of one or more of the factors enumerated in Table 1. For example, Gerald Dworkin addresses cases involving dangers which may not be accurately evaluated by the person involved—for example, cigarette smoking.[12] He identifies a number of possible cases: (1) A person may not know the relevant facts—for example, that smoking between one and two packs a day shortens life expectancy 6.2 years; that there are costs and pain entailed in illness caused by smoking. (2) A person may know the facts, wish to stop smoking, but not have the requisite willpower. (3) A person may know the facts but not have them play the correct role in his calculation because, say, he discounts the danger psychologically, since it is remote in time, or inflates the attractiveness of other consequences of the decision, which he regards as beneficial.

Presumably, among smokers, all three fact patterns, and others, including purely voluntary choices that may subjectively enhance personal welfare,[13] obtain. According to Dworkin, case one justifies education, warnings, and so forth; case two may justify more coercive measures because coercion is being used merely to enable people to carry out their own goals. In case three, a good is being imposed on someone contrary to his own wishes, but one might argue that an accurate accounting on his part of the consequences of his action would lead him to reject his current course of action, and coercive intervention thus enables him to realize the preferences he would be likely to hold if his assessment of the facts were free of bias. But a single policy measure is unlikely to be fully responsive to all three categories of cases and may violate voluntary choices in other cases. Dworkin, in a subsequent article, addresses the case of mandatory motorcycle helmet laws.[14] The laws might attract, in his view, one of three possible responses: (1) that helmetless motorcycle riding is typically involuntary, that is, it reflects an insufficient appreciation of the risks; (2) that helmetless motorcycle riding, though typically voluntary, should be banned, but on grounds other than hard paternalism, for example, in terms of the interests of third parties who have to underwrite the costs of accidents or bear the psychic costs of observing their consequences; or (3) that restrictive statutes are morally unjustified because they infringe personal sovereignty, and alternative, less coercive measures should be adopted to increase safety. Dworkin is inclined to the view that responses one and two may justify restrictive interventions. Feinberg, however, is unconvinced that the case for mandatory helmet laws is made: third-party psychic costs and public sector financial costs, if a basis for intervention, would transform large domains of self-regarding conduct into other-regarding conduct and would again justify sweeping interference with individual preferences.[15] He would restrict the state to its role in educating, testing, licensing, taxing, and insuring motorcycle riders.[16] In the exercise of these functions, motorcyclists could be exposed to information about the consequences of not wearing helmets, presented in very graphic form if need be, and perhaps could be subjected to differentiated accident and health insurance premiums. Such policies would largely meet responses one and two, while avoiding three.

Sunstein, in contrast, argues for a substantial role for legal paternalism in settings such as this.[17] He maintains that laws may reflect the majority's "preferences about preferences," or second-order preferences at the expense of first-order preferences.[18] This phenomenon—voluntary foreclosure of consumption choices—is the political analogue of the story of Ulysses and the Sirens.[19] Such measures may be regarded as partly an effort by the public to protect itself against its own misguided choices—a kind of social insurance policy. Examples given by Sunstein are laws requiring non-entertainment broadcasting on television, preventing the advertising of cigarettes, requiring the wearing of seatbelts, and outlawing the use or possession of narcotics. How one goes about ascertaining individuals' second-order preferences is not elaborated by Sunstein; without an appropriate process delineated, almost any kind of over-riding of first-order preferences could be justified on this basis.

Sunstein also argues that preferences are often induced by the act of consumption itself and are not prior or exogenous to it. The most familiar case is addiction: the problem is that an addict might continue (rationally) to consume even though he would have preferred not to have become involved with the object of his addiction in the first place. A weaker case is habit, which might continue to produce behaviour that an actor armed with perfect information would prefer to avoid. Myopia (refusal to engage in an activity with high long-term benefits because of its short-term costs) is in some respects a more general case of habit. But whereas habit-breaking is typically designed to prevent dangerous activity, efforts to overcome myopia tend to involve attempts to force people to engage in beneficial conduct. Obvious examples of addiction are drug, alcohol, and tobacco consumption. Sunstein defines addiction as a process in which the subjective costs of not consuming a particular good increase dramatically over time, whereas the subjective benefits of consumption decrease or remain stable. If the subjective benefits of use decrease over time, it may be reasonable to assume that the consumer would have preferred not to have become involved with the good in the first place. An example of a habit would be people's failure to use seatbelts because the initial costs of breaking the habit of non-use are high; but after repeated use of seatbelts—perhaps because of mandatory use laws—these subjective costs diminish sharply: people become habituated to buckling-up, and use turns out not to be particularly bothersome. A legal rule requiring seatbelt use might thus be socially optimal because a rule breaks the habit which is responsible for the initial subjective costs of seatbelt use. In the process, subjective preferences change dramatically. Examples of myopia given by Sunstein include cases where patients are unwilling to follow doctors' recommendations but are sometimes forced to do so and are eventually grateful that they were. Non-entertainment programming that may be required on radio and television, and sometimes may be made the exclusive available option, might be justified on the same basis. Exposure to alternative forms of programming may over time change subjective preferences.

As with Sunstein's category of second-order preferences over-riding first-order preferences, addictions, habits, and myopia appear to provide an open-ended justification for over-riding preferences in a wide range of circumstances, without any tractable principles constraining intervention.

Endogenous (Contingent) Preferences

The exogeneity of preferences in the neo-classical economic paradigm and the primacy accorded to the value of individual autonomy in most liberal theories have been challenged from various quarters. For example, from within economics, John Kenneth Galbraith in his well-known book *The Affluent Society*,[20] contested two basic propositions of economics: the first is that the urgency of wants does not diminish appreciably as more of them are satisfied; the second is that wants originate in the personality of the consumer, and the task of economic organization is merely to seek their satisfaction. Galbraith argues that if an individual's wants are to be considered urgent they must originate with him. They cannot be urgent if they must be contrived for him. And above all, they must not be contrived by the process of production by which they are satisfied. He claims that this means the whole case for the urgency of production, based on the urgency of wants, cannot be sustained. One cannot defend production as satisfying wants if that production creates the wants. One can no longer assume that welfare is greater at a higher level of production than at a lower one. Galbraith refers to the way that wants depend on the process by which they are satisfied as the "Dependence Effect." His argument is essentially an empirical claim that in more affluent societies the production, marketing, and advertising of goods and services precedes the demand for them and creates that demand, reinforced by motivations such as imitation and envy on the part of consumers.

In a vigorous critique of Galbraith's argument, Hayek[21] concedes that we would not desire many of the amenities of civilization if we did not live in a society in which others provide them. Innate wants are probably confined to food, shelter, and sex (procreation); the rest we learn to desire because we see others enjoying them. To say that a desire is not important because it is not innate is to say that the whole cultural achievement of humanity is not important. Hayek goes on to argue that an individual's desire for literature, music, art, and so on probably does not originate with him in the sense that this want would exist if literature, art, and music were not produced. In other words, the knowledge of what is being or can be produced is one of the many factors that influence what people will want. He claims that it would scarcely be an exaggeration to say that contemporary "man," in all fields where he has not yet developed firm habits, tends to find out what he wants by looking at what his neighbours do and at various displays of goods and services; he then chooses what he likes best. In other words, Hayek poses the question of what the significance is of conceding that preferences are culturally endogenous or, if one wishes, socially constructed. For Galbraith, the implication is that we should allocate fewer of our resources to material production of goods and services through the market and allocate more of our resources to public production—through the government—of education, health care, and a variety of other public goods. Hayek views this as an attempt to justify the use of coercion to make people employ their resources for purposes for which Galbraith has an individual preference.

A more radical critique of the assumption of the exogeneity of preferences or the primacy of individual autonomy has been made from a communitarian perspective. Communitarians, such as Michael Sandel,[22] Alastair MacIntyre,[23] and Charles Taylor,[24] are critical of what they view as an impoverished, pre-social, atomistic conception of human identity which fails to acknowledge the extent to which individual identities are shaped and constituted by their particular social, historical, cultural, and linguistic contexts. Given the contingency of these circumstances, the claim for the validation of existing preferences is also contingent because communities, through their collective choices, may decide to adopt some new conception of the common good, and preferences are likely to adapt accordingly as individuals participate in this process of political reconceptualization of their community values.

Feinberg's reply[25] to this critique of classical liberalism is to concede that in part it is justified; however, while accepting the essentially social nature of man, he argues that it is still plausible to retain a doctrine of the human right of autonomous self-government within the private sphere. His argument essentially rests on viewing liberalism as a doctrine about the uses and limits of state power and not about the importance of the role of participation in various communities of interest in the shaping of human identities. He argues for a form of pluralism where, on the one hand, membership in a large array of intermediate sub-communities of all kinds, often overlapping in their memberships, is available to all individuals, while resisting any conception of a uniform and monolithic comprehensive public community on the other, which risks an authoritarianism that is antithetical to even socially relative concepts of autonomy. The psychological need for a unifying ideology amid this diversity—in this community of communities— would be satisfied by a liberal state built on a creed of mutual tolerance and respect for rights.[26]

Thus, like Hayek in his debate with Galbraith, Feinberg in his rejoinder to Sandel and other communitarians adopts a strategy of confession and avoidance. That is, even if one acknowledges the socially relative nature of preferences, it does not follow that the state, as representative of the larger national community, thereby acquires the right to impose a uniform set of preferences on all its citizens. Rather, it should maintain neutrality among different conceptions of the good life.

Sunstein argues a somewhat more eclectic case for disregarding preferences.[27] In addition to arguing that existing preferences may be induced by consumption choices and not be exogenous to them, as noted above, he argues that preferences which reflect existing legal structures may be suspect in various ways: adaptive preferences, or preferences that result from the lack of available opportunities; endowment effects, or preferences that are attributable to ownership or non-ownership; and ideology, amounting to interest-induced beliefs on the part of the well-off and adaptive preferences on the part of the worse off. All these effects might be regarded as cognitive defects to which the legal system should and sometimes does respond.

The phenomenon of adaptive preferences results from the fact that what people want is sometimes a product of what they can get.[28] Although preferences that have adapted to the absence of opportunities are in important respects welfare promoting, because they diminish frustration and envy and prevent people from cursing a fate that they perceive themselves as powerless to change and in this sense reduce cognitive dissonance, if such preferences are not part of conscious character planning and if they arise during a process of conditioning over which people exercise little or no control, there is an important sense in which the resulting preferences are not autonomous. Those preferences are produced by a lack of opportunities which, if they were available, would result in a different preference structure. For example, the hostility of many women "trapped" in traditional relationships or roles to equal rights legislation may result from the cognitive dissonance produced by new conceptions of the role of women.

With respect to endowment effects, social psychologists and experimental economists have demonstrated that people sometimes value things once they have them much more highly than they value those same things when they are owned by others.[29] Endowment effects may result in part from cognitive processes whereby people prefer received income to opportunity income because of psychological attachments. Such effects represent an effort to adapt preferences to the existing distribution of goods and legal entitlements. Thus, preferences that are both endogenous to and subject to distortion by the legal status quo do not provide a strong justification for preservation of the status quo.

With respect to the influence of ideology on preferences, ideology (reflected in existing legal structures) can be understood as a kind of cognitive distortion on the part of both its victims and its beneficiaries. From the standpoint of victims, ideology is part of the general category of adaptive preferences. People may become content with the status quo, even a status quo in which they are oppressed, because they believe that it cannot be changed; here again they are engaged in dissonance reduction.

Sunstein frankly acknowledges the dangers entailed in a socially contingent theory of preferences:

> Lurking beneath the surface, however, is a serious risk: the recognition that desires are social constructs, or are distorted by various factors, may tend to undermine the notion of autonomy altogether. If the ideas of endogenous preferences and cognitive distortions are carried sufficiently far, it may be impossible to describe a truly autonomous preference. No desire is unaffected by social forces. If the notion of autonomy is abandoned, the realm of permissible legal interferences may become limitless—hardly a comforting prospect. It is difficult indeed to generate a baseline from which to describe genuine autonomy, and an approach that tries to abstract entirely from social pressures is unlikely to be fruitful.[30]

In a later essay, Sunstein acknowledges the Scylla and Charybdis that he finds himself between:

> In deciding whether and when to disrupt voluntary transactions, it would be a large mistake to believe that there is a pre- or post-social standard of autonomy that might be used as the basis for political criticism. Thus notions of adaptive preferences, or preferences about preferences, must not pretend to depend on a regulative ideal of pure self-creation or of a contextual selection of preferences. A positive definition of autonomy is likely to be chimerical.

But it would be an equally large mistake to abandon the idea of autonomy altogether. There is a substantial difference between a preference that results from the absence of available opportunities, or a lack of information about alternatives, and a preference that is formed in the face of numerous opportunities and all relevant information.[31]

Although avoiding both these polar errors seems intuitively appealing, Sunstein offers very little in the way of a set of tractable principles that provide much purchase on when private preferences should be over-ridden. That is, how does one go about ascertaining whether or not preferences are adaptive? The calculus is rendered even more complex by his concluding acknowledgement in the later essay that even if private preferences can be viewed as flawed in any of the various respects which he identifies, collective action may also be flawed in different ways as a result of political faction-alism and the influence of self-interest in the political process. In other words, however flawed private preferences may be, there is always the possibility that government action may make things worse rather than better. Moreover, even setting aside factionalism and self-interest in the political process, we are faced with a serious circularity problem. If individual preferences may be flawed in all the ways that Sunstein describes, would we not suppose that the preferences of legislators, bureaucrats, regulators, and judges would be subject to the same infirmities? Why isn't this a quintessential case of the socially constructed blind leading the blind, unless we make the precarious assumption that when we aggregate preferences in collective decision making, all the sundry flaws and biases in individual preferences get neutralized in one "genuine" collective preference? Or as Eric Mack puts it (perhaps too strongly): "If the problem is that people are such knaves or fools that they cannot recognise or will not choose these components of human flourishing, then who is to be entrusted to design and enforce limitations on the market that will advance genuine personhood and community?"[32]

There is a further and in some ways more fundamental circularity problem with theories of endogenous preferences: presumably *any* form of social, economic, or legal organization will be vulnerable to the same claim, so that the validity of individual preferences will be open to challenge ad infinitum.

Ad Hoc (Intuitive) Paternalism

In the face of these difficulties of formulating general principles for justifying paternalistic over-riding of preferences, both Duncan Kennedy[33] and Robin West[34] advocate a case for ad hoc, or intuitive, paternalism, reflecting in effect the fourth view of the relationship between personal autonomy and personal good noted by Feinberg. Kennedy argues that principled anti-paternalism collapses once incapacity is acknowledged as an exception, for example, in the case of minors and mental incompetents. However, principled paternalism also collapses, according to Kennedy, once one recognizes the repugnant implications of pervasive authoritarianism. This leads Kennedy to endorse a form of ad hoc paternalism premised on moral intuition on a case-by-case basis where the basis of paternalism is "inter-subjective" unity of the actor with the other—identification and intimate knowledge by the actor of the person on whose behalf he or she seeks to act. But, according to Kennedy, the most fundamental characteristic of social life in our form of capitalism is social pluralism, which he claims is a euphemism for social segregation and consequent ignorance and fear of one group for another. He concludes:

> The only way to reduce the risk of making mistakes for which one is responsible no matter how good one's intentions is to deal with people who are not at a great distance, who are not strangers. If the others in whose interests you have to act are mobilized, it's more likely that you will have some intuitive knowledge of them, because they will have the means of group expression. It's more likely that they will be able to tell you what to do and correct you when you do it wrong, so that you do not make mistakes on their behalf. And if they are mobilized, there is more chance they will be able to dispense with your services. That is the true paternal goal: that the other should surpass you both in knowledge and in power and share both.[35]

This view of paternalism is, of course, highly political.

Robin West proposes that judges adopt an approach of "sympathetic understanding."[36] Ironically, West illustrates this approach by citing Adam Smith in *The Theory of Moral Sentiments*:

> By (an act of sympathy) we place ourselves in his situation, we conceive of ourselves enduring all the same torments, we enter as it were into his body, and become in some measure (the same person with) him, and thence form some idea of his sensations, and even feel something which, though weaker in degree, is not altogether unlike them. His agonies, when they are thus brought home to ourselves, when we have thus adopted and made them our own, begin at last to affect us, and we then tremble and shudder at the thought of what he feels. For as to be in pain or distress of any kind excites the most excessive sorrow, so to conceive or to imagine that we are in it, excites some degree of the same emotion, in proportion to the vivacity or dullness of the conception.[37]

As with Kennedy, West attributes many of our preferences to social structures which are antithetical to our own interests.[38] One example West uses is the preference of a community to live in a society free of homosexuality. This preference may not be in the true interest of the community, but it reflects the socialization of its members by a homophobic environment.[39] However, West differentiates herself from modern critics of preference sovereignty who have argued that a judge should make paternalistic determinations by reasoning deductively from general conceptions of human flour-ishing or civic virtue.[40] West is critical of this approach, mainly because she sees no reason for entrusting this role to a judiciary, most of whom are in the upper echelons of a classist, racist, and patriarchal society,[41] rather than leaving this role to private contracting parties or legislators. She claims, however, that the "story-telling" or personal revelation character of the private law adjudicative process renders it more amenable to inductive judgements based on sympathetic understanding or inter-subjective unity.

West fails to explain how judges who are unable to define representative notions of civic virtue and human flourishing will be able to identify with the experience of people who are entirely unlike themselves. West's opti-mism that judges both desire and are able to understand sympathetically the daily trials and tribulations of, for example, inner-city youth, indigent wo-men who become surrogate mothers, or gay men who wish to freely express their sexuality, is puzzling. Furthermore, implicit in her distinction between conceptions of inter-subjective unity or sympathetic understanding and a more general conception of human flourishing is the suggestion that these two approaches are disconnected—that one's interpretation of another's plight is not influenced by one's conception of human flourishing. This is a separation of passion and reason which seems at odds with West's general theoretical orientation. Moreover, with both Kennedy and West, it is diffi-cult to understand how inter-subjective unity or sympathetic understanding can be achieved without substantial deference to the underlying preferences, values, or goals of the individuals who are engaging our concern. The total renunciation of their preferences, values, or goals, and the substitution of external preferences, values, or goals is patronizing and authoritarian rather than sympathetic and inter-subjectively unifying.

Bad Preferences

An ironic convergence of views is observable in communitarians such as Sandel[42] and Radin,[43] on the one hand, and political conservatives and liberal theorists such as Irving Kristol and James Q. Wilson, on the other, in their commitment to a concept of the personal good or civic virtue (legal moralism?), against which private preferences are to be evaluated and, if necessary, over-ridden. For example, Kristol,[44] in a passionate defence of the case for censorship of pornography, argues that pornography debases and brutalizes our citizenry. Its whole purpose is to treat human beings ob-scenely, to deprive human beings of their specifically human dimensions, and to reduce men and women to some of their mere bodily functions—to their animal components, where human relationships have been debased into a crude animal connection. Kristol rejects what he calls the "managerial conception" of democracy, where democracy is seen as nothing but a set of rules and procedures whereby majority rule and minority rights are reconciled into a stable equilibrium. He claims that the purpose of democracy cannot possibly be the endless functioning of its own political machinery. The purpose of any political regime is to achieve some version of the good life and the good society and to educate its citizenry in what used to be called "republican virtue."[45]

James Q. Wilson[46] argues similarly in defending the case for criminalization of narcotics. He argues that society is not and could never be a collection of autonomous individuals. We all have a stake in ensuring that each of us displays a minimum level of dignity, responsibility and empathy. He argues that dependency on certain mind-altering drugs is a moral issue and that their illegality rests in part on their immorality. Legalizing them would undercut, if not eliminate altogether, the moral message. Wilson concludes:

> That message is at the root of the distinction we now make between nicotine and cocaine. Both are highly addictive; both have harmful physical effects. But we treat the two drugs differently, not simply because nicotine is so widely used as to be beyond the reach of effective prohibition, but because its use does not destroy the user's essential humanity. Tobacco shortens one's life, cocaine debases it. Nicotine alters one's habits, cocaine alters one's soul. The heavy use of crack, unlike the heavy use of tobacco, corrodes those natural sentiments of sympathy and duty that constitute our human nature and make possible our social life.
>
> Human character is formed by society; indeed, human character is inconceivable without society, and good character is less likely in a bad society. Will we, in the name of an abstract doctrine of radical individualism, and with the false comfort of suspect predictions, decide to take the chance that somehow individual decency can survive amid a more general level of degradation?[47]

More generally, it might be argued that just as parents often feel morally entitled, indeed, obligated, to intervene with their children to curb self-destructive or debasing impulses, such as pulling wings off flies or being cruel to pets or to other children, not eating or sleeping properly or keeping themselves clean, engaging in dangerous or anti-social activities, not helping with family chores or doing homework—society is entitled and obliged to suppress at least extreme forms of self-destructive or debasing impulses when observed on the part of individuals who are members of it: "we are each our brother's keeper." But when does moral guidance and moral direction in the family become authoritarianism (or legal moralism) in the community at large? Interestingly, Mill himself equivocated in his opposition to paternalism in his famous example of slavery contracts:

> The ground for thus limiting this [the would-be slave's] power of voluntarily disposing of his own lot in life is apparent, and is very clearly seen in the extreme case. The reason [in general] for not interfering, unless for the sake of others, with a person's voluntary acts is consideration for his liberty. His voluntary choice is evidence that what he so chooses is desirable, or at least

endurable, to him, and his good is on the whole best provided for by allowing him to take his own means of pursuing it. But by selling himself for a slave, he abdicates his liberty; he foregoes any future use of it beyond the single act. He therefore defeats, in his own case, the very purpose which is the justification of allowing him to dispose of himself. He is no longer free, but is thenceforth in a position which has no longer the presumption in its favor that would be afforded by his voluntarily remaining in it. The principle of freedom cannot require that he should be free not to be free.[48]

The most straightforward interpretation of Mill's views on slavery contracts seems to be that he regarded such contracts as inconsistent with basic notions of individual self-fulfillment or perhaps human flourishing. But then, as various commentators have pointed out,[49] how would he be able to avoid the slippery slope argument that all kinds of other conduct, such as the use of narcotic drugs, cigarettes, and alcohol, are also often highly self-destructive and likely to reduce dramatically the scope of one's future liberties? It might be rejoined that slavery contracts are such an extreme case of future liberty-restricting conduct that in most instances where they might be observed one should infer either coercion, ignorance of relevant facts, or cognitive deficiencies, and that this presumption is so strong that it is not worth investigating each case to determine whether it might fall outside the presumption.[50] Indeed, courts have often taken a similar view in striking down restrictive covenants in employment and exclusive service contracts.[51] Kristol and Wilson might well adopt a similar view with respect to pornography and narcotics.[52] As argued in Chapter 3, the difficulty with this position is that at base it entails a form of moral majoritarianism where activities are condemned as "free-floating evils," irrespective of any demonstration of harm to third parties from them. The limits on this kind of collective intervention in the domain of individual choices are far from self-evident.

• • •

In private law adjudication of contractual disputes where paternalism in one form or another (including incapacity; the doctrine of unconscionability; the doctrine of unreasonable restraint of trade) is raised as a defence to contract enforcement (in contrast to broader issues of legislative and regulatory policies grounded in paternalistic concerns instanced throughout this chapter), one might, to restrict the domain of judicial inquiry to tractable proportions and to recognize some limits on the political legitimacy of courts, accept the distinction, drawn by Feinberg and recognized by Sunstein, between a preference that results from the absence of available opportunities, or a lack of information about alternatives, and a preference that is formed in the face of numerous opportunities. In addition, it would seem appropriate to be sensitive to the problem of cognitive deficiencies that lead to sharply diminished capacity on the part of given individuals—relative to average members of the contracting universe who enter into the class of transactions in question—to process and evaluate information about a given contract and alternatives thereto. With paternalistic concerns so circum-scribed in private law contract adjudication (for example, in terms of the scope of a defence of unconscionability), we are largely remitted to the domain of coercion and asymmetrically imperfect information (canvassed in previous chapters).

In resolving issues of paternalism more generally in public policy-making, it is impossible to sustain a sharp and clear divide between the domains of private and public ordering. However, even in this broader context, beyond the first two categories of paternalism—cognitive incapacity and choices that do not reflect underlying preferences—the case for paternalistic legal interventions on grounds of contingent, adaptive, or bad preferences be-comes much more problematic and the burden of justifying intervention correspondingly much stronger, simply because clearly definable individual preferences are being repudiated in the absence of readily identifiable forms of coercion or information failure.

Milton Friedman appropriately acknowledges the unavoidable anguish that economic and philosophical liberals confront on the issue of paternal-ism:

> The paternalistic ground for governmental activity is in many ways the most troublesome to a liberal; for it involves the acceptance of a principle—that some shall decide for others—which he finds objectionable in most applications and which he rightly regards as a hallmark of his chief intellectual opponents, the proponents of collectivism in one or another of its guises, whether it be com-munism, socialism, or a welfare state. Yet there is no use pretending that problems are simpler than in fact they are. There is no avoiding the need for some measure of paternalism. As Dicey wrote in 1914 about an Act for the protection of mental defectives, "The Mental Deficiency Act is the first step along a path on which no sane man can decline to enter, but which, if too far pursued, will bring statesmen across difficulties hard to meet without consid-erable interference with individual liberty." There is no formula that can tell us where to stop. We must rely on our fallible judgment and, having reached a judgment, on our ability to persuade our fellow men that it is a correct judgment, or their ability to persuade us to modify our views. We must put our faith, here as elsewhere, in a consensus reached by imperfect and biased men though free discussion and trial and error.[53]

Ironically, this conclusion does not seem strikingly dissimilar from that espoused by Duncan Kennedy.[54]

CHAPTER EIGHT

Consideration

The Nature of the Conceptual Problem

I return to the statement by Milton Friedman in *Capitalism and Freedom:* "The possibility of coordination through voluntary cooperation rests on the elementary—yet frequently denied—proposition that both parties to an *economic transaction* benefit from it, provided the transaction is bilaterally voluntary and informed."[1] On this view, promises or commitments made in the course of *economic transactions,* because of their supposedly mutually beneficial qualities, are singled out for specially privileged legal recognition. This view finds an important parallel in the law of contracts, where conventional legal doctrine asserts that a promise is not binding without consideration, with consideration being defined as something either given or pledged in exchange for a promise. Thus, though this chapter is not strictly about limits on freedom of contract, it is about the closely related issue of limits on freedom of promising. The central question raised by the privileged status accorded to bargained-for promises in both economic and legal theory is: why should promises have to be *paid for* in order to be binding?

In addressing this question, we need to have recourse to a more general theory of promise-keeping. While a number of such theories have been advanced,[2] in accordance with the general theme of this book I identify two broad categories of such theories: autonomy-based theories and welfare-based theories. Autonomy-based theories take the position that individual freedom would be unjustifiably restricted if promises were not binding, because individuals would be deprived of the freedom to place themselves under a moral, and indeed legal, obligation with respect to their future conduct. For example, Fried argues[3] that restrictions involved in promising are restrictions undertaken for the purpose of increasing one's options in the long-run, and thus they are perfectly consistent with the principle of autonomy—consistent with respect for one's own autonomy and the autonomy of others. However, as he acknowledges, though this may be true in the long-run for most parties, in particular transactions advantages may accrue to a given party from breach. To proscribe breach in these cases is to court the dangers of espousing some form of rule utilitarianism, even though in the case at hand, at least one party's utility would be reduced by performance, or perhaps in a particular case enforcement of a promise may reduce net utility, whatever one might say about promise-keeping generally. If exceptions are made in such cases, rule utilitarianism risks collapsing into act utilitarianism. In recognition of this danger, Fried moves to a different ground for enforcing promises. He argues that the obligation to keep a promise is grounded not in arguments of utility but in respect for individual autonomy and trust. An individual is morally bound to keep his promises because he has intentionally invoked a convention whose function it is to give grounds—moral grounds—for another to expect the promised performance. To renege is to abuse a confidence he was free to invite or not, and which he intentionally did invite. Thus, Fried argues, there exists a convention that defines the practice of promising and its entailments. This convention provides a means by which a person may create expectations in others. By virtue of the basic Kantian principles of trust and respect, it is wrong to invoke that convention in order to make a promise and then break it.

Several difficulties arise with this kind of theory. First, Fried is required to have resort to some rather vague social conventions to define the practice of promising and its entailments. In other words, his theory appears to entail a resort to external values to specify when promises should or should not be enforced, rather than deriving an internally generated set of implications purely from the premise that contract rests on individual autonomy and consent. Moreover, the resort to social conventions poses a difficult sociological enquiry for courts in determining exactly what the prevailing social conventions are.[4] Second, even if these can readily be established, there is nothing in Fried's theory, as both Buckley[5] and Craswell[6] point out, that permits one to evaluate whether the prevailing social conventions are good or bad. Buckley argues[7] that though promises made within such conventions may be content-independent, the reason we have collectively adopted a social convention of promise-keeping in a broad range of circumstances cannot simply be that the more choices open to individuals, the better; we must justify which kinds of additional choices are better than fewer choices of given kinds, which he claims requires a consequentialist justification—in his case a utilitarian justification. A third problem with autonomy theories of the kind advanced by Fried is that if the obligation to keep one's promises flows merely from the fact of an autonomous choice to assume such obligations, this leads to a subjective theory of promissory intent—which Fried indeed adopts—and the rejection of an objective theory of intent. As Barnett points out,[8] this yields a one-sided theory of individual autonomy, given that a promisee may reasonably rely on what appears to be an external manifestation on the part of the promisor of an intention to be legally bound, even though subjectively the promisor intends otherwise. Barnett, by way of an alternative to Fried's autonomy theory, offers a consent theory of contract based on a theory of the acquisition of entitlements, where for both the initial acquisition of entitlements and the voluntary transfer thereafter, external manifestations of intention, objectively interpreted, are what lead to entitlements. He argues that this consent-based theory of contract is more respectful of the autonomy of both promisor and promisee and the inter-relational nature of the promissory process.

A second category of theories of promise-keeping is welfare-based and argues that making promises and enforcing them increases social welfare.[9] In reciprocal relationships, if promisees could not rely on promises, they would either pay less for promises or enter into fewer promissory relationships, in which event both promisors and promisees would be worse off. In non-reciprocal relationships, at least where interdependent utility functions are involved (the promisor derives utility from enhancing the utility of the promisee), both parties may again be rendered worse off if beneficial forms of reliance are discouraged.

There are two principal difficulties with this second class of promise-keeping theory.[10] First, there is a substantial element of circularity to it. Whether it is reasonable to rely on a particular promise, and to what extent, depends on a prior determination of what kinds of promises are legally binding. Any reliance on a type of promise that is not legally binding is reliance for which the promisor cannot reasonably be held responsible. Thus, the mere fact of reliance provides little or no purchase on the question of which promises should be legally enforceable. A second problem is that if we are so confident that we can evaluate the welfare effects of different types of promises, why do we need the institution of promising at all? Why not simply re-allocate resources in society by fiat so as to achieve this welfare-maximizing end-state?

Under both classes of theories, three questions of descending generality have to be answered: Why should promises be kept? Which promises should be kept? And to what extent should promises be kept? On Fried's autonomy or will-based theory, if an individual elects to make a promise that he intends to be legally bound by, it apparently follows that either the promise should be specifically performed or expectation damages should be awarded on breach, so that one way or the other the promisee receives the full value of the promise.[11] Craswell rightly regards this conclusion as not warranted by the premise, in that almost any remedy for breach—specific performance, expectation damages, reliance damages—makes a performance non-optional to some extent, and a promisor who intends to be legally bound by his promise could intend to be bound to any of these extents.[12]

On the second class of theory, welfare analysis suggests that no given remedy for breach is optimal in all circumstances.[13] Expectation damages may be effective in ensuring that only efficient breaches of contract occur— breaches where the promisee is rendered no worse off from the breach by receiving his expectation, while the promisor may realize gains from recontracting with a third party even after expectation damages are paid. However, expectation damages, while inducing appropriate precautions against inefficient breach by the promisor, may induce excessive reliance by the promisee, who will ignore the possibility of an efficient breach and make expenditures that subsequently prove to have much lower social value. Full reliance damages may be inefficient as a remedy for breach if they are less than expectation damages: the promisor will be able to ignore part of the promisee's surplus from the exchange. Full reliance damages may also induce wasteful reliance, indeed, in some cases, reliance beyond that induced by the expectation measure. In many instances, as Fuller and Perdue long ago pointed out in a classic article,[14] reliance damages and expectation damages may be equivalent, in that the promisee, in reliance on the promise, may have forgone similar opportunities in the market. Here his reliance costs are his opportunity costs.

According to Goetz and Scott,[15] the damage measure for breach of a promise should be designed to minimize precaution costs. If all promises, especially all non-reciprocal promises, were enforced to the full extent of expectation damages, this might induce excessive reliance by promisees in cases where the promisor wished to provide for various "regret contingencies," in which event he would not want to keep his promise. In response to the prospect of expectation damages for breach, the promisor may make either fewer or lower quality promises, by qualifying his commitments in various ways. However, non-enforceability of such promises, while relieving promisors of the costs of regret contingencies by transferring them to promisees, may cause promisees to adopt self-precautions against the contingency of breach, in effect by making sub-optimal investments in beneficial reliance. Thus, a complicated calculus is entailed in structuring a remedy for breach of various classes of promises that will ensure beneficial levels of reliance by promisees, avoid wasteful forms of detrimental reliance in the event of breach, and not excessively discourage the number or quality of commitments made by promisors.

Applications

Bargained-for Promises

Both autonomy and welfare theorists generally find bargained-for promises relatively unproblematic. First, promises made in an arms-length bargain setting, where commitments are made in return, are usually interpreted as manifesting an intention to be legally bound. Acceptance by the promisor of the reciprocal commitments of the promisee generally signifies that he intended to make a binding commitment. Had he not intended to do so, and made this clear to the promisee, it is unlikely that in most typical commercial settings the promisee would have been prepared to make any reciprocal commitment to the promisor. In such settings, it is also argued that expectation damages, for reasons noted above, are often an appropriate way of compensating the promisee in the event of breach by the promisor. Moreover, it is argued that in reciprocal bargaining relationships, to the extent that the expectation measure of damage does not reflect the parties' mutual wishes, they are free to bargain for some other remedy or measure of damage on breach.[16] Obviously, the more stringent or expansive the remedy available to the promisee on breach, the more he will have to offer the promisor by way of a reciprocal commitment.

One way autonomy and welfare theories of promising might differ in the bargained-for promise context is with respect to allegedly one-sided bargains. Autonomy theorists would be highly deferential to the subjective valuations by the parties of the considerations being exchanged, in the absence of coercion, information failures, and so on, while some welfare (end-state) theorists would be concerned that in a bargaining setting, where the parties are dealing with each other at arms-length and where any inference of an intended gift is implausible, rules of substantive fairness should ensure that the values exchanged are roughly equivalent. Gordley's theory of equality in exchange, discussed in Chapter 5, is one such theory.[17] This would require the courts to police bargains for the adequacy of consideration—a role that historically they have claimed to eschew—although modern doctrines of unconscionability have increasingly concerned themselves with not only procedural unconscionability but substantive unconscionability of the kind that may be reflected in gross inequalities in values exchanged.[18]

Contract Modifications

Traditional contract doctrine stipulated that a promise given in exchange for a promise to perform an existing contractual obligation is unenforceable.[19] This is often referred to as the "pre-existing duty" rule. Thus, for example, where one party agreed to pay more, or accept less, than the contract initially contemplated, and the other party offered no fresh consideration for the additional payment promised or the complete or partial waiver of the initial obligation, the first party's promise was presumptively unenforceable. This doctrine has been substantially modified in various respects over time, the most prominent exception being the emergence of the doctrine of promissory estoppel. As formulated in section 90 of the U.S. Restatement (2nd) of Contracts: "A promise which the promisor should reasonably expect to induce action or forbearance on the part of the promisee or a third person and which does induce such action or forbearance is binding if injustice can be avoided only by enforcement of the promise. The remedy granted for breach may be limited as justice requires." More specifically, in the context of contract modifications, section 89(a) of the Restatement (2nd) provides: "A promise modifying a duty under a contract not fully performed on either side is binding (a) if the modification is fair and equitable in view of circumstances not anticipated by the parties when the contract was made." In the famous English case of Central London Property Trust Limited v. High Trees House Limited,[20] Lord Denning developed and applied a principle of promissory estoppel in a case where the plaintiffs, who had leased a block of flats to the defendants for an annual rental, agreed to accept a reduced rent when, following the outbreak of World War II, only about one-third of the units in the building had been let. In a subsequent action by receivers for the plaintiffs to recover the shortfall, Lord Denning held that the plaintiffs were bound by the commitment they had made to the defendants, at least for the duration of the wartime conditions or until the flats were fully rented (whichever came first). He stated that the relevant principle was that where "a promise was made which was intended to create legal relations and which, to the knowledge of the person making the promise, was going to be acted on by the person to whom it was made, and which was in fact so acted on,"[21] the promise must be honoured.

Autonomy theorists would have little difficulty endorsing the enforceability of contract modifications, even when not supported by fresh consideration, if one of the parties chooses to make a new commitment to the other party which she intended to be legally binding. In a bargaining setting, it is probably reasonable in most cases to infer an intention to be legally bound. However, as noted in Chapters 4 and 6, problems arise in the case of pure strategic contract modifications, which are the result of opportunistic or coercive exploitation by one party of another's temporary dependency, although a rule of non-enforceability can be reconciled with autonomy theories by resort to notions of coercion and arguably with welfare theories if the risks of strategic behaviour raise the joint costs of contracting *ex ante*.[22] As noted further in Chapter 6, more complex problems arise with contract modifications that are negotiated as responses to changes in the economic environment of the contract, which might, on the one hand, be viewed as a reasonable reallocation of unforeseen risks, but on the other hand may reflect strategic reallocation of previously assigned risks, where the promisee exploits the promisor's contractual dependency on him and lack of adequate remedies for breach to reassign a risk, again implicating theories of coercion and welfare concerns pertaining to the impact of strategic behaviour on the joint costs of contracting.

Gratuitous Promises under Seal

Where a gratuitous promise is embodied in a document under seal, the law traditionally enforces such a promise as if it were a contract. That is, it is assumed that the promisor intended to be legally bound and the full expectancy interest of the promisee is protected. Fuller identified three basic functions that are performed by legal formalities.[23] First, an evidentiary function is served by legal requirements that provide evidence of the existence and purport of the undertaking in the event of controversy. Second, formality requirements may also perform a cautionary or deterrent function by acting as a check against inconsiderate action. Third, formality requirements may serve a channelling function by marking or signalizing the enforceable promise and thus furnishing a simple and external test of enforceability by offering parties a legal framework into which they can fit their actions in order to achieve a legally effective expression of intention. The last of these three rationales is particularly pertinent to the issues addressed in this chapter.

United States and Anglo-Canadian contract law regarding gratuitous promises under seal has diverged over time. The institution of the seal is still freely available and widely used in Anglo-Canadian jurisdictions, although it has been repealed by statute in about two-thirds of the American states. Eisenberg appears to support the demise of the seal in the United States:

> Originally, the seal was a natural formality—that is, a promissory form popularly understood to carry legal significance—which ensured both deliberation and proof by involving a writing, a ritual of hot wax, and a physical object that personified its owner. Later, however, the elements of ritual and personification eroded away, so that in most States by statute or decision a seal may now take the form of a printed device, word, or scrawl, the printed initials "L. S.," or a printed recital of sealing. Few promisors today have even the vaguest idea of the significance of such words, letters, or signs, if they notice them at all . . . Considering this drastic change in circumstances, the rule that a seal renders a promise enforceable has ceased to be tenable under modern conditions.[24]

Eisenberg resists the view that some new formality, with less ambiguous significance for promisors than the formality practices that have evolved over time in the United States, should be reinstituted. He claims:

> As a practical matter, such a form would be primarily employed to render donative promises enforceable. Both morally and legally, however, an obligation created by a donative promise should normally be excused either by acts

of the promisee amounting to ingratitude, or by personal circumstances of the promisor that render it improvident to keep the promise. If Uncle promises to give Nephew $20,000 in two years, and Nephew later wrecks Uncle's living-room in an angry rage, Uncle should not remain obliged. The same result should ordinarily follow if Uncle suffers a serious financial setback and is barely able to take care of his immediate family, or if Uncle's wealth remains constant but his personal obligations significantly increase in an unexpected manner, as through illness or the birth of children.[25]

Eisenberg points out that both the French and the German Civil Codes, while providing special forms that enable a donative promise to be rendered legally enforceable, also provide extensive treatment of improvidence and ingratitude as defences. However, he takes the view that inflicting on courts the burden of inquiry into issues of improvidence and ingratitude and the uncertainty inevitably associated with such enquiries renders the game not worth the candle.

Autonomy theorists would surely take strenuous issue with Eisenberg's position. Assuming that the device of the seal does carry unambiguous connotations of an intention to be legally bound, as the relatively demand-ing seal formalities seem to entail in Anglo-Canadian jurisdictions, if the promisor chooses to invoke this convention, he should be legally able to bind himself. It would also seem to follow, at least on Fried's view, that the appropriate remedy for breach is expectation damages—only this remedy renders the promise fully enforceable. This, in fact, reflects established doctrine. Eisenberg also seems to accept the case for expectation damages for breach of sealed promises if the institution is to be retained.[26]

Welfare theorists may have more difficulty rationalizing the enforceability of sealed promises. Because of the non-reciprocal nature of such promises, it may be difficult to determine whether they are welfare-increasing. That is, when one contrasts sealed promises with bargained-for promises, it may be difficult to conclude that the promisee values the resources being trans-ferred more highly than does the promisor. In this sense, one might view the promise as a "sterile transmission," or merely a redistribution of resources, that may or may not be welfare-enhancing, and on which the legal system is not justified in expending social resources. Alternatively, one would need to argue that the promisor, at least, regards the resources as serving a more valuable function in the hands of the promisee than in his own hands, and that his judgement should be respected, but this is simply a restatement of the autonomy justification for enforcing such promises. Moreover, it does not offer any distinctive welfare justification for why advance *commitments* to make gifts should be enforced when the promisor subsequently changes his mind.

Shavell has argued[27] that where donees do not know whether a donor is altruistic or a masquerader, in the absence of enforceable contracts the only possible outcome is a pooled outcome in which masqueraders mimic altruistic donors. If the percentage of masqueraders in the population is sufficiently high, altruistic donors will want to induce donees to raise their reliance, reflecting interdependent utility functions. Thus, altruistic donors will distinguish themselves by making contracts to give gifts. However, if courts cannot easily verify the occurrence of contingencies that a donor would want to release him from his obligations, the donor may be made worse off by being legally bound to give a gift. In this case, a legal rule that renders a donor who announces his intentions to give a gift obligated to do so can have two consequences. One is that the donors will announce their intentions despite their resulting legal obligation. In this case donors are made worse off, but donees are made better off. The other possibility is that donors will refrain from announcing their intentions in order to avoid becoming legally bound. In this event, both donors and donees are made worse off by the rule.

With respect to the remedy for breach of a gratuitous promise under seal, welfare theorists may also encounter more difficulty than autonomy theorists in rationalizing the case for awarding expectation damages. The theory of efficient breach, whatever its merits in a conventional commercial setting, does not seem to have much relevance to the sealed promise context. Suppose, for example, that a promisor initially promised a stream of payments under seal to a local symphony orchestra, but now decides that the local opera company could more productively use his support. How is a judgement as to which is the more highly valued social use rendered more robust by requiring him to continue his support for the symphony (or pay equivalent damages) before he can support the opera? This is unlike the conventional example of the widget manufacturer who wishes to breach with the first buyer in order to reallocate manufacturing resources to more profitable uses and is prepared to pay-off the first buyer to the extent of any forgone profits of the latter, after mitigation. In the symphony/opera case, there is no way of leaving the symphony unaffected, short of providing all the resources originally committed to it. This may not be true of a gratuitous promise of services, where on breach the promisor may be able to compensate the promisee for the lost expectancy and still find it worthwhile to employ the services elsewhere. If, however, the promisor's financial resources permit only one or the other charitable activity to be supported, this seems to entail a Kaldor-Hicks welfare judgement, rather than a Paretian judgement. But if a court is confident that it can make such a judgement, and if this judgement favours the opera, then it should allow the promisor to breach his promise to the symphony orchestra without payment of any damages at all. However, such a solution would entirely ignore the joint *ex ante* interests of promisor and promisee to provide for and indeed encourage some degree of reliance on the promise. As we have seen, both expectation and full reliance damages may induce excessive reliance so that one might wish to settle for some form of "reasonable reliance," as Goetz and Scott propose,[28] although just what form an operational rule to this effect would take is far from clear.

It should be added that contract doctrine treats completed gifts the same as gratuitous promises made under seal—that is, as binding and irrevocable—presumably on the grounds that the actual handing over of the gift manifests a clear, deliberate, and unambiguous intention to be bound by the gift, without proof of any specific form of reliance by the donee, and without limiting her claim to retain the gift to demonstrated reliance costs up to the time of any revocation of it.

Informal Promises to Charities

Here, as with the treatment of promises under seal, American and Anglo-Canadian contract doctrine significantly diverges. Under section 90 (2) of the U.S. Restatement (2d) of Contracts, "A charitable subscription is binding . . . without proof that the promise induced action or forbearance." Conversely, the Supreme Court of Canada in Dalhousie College v. Boutilier Estate[29] held that a promise to commit funds to a general fund-raising drive that had been mounted by Dalhousie College was unenforceable, given the lack of any specific request by the promisor to the promisee to make particular commitments on the strength of the promise, and given the absence of evidence of any specific or identifiable forms of reliance by the promisee on the particular promisor's pledge. In this case, the promisor had suspended performance of his promise pending recovery from personal financial reverses, and his estate refused to perform after his death.

From an autonomy perspective, at first sight the American position seems easier to defend. If a promisor manifests an unambiguous intention to be legally bound by a promise to a charity, even though the promise is not under seal, there seems to be no reason why the promisor's intention should not be respected. Equally, from a welfare perspective, it may be the case that enforcement of such promises increases social welfare. Posner gives the following example:[30] A promises to give a thousand dollars a year for the next twenty years to the Symphony Orchestra (B). The value of the gift to B is the discounted present value of a thousand dollars to be paid yearly over a twenty-year period. Among the factors that will be weighed by B in discounting these expected future receipts to present value is the likelihood that at some time during the twenty-year period A will discontinue the annual payments. Depending on B's estimation of this risk, the present value of the gift of a thousand dollars a year may be quite small. But suppose the gift is actually worth more to B because A is certain to continue the payments throughout the entire period, though this fact is not known to B. If A can make a binding promise to continue the payments in accordance with his intention, B will revalue the gift at its true present worth. The size of the gift (in present value terms) will be increased at no cost to A, thus increasing social welfare. By legally deeming such a promise unenforceable, A must confront the alternatives: he can either promise a larger gift, the discounted value of which would equal the true value as known to A, or substitute a one-time transfer, which for tax, liquidity, or other reasons[31] may have a lower present value than an enforceable series of future gifts (although it would be greater than that of a declared but unenforceable intention to make a series of future gifts).

However, further analysis reveals a range of complexities here. The failure to invoke the mechanism of the seal (where available) may suggest an ambiguity in the promisor's intentions. Perhaps she was unaware of the mechanism, or at the time of making the promise found it inconvenient to have the promise sealed, or the transaction costs entailed discouraged such action but the promise was still meant to be legally binding. Alternatively, the non-invocation of the seal might lead to an interpretation of the promise as no more than a "best efforts" promise to perform unless some set of adverse financial or personal contingencies arose, or a promise to perform only as long as the promisee is using the resources in ways that the promisor finds worthwhile or productive; or yet again, the promise might be interpreted as totally contingent (a "present intentions" commitment), allowing the promisor to change her mind at any time for any reason at all, including if she should find a preferred charity or suffer financial impecuniosity as a result of a disastrous gambling spree. In other words, the kinds of qualifications noted by Eisenberg in connection with the German and the French Civil Codes cannot ultimately be avoided. In those American states that have abolished the seal, all these same ambiguities arise, though perhaps here the situation is further complicated by the lack of presumption, one way or the other, in interpreting an unsealed promise in favour of a charity as legally binding or not. Determining which of the three possible sets of intentions might have been present and implying an operational term into a "best efforts" promise to put some limits on the grounds for exit suggest significant transaction and error costs in judicial determinations. If unsealed promises to charities can, however, be identified where the promisor "really meant" to be legally bound, then it is not clear on what basis one could justify a different remedy for breach than in the case of sealed promises, that is, expectation damages. But the problem remains, how to identify such promises?

On this question, the relationship between the issue of what kinds of promises should be enforced and the extent to which various kinds of promises should be enforced, noted by Eisenberg[32] and explicated more fully by Goetz and Scott,[33] becomes central from a welfare perspective. If it is not reasonable to interpret the promise as intended to be legally binding, but rather as either a "best efforts" promise or a "present intentions" commitment, then it is not clear why the existence of reliance advances the case for enforceability. A promisee, making his best judgement as to the probability of performance, commits on that basis. Any more extensive commitments constitute unreasonable reliance. And, moreover, reliance commitments reflecting only the expected value of the promise (discounting for the probability of non-performance) should not be the legal responsibility of the promisor. Although rational, in the sense of reflecting a reasonable *ex ante* estimate of the likelihood of performance by the promisor, they are not commitments for which the promisor accepted any legal responsibility. However, if the promise was intended to be legally binding, then even in the absence of any reliance, it is difficult to see why the case for enforceability is any weaker than that for sealed promises or, for that matter, fully executory informal bargains, or why the remedy for breach should be any different than in those cases (expectation damages). It is true that the failure to invoke the mechanism of the seal, where available, may raise serious doubts as to the promisor's intentions, but these doubts are not resolved by inquiring into whether there was reliance or not, because some degree of reliance is consistent with any of the three possible interpretations of the promisor's commitment: a promise made with the intention of being legally bound; a "best efforts" promise; or a "present intentions" commitment. This reflects the problem of circularity inherent in reliance theories of promise-keeping.

In attempting to resolve this conundrum, Goetz and Scott argue that in the case of non-reciprocal promises, some form of reasonable reliance measure of damage may be socially optimal, in that this discourages excessive reliance by promisees yet encourages some forms of beneficial reliance; at the same time, it discourages excessive precautions by promisors that might be entailed in an expectation measure of damages, such as making fewer or lower quality (more conditional) promises.

One might argue, however, that an expectation measure of damages would serve the function of a penalty default rule, as discussed in Chapter 5, by creating stronger incentives for promisors to clarify their intentions (for instance, as to regret contingencies) where their subjective intentions are revealed to be at variance with objective interpretations of their intentions upon application of commonly understood meanings of the language that they have employed in their promises. In other words, if they have a better appreciation than promisees of contingencies that may affect their ability or willingness to fulfil a promise, this information asymmetry may be reduced by penalizing non-disclosure through expectation damages. This disclosure, of course, comes at a cost, in terms of both the transaction costs entailed in writing a more fully specified promise and the adjudication costs entailed in interpreting the scope and application of the conditions incorporated. Where conditions have not been included because of the transaction costs entailed, expectation damages may then induce excessive reliance by promisees. Moreover, where promisors are, on average, more risk averse than promisees, which may be the case in informal promises to charities that typically hold a "portfolio" of charitable commitments, expectation damages may not be an optimal form of risk allocation.

The Goetz-Scott proposal violates autonomy-based theories of promisekeeping of the kind advanced by Fried, in that some promisors will be bound by promises that they did not intend to be legally binding. Their solution also seems to be in some tension with Barnett's consent-based theory of promise-keeping, which justifies the invocation of objective theories of intent. Even if one can identify some sub-set of non-reciprocal promises where the promisor has manifested an intention to be legally bound, applying appropriate interpretive conventions, it is also not clear how the fact of reliance by the promisee on the promisor's commitment, or the prospect of liability for reasonable reliance costs, in any way advances this interpretive exercise. If such promises can be independently identified, then it is not clear how one could justify a different remedy for breach than that employed in the case of promises under seal, that is, expectation damages.

Thus, from a welfare perspective, choosing between the American and the Anglo-Canadian rules on charitable pledges reveals serious indeterminacies. Arguably, the U.S. rule may reduce charitable giving on net since the subsequent freedom of action of many donors is reduced. The fact that in Anglo-Canadian jurisdictions charities so rarely obtain promises of donations under seal, where the seal is readily available, may suggest that they believe they are likely to raise more donations on net by giving donors the ability to terminate pledges if a donor's changed circumstances or a donee's conduct render this expedient (unless the transaction costs entailed in sealing charitable promises can explain the rarity of the practice). Thus, the net welfare effects of either an across-the-board rule of legal enforceability (even absent requested or specific reliance) or a rule of unenforceability of unsealed promises to charities are far from clear. One might consider the advantages of legal rules offering charities and donors a menu of options. For example, charitable pledges might be required to carry one of several stipulated designations: "This pledge is legally enforceable"; "This pledge is legally unenforceable"; "This pledge is legally enforceable except in the event of the donor's unemployment or serious illness in his immediate family" (this last category raises serious interpretative problems that courts arguably should not be burdened with).

Intra-Familial Promises

This class of case has proved especially problematic for the courts and also raises difficult problems for competing theories of promise-keeping. Traditionally, the courts have shown a substantial degree of reluctance in enforcing intra-familial promises. For example, in the famous decision of Atkin L.J., in Balfour v. Balfour,[34] the plaintiff sued the defendant (her husband) for money she claimed was due her in respect of an oral agreement that she receive an allowance of thirty pounds a month. This agreement was entered into between husband and wife in circumstances where she had to remain in England for medical reasons, while he was required to return to Ceylon to resume working. Subsequent to the agreement, the parties decided to terminate their relationship. Atkin L.J. held that the agreement was unenforceable:

> To my mind it would be of the worst possible example to hold that agreements such as this resulted in legal obligations and could be enforced in the Courts. It would mean this, that when the husband makes his wife a promise to give her an allowance of thirty shillings or two pounds a week, whatever he can afford to give her, for the maintenance of the household and children, and she promises to apply it, not only could she sue him for his failure in any week to supply the allowance, but he could sue her for non-performance of the obligation, express or implied, which she had undertaken on her part. All I can say is that the small Courts of this country would have to be multiplied one-hundred fold if these arrangements were held to result in legal obligations . . . The common law does not regulate the form of agreements between spouses. The promises are not sealed with seals and sealing wax. The consideration that really obtains for them is that natural love and affection which counts for so little in these cold Courts. The terms may be repudiated, varied or renewed as performance proceeds or as disagreements develop, and the principles of the common law as to exoneration and discharge and accord and satisfaction as such find no place in the domestic code. The parties themselves are advocates, judges, Courts, sheriff's officer and reporter. In respect to these promises each house is a domain into which the King's writ does not seek to run, and to which his officers do not seek to be admitted.[35]

The courts now generally take the position that separation agreements entered into between spouses following marriage breakdown are legally enforceable. For example, in Merritt v. Merritt,[36] Lord Denning distinguished cases such as Balfour v. Balfour, where the parties at the time of entering into the agreement were living together in amity, from cases where the parties were separated or about to separate. He said, "When husband and wife, at arm's length, decide to separate and the husband promises to pay a sum as maintenance during the separation, the court does, as a rule, impute to them an intention to create legal relations."[37]

This distinction seems to be a supportable one on either of the two major classes of theories of promise-keeping, at least in some range of cases. With intra-familial arrangements, it is often difficult to determine whether the promisor was manifesting an intention to be legally bound unconditionally, or whether the promise was conditional on factors pertaining to her future financial circumstances or the future conduct of the donee. Moreover, as Goetz and Scott point out, from a welfare perspective, extra-legal sanctions against breach are often effective in these situations because promisors generally care about the welfare of promisees: "In contemplating a promise, the promisor may regard costs suffered by the promisee as equivalent to costs suffered by himself. The promisor will have already taken into account the prospective detrimental reliance of the promisee. Thus, the need for a legal sanction to reflect the promisee's interests is obviated."[38] In other words, the social costs entailed in invoking legal sanctions may not be warranted. However, separation agreements entered into following marriage breakdown are typically viewed by the parties as a substitute for legal proceedings yielding binding court orders, and it seems reasonable to interpret their actions as manifesting a joint intention to be legally bound by such an agreement. Moreover, the extra-legal sanctions that conduce to performance are obviously inoperative once a relationship has broken down.

Other cases are not so easily resolved. For example, in Jones v. Padavatton,[39] a mother agreed to support her daughter through law school, encouraging her to give up a well-paid job and an apartment in Washington, D.C., and move to England to study; then, following a disagreement, the mother terminated the support. The majority of the English Court of Appeal held that the undertaking was not intended to be legally binding, for reasons of the kind offered by Atkin L.J. in Balfour v. Balfour. Salmon L.J., however, held that the promise was legally binding, because of the substantial and irreversible reliance costs that the daughter had incurred at the mother's request in abandoning her career and apartment in Washington, but that it was subject to an implied term that support would be forthcoming only for the normal duration of the program of study, which the daughter had exceeded. Here, as was the case in Balfour v. Balfour, though the agreement was initially entered into in amicable circumstances, the subsequent rupture of the relationship meant that the normal familial, extra-legal sanctions against breach ceased to be operative, thus suggesting that the distinction Goetz and Scott draw between intra-familial arrangements and others on this account may be too sharp. Given that any time family members end up in court over a disputed promise their relationship is likely to have been ruptured, it is not clear that the existence of extra-legal sanctions in the case of intact relationships has much to say about the legal enforceability of intra-familial arrangements once a relationship has been terminated.

Related issues were posed in a famous American case, Hamer v. Sidway,[40] where an uncle promised his nephew five thousand dollars if he would refrain from drinking, using tobacco, swearing, and playing billiards or cards for money until he reached twenty-one. The nephew refrained from these activities as requested, but the uncle died before making payment, and his estate refused to honour the promise. In this case, the court enforced the promise, on the grounds that the uncle had benefited from the nephew's behaviour and that the nephew had restricted his freedom of action in reliance on the uncle's promise. It is notable that the court was not concerned with inquiring into the scale of the nephew's reliance costs: "We need not speculate on the effort which may have been required to give up the use of those stimulants."[41] In other words, the nephew received full expectation damages. Indeed, at least according to Fried, autonomy theories of promise-keeping would seem to require this result. Welfare theorists, who favour rules that promote socially optimal levels of beneficial reliance on gratuitous promises, would probably be forced to concede that calculating reliance costs in such situations is a next-to-impossible task, and that in the interest of conserving judicial resources and minimizing error costs, expectation damages may have to be substituted. This problem seems much more general than either Goetz and Scott or Eisenberg—proponents of reasonable reliance measures of damages in the case of non-reciprocal promises outside the context of commercial relationships—seem prepared to concede. That is, in most cases, expectation damages will be easier to measure than reliance damages. An example given by Eisenberg is suggestive of the generality of the problem:

Uncle promises to give Nephew the amount of his expenses, up to $1,000 for a four-week vacation in New York City. Nephew purchases a round-trip plane ticket for $250 and goes to New York. After he is there for 10 days, and has spent another $250 on hotels, meals, and entertainment, Uncle calls, and says, "I am not giving you any more money than you have already spent. Come back now, or pay for the rest of your vacation yourself." Nephew's financial loss is only $500, for which Uncle should obviously be liable. But suppose further that Nephew is entitled to only one four-week vacation each year, and except for Uncle's promise of a full four weeks in New York, he would have gone back-packing with friends who have now set off without him. On these facts, Nephew has incurred a non-financial opportunity cost equal to the utility of his back-packing vacation offset by the utility of the vacation he actually gets. Assuming this element of damage was reasonably foreseeable, should Uncle be liable for that cost as well?[42]

Eisenberg concedes that it is arguable that since we do not know if a promise of less than $1,000 for a four-week vacation would have been sufficient to induce Nephew to go to New York, the only way to ensure that Nephew is fully compensated is to enforce Uncle's promise to its full extent. However, he concludes that requiring full enforcement of a donative promise whenever a relying promisee has incurred any non-financial cost, regardless of its nature or extent, is "strong medicine" where the promise was founded on a generous impulse, the promisee's financial costs are accounted for, and the non-financial costs seem questionable or insubstantial: "Broadly speaking, expectation should be employed as a surrogate for measuring the cost of reliance only if those costs appear significant, difficult to quantify, and closely related to the full extent of the promise."[43] In this example, Eisenberg views expectation damages as inappropriate, because Nephew's only non-financial cost is his loss of the opportunity to take a different vacation. This conclusion does not seem particularly persuasive or principled and suggests a high degree of arbitrariness in determining when one should switch from reliance damages to expectation damages because of relative ease of measurement.

The relevance of demonstrated reliance by promisees on promises in intra-familial contexts, with respect not to the appropriate remedy, but to the prior question of whether the promise should be legally enforceable at all, creates many of the same problems of indeterminacy noted earlier in different contexts. For example, suppose that an uncle promises his nephew $1,000 as a Christmas present, with no explicit conditions attached, and the nephew buys a new suit for $500 on his credit card before Christmas Day. The gift does not materialize on Christmas Day and is in fact revoked. If the uncle really meant to be legally bound by his promise, as in Hamer v. Sidway, it would seem difficult to justify a remedy different from the expectation damages awarded for breach of an unrelied-upon promise under seal. To give the nephew full reliance damages puts a premium on precipitate action and penalizes more circumspect promisees who do not rely at all until the promise is fulfilled. What constitutes "reasonable" reliance in this context is not clear. If, however, the promise was not intended to be legally binding, but was instead a "best efforts" promise or a "present intentions" commitment, then any reliance ought reasonably to be influenced by the probabilities of performance; and if performance does not materialize, the donee should have no cause for complaint. This is similar to the case of promises to charities where, if such promises are performed (say, 70 percent of the time), charities may reasonably make advance commitments against such expectations but should have no legal grounds for complaint, simply on the basis of probabilistic reliance, in the balance of cases where the pledges are not performed. Thus, it is again not clear how the presence or absence of reliance advances the inquiry into whether the uncle in making the promise to the nephew was manifesting an intention to be legally bound.

However, Barnett cites an example where the existence of reliance by the promisee, combined with knowing acquiescence by the promisor, may avoid this problem of circularity and yield a reasonable inference that the promisor did intend, or should objectively be construed as intending, to be legally bound:

> Suppose that A makes a substantial promise to B—for example, a promise to convey land. The promise is clear, but it is ambiguous as to its intended legal effect. Does A intend to be bound and subject to legal enforcement if she reneges, or is she merely stating her current view of her current intentions? Now suppose that B announces to A his intention to rely on A's promise in a substantial way—for example, by building a house on the land—and that A says nothing. Suppose further that B commences construction and observes A watching in silence. It would seem that under such circumstances A's ambiguous legal intent has been clarified. By remaining silent in the face of reliance so substantial that B would not have undertaken it without a legal commitment from A—A could not reasonably have believed that B intended to make a gift to her of the house—A has manifested an intention to be legally bound. In this manner, a promisor's silence while observing substantial reliance on the promise by the promisee can manifest the promisor's assent to the promisee. In a consent theory, if consent is proved, then enforcement is warranted even if a bargain or a formality is absent.[44]

A more fundamental problem that arises with intra-familial promises, as in Jones v. Padavatton and Harmer v. Sidway, is the distinction between gratuitous promises not intended to be legally binding and conditional promises or unilateral contracts ("If you find my lost dog, I will pay you $100") which in many contexts are conventionally enforced. Muris persuasively argues[45] that where performance of the condition by the donee confers additional subjective value on the *promisor,* beyond the value that the latter would derive from making an unconditional gift to the donee, performance of the condition should be treated as consideration for the promise. Thus, if a reasonable interpretation of the conditional promises in Jones v. Padavatton and Hamer v. Sidway was that performance of the condition by the donee conferred value not only on him or her but also on the promisor, the promises should be enforced. In other words, these cases should not be viewed as involving non-reciprocal promises. This approach might be extended to some charitable pledges with specific conditions attached as to the expenditure of the donations, although Williston long ago acknowledged[46] the difficulties of determining when performance of conditions in non-bargained-for unilateral promises can properly be construed as conferring additional value on promisors.

Promises in Return for Past Benefits Conferred: "Moral Consideration"

To take an example from Fried,[47] a workman throws himself in the way of a falling object, saving his employer's life but suffering disabling injuries as a result. The grateful employer subsequently promises the employee a pension which, following the employer's death, his executors refuse to continue on the grounds that it was promised without consideration. From an autonomy perspective, if the employer intended to be legally bound (Fried) or at least if his conduct manifested an intention to be legally bound (Barnett), it would follow that he should be liable, presumably on Fried's view, for full expectation damages. From a welfare perspective, the case may not be so simple: one would want to ask whether enforcing promises of this kind is likely to engender more acts of rescue in similar circumstances, or whether this may lead to fewer or more complicated conditional (and hence lower quality) promises being made. In addition, even if such a promise is held enforceable, there is still the question as to what the appropriate remedy is for breach. If, from a welfare perspective, it is argued that the objective is to promote optimal reliance on gratuitous promises and to protect reasonable reliance costs where these are incurred, how would one go about measuring the promisee's reasonable reliance costs in this case? Or would pragmatic considerations bearing on ease of measurement dictate, as Goetz and Scott and Eisenberg might be inclined to concede, the application of an expectation measure of damages?

A general comment on these various examples of unsealed non-reciprocal promises is warranted. Substantial difficulties have been noted in determining whether a promisor really intended to be legally bound in such cases. Why is it that we are much less impressed with these difficulties in informal bargain settings with or without demonstrated reliance? For example, I order by telephone a shipment of coal for my factory from my local coal merchant, delivery a month hence, with payment on delivery. I subsequently discover a cheaper source of coal and cancel the order before any specific reliance by the coal merchant has occurred. The law of contracts would routinely hold that my placement of the order entailed a legally binding, non-contingent promise to accept and pay for the coal on the agreed delivery date and would award expectation damages (forgone profits) for breach, without proof of detrimental reliance. We would not typically interpret my order as a "best efforts" promise or a "present intentions" commitment— both plausible interpretations of promisors' intentions in the unsealed gratuitous promise cases. Why is this? The answer would seem to be that in self-interested bargaining settings it is reasonable, indeed necessary, for me to make firm commitments if I want to induce merchants with whom I deal to take optimal precautions to ensure that they have the capacity to perform their side of an executory bargain, in this case by ensuring that they have enough coal on hand or under order to meet all reasonable future commitments. In many non-reciprocal promise settings such as charitable pledges, however, where altruism is assumed to be the primary motivation for a promisor's actions, promisors in many contexts can readily foresee future contingencies, such as medical misfortunes and financial reverses, where their own interests or those of their immediate family must be placed above those of more socially distant donees. In other words, altruism is in more constrained supply than self-interest. Thus, contrary to Fried's view, it seems likely that "promises" in the bargain and non-bargain settings—self-regarding and other-regarding promises—will frequently, perhaps systematically, exhibit sharply different properties, thus providing some semblance of a rationale for the traditional requirement of consideration as a condition of enforceability.[48]

. . .

Fried concludes on the doctrine of consideration:

> [T]he standard doctrine of consideration . . . does not pose a challenge to my conception of contract law as rooted in promise, for the simple reason that that doctrine is too internally inconsistent to offer an alternative at all. The matrix of the inconsistency is just the conjunction of propositions A and B. Proposition B [that the courts will not investigate the adequacy of consideration] affirms the liberal principle that the free arrangements of rational persons should be respected. Proposition A [that a promise in order to be enforceable requires consideration], by limiting the class of arrangements to bargains, holds that individual self-determination is not a sufficient ground of legal obligation, and so implies that collective policies may after all over-ride individual judgment, frustrating the projects of promisees after the fact and the potential projects of promisors. Proposition A is put forward as if it were neutral after all, leaving the parties their "freedom of contract." But there is a sense in which any promisor gets something for his promise, if only the satisfaction of being able to realize his purpose through the promise. Freedom of contract *is* freedom of promise, and . . . the intrusions of the standard doctrines of consideration can impose substantial if random restrictions on perfectly rational projects.[49]

Kull similarly argues[50] that the view that gratuitous promises should not be enforced because they are of marginal economic significance or are trivial is inconsistent with the law relating to private transactions, which makes no distinction in principle between the significant undertaking and the trivial one. It is for individuals to decide whether a promise is worth making and whether it is worth enforcing by legal process. Nothing justifies the conjecture that a gratuitous transfer produces less economic utility than otherwise comparable transactions in the bargain context. If gratuitous transfers are not regarded as intrinsically inferior, then considerations of private autonomy should, on their face, apply with equal force to justify the enforceability of gratuitous and compensated undertakings. A rule of enforceability thus secures a greater degree of choice for promisors, who select a level of certainty at which they wish to warrant their statements on intention and freely assume the associated cost. The risk that promisors may subsequently regret their promises is as irrelevant as it is in the case of bargained-for promises. If contract law exists to extend the potential reach of private action, rather than to protect individuals against the consequences of their own acts, gratuitous promises (seriously intended) should clearly be enforced. If people who make gratuitous promises are presumed to be as rational as those who make bargain promises—and no more in need of special protection—then their promises have no less claim on social resources devoted enforcement. According to Kull, the fundamental misconception of the older, paternalistic reasoning about gratuitous promises was that it saw the enforcement of such promises as a detriment to those who make them, when on the contrary, a rule of non-enforceability penalizes gratuitous promisors by restricting the terms on which they may manage their own affairs.

This view is unsatisfactory in two fundamental respects. First, an autonomy-based theory of promise-keeping provides absolutely no assistance in determining, at least outside the context of sealed promises, which gratuitous promises can reasonably be interpreted as intended to be legally binding and which cannot. This problem is exacerbated by Fried's rejection of an objective approach to the interpretation of promissory intention—a problem avoided in Barnett's consent theory of promissory obligation. But even objective theories of intention are contingent on social (linguistic) conventions governing the legal connotations of language. Thus, objective theories of intent risk some of the same problems of circularity that Barnett attributes to reliance or welfare theories—that is, do parties understand certain language to have particular legal connotations because the law says so, or does the law attach certain legal connotations to particular language because the parties believe that the language has these connotations?[51] Second, the choice of remedies for promissory breach is not necessarily resolved by reference to autonomy considerations if one accepts Craswell's argument that almost any remedy for breach renders performance of promises non-optional to some extent, so that a promise to be legally bound does not necessarily resolve the question of the extent to which the promisor intended to be legally bound.

Conversely, welfare-based theories of promise-keeping pose their own set of indeterminacies. That is, if the objective of legal rules in this context is "maximizing the net social benefits of promissory activity—the benefits of the promises minus their costs"—[52] or regulating promises so as to "maximize the net beneficial reliance derived from promise-making activity,"[53] difficulties arise in determining which legal sanctions optimize the interactions between promisor and promisee and minimize precaution costs for both parties. Moreover, there is a tendency to elide the questions of which unilateral promises should be enforceable and the extent to which they should be enforceable. The fact that some reliance has occurred does not demonstrate that either promisor or promisee understood a promise as legally binding; nor is it a principled compromise to resolve ambiguities on the first question by adopting an intermediate solution on the second: if we cannot determine whether the parties understood a particular promise as binding at all, we will hold the promisor only a little bit bound.

Fried suggests that movements in the law imply that we may have, in the not too distant future, a more candid set of principles to determine what promises should be enforceable in terms of the fairness of each type.[54] He concludes that we are moving in that direction as a result of a more open willingness to stigmatize certain promises as unfair or unconscionable and to deny enforcement on that ground rather than on the ground of insufficient consideration.[55] Eisenberg similarly concludes:

> The common law, under the influence of the axiomatic school, adopted a posture in which the threshold for enforceability of promises was set relatively high. Once that threshold was crossed, however, defences based on unfairness were seldom permitted, and promises were normally to be enforced to the full extent of the promisee's expectation. A sounder posture is to set the threshold for enforceability relatively low, but to carefully scrutinize enforceable promises for violation of discrete unconscionability norms, and to tailor the extent of enforcement to the substantive interest that enforcement is designed to protect.[56]

While Fried and Eisenberg may have some grounds for arguing for dissolving the concept of consideration into functionally more relevant doctrines, as I have shown in previous chapters one should not lightly assume that these issues are more tractable than consideration issues. But, in any event, the two core issues posed by unilateral "promises" cannot ultimately be avoided: when to treat them as legally binding, and what remedies to provide for their breach. Neither of these issues can readily be subsumed into other doctrinal or conceptual categories of contract law.

The core of the conundrum reduces to this: Reasoning from reliance to obligation, the fact of reliance—even reasonable (probabilistic) reliance—proves nothing about a donor's intention to be legally bound or a donee's reasonable understandings of this. Reasoning from the fact of an intention to be legally bound to the remedy for breach tells us nothing about the extent to which a donor intended to be legally bound. Once we accept that donors should be legally free to fashion whatever commitments they find congenial, it becomes clear that the role of the law in this context is to provide non-mandatory default rules in the case of incomplete promises. This implicates many of the issues canvassed in Chapter 6. Because of a greater degree of ambiguity about a promisor's intention in the case of unilateral promises compared to bargained-for promises, I would argue that it is crucial that the law offer a clear signalling mechanism for donors wishing to make unconditionally binding legal promises. In this respect, a mechanism like the promise under seal seems an indispensable additional legal option that should be available to promisors (and promisees). The abolition of the seal in a majority of American states seems seriously misconceived. In the case of charitable pledges, a stipulated set of legal designations that are clear and widely understood may serve the same function. If an appropriate formality is available, then informal gratuitous promises, outside the bargain context, whether relied on or not, might be made legally unenforceable, except in the case of conditional promises where it seems reasonable to infer that performance of the condition by the donee confers significant additional subjective value on the *promisor* beyond that associated with an unconditional promise. This set of rules would not preclude probabilistic reliance, but at the donee's risk in the case of executory promises. Where benefits have been conferred under an unenforceable promise prior to revocation, the donor should not be entitled to claim restitution; rather these benefits should be treated as a completed gift.

In the case of gratuitous promises that meet relevant formality requirements, the default rule for breach—currently the expectation interest—needs to be addressed. There are four reasons the prevailing rule may not be appropriate. First, the theory of efficient breach seems to have no application to gratuitous promises for monetary payments and hence cannot sustain the case for the expectancy measure. Second, the argument that the expectation measure often appropriately measures reliance costs in market exchanges also has no application to gratuitous pecuniary promises: recipients of donations typically incur no opportunity costs in accepting one donation in the sense that they are thereby constrained to forgo others. Third, the expectation measure, as with the full reliance measure, may induce excessive reliance by failing to discount for the possibility of breach. Fourth, recent empirical evidence suggests that individuals commonly attach a higher value to out-of-pocket costs than to forgone opportunities. Thus, the former may warrant more serious legal protection than the latter.[57] These last two factors are common to gratuitous and bargained-for promises, but in the case of gratuitous pecuniary promises are not qualified by the first two factors. These arguments might lead us to adopt a reasonable reliance measure as the default rule. However, there are several compelling countervailing arguments. First, some donors may want donees to be able to rely up to the full value of the expectation: given interdependent utility functions both may be made better off if the donee is unconstrained in the timing and extent of his expenditures, up to the measure of the expectancy. Second, expectation damages can be viewed as a penalty default rule designed to induce promisors to communicate to promisees the precise contingencies in which they wish to reserve the right to revoke a promise. Third, measuring reasonable reliance costs in the case of gratuitous promises seems often to be a highly speculative exercise, and promisors should not be encouraged to cast this burden *ex post* on the subsidized court system. On balance I favour the expectancy measure as the default rule for breaches of sealed gratuitous promises, provided that the promisor remains free to stipulate some other measure if he chooses (for example, actual reliance expenditures to the date of breach not in excess of the expectancy). I take this position mainly because the expectancy measure is easiest to define and administer, and if the promisor prefers some other measure, he should bear the costs of stipulating the alternative.

CHAPTER NINE

Discrimination

The Nature of the Conceptual Problem

In this chapter, I will address the question of discrimination in contracting—either in the choice of one's potential contracting partners, or in the terms on which one is prepared to contract with particular contracting partners. In one sense, of course, all contracting involves discrimination. Given an assumption of scarcity, if I sell my house to you, I cannot sell it to somebody else; if I employ you, and I have only a limited need for labour, I cannot employ somebody else. Even where I choose to contract with a particular party, I may set different terms of trade than I would if I were entering into a similar transaction with somebody else—for example, because the party with whom I am contracting presents more risks to me or imposes a greater cost on me than alternative contracting partners.

However, beyond these endemic forms of discrimination in a market system, a sub-set of discrimination engages special concerns. At the most basic level these involve what are often referred to as "invidious" forms of discrimination, where holding all other characteristics of potential contracting parties constant, I would, if legally unconstrained, choose to discriminate in my contractual activities because of largely ascriptive characteristics of potential contracting partners, such as race or gender. Where the legal system over-rides my right to make autonomous choices, or to act on my personal preferences, with respect to my contracting partners or the terms on which I choose to interact, it is unavoidably making a moral judgement about the quality of my preferences. Domestic human rights or civil rights legislation in most market economies throughout the world extensively constrains my ability to discriminate in these contexts. However, the legitimate scope of such laws is highly contestable. For example, typically such laws do not impinge on family relations—whom I may marry, whom parents may choose or choose not to adopt, which strangers a family may wish to invite into their home or to make part of their family. Similarly, certain private clubs or associations may be entitled to establish terms of membership, for example, a men's or women's club or association or an ethnic club or association, which precludes membership to outsiders lacking the relevant ascriptive characteristics. Even in more commercial contexts, such as selling or renting accommodations, selling goods or services, and employment relations, much debate surrounds whether illegitimate forms of discrimination should be confined to cases where individuals deliberately engage in invidious forms of discrimination (disparate treatment); or whether the law should reach so-called statistical forms of discrimination that are "effect" rather than "intent" based (disparate impact); or whether the law should go further still and require individuals in various contexts to engage in so-called reverse discrimination or affirmative action in order to redress historical forms of invidious discrimination that previous generations have pursued and that have left a legacy of unequal opportunity or participation by certain historically disadvantaged groups in economic, social, and political activities.

Although determining a normatively defensible role for the state in constraining various forms of private discrimination raises many controversial issues, an important incongruity emerges when one examines the role of the state in regulating private interactions that involve parties beyond a state's borders. In particular, international trade regulation in most market economies exhibits strongly discriminatory characteristics, in that transactions that would be regarded as routine and unexceptionable between citizens (such as, say, buying and selling shirts or shoes), are commonly heavily constrained by law where the potential contracting parties are non-citizens. Here, in sharp contrast to the role the state plays in enacting and enforcing domestic human rights legislation, the state compels me by law to discriminate in favour of my fellow citizens and against foreigners, even where, as a matter of autonomous choice or personal preference, I would rather not discriminate. Is there any justification for discriminatory international trade laws? I will return to this question later in the chapter.

Beyond legally mandated forms of discrimination constraining citizens' commercial dealings with aliens, a parallel set of issues arises with legally mandated constraints on the freedom of individual citizens to associate with whom they please, especially with individuals who are at present foreigners or non-citizens of one's country. That is, why should I not be allowed to hire anybody I please, from any part of the world I please, to come to my country and work for me, or sell him my house or business, or otherwise associate with him? Also, when one examines the immigration policies of most market economies, it becomes clear that typically quite severe restrictions are imposed on my freedom to associate with non-citizens. Not only is the total size of the immigration intake tightly regulated in most countries, but very detailed laws generally prescribe the composition of the permissible intake. That is, the collectivity determines for me who I am permitted to invite to associate with me as a fellow citizen. Many of the conditions imposed, either directly or indirectly, on the entry of potential immigrants entail forms of discrimination that would be regarded as highly invidious if engaged in in domestic contexts.

Private Discrimination: Human Rights Laws

The Contours of the Problem

The issue of discrimination, or its converse—equality rights—in both public and private sectors has emerged as one of the most difficult domestic policy issues now facing many industrialized societies. Despite trends towards privatization and deregulation of many economic activities that developed in these societies in the 1980s,[1] the issue of discrimination, particularly in labour markets, has attracted increasing regulatory and policy attention from governments in these societies. Along with environmental policy, it is clearly one of the most rapidly growing areas of state regulation, reflected in the enactment of civil rights and human rights legislation, comparable worth or pay equity legislation, and the adoption or mandating of affirmative action programmes in both the public and the private sectors. Although these legislative initiatives are often broader in scope, their primary operational focus is discrimination on the basis of race or gender in the workplace; they address such issues as hiring, firing, promotion, and wage rates and working conditions. Obviously, the focus of these legislative initiatives is groups which have historically suffered from systemic disadvantage or oppression. In North America, these groups most prominently comprise blacks, women, and Native Americans. The historical circumstances of each of these groups, and indeed their future aspirations, often differ in important ways. For most blacks and women, the historical denial of participation in the mainstream of economic, political, and social life, and aspirations to enjoy the benefits and advantages of fuller integration into what previously have been white, male-dominated spheres of activity, describe the problem and the agenda. In the case of Native Americans, the agenda is much less integrationist, with many Native Americans instead aspiring to revive and revitalize traditional communal living arrangements on reserves, through enhanced forms of self-government. With respect to women, while many areas of economic, political, and social activity are still largely dominated by white males, female participation in both post-secondary educational programmes and the labour force more generally has dramatically increased over the last thirty years.[2] Unfortunately, there has been less significant progress in the case of America's blacks, and we are faced with the acute challenge of designing a set of integrationist policies that are responsive to the legacy of slavery and subjugation which has characterized the history of the black race in North America.

The statistics on the current economic and social status of blacks paint a grim picture. Blacks are more than twice as likely as whites to be jobless. The median black family income is 56 percent of a white family's. Nearly a third of all blacks, as opposed to 10 percent of whites, live below the official poverty line—among them 45 percent of all black children, as opposed to 15 percent of white children. A newborn black baby is twice as likely as a white baby to die before its first birthday. Half of all black children (as against 16 percent of white children) live in families headed by a woman, and two-thirds of these children live below the official poverty line. Two-thirds of black babies are born to unmarried mothers. The thirty-one million or so blacks compose 12 percent of America's population, but constitute nearly half its prison population. A black man is six times as likely as a white man to be murdered. Homicide is the leading cause of death for young black men. In Washington, D.C., in 1989, nearly four times as many black men were jailed in the district's prisons as graduated from public schools. Black men account for 2 1/2 percent of America's college students (and declining), but 40 percent of its prison inmates. Nearly one black man in four is either in prison, on parole, or on probation. Nearly half the black teenagers in the city of Chicago fail to graduate from high school. In real terms, median black family income in the Midwest has fallen by almost a third in the past twenty years.[3] In the 1950s the unemployment rate among black youths was close to that of white youths; in 1987, the rate was twice as high, despite significant narrowing of the education gap.[4]

Although many of these appalling numbers are obviously a legacy of discriminatory and segregationist policies adopted by the state in the past, the abolition of slavery following the Civil War, the gradual repeal of Jim Crow and similar state laws, the abrogation of the "separate but equal doctrine" by the U.S. Supreme Court in 1954 in Brown v. Board of Education,[5] and the enactment of civil rights legislation in the early 1960s have largely removed the state as a direct agent of domestic discrimination. For those who take the view that the principal cause of the depressed economic and social status of blacks historically has been the existence of discriminatory state policies and that, conversely, the repeal of these policies would unleash a liberating set of dynamics in which unconstrained or undistorted private market activities would place members of the black community on an upward trajectory as they have many immigrant minorities after their arrival in the United States,[6] the facts stated above are chastening. Can we in fact assume that private markets and unconstrained freedom of contract will, of their own motion, quickly redress the consequences of past systemic discrimination sanctioned and effectuated by the state? A recent arresting study using trained testers with common negotiating scripts, reports that in buying new cars from dealerships in Chicago, white women had to pay 40 percent more than white men; black men had to pay more than twice the markups of white men; and black women had to pay more than three times the markup of white men.[7] This, along with the other evidence cited above, suggests caution in accepting such an optimistic assumption.

Normative Dilemmas

The central issue that normative theory must address in the current context is what role the state should play, if any, in espousing or promoting laws or policies that are designed to penalize, and hopefully eliminate altogether, forms of *private* discrimination. None of the major normative theories referred to previously in this book, and discussed further below, would countenance the state's adopting policies that deny the equal moral agency of every citizen. Autonomy theories would view such policies as an attempt by the collectivity to interfere with the right of every individual to choose her life plan for herself. Welfare theories would tend to stress different considerations. Utilitarian theories are probably the most ambiguous in this respect, in that though they would typically insist that everybody's preferences should count for one and not more than one (thus ruling out political disenfranchisement of any segment of the population), if the majority of the population were to favour discriminatory state policies that are directed to a small minority of the population, it is not so clear what basis exists for objection to such policy. Distributive justice theories of a social contractarian orientation stress the principle of equality of opportunity, which would clearly be denied by the adoption of collective policies designed to disadvantage particular groups in the community. Communitarian theories would stress that the very notion of a political community implies equal rights of participation in both public and private spheres of activity for all members of the community. What is striking about all these theories is that they espouse, in one form or another, some notion of equality. Given this commonality, why should the formulation of anti-discrimination policies prove one of the most contentious and divisive issues of our time? On closer scrutiny it becomes apparent that the concepts of equality embodied in these various normative theories differ significantly, particularly with respect to appropriate collective responses, if any, to *private* forms of discrimination.

AUTONOMY THEORIES
Classical liberal or libertarian theories of the kind most prominently articulated in recent times by authors such as Robert Nozick[8] provide a very narrow ledge on which to gain any purchase on private acts of discrimination. As we have seen in earlier contexts, these theories stress the right of each individual to choose for herself whatever life plans or conception of

the good she finds most congenial, unconstrained by alternative conceptions of the good espoused or imposed by others. A central role played by actual consent in interactions between individuals provides a very broad latitude for individuals to choose as they please what contractual or associational relationships they will pursue with others. If an individual should choose not to interact with another because of a distaste for the latter's race or gender, that is the individual's private business. Epstein argues in a recent book, "An antidiscrimination law is the antithesis of freedom of contract, a principle that allows all persons to do business with whomever they please for good reason, bad reason or no reason at all . . . The first question to be asked in any public debate is *who* shall decide, not *what* shall be decided. On the question of association, the right answer is the private persons who may (or may not) wish to associate, and not the government or the public at large."[9] This view is reflected in the famous (notorious) decision of the Supreme Court of Canada in 1940 in Christie v. York Corporation,[10] where a tavern operator had refused to serve a black man because of his colour and the latter sued for damages in tort for the humiliation he had suffered. In rejecting his claim, the majority of the Court stated: "We ought to start from the general proposition that the general principle of law . . . is that of complete freedom of commerce. Any merchant is free to deal as he may choose with any members of the public. It is not a question of motives or reasons for deciding to deal or not to deal; he is free to do either."[11]

An editorial note accompanying the reported decision renders explicit a common perception of the implications of this decision: "This would appear to be the first authoritative decision on a highly contentious question and is the law's confirmation of the socially enforced inferiority of the coloured races."[12]

Two important and difficult qualifications to the general libertarian position require comment. Nozick himself acknowledges that if initial property rights have been obtained through an unjust form of acquisition, then rectification of this injustice is warranted—often referred to as a form of compensatory or corrective justice. However, in determining what is a just or unjust initial acquisition of entitlements, it must be acknowledged that neither Nozick nor most other theorists have offered a convincing or at least operational theory. In part, the problem is one of infinite regress, that is, an improper confiscation by group A of entitlements belonging to group B in the relatively recent past may have been preceded by an improper confiscation by group B of entitlements from group C in the more distant past, and so on.[13] However, in the context of the plight of American blacks, it can scarcely be denied that slavery in the first instance and a vast array of discriminatory state policies that remained in place or were introduced after the abolition of slavery could reasonably be viewed as an unjust form of confiscation, particularly with respect to the human capital of blacks who were exploited under these regimes. Even if we are agreed that an initial acquisition of entitlements was unjust, the further question must be confronted of what form appropriate rectification might now take.

The second important qualification to classical autonomy theories as they might apply to the context of private discrimination is the harm principle, discussed at some length in Chapter 3. Here, it might be argued that when A chooses not to hire B or to serve B because of a distaste for B's race or gender, this, in the first instance, causes harm to B in that A's actions frustrate B's ability to pursue life plans of his choosing; it thus violates B's autonomy and, more broadly, harms a range of third parties who are not directly implicated in the interaction between A and B, but who may be offended by A's action. Both these conceptions of harm are highly problematic within standard autonomy theories. As Gardner points out:

> Requiring citizens to adopt a policy of equal respect would be wholly inconsistent with any commitment to allowing their personal preferences and projects to prevail, for such a policy would stipulate that personal preferences be excluded from every social practice, and would eclipse all spheres of individual judgment. It follows that liberals cannot properly require us to desist from discriminating merely because, by discriminating, we fail to treat fellow citizens with equal respect.[14]

In other words, classical autonomy theories emphasize negative notions of liberty, where the state or third parties are not entitled to interfere with my pursuit of chosen life plans, provided that my choices do not involve positive actions that impact on the interests of others; however, this constraint does not embody a positive duty on my part to take affirmative actions to assist or enable others to pursue life plans of their own in priority to my own preferences as to how I wish to use my own resources.[15]

The indirect harm to third parties who may be offended by A's decision to refuse to interact with B because of B's race or gender raises the problem of majoritarian moralism, discussed in Chapter 3. If the "bare offense" caused to third parties by A's decision to discriminate against B provides a normative justification for intervention by the state in suppressing or over-riding A's choices, then A's sphere of autonomous choices would be radically undermined not only in the present context but in many others. As we have seen in some of these other contexts, if third parties generally are offended by homosexual relationships (perhaps the society is largely homophobic), then a decision by A to enter into a homosexual relationship with B that offends these third parties would be objectionable. Similarly, in the present context, a decision by A to interact with B, despite the fact that most members of the community are offended by certain interactions with blacks or women, would provide a basis for over-riding these choices by A and B. Thus, any conventional understanding of classical autonomy theories would provide very limited scope for state intervention to constrain private acts of discrimination.

As in other contexts, I include under welfare theories any end-state or consequentialist theory, in contrast to the deontological character of autonomy theories. In the discrimination context, I review utilitarian theories, related efficiency theories, distributive justice theories, and communitarian theories.

Utilitarianism. Utilitarian theories, unlike autonomy theories, can readily countenance the over-riding or suppression of individual preferences if a proposed course of action would, on balance, promote the general social welfare. In the discrimination context, this immediately suggests possibilities for the adoption of collective policies designed to penalize or eradicate private forms of discrimination if, on a general utilitarian calculus, this was to be thought likely to enhance the general social welfare. However, a number of problems must be confronted in applying a utilitarian framework to problems of discrimination. First, conventional utilitarian theories take preferences as given in undertaking the felicific calculus. Apart from problems of preference revelation, aggregation, and comparison, utilitarianism is clearly a double-edged sword in the discrimination context. Although it provides a normative basis for taking into account preferences of every member of the political community, and not just those of the parties immediately affected by an interaction or a withheld interaction, including third party disutilities of the kind ruled out by most autonomy theories, there is a social and historical contingency to such a calculus that renders the outcome highly speculative, and indeed uncongenial, in many settings. For example, in a predominantly racist community, such as that of the U.S. South until recent decades, depending on the intensity of preferences on either side of the racial fault-line, it seems entirely plausible to suppose that a utilitarian calculus would justify all kinds of state-sanctioned discriminatory policies.

Various efforts have been made to forestall this possible implication of the application of a utilitarian framework to the problem of discrimination. All these efforts, in one way or another, involve discounting certain kinds of preferences. For example, Dworkin[16] has argued that a critical distinction must be drawn between *personal* and *external* preferences. The personal preferences of an individual relate to his own enjoyment of some goods or opportunities, whereas an external preference relates to the assignment of goods and opportunities to others. Dworkin argues that utilitarian theory owes much of its popularity to the assumption that it embodies the right of citizens to be treated as equals. If the utilitarian argument counts external preferences along with personal preferences, then the egalitarian character of that argument is said to be corrupted.

Although superficially attractive, this argument quickly encounters a number of formidable problems. For example, though it may rule out external preferences on my part that imply contempt for blacks or women and that disapprove of social situations in which the races or genders interact in various ways, it would also seem to rule out altruistic or moralistic preferences on my part as to how I would like to see the lot of others with whom I do not directly interact improved. Moreover, as Dworkin acknowledges, disentangling personal from external preferences, when they are often inextricably tied together, may make determining which preferences should be ruled out close to impossible.

Another line of argument that has been advanced for escaping the implications of taking all preferences as given where this may lead to utilitarian support for racist policies is to view many preferences as socially contingent or endogenous.[17] For example, Sunstein argues that discriminatory preferences often reflect socialization processes that lead to irrational preferences which, when confronted with a different social experience or empirical world, may be quickly and relatively painlessly modified—perhaps by way of an analogy to initial resistance on the part of many drivers to wearing seatbelts who, when confronted with the actual experience as the result of mandatory seatbelt laws, quickly find that the costs and inconvenience entailed have been initially exaggerated, and adapt their preferences accordingly. On this view, the law may have an important role to play in shaping preferences.[18] For example, a recent study by the Economic Council of Canada found that discriminatory attitudes by residents to immigrants of different racial, ethnic, or cultural backgrounds seem to decline markedly with increased contact (the so-called contact hypothesis).[19] Conversely, Akerlof argues, many minorities, by way of reducing cognitive dissonance, may adapt their preferences so as to view jobs which they consider to be unattainable because of discrimination to be unattractive jobs, and thus the intensity of their opposition to discrimination in the workplace is reduced accordingly. However, if these jobs are thought to be attainable by minorities, they would reevaluate their perception of the attractiveness of such jobs. Thus, so the argument goes, we should be sceptical about accepting as given existing preferences on either side of the racial (or gender) fault-line. Again, as with Dworkin's argument, this seems at least superficially appealing; but, as I argued in Chapter 7, it has no natural limits to it and seems to be an invitation within a utilitarian framework for the decision-maker (the government) to play fast and loose with which preferences it chooses to count and which to ignore.

If we assume, in contrast to the preceding discussion, that the society in question is predominantly comprised of anti-racists or anti-discriminators, utilitarianism may pose a different set of problems. Now, we can envisage the utilitarian calculus justifying very aggressive anti-discrimination policies, even if these entail imposing special burdens on individuals or sub-groups of the community who are singled out as means for some greater social ends. This problem manifests itself acutely in certain affirmative action programmes, where employers and disappointed applicants who have been displaced by minorities (the so-called innocent white male problem) would often view themselves as having been singled out to bear a disproportionate share of the burden of policies adopted by the collectivity in the service of some general social welfare objective. That is, these individuals may well view their ability to pursue life plans of their choosing as seriously compromised, from an autonomy perspective, by the adoption of anti-discriminatory social policies.

Efficiency. The conventional efficiency perspective on adopting anti-discrimination laws to constrain private acts of discrimination reflects a high degree of circumspection as to both the efficacy and the necessity of such policies.[20] This view rests on two main premises.

First, it is argued on conventional utilitarian grounds that we must take existing preferences as given, including tastes for discrimination on the part of employers, employees, or customers.[21] If an employer, owing to his personal taste for discrimination, or because of a taste for discrimination by employees or customers, is prepared to forgo monetary income that might be derived from hiring blacks or women or servicing the needs of such customers in order to indulge these tastes for discrimination, then the costs and benefits of anti-discrimination laws as applied to private market activities entail balancing the gains to the victims of such discrimination against the costs to employers, in terms of both pecuniary and non-pecuniary impacts. If, for example, one assumes a case where an employer has a personal taste for discrimination and prefers to hire whites over equally or more productive blacks, then the costs to the employer of hiring a black (pecuniary and non-pecuniary costs) must exceed the gains to the black from being hired, otherwise the black would be able to strike a contract with the employer whereby the former would forgo some part of the wages payable to white workers in order to compensate the white employer for the psychic costs of hiring him. That such deals are not common leads to the implication that anti-discrimination laws which compel non-discriminatory hiring and non-discriminatory wage terms will generate more social costs than benefits. To most readers, this implication will seem extremely uncongenial, but it reflects the more general dilemma associated with any utilitarian theory that, by definition, is preference-driven.

The alternative premise upon which conventional efficiency theorists rest their circumspection towards anti-discrimination laws is that in competitive markets they are unnecessary. Here, the argument is that employers who refuse to hire black workers whose marginal revenue product exceeds their wage or who decline to serve black customers are forgoing profits and will, over time, be driven from the market by non-discriminatory firms which are prepared to lower their costs or increase their productivity through the hiring of appropriately qualified blacks or increase their profits through the servicing of black clientele—profits that firms with discriminatory proprietors are denying to themselves.[22] This argument is not so much that antidiscrimination laws are inefficient as that they are unnecessary, and given that their administration entails some costs, including error costs, these laws may simply impose a deadweight social cost on the community. Moreover, to the extent that these laws, by accident or design, reach further by addressing not only cases of invidious discrimination but noninvidious, cost-based forms of discrimination (including mandatory hiring of less productive workers), firms will engage in various substitution strategies (such as relocating plants to areas with few blacks) that will largely frustrate these larger aims of the law and will entail various efficiency losses beyond those associated with the direct administrative costs of the law.[23]

These efficiency arguments have not gone unchallenged. First, as Donahue has persuasively contended,[24] there is a serious tension between the two arguments. If the second argument is correct, then the existence of discrimination in private markets is a disequilibrium condition, which will eventually be eliminated as competitive market forces drive discriminators from the market. This entails a dynamic view of markets, in contrast to the static view that underlies the first argument, and emphasizes Kaldor-Hicks more than Pareto efficiency considerations. Indeed, if the second argument is approximately accurate, Donahue argues that, as a matter of both theory and reasonable empirical conjecture, laws that force markets to the equilibrium condition more quickly are likely to generate substantial net social benefits over costs. Moreover, careful empirical evidence assembled by Donahue and Heckman[25] on the impact of the Civil Rights Act of 1964 on the economic status of blacks in the South in the decade 1965 to 1975 suggests a substantial impact of this law—an enhancement of status that is not sufficiently explained by alternative theories such as out-migration or improvements in the quality and quantity of black education. The Civil Rights Act by prohibiting, *inter alia,* discrimination in employment decisions is viewed by Donahue and Heckman as part of "a multipronged federal effort that enlisted willing employers who needed an excuse for doing what they wanted to do anyway."[26] Social conventions that attracted significant costs in terms of third party reactions to any employer's breaking these conventions created a collective action problem, where first movers were likely to be heavily penalized. The enactment of civil rights and related legislation effectively addressed this problem.

In addition to Donahue's argument for expediting the realization of an efficient equilibrium, other commentators have made the argument that competitive markets, in and of themselves, may not gravitate towards this equilibrium. For example, MacIntosh argues[27] that even competitive markets, including labour markets, may be afflicted by a relatively persistent adverse selection problem pertaining to the hiring of previously disadvantaged minorities. He argues that it may be privately rational (and non-invidious) for an employer to rely on various statistical proxies for evaluating potential employee productivity, rather than investigating each applicant's personal credentials and characteristics in detail. For example, in insurance markets it is commonplace for insurers to use age and sex as important proxies in defining risk pools, say, for automobile insurance, life insurance, and pensions. In the case of automobile insurance, young male drivers, as a class, present a higher average risk than other classes of drivers, and since it is costly to investigate the underlying driving propensities of each driver in this risk class, group-based characteristics may represent an efficient decision rule. However, in the case of labour markets, MacIntosh argues that these statistical proxies, though perhaps privately rational, may be socially inefficient. For example, suppose it to be the case that because of prior deprivation and denial of educational opportunities blacks on *average* are less well qualified (less productive) than whites on *average* for a particular class of job, an employer may use race as a proxy in making hiring decisions. This means that a particularly well qualified black who is as or more productive than any white applicant is unlikely to be hired. This in turn implies that the rates of return to investments by blacks in educational or other relevant forms of credentialling are likely to be lower on average than for whites, and over time will reduce the incentives for blacks to make these kinds of investments in their human capital, thus reinforcing the accuracy of the original statistical proxy. Even if the original statistical proxy is inaccurate, the fact that blacks are never or rarely hired means that employers will seldom be confronted with disconfirming evidence, so that even an initially inaccurate proxy may persist indefinitely in the market (and over time become accurate), having the same deleterious dynamic effects of discouraging investment by blacks in their human capital and leading in both cases to a form of low-level investment trap entailing incomplete realization of the economic and social potential of blacks—a cost not only to them but to society at large.

One might argue (as Epstein does) that in competitive markets, there would be incentives for employers to invest resources in developing more refined screening techniques for new employees or hiring intermediaries who have expertise in matching employers and employees.[28] However, though this may be socially desirable, each employer may find that she confronts a positive externality with respect to investments that she might make in gathering more accurate information on individual job applicants. That is, suppose an employer interviews each applicant individually and develops a substantial information bank on each individual's qualifications and then chooses to hire a black the employer regards as having superior qualifications to average blacks in the pool and to available white applicants. Here, she runs the risk that other employers will simply hire the employee away, in effect free-riding on the first employer's investments in screening activities. It is possible that contractual arrangements between the first employer and the minority employee could reduce this free-riding risk by other employers, but courts have traditionally been sceptical of employment contracts that contain covenants which penalize employee exit.[29]

Epstein also argues that even after efficient sorting takes place, residual discrimination may in fact often be rational (or efficient). In long-term contractual relationships that are governed by both formal and informal norms, he argues that the greater the variance in preferences among employees, the greater the cost to employers in setting and enforcing workplace norms. Voluntary sorting can reduce the cost of making and enforcing group decisions, through promoting more homogeneous preferences and so-called interactive efficiencies.[30] These efficiencies have been claimed by other authors to be explanations for the dominance of Chinese middle-men in the Malaysian economy and Jews in the New York diamond trade.[31] They may also explain the close ethnic affinities maintained among employers and employees by many small businesses run by immigrant families in North America. Even if we concede the possibility of rational discrimination in some contexts, the question arises whether discrimination specifically towards blacks (and women) by white employers can be explained in these terms in many contexts, or whether the explanation instead lies in invidious tastes for discrimination among employers, employees, or customers. The argument can too easily be invoked to rationalize the latter, and it risks resurrecting a version of the "separate but equal" doctrine adopted by the U.S. Supreme Court in Plessy v. Ferguson[32] and now almost universally discredited.

Distributive Justice. There are several versions of distributive justice theories. However, unlike autonomy theories, and like utilitarian and efficiency theories, they share the common property of involving end-state principles.[33] For example, Buchanan[34] extends the efficiency criterion to constitutional rules and would evaluate social arrangements in terms of their consistency with such rules, which are efficient in that they receive the potential or actualized agreement of all parties involved. He argues that the principle of "equal treatment for equals is a necessary element in any set of rules for social order in the community that makes any claim to fairness and that such a principle would tend to emerge from the conceptualized contractual agreements among all persons."[35] He interprets equal treatment as requiring "the absence of effects on expected values that are exerted by elements external to the persons themselves and discriminatorily distributed amongst persons."[36] In a society whose members agree to constrain themselves to equal treatment of equals, individuals would be guaranteed job and work assignments unaffected by tastes for discrimination. Buchanan is prepared to argue that in a world where employers initially have no information about the potential productivity of entrants, and where various groups differ in average productivity although individual productivity overlaps, there may be a case for imposing a temporary quota regime for a demonstration period; during this time employers would be constrained to hire new entrants in proportion to the relevant numbers of the two groups in the inclusive set and to pay first period wages equal to the average productivity of all members of the inclusive set. After the demonstration period is over, presumably employers would be able to identify more productive individual members of each group and treat them equally.

Buchanan's constitutional rules are voluntarily chosen by actual members of society who are fully aware of their own interests. However, one step earlier, at a pre-constitutional stage, individuals may be assumed to conclude a hypothetical social contract specifying the principles underlying the legal-institutional-constitutional system. John Rawls' theory of justice[37] is such a theory, where behind a veil of ignorance that he imposes on individuals, they are unaware of morally irrelevant characteristics such as race, class, sex, economic position, and other individual endowments. According to Rawls, behind this veil of ignorance three principles of justice would be unanimously agreed to: the principle of equal liberty; the principle of equal opportunity; and the difference principle specifying that the allocation of all other primary goods should be to the greatest benefit of the least advantaged and inequalities tolerated only to the extent that they satisfy this principle. Rosenfeld[38] more recently has refined these contractarian theories in the discrimination context by developing a principle of justice as reversible reciprocity within a diological process, making genuine reversals of perspective possible.

More radical distributive justice perspectives would stress less equality of opportunity and more equality of outcome and, for example, would be sceptical of affirmative action programmes that have as their principal aim facilitating the entry into economically and socially privileged occupations of members of previously disadvantaged groups, where their effectiveness would simply be to reinforce and perhaps exacerbate previous, more fundamental, patterns of inequality.[39]

Whatever the particular implications of given theories of distributive justice, as Gardner points out:

When liberals cite distributive justice as a legitimacy principle, they mean it to authorize the correction of existing patterns of advantage and disadvantage exclusively. They do not mean the principle to respond to information of certain other kinds about the various citizens involved such as their past conduct or their personal responsibility for the existing patterns. To respond to such further factors would be to go beyond a response to the injustice of particular states of affairs, and to engage instead in a consideration of how, and by whose agency, they arose.[40]

However, Gardner goes on to demonstrate persuasively that the compensatory or corrective justice theory—that is, rectification of past harms—that many liberals, including libertarians such as Nozick, recognize, and most theories of distributive justice, which many liberals also recognize, are in fundamental tension with one another:

> [S]ince the moderate liberal theory of distributive justice treats it as an end-state principle, and the moderate liberal view of the harm principle associates it with past harmful actions and state responses to culpability, there is no point at which the two principles could be said to be joined, to be continuous. Given a single practice which could be a harm, or could be an injustice, there is no single state response which is a legitimate application of the harm principle and a legitimate implementation of distributive justice. So, as we saw with positive discrimination and with the problem of justifiability, an application of the liberal harm principle will be incoherent and arbitrary from the perspective of liberal distributive justice, because it will look to past behaviour: meanwhile, redistribution will not cohere with the harm principle, because it will look only to the justness of end-states, ignoring how they came about. The two principles are radically discontinuous.[41]

These principles are unlikely to cohere in their prescriptive implications for the consequences of discrimination, because a compensatory or corrective justice perspective would require clear identification of both victims and wrongdoers, with respect both to past acts of discrimination and to current acts. In the case of historical instances of discrimination, neither the immediate victims nor the immediate wrongdoers are likely to still be alive, making a redressing of past grievances impossible. With respect to current acts of discrimination—defined here as invidious forms of discrimination that entail treating individual members of certain groups as inherently unequal or inferior—sanctions against private discriminators might be justifiable on a narrowly defined contextual version of the harm principle that is (in Gardner's words) tied to "the degradation suffered by those whose race or gender have been devalued, and the cultural meaning which race and gender have, on that account, assumed for us."[42] The distributive justice principle, however, potentially cuts much more broadly. Because it looks to the future rather than the past, in the sense that we want a better distribution tomorrow than we have today, irrespective of who or what accounts for today's distribution, it is easy to see a wide range of policies as justified on distributive justice grounds, including direct forms of redistribution through the tax and transfer system, or the provision of enhanced public services, such as education to disadvantaged minorities, or the outlawing of various forms of statistical discrimination that, though not maliciously motivated, have a disparate impact on historically disadvantaged and oppressed groups. The most controversial extension of the distributive justice perspective is the adoption of affirmative action programmes.

These programmes, at least in strong-form versions, go beyond sanctioning invidious or statistical discrimination and require public institutions such as universities, and arguably private employers, to hire members of historically disadvantaged groups, such as blacks and women, even if on an assessment of their individual merits (thus setting aside the issue of statistical discrimination) they are not as well qualified for the position in question as individual members of other groups. Here, most forms of the distributive justice principle begin to encounter difficulties. First, individual members of the community (say, employers) or so-called innocent white males are singled out to bear the burden of society's commitment to the distributive justice principle. Moreover, in the case of disappointed applicants for jobs or university positions from previously dominant groups, it is likely to be the least well endowed of these applicants who will bear the burden of the redistribution programme. In turn, the principal beneficiaries of these programmes will often be the better endowed members of the historically disadvantaged groups. In addition, affirmative action programmes by definition will not reach equally disadvantaged members of non-targeted groups, such as poor whites or members of other minority groups. Thus, both the vertical and the horizontal equity properties of affirmative action programmes are open to challenge, rendering the distributive justice rationale for such programmes necessarily contentious.

Communitarianism. Gardner, drawing on the work of Raz,[43] argues that a conception of autonomy is possible that reconciles both the harm (or compensatory/corrective justice) principle and the distributive justice principle. For Raz, the idea of autonomy is not one which requires unfettered personal choice, but is instead the repository of shared cultural values. The liberalism at stake here involves a recognition that autonomous persons, capable of self-creation, are not themselves self-created. This implies a creative function for the state. The conception of autonomy which the state is to promote is not invented or revealed, but is already defined in our existing cultural institutions and is part of our shared heritage. The authority of government is associated with creation as a product of interpretation, the creation of a culture which is as close as possible to that pluralistic and tolerant culture which it already understands itself, collectively, to be. Thus, anti-discrimination policies consist of two methods with a single end in view, namely, the enhancement of a valuable autonomy of citizens and the implementation of the ideal that the culture is one of competitive pluralism and mutual toleration, but also one of participation and unavoidable commitment. The exclusion or marginalization of racial minorities, women, or religious groups is inconsistent with the pursuit of such a culture. Thus, according to Raz and Gardner, the state has its own responsibility of providing or ensuring the conditions necessary for the valuable flourishing of its citizens. Readers will immediately recognize connections here with the theory of human flourishing espoused by Margaret Radin in the commodification context, and the theory of egalitarian liberalism espoused by Dyzenhaus in the pornography context (discussed in Chapters 2 and 3 respectively). For Gardner at least, this contextual or cultural theory of autonomy justifies the state's placing special burdens on employers, given their centrality as institutions in our culture, as distributive agencies of the state itself.[44] Although this view would certainly justify prohibitions on various forms of private statistical discrimination, it is not so clear whether it would also justify strong-form versions of private sector affirmative action programmes.

Normative Dilemmas, Empirical Uncertainties, and the Choice of Policy Instruments

INVIDIOUS DISCRIMINATION

In attempting to identify strong convergences and divergences among these competing perspectives, it is useful to review possible policy responses to different classes of discrimination. In invidious discrimination, which implies a deliberate treatment of members of particular groups as inherently unequal or inferior, a tightly contained harm principle that focuses on such behaviour towards groups that have historically been treated in this way and thus disadvantaged would perhaps—even on some classical liberal views—justify a form of legal prohibition, because such behaviour is inconsistent with the discriminator's own claims that he has a right to be treated as an equal moral agent. A utilitarian-*cum*-Kaldor-Hicks efficiency perspective would probably militate in the same direction, if one believes that competitive markets would in due course reach this outcome themselves, and if one accepts the kind of empirical evidence adduced by Donahue and Heckman as to the effects of the Civil Rights Act on the economic status of blacks in the South. Most distributive justice perspectives are not inconsistent with this perspective, although they tend to take a more systemic view. Communitarian (contextual or cultural) theories of individual autonomy would clearly support state intervention in these cases.

STATISTICAL DISCRIMINATION

Somewhat more complex issues are raised by cases of so-called disparate impact or statistical discrimination, where the alleged discriminator is not engaging in invidious discrimination but is instead employing statistical proxies that yield disparate and adverse impacts on historically disadvantaged groups. The case for intervention seems clearest where even though statistical proxies accurately capture average and relevant qualities or productivity of members of different groups, the distribution of these qualities or characteristics across the groups significantly overlap, and more individualized decision-making would identify members in the historically disadvantaged group with the relevant credentials or characteristics that would enable them to do the job at hand as well or better than any member of the advantaged group. Other cases are less straightforward. Some proxies may not obscure significant overlapping productivity in terms of what qualities the proxies are indirectly trying to measure. Rather, the objection is that the proxy, which excludes all or most members of some groups, does not reflect an adequate conception of the qualifications required for a particular job. For example, suppose a police department specifies height and weight requirements in new recruits which most women and Asians or Hispanics cannot meet. One might argue that individual applicants from any of these groups should be entitled to demonstrate the requisite physical strength or skills directly, rather than through indirect size and weight proxies. Alternatively, one might argue that physical strength or skills are not indispensable to the tasks that many police officers are called upon to perform, and that indeed other qualities, such as the ability to relate to minorities, or to conciliate domestic disputes, or to relate to troubled teenagers, may enhance performance on the job. In this case, both the proxies and the qualities for which they are indirect indices are inappropriate or incomplete and reflect a conception of merit that is consciously or unconsciously biased by, and in favour of, the dominant group.

In both kinds of cases, because the discriminator may not intend to treat members of the historically disadvantaged group as inherently unequal or inferior, but may simply be adopting a proxy as a matter of convenience or convention, classical autonomy theories may have more difficulty accommodating the case for legal intervention. However, as argued above, utilitarian or Kaldor-Hicks efficiency arguments can be marshalled for outlawing statistical proxies, both in cases of overlapping distributions of qualifications among members of different groups and in cases where proxies are measuring inappropriate or incomplete indices of merit to enhance long-run social welfare or efficiency. Distributive justice theories of a social contractarian kind advanced by scholars such as Buchanan, Rawls, and Rosenfeld would clearly support legal intervention in such cases in order to preserve or promote the value of equality of opportunity. Communitarian theories would even more strongly favour intervention.

I am purposely not including in the category of statistical discrimination a mere failure by employers or educational institutions to hire or admit individuals in proportion to the percentage of the national or local population that their minority group constitutes, in the absence of proof that inappropriate proxies of the kind described above have been employed. To view statistical discrimination as extending so broadly is largely to elide this category with affirmative action, to which I now turn.

AFFIRMATIVE ACTION

When we move from legal interventions directed at current forms of invidious discrimination or statistical forms of discrimination to strong-form affirmative action programmes, we can immediately see why these provoke so much public controversy and have engendered, particularly in the United States, a tortured and largely incomprehensible body of constitutional and civil rights case-law.[45] From the classical autonomy point of view, firms or individuals are required to accept obligations in terms of hiring in contexts where a failure to hire a member of a disadvantaged group does not reflect either a deliberate intention to treat all members of such a group as inherently unequal or inferior or even to employ statistical proxies that may disadvantage particular members of such groups in cases where the distribution of talents or qualifications overlap the membership of more than one group, but instead entail an affirmative obligation to hire someone whom the employer does not regard, as a matter of individualized judgement, to possess talents or qualifications equal or superior to those of other applicants. It is true that the concept of merit is somewhat subjective,[46] and one can reasonably argue that a slightly less well qualified applicant for a job or a place in a professional school may nevertheless possess superior merit in other dimensions, in terms of, say, an ability to empathize better with members of her racial group than can members of other groups.[47] However, on any conventional version of liberal theory that emphasizes individual autonomy, these decisions as to merit in contractual or associational relationships would be made by the individuals concerned, subject only to the constraint, suggested above, that this not violate a tightly contained harm principle designed to avoid either deliberate or statistical forms of discrimination against historically disadvantaged groups. In a utilitarian or Kaldor-Hicks efficiency framework any evaluation of the social costs and benefits of strong-form affirmative action programmes seems hopelessly indeterminate.[48] On the positive side of the ledger, reasonable arguments can be made that such programmes may provide important forms of role-modelling, may increase the richness and diversity of, for example, student bodies, and thus the learning experience for everyone, may promote greater racial equality and harmony and social stability in the long-run, and so on. On the negative side of the ledger, reasonable arguments can be made that strong-form affirmative action programmes perpetuate and indeed reinforce social pre-occupations with racial distinctions and divisions, stigmatize the beneficiaries of such programmes both in their own eyes and in those of others through widely held perceptions that they are of inferior merit and hold their positions only because of preferential treatment; that such programmes impose productivity costs on employers and ultimately their customers; and that the potential of displaced applicants will not be fully realized. Most of these claims on both the positive and the negative sides of the balance sheet for affirmative action programmes are ultimately empirical at base, and very little is known at this time, with any confidence, about the magnitude of the various claimed effects or how they net out against one another.[49]

With respect to possible distributive justice rationales for affirmative actions programmes, as noted above, difficulties present themselves on both sides of the equation. First, such programmes seem to impose a special "tax" on less well endowed members of the dominant groups (for example, on less well endowed innocent white males) and appear principally to benefit better endowed members of disadvantaged groups while excluding disadvantaged members of other groups altogether. However, there are countervailing arguments in both cases. With respect to the innocent white male problem, it can reasonably be argued that affirmative action pro-grammes put such individuals in no worse position than they would have been in had members of disadvantaged groups not been afflicted with the legacy of earlier forms of discrimination. With respect to the argument that such programmes benefit only better-endowed members of disadvantaged groups, if one accepts the role model argument, then in a more dynamic framework one would hope that these role models would over time attract a broader cross-section of members of disadvantaged groups into the occupations to which the affirmative action programmes are directed. According to Rosenfeld, his theory of justice as reversible reciprocity would support some forms of affirmative action programmes through hypothetical agreement of all the affected individuals as they envisage the implications of role reversal.[50]

SUPPLY-SIDE POLICIES
A final class of policy response would focus not on the demand side but on the supply side and would commit substantial public resources to enhancing the quality of education, housing, health care, transportation networks, law and order, and so forth in black communities. That is, problems of disad-vantage would be attacked at a much earlier juncture than is the case with affirmative action programmes. From a classical liberal perspective, the wealth redistribution entailed in enhancing the ability of members of one

group to realize their life plans at the expense of the ability of members of other groups to do the same would be viewed as suspect, unless a very broad understanding of rectification obligations for past wrongful acquisitions is adopted. From a utilitarian or Kaldor-Hicks efficiency perspective, social investments of this kind may very well have positive long-term social pay-offs, although the design of appropriate programmes and their likely efficacy would raise complex empirical questions that, by their nature, are difficult to resolve conclusively. From a distributive justice perspective, supply-side oriented policies are attractive because the costs of these programmes would be largely underwritten by better-endowed members of the community and in turn would be designed to benefit a wide cross-section of members of disadvantaged groups. However, by nature, such programmes are likely to entail only long-run pay-offs, so that a generation (and probably more) of members of disadvantaged groups are likely to be sacrificed, in direct contrast to the sacrifices demanded of others (innocent white males) under affirmative action programmes. Moreover, to the extent that one views as plausible adaptive preference arguments on both the demand and the supply side of many labour markets, it may be the case that supply-side ("push") policies are only likely to be fully effective in the long-run if complemented by short-run demand-side ("pull") policies, including affirmative action policies.[51]

Communitarian theories of contextual or cultural concepts of autonomy would undoubtedly favour strong collective commitments to supply-side policies, while perhaps acknowledging ambivalences similar to those of distributive justice theories towards strong-form demand-side policies.

THE OPTIMAL MIX OF POLICIES

Where does all this leave us? It might be felt that the normative theorizing surrounding the issue of discrimination—in particular, private acts of discrimination—is both ethereal and indeterminate. However, the various perspectives canvassed above in fact reflect views that are intensely held (albeit perhaps at a more intuitive level) by substantial segments of the population in most communities, so that we cannot afford to dismiss the challenge of developing a normatively coherent perspective on the case for anti-discrimination laws as applied to private conduct. In terms of forging some common ground among these various perspectives, which all adopt in one form or another the concept of equality as a central premise, I believe that the following set of policy orientations reflect the contours of the widest potential range of convergence. First, invidious forms of discrimination should attract strong public and private legal sanctions.[52] Even classical liberals, who emphasize the centrality of autonomy values, should be prepared to accept a harm principle that recognizes a failure to accept the equal moral agency of other individuals as a transgression of this principle. The very claim of autonomy, even in its most austere form, surely demands this degree of reciprocal recognition. The issue of statistical discrimination is somewhat more complex, but if we accept the importance of social, cultural, and historical contexts, the use of either direct or indirect statistical proxies that systematically encumber individual members of historically disadvantaged groups where these members possess overlapping competencies with members of other groups should not be tolerated, whether these statistical proxies are on average accurate or not. However, as the empirical evidence on the impact of the Civil Rights Act on the economic status of blacks shows,[53] despite the initial influence of the Act, it appears to have had little or no impact on the status of blacks after the first decade of its enactment, so that attacking these two forms of discrimination (the primary focus of the Act) is clearly not enough. With respect to further demand-side policies, strong-form affirmative action programmes create major moral dilemmas for most of the normative theories canvassed above. I believe that the severity of these dilemmas can be mitigated in several ways.

First, affirmative action programmes should be voluntary to the greatest extent possible.[54] I believe that appropriate state agencies, comprising representative bodies of citizens, might, with judiciously chosen and flexible bench-marks in mind, attempt to negotiate affirmative action programmes with at least larger employers, and educational institutions, bearing in mind that bench-marks will have to vary from location to location, occupation to occupation, and discipline to discipline, reflecting differing regional demographics and the reality that cultural preferences for different occupations or disciplines are probably not entirely an artifact of social construction. For example, if blacks are generally less interested than whites in pursuing careers in medieval studies or classical Latin and Greek, but more interested in pursuing careers in law or medicine, relevant bench-marks should realistically reflect these differences. National quotas or standards[55] seem much too crude to accommodate these locational and vocational differences.[56] In the fashioning of these bench-marks, criteria that do not strain too severely legitimate conceptions of merit should govern the choices. For example, bench-marks or targets should not impose substantial costs on employers or substantially deviate from what would otherwise be appropriate standards for admission to educational programmes. I recognize that "substantial" is a highly subjective term, but on the assumption that invidious and statistical discrimination have been otherwise addressed, substantial deviations from legitimate merit-based criteria are likely to attract sharply diminished social support, in part because they impose disproportionate costs on sub-sets of the population.

What would be the sanction for employers who refuse to negotiate voluntary contracts in which targets were set for enhancing minority hiring over time? Here, it seems to me, much less weight than in the past should be placed on the force of legal sanctions. Rather, much greater weight should be placed on the dissemination of information—information about which employers have refused to negotiate affirmative action programmes and their current employment record with respect to racial minorities and women; which employers have failed to realize targets previously agreed to and their employment record with respect to racial minorities and women. Systematic collation and public dissemination of this information in readily accessible and comparative form by region, industrial category, and discipline would then permit individual citizens, as present or potential shareholders, as present or potential employees, or as present or potential customers to determine what relationship, if any, they wish to pursue with firms in the light of their employment record. An employer entering into a contract with an appropriate state agency under which commitments are made as to racial and gender hiring targets should be immune from public and private legal sanctions for statistical discrimination (disparate impact) but not invidious discrimination (disparate treatment), as long as the targets are being met. This approach is sensitive to individual autonomy concerns, and it gambles on the fact that an overwhelming majority of the population support strong anti-discrimination laws and will, as individual economic agents (as opposed to voters), be prepared, so to speak, to put their money where their mouths are (as with consumer preferences for environmentally friendly products).

A second strategy with respect to affirmative action programmes that seems to me appealing in terms of narrowing divergences among the major normative perspectives reviewed above is to seek out means for spreading the costs of these programmes more broadly.[57] For example, a collective commitment to provide resources to add additional places for minorities in university programmes, such as professional schools, and wage or training subsidies to employers who are prepared to add minorities to their payrolls, has the potential for mitigating both the disproportionate burden otherwise borne by employers in some contexts and the so-called innocent white male phenomenon. Although it is true that these additional opportunities financed out of collective resources could be made available to all, the empirical evidence briefly reviewed in earlier chapters on widely held perceptions of fairness suggests that forgone opportunities of potential gains are not as deeply felt as losses of what are perceived to be existing entitlements. I appreciate that designing these "add-on" programmes is not straightforward, particularly in the private sector, where it would be difficult to ensure that employers are indeed creating additional opportunities for members of minorities, rather than simply transferring the cost of employment decisions that they would have made anyway to the public purse. However, these problems do not seem so intractable that sensible schemes to mitigate them could not be designed.

A third feature of a defensible affirmative action strategy that must be addressed is its breadth of coverage. Although the question of which groups are to benefit from such a programme is highly sensitive, if the focus of the programme is not to be excessively diffused, if the burden it is asked to bear is to be kept manageable, and if a bureaucratic swamp is to be avoided, priorities have to be chosen. Given both the history of slavery and subjugation to which blacks have been subjected and contemporary indicators of the grim legacy of this history for their social and economic status, blacks seem to me to have a preeminent claim to affirmative action. This may imply leaving outside the scope of most affirmative action programmes (but not other prohibitions against discrimination) other visible minorities, women, the mentally and physically handicapped, and gays and lesbians. This proposal will provoke strong dissent, but asking affirmative action programmes—controversial in any context—to bear the burden of redressing all of society's injustices is to risk achieving nothing. The political and economic capital they entail is too scarce to bear this burden.

A fourth desirable feature of a concerted affirmative action strategy, but only if implemented as part of a broader mix of policies—most crucially supply-side policies—would be to explicitly and legally time-limit or sunset it from the outset, for example, to confine its operational life to two decades, so as to provide time for supply-side policies to take hold but also so as to avoid stretching the fragile social consensus supporting such programmes beyond the breaking point. When such a strategy has expired, it would seem desirable to allow both private and public employers to continue experimenting with different forms of affirmative action programmes if they so wish, preferably following discussions and negotiations with their workforces,[58] given how little we know about what policies will or will not work in redressing the consequences of racial discrimination. U.S. Supreme Court decisions currently seem to largely take this view in the case of private sector affirmative action programmes, but it is not clear why public sector employers or educational institutions should not (despite decisions like *Bakke*[59]) be equally free, although not legally obligated, to engage in similar experimentation.[60] Beyond the time-frame of the state-orchestrated affirmative action strategy, the state's only continuing role (other than enforcement of invidious and statistical discrimination laws) might be to collect and publicly disseminate comparative information about private and public employers' records on employment of blacks.

Beyond these demand-side policies, it seems absolutely crucial to place a heavy relative emphasis on supply-side policies.[61] Massive migration of blacks from the South in the two decades after World War II dramatically transformed the demographic character of many U.S. cities: Chicago grew from 8 percent black in 1940 to 40 percent in 1980; Cleveland from 10 percent to 44 percent; Washington from 28 percent to 70 percent.[62] This movement has unfortunately been followed by white flight to the suburbs,[63] along with many economic activities and jobs, and the disappearance of well-paid blue collar jobs in many manufacturing ("smoke stack") industries, in part as a result of increased import competition. As a matter of normative theory, distributive justice policies that spread the costs broadly among the advantaged classes and distribute the benefits broadly among the disadvantaged class or classes have very strong appeal. Moreover, empirically, the evidence seems to suggest that demand-side regulation, no matter how strong, has major limits in terms of efficacy. This is not surprising. Policies that attack a problem at the back-end, where members of disadvantaged groups have been allowed to live through their formative years in circumstances of deprivation, and then subsequently seek to redress the consequences, seem almost certain to be less effective than attacking the problem closer to its source.[64] However, policy design in this context is not straightforward. As the mixed record of the so-called Great Society programmes of the 1960s indicates, simply throwing money at problems relatively indiscriminately is unlikely to be effective (the performance of HUD in the low-income housing field provides one example). However, a wide range of initiatives might sensibly be contemplated with respect to the quality of public education in the city cores, pre-natal and post-natal care programmes, early childhood (pre-school) educational programmes, enhanced elementary school facilities for learning disadvantaged children, improved transportation networks with the suburbs (where better paying jobs are increasingly located), improved law and order services in inner-city neighbourhoods, enhanced health care facilities, and so on. In many cases, appropriate government agencies could contract with local community groups to provide innovative programmes in these areas. In other contexts, experimentation with school voucher systems, with enhanced voucher benefits for members of disadvantaged groups, may be worth experimenting with to encourage both competition and diversity in responses to the needs of these groups. If there is to be a "peace dividend" from the end of the Cold War, these are surely the priority claims.

WILL THE CYCLE BE UNBROKEN?

The Economist—not a journal known for its radical positions on economic or social issues—in a series of recent articles about "America's Wasted Blacks" wrote:

> The slums in America's great cities are shameful. They are a damning indictment of the richest country in the world. The problems that fester in them are not peripheral: they constitute America's main domestic challenge today. The nation now has a quarter of a century's worth of anti-poverty experiments.

That poverty persists despite these efforts is less a reason to give up than a reason to learn from what works and what does not . . . America cannot afford to let down its blacks for much longer.[65]

In 1965, Lyndon Johnson told Congress that "If we stand passively by while the center of each city becomes a hive of deprivation, crime and hopelessness . . . if we become two people, the suburban affluent and the urban poor, each filled with mistrust and fear for the other . . . then we shall effectively cripple each generation to come." A generation has passed, and the crippling goes on.[66]

Trading with Aliens: International Trade Policy

The Basic Theory of International Trade

The basic economic theory of the mutual gains realizable from international trade, despite many modern refinements and elaborations,[67] is simply an aspect of the more general economic theory of the mutual gains from exchange in any voluntary contractual relationship. These gains were long ago demonstrated by Adam Smith in *The Wealth of Nations,* and his famous pin-making example still serves to illustrate the gains to be realized from specialization and exchange. Few of us find it rational to grow all our own food, make all our own clothing, build our own shelter, administer our own medical services, and so on. In its extreme form, this kind of self-sufficiency or autarky entails an existence similar to that of the hermit or caveman. In fact, most of us specialize in producing goods or services for others and sometimes for ourselves but buy goods or services for other needs from producers who specialize in their production. But if this kind of specialization within communities is rational, Smith argued that specialization and exchange among members of different communities is equally rational. He rejected then current mercantilist notions that buying imports transferred scarce gold currency into foreign hands, diminished national wealth, and reduced domestic employment. Thus, on Smith's theory of the gains from specialization, it makes no sense for Canadians or Americans to attempt to produce their own rice or pineapples if these can be purchased from foreigners more cheaply because of different endowments in climate, soil, skills, and so on. Alternatively, it may make no sense for producers in these foreign countries to build their own telephone systems or hydro-electric generators if we can supply them at a higher quality or lower price.

David Ricardo early in the nineteenth century extended Smith's theory of absolute advantage into a theory of comparative advantage which sought to demonstrate that even countries that are less efficient than other countries in everything they produce will still find it rational to trade.[68] He advanced this theory by means of a simple example. In his example, England could produce a given quantity of cloth with the labour of one hundred men. It could also produce a given quantity of wine with the labour of one hundred and twenty men. Portugal, in turn, could produce the same quantity of cloth with the labour of ninety men and the same quantity of wine with the labour of eighty men. Thus, Portugal enjoyed an absolute advantage over England with respect to the production of both cloth and wine; that is, it could produce a given quantity of cloth or wine with fewer labour inputs than England. However, Ricardo argued that trade was still mutually advantageous: when England exported to Portugal the cloth produced by the labour of one hundred men in exchange for wine produced by eighty Portuguese, it imported wine that would have required the labour of one hundred and twenty Englishmen to produce. As for Portugal, it gained by the labour of its eighty men cloth that it would have taken ninety of its labourers to produce. Both countries are thus better off through trade. Another way of understanding the intuition is to imagine the following simple domestic example.[69] Suppose a lawyer is not only more efficient in the provision of legal services than her secretary, but is also a more efficient secretary. It takes the secretary twice as long as the lawyer to type a document. Suppose, more specifically, that it takes the lawyer's secretary two hours to type a document that the lawyer could type in one hour, and that the secretary's hourly wage is twenty dollars, while the lawyer's hourly rate is two hundred dollars. It will benefit the lawyer to hire the secretary and pay her forty dollars to type the document in two hours and sell for two hundred dollars the hour of her own time that would otherwise have been spent typing the document. In other words, both the lawyer and the secretary gain from this exchange. These examples, in an international trade context, generalize to the proposition that a country should specialize in producing and exporting goods in which its comparative advantage is greatest, or comparative disadvantage is smallest, and should import goods in which its comparative disadvantage is greatest.

An unfortunate semantic legacy of Ricardo's demonstration of the gains from international trade that has been perpetuated in the terminology of trade literature and debate is that in international trade *countries* are trading with each other. This, of course, is rarely the case. As in purely domestic exchanges, *private economic actors* (albeit located in different countries) are trading with each other. In its most rudimentary form, international trade theory seeks only to demonstrate that free international trade dramatically broadens the contract opportunity set available to private economic actors and hence, the mutual gains realizable from exchange as parties with different endowments of specialized skills or resources are able to reap the gains from their differential advantages and disadvantages through trade.

It may be argued that in international exchanges, in contrast to domestic exchanges, part of the gains from exchange are realized by foreigners, and that a country would be advantaged by capturing all the gains from exchange for itself. However, this raises the question of whether the domestic gains forgone by foreign trade are greater or less than the additional gains from purely domestic exchange. As a matter of simple economic theory, the gains to domestic consumers from foreign trade will almost always be greater than the additional gains to domestic producers from purely domestic trade. This is so because higher domestic than foreign prices will entail a transfer of resources from domestic consumers to domestic producers (arguably creating matching decreases and increases in welfare), but *in addition* some domestic consumers will be priced out of the market by the higher domestic prices and will be forced to allocate their resources to less preferred consumption choices, entailing a dead-weight social loss. An alternative way in which to conceive of the net domestic loss from forgone foreign exchange opportunities is to ask what compensation domestic producers would need to offer domestic consumers to render them indifferent to these forgone opportunities. Presumably only domestic prices that matched foreign producers' prices would achieve this end. These simple theoretical propositions, as we shall see, are amply borne out by the evidence.

The Historical Experience

The history of the application of the free trade idea in national and international policy-making in the intervening two centuries since the publication of *The Wealth of Nations* has been a checkered one.[70] Perhaps the low point was the infamous Smoot-Hawley tariff, adopted by the United States in 1930, which raised duties on imports to an average of 60 percent. This piece of protectionist legislation is widely accepted by economists as having severely aggravated the Great Depression. By inducing similar retaliatory measures by other countries, it caused international trade to come largely to a standstill.

Although this experience continues to hold important lessons for us today, I wish to focus on the decades following World War II. In 1947, as part of the Bretton Woods Agreement for post-war economic reconstruction, the General Agreement on Tariffs and Trade (GATT) was entered into by about twenty of the world's major trading countries. This agreement sought to outlaw discriminatory trade restrictions and to facilitate the successive lowering of tariffs and other trade barriers through multilateral negotiations.[71] In the course of seven subsequent negotiating rounds now involving almost one hundred countries, customs duties and import taxes have dropped dramatically. Worldwide, average tariff rates on manufactured goods have fallen from 40 percent in 1947 to between 5 and 6 percent in 1987.[72] The 1988 Free Trade Agreement with the United States, which precipitated the most passionately contested Canadian general election in recent decades, will see remaining tariffs between the two countries cut to zero over a ten-year period and various non-trade barriers to trade substantially reduced. The current Uruguay multilateral round of GATT negotiations is also likely to further lower tariffs and other trade barriers globally. From a global welfare perspective, multilateral trade liberalization is strongly preferable to regional trade liberalization because regional trading blocs inherently discriminate in favour of members and against more efficient non-members—that is, they involve trade diversion as well as trade expansion.[73]

From a Canadian perspective (which in most respects can be viewed as representative of the experience of other developed countries) what have been the implications of this unprecedented reduction in tariffs on both imports and exports since World War II?[74] Between 1947 and 1986, Canada's merchandise imports grew by 552 percent in real terms, and its merchandise exports by 564 percent in real terms. For Canada, post-war multilateral trade liberalization has to a large extent entailed bilateral trade expansion with the United States.

The Impact on Employment

What has happened to the welfare of Canadians during this period of trade liberalization? From 1947 to 1986, per capita GDP in Canada rose in real terms from $7,402 to $19,925 (1986 $)—an increase of 169.2 percent. Total employment grew from 4,821,000 in 1947 to 12,295,000 in April 1988 (an increase of 155.0 percent), with manufacturing employment rising 88.7 percent from 1,131,750 to 2,136,000 during this period. At the same time, of course, Canadian consumers have enjoyed dramatically increased product choices and lower product prices because of imports. Although it would be naive to suggest that these increases in jobs and incomes are wholly or even primarily attributable to trade liberalization and expansion, at least the opposite proposition so often asserted—that continued trade liberalization is likely to reduce real incomes and employment—is revealed to be unfounded. Although trade liberalization can and does have negative impacts on jobs and wages in particular domestic sectors which are vulnerable to imports, the net effect on jobs and wages economy-wide has been strongly positive. For workers in sectors adversely impacted by imports, generous and well-conceived domestic adjustment assistance programs, rather than trade protection, can deal most effectively with transition costs.

The Impact on Social Policies

Not only has the post-war period of trade liberalization seen these enormous increases in real incomes and employment, but it has also simultaneously witnessed the emergence of the modern welfare state. Public expenditures in Canada on education have risen from $147 per capita in 1947 to $1,237 per capita in 1983–1984 in real terms (1986 $), or from 1.99 percent of GDP to 6.79 percent. Public expenditures on health care have risen from $54 per capita in 1947 to $1,202 per capita in 1985 in real terms (1986 $), or from 0.72 percent of GDP to 6.18 percent. Direct financial benefits paid to Canadians under various social welfare programs amounted to $49,136 million in 1985, compared with 1947 expenditures of $3,838 million on all "public welfare" programs (including health) (1986 $). Federal transfer payments to the provinces have risen from the equivalent of 0.12 percent of GDP in 1947 to 4.04 percent in 1986. Public expenditures on cultural activities have risen from negligible amounts in 1947 to 0.74 percent of GDP in 1984–1985. Over the same period, greatly increased regulatory attention has been paid to occupational health and safety and environmental issues. Trade liberalization and trade expansion have not been inconsistent with these redistributional, social, and cultural policies. History again reveals this fear to be a phantom. Indeed, the simple truism is often overlooked that only relatively prosperous countries can afford generous social policies. Impoverished third-world countries do not have such policies, not because they lack commitment to them in principle, but because they do not have the wealth to afford them. Creating wealth is a precondition to redistributing it.

Thus, nothing in the theory or history of trade liberalization and expansion is inconsistent with increasing real incomes and employment or compassionate and civilized social and cultural policies. In fact, we have every reason to believe that only by exploiting our comparative advantage to the fullest can we sustain increasing prosperity and the social policies that such prosperity makes possible.

The Impact on Cultural Diversity

A communitarian perspective, which figured prominently in the Canada-United States free trade debate, emphasizes the dangers to national cultural identity presented by free trade and full international mobility of labour and capital. Distinctive ways of life and cultural values are threatened by the homogenizing effects of economic and technological imperialism. This point of view, which has its roots in the critique by Rousseau and the nineteenth-century political romantic movement of classical political economy, and also in the Jeffersonian alternative to the commercial republic, has found its leading Canadian exponent in the philosopher George Grant.[75]

One must find somewhat unrealistic the romanticized "closed community" conception of contemporary critics of liberalism. Traditional closed societies may have preserved distinctive customs and beliefs against external influences, but only at the cost of racial, religious, and ideological intolerance, and of significant limits on individual self-development. If we were really to avoid the consequences of contemporary cosmopolitanism, trade barriers would hardly be enough—we would need strict censorship, exit visas, limits on ethnic diversity, and other measures aimed at maintaining the "closedness" of the community.

In any event, in the post-war decades, when we have witnessed such enormous increases in international trade, particularly bilateral trade, we have simultaneously witnessed the flowering of nationalism in Quebec and the increasingly confident assertion of a distinct French-Canadian cultural and linguistic identity. In this same period, we have also witnessed an enormous influx of immigrants from a great diversity of cultural backgrounds that has immeasurably enriched Canada's multicultural mosaic, rendering Canada one of the most vibrant and tolerant cosmopolitan societies in the world. This is not the traditional Canada that George Grant so nostalgically recalled in *Lament for a Nation*,[76] but neither have we become part of a homogenized, universalistic American culture as he portended. We are and will remain a profoundly different society, as a comparison of daily life in Windsor and Detroit or Toronto and Buffalo should convince the doubtful reader. There are surely deeper measures of a society's cultural evolution than how many minutes are occupied by which country's soap operas on local commercial television networks. Although liberal trading policies cannot claim direct credit for our increased cultural diversity and distinctiveness, a close intellectual concomitant of liberal trading policies— more liberal immigration policies—clearly can claim substantial credit. It is not philosophically consistent to urge open and liberal immigration policies but to advocate at the same time closed and illiberal trade policies that deprive potential immigrants of economic opportunities in their home countries, thus leaving them with no option but to sever their roots and emigrate.

The Rise of the New Protectionism

Despite both the theoretical and the empirical support that exists for the virtues of free trade, the last decade and a half—a period when the global economy experienced two oil price shocks, three world-wide recessions, and the rise of Japan and the other NICs—has simultaneously witnessed a sharp increase in the use of quantitative restrictions: quotas, voluntary export restraints (VERs) and orderly marketing agreements (OMAs), typically negotiated on a bilateral basis outside the safeguard provisions (Article XIX) of the GATT and in clear violation of its letter or spirit.[77] The increasing significance of non-tariff barriers to trade (NTRs) is well captured in Figure 7.

In addition to the increase in the use of quantitative restrictions, various forms of contingent protection—most notably anti-dumping (in the United States, the E.C., Australia, and Canada) and countervailing duties (almost exclusively in the United States)—have been increasingly applied by governments, especially with respect to the trade values covered, against allegedly dumped or subsidized imports.[78] In 1985, a full 5 percent of U.S. imports were challenged under at least one of the U.S. trade remedy laws.[79]

Many of the new forms of protectionism and indeed residual aspects of the old protectionism are directed by developed countries against imports from Japan, from newly industrializing countries (NICs) predominantly

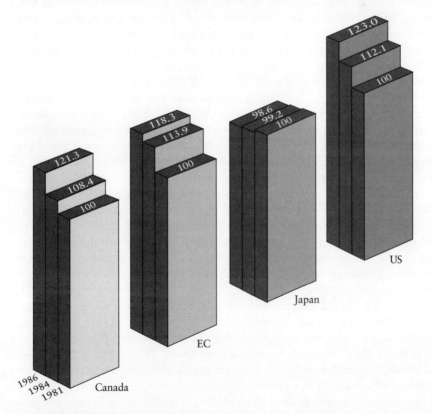

Figure 7. Import-coverage indexes of selected non-tariff barriers in Canada, the European Economic Community (excluding Portugal and Spain), Japan, and the United States for the years 1981–1986, where 100 is the index for 1981.

located in South East Asia, and from Third World or developing countries.[80] Border restrictions and domestic subsidies severely restrict imports of sugar, rice, cotton, tobacco, beef, and vegetable oils from developing countries. With respect to processed agricultural products, including non-competing tropical agricultural commodities and processed natural resources, developed countries often apply escalating tariffs to these products, depending on the stage of processing they have attained prior to importation, in order to protect processing activities in developed countries, and thus deny developing countries the opportunity of building processing industries of their own. With respect to manufactured goods, tariffs on textiles, clothing, rubber, leather, and footwear are systematically higher than tariffs on other manufactured goods. Moreover, non-tariff barriers, including quotas, imposed by developed countries on developing countries' manufacturing exports are especially severe. These non-tariff barriers to trade apply particularly to textiles, clothing, steel, footwear, consumer electrical and electronic goods, motor vehicles, ships, and chemicals.[81] Reflecting a massive exercise in hypocrisy, the costs of protectionist policies imposed by developed countries on developing countries exceed the entire value of foreign aid provided to these countries.[82]

Many of the arguments invoked to justify these trade restrictions are spurious. For example, it is often argued that it is unfair for workers in industrialized countries to have to compete with imports from Third World countries, where wage levels are much lower. But lower wage costs are one of the principal comparative advantages that these countries possess and are no different conceptually from Canada or the United States possessing a comparative advantage, through good fortune, in certain kinds of natural resources. It is no more unfair for us to exploit that comparative advantage than it is for developing countries to exploit theirs in terms of the availability of a large, unskilled, and relatively low-cost labour force. To deny them the opportunity to exploit this comparative advantage is to deny them the opportunity to get on the same escalator that we rode in the earlier stages of the industrial revolution. Moreover, it does not necessarily follow that because wage costs are lower in these countries we cannot compete with them. If, because of higher capital intensity, superior education or job skills, and greater technological and managerial sophistication and innovation, the productivity of labour is greater in industrialized countries, this will in many cases more than offset differences in wage costs. Where this is not so, we should reallocate our resources to other activities where we possess a comparative advantage. It is also sometimes argued that it is unfair for consumers in industrialized countries to take advantage of imports that are produced by low-cost labour. But, given the paucity of other economic opportunities in many of these countries, it is not clear how we advance the welfare of workers in these countries by denying them jobs at all.

A burgeoning political discourse surrounding the notion of "fair" (or "unfair") trade, or "level playing fields," raises analogous arguments in other contexts. For example, it is now often argued that lax environmental laws, child labour laws, and workplace safety laws in many developing and other countries constitute unfair forms of implicit subsidies to producers in these countries relative to producers in developed countries who must meet more demanding (and costly) standards. Alternatively, it is argued that as a matter of paternalism we should insist, out of concern for the welfare of various groups in developing countries, that they adopt standards similar to ours as a condition of the right to trade with us. However, given the impossibility of complete harmonization of all domestic policies in every trading nation that may, directly or indirectly, affect comparative advantage (that is, most domestic policies), trade protectionism quickly becomes the default option.[83]

Whatever the impact of trade restrictions imposed by industrialized countries on Third World countries, the trade restrictions make no sense in terms of the importing countries' own welfare. For example, it makes no sense to "tax" U.S. consumers of specialty steel $1 million per year for each job preserved in the domestic specialty steel industry when the average compensation per worker was less than $60,000, or to "tax" U.S. consumers of automobiles $160,000 per year for each job preserved in the domestic auto industry when the average annual compensation of U.S. autoworkers is less than one quarter of this figure.[84] Equally, in a Canadian context, it makes no sense to "tax" consumers of footwear between $53,668 and $69,460 per year for each job saved in the industry when average earnings per worker at the time of the estimates were $7,145 p.a., or to "tax" consumers of textile and clothing between $40,600 and $50,982 per year for each job saved when the average earnings per worker at the time of the estimates were $10,000 p.a., or to "tax" consumers of automobiles between $179,000 and $226,394 per year for each job saved when average earnings in the industry at the time of the estimates were between $29,000 and $35,000.[85] Even a 100 percent wage subsidy for workers threatened with job displacement by imports would, at the limit, be socially less costly than these trade restrictions.

Ethical Perspectives on Trade and Adjustment Policies

An ethical perspective on trade and adjustment policies has more elusive implications for policy than the economic perspective, in part because there are many ethical paradigms. Utilitarianism in many ways provides the underpinnings for modern welfare economics and would tend to suggest similar implications to the economic perspective. One difference is that utilitarianism would be unlikely to distinguish, as an efficiency perspective would typically do, between the social and the private costs of adjustment—both are sources of individual disutility and should be weighed against the gains in utility to other members of the community from trade liberalization in arriving at a determination of whether average utility (not simply income) has been increased.[86] The private and psychic costs of change may be substantial[87] and may significantly narrow the gap between the gains to consumers from trade liberalization and the benefits of trade protection as reflected only in incomes preserved.

A Kantian social contract perspective, at least in its modern Rawlsian version,[88] would take the view that behind the hypothetical veil of ignorance, where the social contract is constructed and where our individual lots in life and endowments are not known, we would all agree that no collective policy should be pursued that does not improve the lot of the least advantaged. In other words, we would all agree to a form of social insurance against the risk of finding ourselves in the position of the least advantaged. However, Rawls accepts that not every transaction or policy in society must meet this standard, provided that the basic structural rules of society are compatible with it. Thus, though trade liberalization may sometimes impose disproportionate costs on some of the least advantaged groups in society, it seems reasonable to infer that Rawls would accept that instruments other than trade protection may more efficiently meet his distributive justice goal without sacrificing the increases in the welfare of others that trade liberalization may entail.

A major difficulty with both the utilitarian and the social contract ethical perspectives, in the international trade context, is that it is not clear why (as is often assumed) national boundaries should be assigned any special ethical significance.[89] If a global perspective is adopted, then utilitarianism would require that the disutility caused to individuals in foreign countries from domestic trade restrictions should be weighed in the utilitarian calculus. If one accepts the declining marginal utility of money and the fact that interpersonal comparison of utilities is possible (which is admittedly controversial), one might argue that the disutility caused to low-income foreign workers from domestic trade restrictions should be assigned special weight.[90] Similarly, a global social contract perspective would require that the lot of the least well endowed globally should be given a special ethical pre-eminence. In both cases, a global perspective would seem to militate strongly against the maintenance of trade restrictions by industrialized countries against NICs and LDCs, or at least that foreign aid of equivalent value to the latter of trading opportunities forgone would be ethically dictated.[91] However, aid on this scale is likely to exceed the compensation required to meet all losses to domestic interests in industrialized countries from trade liberalization. Moreover, it is not clear what purposes might be specified for the aid if production of exports displacing domestic production in the importing country is foreclosed.

A third ethical perspective which has gained considerable attention in recent years is that of communitarianism. Communitarians see the autonomous individual self of liberal theory as reflecting an impoverished conception of human life. According to this perspective, it is "constitutive attachments" to particular communities, groups, and institutions which make human life rich and which are formative of true human identities.[92]

In a number of respects the communitarian perspective may suggest policies which diverge considerably from those driven by utilitarian or liberal individualist perspectives. Whereas the latter are able to conceptualize the psychic costs of change as real costs, which may merit compensation, for the communitarian the "exit" option—even when accompanied by such compensation—may still seem unjustified, if exit involves severing the bonds to extended family, neighbourhood, region, or colleagues. Loss of a significant part of one's human identity may simply not be compensable through redistributive policies. Policies which enhance the stay option may be preferred, where they are able to keep intact the attachments which, according to the communitarian, make life worth living. Still, even here certain "stay" instruments would be preferred over others. For example, programmes which create long-term jobs through subsidies would be preferable to trade restrictions. Trade restrictions, unlike labour subsidies, need not prevent firms from replacing labour with capital in the production process and hence are an uncertain hedge against the kinds of employment dislocations which communitarians seek to prevent. The rents that firms, including foreign firms, capture from trade restrictions may well be invested abroad or in other industries or regions of the country that are not in decline, rather than used to preserve or create employment opportunities in the affected area. Retraining policies which permit workers to find jobs in the same locality would be both attractive to communitarians and broadly consistent with the "exit" option in the strict sense of exit from the industry that is in decline.

Of course, not all the humanly significant attachments will be preserved (the workplace will change and with it, co-workers), but as Sandel admits, "Each of us moves in an indefinite number of communities, some more inclusive than others, each making different claims on our allegiance."[93] It would be difficult even for a committed communitarian to argue that the government should intervene to prevent all changes in these various interwoven loyalties and ties.

Within the mainstream of policy debate in liberal democratic societies, all three ethical perspectives have prominence and the legitimacy that comes from expressing the felt needs of a substantial number of voting citizens. This pluralism is also reinforced by the reality that each perspective taken to its extreme would self-destruct or lead to a result so intolerable to a large number of citizens that it would disenfranchise their needs. A pure aggregate efficiency perspective, with no concern for the distributive consequences of adjustment, would lead to the kind of gap between rich and poor which, as the overwhelming public support for a wide range of social welfare policies suggests, has become intolerable to a majority of citizens. By contrast, a society that totally neglected the efficiency consequences of its decisions in favour of redistributive or communitarian goals would eventually find itself with a very small pie left to distribute, as well as with communities dying from stagnation rather than from too rapid change.

Similarly, complete exclusion of community concerns would be a disenfranchisement of important needs. Economists and liberal individualists tend to view mobility between jobs and regions as enhancing human autonomy and choice. Yet one does not need to accept the more extreme claims of communitarianism to recognize that the rapidity of change and the abrupt manner in which it dissolves long-standing relationships and routines may outweigh possible long-term benefits, particularly for older members of the workforce. Olson notes that societies characterized by high levels of geographical and employment mobility, and by rapid economic change, also typically experience certain concomitant social costs—including high suicide, divorce and mental illness rates, and serious problems with alcohol and drug abuse.[94]

These considerations suggest a significant role for communitarianism in the formulation of adjustment policies. To economists, of course, policies which actually retard the speed of a market-driven reallocation of labour and capital are less justifiable than those which are merely compensatory. But in a morally pluralistic society, it is not enough simply to "pay off" the losers—the values they hold dear must continue to have a legitimate place in the policy process.

From each of the three ethical perspectives (utilitarianism, social contractarianism, and communitarianism) there is an argument for government intervention to address trade-induced employment dislocations. The argument rests on the consequences of such dislocations for workers, their families, and their communities. Whereas a total disregard of the consequences of policies for economic efficiency would clearly constitute a form of folly, it is entirely understandable that voters will make some sacrifice of efficiency in order to preserve community stability or to enhance social justice.

The evidence suggests that the dysfunction in the policy process lies in the choice of instruments often employed to vindicate the non-economic ethical goals of protection. Utilitarian, social contractarian, and communitarian ethical theories are all compatible with "net benefit maximization":[95] Because there are scarce resources available with which to achieve legitimate public ends, the particular benefit sought by a given policy should be achieved at the least economic cost, and with the fewest harmful side-effects to other legitimate policy goals.

Certain instrument choices are much more capable than others of reconciling economic efficiency goals and a plurality of the ethical perspectives. From an economic point of view, tariffs in general are less economically pernicious than global quotas, and global quotas are less pernicious than discriminatory quantitative restrictions such as VERs. This ranking is consistent with all three ethical perspectives: the scarcity or cartelization rents which characterize quotas and VERs represent an unjustified transfer of wealth from domestic consumers to domestic and foreign producers.

With respect to industrial subsidies, an economic perspective would suggest that subsidies which provide incentives or compensation to firms to exit from declining industries are the least undesirable instrument. Utilitarians and social contractarians, however, would question the ethical justification for compensating firms for the negative effects of economic change. Communitarians might prefer the economically more pernicious instrument of production subsidies, because they guarantee maintenance of employment in a particular community or region. From all three ethical perspectives, subsidies for modernization would be acceptable if in fact they led to preservation of jobs in a revitalized, newly competitive industry. However, the evidence suggests that where industrial policy has focused on modernization or rationalization, the productivity gains have primarily been realized through shedding of labour by substituting capital. Since from all three ethical perspectives the dislocation effects of change on workers, their families, and communities are of paramount importance, there is reason for concern that modernization subsidies may not in fact retard, and may even accelerate, such dislocation effects. A form of subsidy consistent with all three ethical perspectives would be an incentive to non-declining firms within a given community or region to retrain and employ displaced workers. Assuming new, permanent jobs were thus created—which would depend on whether the elasticity of the firms' demand for labour is greater than for firms in the declining industry—this kind of subsidy would be preferable from an economic perspective to production subsidies to the declining industry and would be broadly consistent with the exit option.

In labour market adjustment policies, the economically optimal instrument would be adequately funded adjustment services, encompassing training, retraining, mobility, and counselling benefits, as well as income support during the job search process. Such assistance would also be consistent with both the utilitarian and the social contractarian ethical perspectives, which view compensation to workers for the real costs of change as the principal goal of industrial policy. From the communitarian perspective, though, adjustment assistance which emphasizes mobility of labour between communities and regions will be counter-indicated. However, adjustment assistance policies which focus on successful relocation of workers *within* a given region or community will be consistent with communitarian goals. From an economic perspective, public sector job creation and income support tied to continued employment of workers in the declining industry are clearly inferior to adjustment assistance. Although communitarians in particular may be inclined to support these policies inasmuch as they keep workers employed within a given community, such policies do not address the long-term economic viability of the community, and they threaten to create permanent dependence on public assistance. Communitarians must be concerned not only about the preservation of community life, but also about its future quality.

This ranking of instruments from the economic and ethical perspectives suggests that some instrument choices are inferior from all perspectives (for instance, discriminatory quantitative restrictions such as VERs). However, the relative desirability of many of the other instruments considered varies depending upon the perspective adopted. Policy-makers must take up the challenge of finding a mix of instruments which more adequately reconciles economic efficiency and a plurality of ethical goals in the particular circumstances of the case.

For instance, in small communities such as Quebec, where textile plants employ a large, middle-aged, unilingual francophone, mainly low-skilled, low-paid workforce, comprising mainly female secondary earners, and where few alternative job opportunities exist within the same locality, trade restrictions (perhaps degressive) or job maintenance subsidies may be the only means of vindicating communitarian goals. In other situations, where a declining firm has a diverse workforce of young, middle-aged and older employees, and where some employment alternatives exist within the community, the margins are wider for a creative instrument mix. The younger workers might be offered adjustment assistance to relocate or to retrain for other jobs within the same community; some, after all, will probably prefer enhanced personal opportunity over community ties. The middle-aged workers might be given jobs elsewhere in the community through an employment creation subsidy, and older workers could be offered an early retirement package, partly subsidized by the government.

The existence of these under-utilized margins for more rational choice in domestic policies challenges the frequent characterization of the New Protectionism as a failure or dysfunction in the international liberal trading order, with *national* self-interest triumphing over global welfare and international legal norms. Nor can the New Protectionism be characterized as a conscious social choice for justice over economic efficiency, since the policy outcomes chosen are often sub-optimal from *both* economic *and* legitimate non-economic ethical perspectives. This evokes a dysfunction in the domestic political process, which produces instrument choices incompatible with any widely held normative concept of the national interest.

The appropriate starting point for reform would therefore be analysis and correction of those aspects of the domestic policy process that produce measures which have relatively high domestic costs and relatively modest, illusory, or redistributively regressive benefits, and which lead to a preference for more over less costly instruments to achieve given objectives.

Living with Aliens: Immigration Policy

Classical free trade theory assumed that goods could often readily be traded across national borders but that the factors of production employed to produce those goods (land, capital, and labour) were fixed and immobile. In the contemporary world, largely as a result of technological changes, this has become dramatically untrue of capital, and much less true of labour. However, the frequent resistance to international mobility of goods is often dramatically intensified in the case of the international mobility of people. Here we move from the domain of international trade policy to the domain of immigration policy.

In the following discussion I will address a question that has confronted all individuals and groups of individuals who, throughout history, have chosen to live in a state of civil society with one another and for whom social, political, and economic relationships are integral to the self-definition of each individual in the community of which they are a part: How does one define and justify the conditions of membership in the community? In the context of the modern nation state, our attention is directed primarily to the substance and procedures of our immigration policies—who may become citizens and who must remain strangers—for nations imply boundaries and boundaries at some point imply closure.

It is a trite truth to observe that we, as Canadians or Americans, are countries of immigrants, as is indeed true of most of the countries of the so-called New World. This does not imply, and has never implied, that entry into our communities is open to all. Indeed, central features of the social, political, and economic history of Canada and the United States have surrounded debates over what the terms of our immigration policies should be. It is an equally trite prediction that immigration issues will continue to dominate debates in the future about what it means to be a Canadian or an American and to be a member of the Canadian or American community.

The Values

LIBERTY

At the heart of debates in all western democracies over immigration policy now, and in the past, lie two core values which stand to some irreducible degree in opposition to each other: liberty and community. Theories of liberty and community each present almost endless variations, but for our purposes, the essence of the two values, in the context of immigration policy, can be fairly readily captured. As Carens points out: "[All liberal] theories begin with some kind of assumption about the equal moral worth of individuals. In one way or another, all treat the individual as prior to the community. These foundations provide little basis for drawing fundamental distinctions between citizens and aliens who seek to become citizens."[96]

Carens goes on to review three contemporary approaches to liberal theory: libertarianism, social contractarianism, and utilitarianism. From the libertarian perspective, exemplified by scholars such as Nozick, individual property rights play a central role. In a state of nature, individuals have rights to acquire and use property and to alienate it voluntarily. The existence of the state is justified only to the extent that it is required to protect property rights and facilitate their voluntary transfer. On this view, if aliens wish to move to Canada or the United States, they should be free to do so, provided that they do not violate anyone else's rights. To the extent that citizens choose to enter into contracts of employment with such individuals, or sell them land, homes, or businesses, the rights of both citizens and aliens would be violated by externally imposed constraints thereon. From a social contractarian perspective, as exemplified most prominently by the writings of John Rawls, an ideal social constitution would be constructed behind a veil of ignorance, where individuals know nothing about their own personal situations, class, race, sex, natural talents, religious beliefs, individual goals, values, talents, and so on. The purpose of the veil of ignorance is to nullify the effect of specific contingencies which put men at odds, because natural and social contingencies are arbitrary from a moral point of view, and therefore are factors which ought not to influence the choice of principles of justice.

As Carens points out, whether one is a citizen of a rich nation or a poor nation and whether one is already a citizen of a particular state or an alien who wishes to become a citizen are specific contingencies of the kind that could set people at odds; a fair procedure for choosing principles of justice should therefore exclude knowledge of these circumstances, just as it excludes knowledge of one's race, sex, or social class. We should take a global, not a national, view of the original position (the "universal brotherhood of man"). Behind this global veil of ignorance, and considering possible restrictions on freedom, we should adopt the perspective of those who would be most disadvantaged by the restrictions, in this case often the perspective of the alien who wants to immigrate. From this point of view, very few restrictions on immigration can be morally justified. Rawls would recognize that liberty may be restricted for the sake of liberty, in the sense that all liberties depend on the existence of public order and security. To cite a metaphor used by Carens, it does no one any good to take so many people into a lifeboat that it is swamped and everyone drowns.[97] But short of a reasonable—as opposed to a hypothetical—expectation of this prospect, largely unconstrained immigration would seem implied by Rawls' social contract theory.

From a utilitarian perspective, the utilities or disutilities experienced by both aliens and citizens would be entered in the calculus.[98] Some citizens would gain from being able to enter into contractual relationships with immigrants; others may lose if wages are depressed through the additional competition immigrants bring to labour markets; and still other citizens as consumers may benefit from access to cheaper goods or services. Against these costs and benefits accruing to citizens must be set whatever costs and benefits accrue to aliens by being permitted entry—in most cases one assumes that the benefits substantially outweigh the costs, otherwise they would presumably not have chosen to resettle in another land. Moreover, to the extent that many aliens will have made the wrenching decision to resettle because of economic privation or religious or political oppression or persecution in their homelands, the gains to them from being permitted to join a new and more congenial community may be substantial. Thus, a utilitarian perspective, though perhaps providing more scope for restrictions on immigration than either the libertarian or the social contractarian perspective, would in general dictate relatively open borders.

COMMUNITY

In opposition to these liberal values stand the core values of community. Here, in the context of immigration policy, it is asserted that control over which strangers will be allowed to enter is a powerful expression of a nation's identity and autonomy—in other words, of its sovereignty. Sovereignty entails the unlimited power of a nation, like that of a free individual, to decide whether, under what conditions, and with what effect it will consent to enter into a relationship with a stranger.[99] The most prominent contemporary articulator of this view is Michael Walzer.[100] In justifying this view, he draws analogies between neighbourhoods, clubs, and families. Although it is true that in the case of neighbourhoods, people are free, in general, to enter and exit as they please, he argues that to analogize nations to neighbourhoods, permitting unconstrained entry by aliens in any number from anywhere in the world would destroy the concept of neighbourhood. He contends that it is only the nationalization of welfare (or the nationalization of culture and politics) that opens the neighbourhood communities to whoever chooses to come in. Neighbourhoods can be open only if countries are at least potentially closed. Only if the state selects among would-be members and guarantees the loyalty, security, and welfare of the individuals it selects can local communities take shape as "different" associations determined solely by personal preference and market capacity.

Walzer claims that if states ever become large neighbourhoods, neighbourhoods would probably become little states. Their members would organize to defend the local politics and culture against strangers. Historically, Walzer claims, neighbourhoods turned into closed or parochial communities whenever the state was open. Thus, Walzer rejects the analogy of states to neighbourhoods and rather analogizes states to clubs and families, where members are free to determine the conditions of membership. Walzer concludes:

> The distribution of membership is not pervasively subject to the constraints of justice. Across a considerable range of the decisions that are made, states are simply free to take in strangers (or not)—much as they are free, leaving aside the claims of the needy, to share their wealth with foreign friends, to honor the achievements of foreign artists, scholars, and scientists, to choose their trading partners, and to enter into collective security arrangements with foreign states. But the right to choose an admissions policy is more basic than any of these, for it is not merely a matter of acting in the world, exercising sovereignty, and pursuing national interests. At stake here is the shape of the community that acts in the world, exercises sovereignty, and so on. Admission and exclusion are at the core of communal independence. They suggest the deepest meaning of self-determination. Without them, there could not be *communities of character,* historically stable, ongoing associations of men and women with some special commitment to one another and some special sense of their common life.[101]

Unlike the liberal theories, which imply no or very few limitations on entry, Walzer's theory, at least without further qualification, appears to permit almost any limitations on entry that a state should choose to impose, including admission policies that are overtly racist. Thus, we are left with two core values which, at the level of abstract articulation, seem to present us with what intuitively are morally unappealing polar choices. In contemplating where reconciliation and qualification may be possible, it is useful to move from the abstract to the concrete and to identify a series of rather specific policy issues that have recurrently arisen in debates over immigration policy in most western democracies.

The Issues

THE SIZE OF THE INTAKE

The issue of the size of the intake of immigrants cannot readily be separated from the composition of the intake, in terms of deducing what kinds of demands the immigrants are likely to make on a particular community. However, to the extent that the two issues can be separated, whatever the composition, the notion that any country could accept and absorb millions of immigrants a year without critical features of its infrastructure collapsing and congestion externalities being created on all sides is unlikely to be readily accepted. One might, of course, argue that a natural equilibrium would establish itself before this happens—if the intake threatens these conditions, some would-be immigrants will abandon an interest in resettling. However, collective action problems may prevent such an equilibrium emerging at all or at any event, quickly or smoothly, and it is not obvious that Rawls' "public order" qualification on the right of entry tells us anything helpful about when congestion externalities have reached the point where the lifeboat metaphor can appropriately be invoked. This concern is somewhat reminiscent of those raised by Thomas Malthus in 1798 in his famous essay *The Principle of Population as it Affects the Future Improvement of Society*. As Heilbroner states the Malthusian thesis:

> [The essay on population claimed] that there was a tendency in nature for population to outstrip all possible means of subsistence. Far from ascending to an ever higher level, society was caught in a hopeless trap in which the human reproductive urge would inevitably shove humanity to the sheer brink of the precipice of existence. Instead of being headed for Utopia, the human lot was forever condemned to a losing struggle between ravenous and multiplying mouths and the eternally insufficient stock of Nature's cupboard, however diligently that cupboard might be searched.[102]

Malthus points out that land, unlike people, cannot be multiplied—land does not breed. Malthus' fears were subsequently proven to be greatly exaggerated, and most dramatically refuted by the settlement of the New World, where increased population through immigration, in terms of increased labour and capital on the supply side and increased aggregate demand on the demand side, made possible the realization of enormous economies of scale and the technological advances that accompanied them. However, as birth rates and destitution levels in many impoverished Third World countries exemplify today, Malthus' concerns were not entirely unfounded, and a totally unrestricted immigration policy may legitimately implicate those concerns. Once some restriction on total intake is recognized as necessary, then the composition of that restricted intake must be addressed.

THE COMPOSITION OF THE INTAKE

A host of complex and morally sensitive issues arises here. With respect to many of them, the core values of liberty and community are likely to yield quite different implications.

A Market in Entitlements. Recalling the discussion of alternative means of allocating scarce lifesaving technology (dialysis machines) in Chapter 2, we can see that one method of allocating scarce entitlements to entry would be for the state to auction off these entitlements on a periodic basis and allocate them to the highest bidders.[103] It could presumably be claimed on behalf of this allocative mechanism that the successful bidders would be those who valued the right of entry most highly, because the opportunities for them following entry are likely to be greatest, presumably reflecting the greater value that present citizens are likely to place on whatever economic activities these successful bidders intend to engage in. Alternatively, it could be cogently argued that this method of allocation of scarce entitlements offends notions of distributive justice by rewarding ability to pay and disregarding claims that other non-citizens might be able to make for entry, on the grounds of, say, economic deprivation, religious or ethnic persecution, or political oppression in their home countries or family reunification, and where, despite their lack of material resources, the opportunity to emigrate may dramatically enhance their individual autonomy and welfare, perhaps to the point of making the difference between life and death.

Lotteries. As with the allocation of scare lifesaving technology, one could employ the mechanism of a lottery. That is, all aspiring entrants would register their applications, and names of individuals in the applicant pool would be drawn on a periodic basis until the total intake for the period was met. This method of allocation would obviously neutralize the role that wealth would play in the allocation of entitlements to entry, but would be entirely insensitive to relative claims of merit or desert that individual members of the applicant pool, and existing citizens, might feel should be vindicated.

Queues: First Come First Served. Scarce entitlements to entry could be allocated on a queuing, that is, first-come first-served, basis, where the order of registration or filing of applications is recorded and applicants are simply selected from the top of the queue until the total, collectively agreed intake for the period in question is met. Although, like lotteries, this method of allocation is wealth neutral, it is vulnerable to all the same objections in that it is entirely insensitive to relative claims of merit or desert that might be asserted by or on behalf of individual applicants.

Once these three methods of allocation are rejected, either in whole or in part, as the primary allocative mechanisms, administrative (merit) allocation is left as the only major alternative. In formulating the criteria for evaluating relative claims of merit or desert in legislation or administrative policies, the normative considerations surrounding the claims of several categories of applicants would have to be addressed.

Applicants Who Pose a National Security Risk. Obviously, no normative theory of immigration recognizes that an invading country is entitled to unopposed entry on the grounds of free movement of people. Similarly, no theory would recognize an obligation to admit subversives committed to overthrowing the state by force. A more difficult question arises with respect to the admission of significant influxes of people who come from non-liberal societies, even if they do not come with any subversive intent. In other words, how tolerant must we be of the intolerant? Carens argues that there may be a case, even from a liberty perspective, for excluding such people where the cumulative effect of their presence may be to undermine the maintenance of liberal institutions. From a communitarian perspective, given that the state, with certain qualifications, can set any conditions of entry that it wishes, exclusion here would be viewed as unproblematic.

Refugee or Asylum Claimants. Aliens who have found their way to our country or are displaced in third countries and seek refugee or asylum status because of the threat of political, religious, or ethnic persecution in their homelands present a morally compelling claim for admission on most theories of immigration. Liberal theories would readily recognize such claims, given the premise of the recognition of the equal moral worth of all individuals and the special concern in Rawlsian social contract theory with the plight of the most disadvantaged. Even on communitarian theories of immigration, at least as articulated by Walzer, a claim arises under the mutual aid or good Samaritan principle, which he believes applies where positive assistance is urgently needed by one of the parties and the risks and costs of giving it are relatively low for the other party. Historically, with some exceptions, refugee or asylum claims have tended to involve relatively small numbers of people at any given time, so Walzer's conditions were often readily satisfied. However, in the contemporary world, with millions of individuals (perhaps as many as fifteen million currently) displaced by war, civil unrest, or religious or ethnic persecution,[104] and with ready means of international mobility, it is not clear how far the principle of mutual aid extends. Walzer states, "I assume that there are limits on our collective liability, but I do not know how to specify them."[105]

Economically Necessitous Aliens. The category of economically necessitous aliens embraces aliens who, because of simple economic impoverishment in their homelands, wish to re-settle in our country (sometimes referred to as "economic refugees"). From a liberal perspective, their claims would be viewed as having different strengths, depending on which strand of liberal theory one espoused. Within a domestic libertarian framework, provided that their entry did not interfere with rights of others, we should admit them. Within a utilitarian framework, much would depend on what they could contribute to our society relative to the costs that they would impose on it, although a global utilitarian framework would also weigh the benefits to them. Within a social contractarian framework they would engage our special concern to the extent that they could properly be characterized as among the least advantaged. In contrast, from a communitarian perspective, Walzer claims that we have very limited obligations to such persons, or at least we are free collectively to take that view.[106] Perhaps we have an obligation to provide foreign aid or, as he argues in his criticism of

234 The Limits of Freedom of Contract

the White Australia policy, where a country has large empty land masses it may have an obligation to share these spaces with necessitous aliens. In his view, to recognize a more general claim would be to invite the prospect of a country's being overrun by almost unlimited numbers of disadvantaged aliens from around the globe who share very little in common with existing members of the community, and who would thus threaten to undermine its sense of community.

Family Members. Both Carens and Walzer recognize that aliens who have family relationships with citizens can make an especially salient normative claim for admission; in Walzer's[107] case because community bonds and affinities are readily embraced by such relatives; and, in Carens'[108] case, presumably because to exclude them would be to deny their equal moral worth, although curiously he suggests that more distant relatives would have a less strong claim. A libertarian perspective on family reunification claimants would readily countenance their admission, provided that they imposed no costs involuntarily on others. The social contractarian perspective might be ambivalent to the extent that family members do not fall within the category of the least advantaged. A domestic utilitarian perspective might again be somewhat ambivalent, particularly in the case of older or infirm family members who might in some cases be expected to contribute little to our society and conceivably make significant demands on us, although a global utilitarian perspective would also weigh the benefits to them.

Culturally Homogeneous Aliens. A complex and sensitive issue arises as to whether a state can morally attach conditions of entry for aliens that are designed to maintain the community's cultural homogeneity. On most versions of liberal theory, such discriminatory conditions are likely to be suspect, in the sense that they do not treat all individuals as being of equal moral worth. From a communitarian perspective, the foundational premise is that the community is free to set any terms of entry that it wishes, particularly where the conditions are designed to reinforce shared, common values. Both core values here encounter difficulties. From a liberal perspective, it is necessary to accommodate the aspirations for national self-determination that independence movements around the world, particularly in the post-war years, have strongly evinced. In the contemporary world, the transformation of Eastern Europe, and the claims for independence or greater autonomy on the part of many groups in these countries, all reflect, to some degree, a claim to an entitlement to recognition and reinforcement of culturally or politically distinct communities. Within Canada, Quebec's claim to being a distinct society, and a potential claim to political independence, with a corollary claim in both cases to being entitled to control the characteristics of its immigrants, rests in large part on the claim to cultural distinctiveness, which may entail exclusionary implications. The claim of Native American or Aboriginal people to self-government, at least on reserves, also rests on a claim to an entitlement to protect and preserve cultural distinctiveness, even where this entails exclusionary elements. Carens, within the liberal egalitarian framework that he adopts, is also prepared to concede that a country such as Japan—one with a long tradition of close cultural homogeneity—might be entitled to maintain a restrictive immigration society, provided that it is applied more or less equally to all aliens.[109]

This proviso is important to him, because he does not want to countenance (as most liberals would not) policies like the White Australia policy[110] (formally abandoned in 1972), which he readily sees as having been motivated by racist sentiments (Canadian immigration policy until 1962 was not substantially different; U.S. immigration policy for most of this century has imposed quotas by country of origin, reflecting the country's ethnic composition in the 1920s). However, an Australian Minister of Immigration once defended that policy in terms that, on the surface, appear to apply to many of the other situations, instanced above, where exclusionary policies may be justified: "We seek to create a homogeneous nation. Can anyone reasonably object to that? Is this not the elementary right of every government, to decide the composition of the nation? It is just the same prerogative as the head of the family exercises as to who is to live in his own house." Or, as one Australian political leader is said to have put the point, with less finesse: "Two Wongs don't make a White."

Carens argues that "difference does not always entail domination. One has to consider what a particular case of exclusion means, taking historical, social, and political context into account. For example, the White Australia policy cannot be separated from British imperialism and European racism. That is why it was never a defensible form of exclusion."[111] Conversely, "Japan's exclusionary policy seems quite different. First it is universal i.e. it applies to all non-Japanese. It is not aimed at some particular racial or ethnic group that is presumed to be inferior, and it is not tied to a history of domination of the excluded."[112] For Walzer,[113] the White Australia policy presents even more serious problems, given his analogy between states and families and clubs, an analogy explicitly drawn by the Australian Minister of Immigration. Walzer is driven to reliance on what appears to be a frivolous qualification of the generally unconstrained right he concedes to states to set the terms of entry by aliens into national communities by suggesting that where a country has large unoccupied land masses, it may have an obligation to share the land even with culturally diverse aliens (a sort of South African "homelands" policy). First, most of the unoccupied land in Australia is unoccupied for a reason—it is desert and largely uninhabitable—and sharing this land with, say, Asians or Africans would be to discharge no moral obligation at all to them. In the terms of the Lockean proviso, "as much and as good" has not remotely been left behind for them. Second, in countries without large unoccupied land masses it would appear to follow from Walzer's position that racially discriminatory admission conditions can be justified in terms of protecting long established community values and characteristics.

Better-Endowed and Less Well Endowed Aliens. Can a country, in setting the terms of admission to the community it represents, morally justify discriminating in favour of more well endowed and against less well endowed aliens (in terms of skills or material resources)? The different versions of liberal theory might respond to this question differently. Within a libertarian framework, it is more likely that better endowed immigrants, in terms of skills or capital, will be able to establish mutually beneficial contractual relationships with existing members of the admitting community; less well endowed aliens presumably pose a greater risk of becoming a public burden in terms of health and education costs, unemployment and social welfare costs, and all these programmes involve coercive forms of redistribution, which libertarians traditionally object to. Within a domestic utilitarian framework, obviously the more that an alien can contribute to the admitting society in terms of skills or capital, and the fewer demands he makes on that society, the more likely it is that the utilitarian calculus will be met, although from a global utilitarian perspective the calculus may go the other way, with special recognition being accorded to the benefits likely to be derived from immigration by less well endowed immigrants.

It bears pointing out in this context that three recent extensive empirical studies (two American, one Canadian) all report strikingly similar conclusions: immigrants in general do not displace indigenous citizens from the labour force, do not depress their wages, have labour force participation rates comparable or superior to those of the indigenous population, and do not engender higher per capita social expenditures.[114] These findings refute many of the more persistent and widely held myths about the domestic effects of immigration. Moreover, from a global perspective, empirical evidence suggests that the economic gains from removing all restrictions on international immigration may well exceed annual world-wide GNP and substantially exceed gains from removing all trade restrictions.[115]

Within a Rawlsian social contract framework, the least well endowed aliens should engage our special moral concern. Moreover, it might be argued that by adopting a preference towards the better endowed aliens, we encourage their exit from their homelands and promote a brain drain or capital drain that reduces the welfare of their communities of origin, which often face severe scarcities of human and financial capital. Carens believes that we cannot justify encroaching on the rights of such individuals on this account, and indeed the evidence of the welfare effects of out-migration on countries of origin is highly indeterminate.[116]

Guest Workers. We are familiar with the contemporary phenomenon of "guest workers" in many countries in Western Europe, where these workers are admitted on a temporary basis for confined categories of tasks, without most of the legal incidents of citizenship,[117] and with no formal assurance of ever being able to qualify for citizenship. Programmes for domestic workers and farm workers in North America possess similar features. However, the phenomenon has historical antecedents—in the past we called such people "indentured workers" or, more bluntly, "coolie labour." In most versions of liberal theory, such arrangements are offensive, simply because they do not treat all individuals as of equal moral worth. This would be particularly so within the libertarian and social contractarian frameworks. A domestic utilitarian framework may be more ambiguous, to the extent that guest worker arrangements are intended to confine aliens to sectors of the economy where indigenous labour is not available, and to prevent competition with, and thus the imposition of costs on, indigenous workers in other sectors. However, on a global utilitarian calculus, given the typical circumstances of most guest workers, net utility would presumably be maximized by expanding their rights to encompass full citizenship. Walzer, from his communitarian perspective, argues that to admit guest workers as residents in one's community and permit them to develop personal, social, and occupational ties as members of that community, but to treat them as a community apart, or as "second class citizens," undermines communal values.[118]

Illegal Immigrants. The category of illegal immigrants embraces those who have taken up residence in a host country without satisfying whatever substantive criteria of permanent admission have been prescribed by law with respect to the various characteristics of claimants described above, or at least without following the procedures that govern those determinations (for example, they are visitors or temporary workers who have outstayed their visas). On the one hand, it can be argued from a liberal perspective that to give priority or preference to immigrants—simply because they are here—over aliens with claims of similar substance who seek admission from outside our boundaries and in accordance with prescribed procedures is to violate the precepts of equal treatment of similarly situated individuals. On the other hand, it might be argued from a communitarian perspective that where illegal immigrants have been resident in the host country for some significant period of time and have established ties and relationships with existing members of the community, perhaps raised children in the host community, and contributed positively to the community in productive ways, through employment or other activities, we have no right to expel them, and indeed perhaps an obligation at some point retrospectively to validate their status by according them citizenship (through amnesty policies), even at the expense of according recognition to a class of intentional lawbreakers and queue-jumpers.

The Historical Experience

From about 1880 to 1920, the Canadian government, through various legal strategies, successively excluded almost all Chinese (through head taxes—the equivalent of tariffs), Japanese (through a voluntary immigration restraint agreement with Japan), and East Indian (through continuous journey restrictions) immigrants from Canada. The preamble to a statute of the British Columbia legislature in 1886 captures the public sentiment of the times:

> Whereas the incoming of Chinese to British Columbia exceeds that of any other immigrant, and the population so introduced are fast becoming superior in number to our own race, are not disposed to be governed by our laws, are dissimilar in habits, are useless in case of emergency, habitually desecrates graveyards by removal of bodies therefrom, and generally the laws governing the whites are found to be inapplicable to the Chinese, and such Chinese are inclined to habits subversive to the comfort and well being of the community.[119]

Prime Minister John A. MacDonald in the same year expressed the following view:

> There is a great deal in the objection taken to unrestricted immigration into British Columbia of people from China. These people are not of our people. They are not of our race. They do not even become settlers. They come to British Columbia and work for a little time, make a little money, and then return to their own country, taking the money with them. Then there are moral reasons, which one need not discuss here, which render the presence of the Mongolian race very undesirable.[120]

Prime Minister MacKenzie King in 1922 said, "If I am correct—and I believe I am—in the assertion that it is a great economic law that the lower civilization will, if permitted to compete with the higher, tend to drive the higher out of existence, or drag it down to the lower level, then we see the magnitude of the question viewed as a great national problem."[121] King reiterated the then familiar contention that "it is impossible to ever hope to assimilate a white population with the races of the Orient"; indeed, to even contemplate assimilation would be to bring Canadians "face to face with the loss of that homogeneity which ought to characterize the people of this country if we are to be a great nation."[122] The massive internment of Japanese Canadians during World War II and the refusal to accept Jewish refugees from Europe before and during World War II ("None is too Many"),[123] consigning many to the Holocaust, along with the long-standing policy of Asian exclusion reflected a community's collective resolve to define its communal values and characteristics. Although communitarianism need not *necessarily* imply these policies, a moral licence to exclude, expel, or intern individuals who are "not like us" carries a much higher risk than liberal values that majoritarian passions and prejudices will over-ride the individual freedoms that are central to the commitment of all liberal theories to the equal moral worth of all individuals. Emphasizing commonalities rather than differences is a natural corollary of liberal values. The atrocities committed over the course of history as a result of tribalism, ethnocentrism, "ethnic cleansing," religious fanaticism, and ideological collectivism (for example, Stalinism) are a tragic testament to this risk. The ethnic and religious conflicts that are currently manifesting themselves in the fragmenting countries of Eastern Europe and the former Soviet Union, the Middle East, Northern Ireland, Africa, India, and other parts of Asia suggest that the lessons of history have not yet been fully learned.[124]

. . .

As one reviews the policy dilemmas in each of the three major areas where issues of discrimination are of central importance—domestic human rights laws, international trade policy, and immigration policy—a major commonality stands out. This is the persistent tendency on the part of democratically elected governments to "back-end" rather than "front-end" their policy responses to the moral dilemmas that each area introduces. For example, in the United States today, almost the entire focus of public debate with respect to domestic anti-discrimination policy pertains to the appropriate role to be assigned to affirmative action programmes. Yet not only are such programmes the most normatively problematic of all possible policy responses, but it also seems clear empirically that, *standing alone,* they are likely to have a very modest impact on the economic plight of blacks, as depicted in the numbing figures presented at the beginning of this chapter. To allow problems of disadvantage and deprivation to fester and deepen during young blacks' formative years and then to attempt to correct the consequences of these disadvantages in adulthood is clearly less likely to be effective than the adoption of a wide range of supply-side policies designed to pre-empt or substantially mitigate these problems in their incipiency. As Stephen Carter (a distinguished black Yale law professor) puts it, affirmative action programmes are an attempt to get "racial justice on the cheap."[125]

Similarly, in the case of adjustment costs entailed in trade liberalization and shifting patterns of international comparative advantage, defensive re-actions, in the form of protectionist policies, typically only defer the necessity for adjustment; but when the need for adjustment is finally confronted, it has often assumed even more severe proportions. Generous adjustment programmes that underwrite the costs of worker retraining and relocation seem much more desirable from most normative perspectives. Moreover, protectionist policies typically impact adversely on foreigners, who often live in less-developed countries. Here, an inability to trade freely with developed countries often translates into greater economic privation at home, which in turn exacerbates problems such as the Third World debt crisis, immigration pressures, and demands for foreign aid, which developed countries must then confront in non-trade related policy contexts, where often the policy options are more costly, less effective, and often less congenial.

Finally, in the case of immigration policy, the enormous volume of refugees or otherwise necessitous persons currently seeking resettlement in developed countries, often from cultural, linguistic, religious, and racial backgrounds that are in many respects quite different from the characteristics of refugee claimants in previous periods[126] and sharply different from the majority of the indigenous populations of developed countries, places great strains on domestic immigration policies in developed countries and the social and political consensus surrounding the appropriate form of these policies. However, it is clear that the level of demands for resettlement would be substantially diminished if developed countries, through appropriate forms of international cooperation, took stronger and more effective policy stances towards human rights violations and political or religious oppression in many countries of origin, adopted more liberal trade policies, provided more generous forms of foreign aid in cases of natural disasters, and provided more effective forms of developmental aid in forms—or with conditions attached—designed to address and, if necessary, discipline the governmental incompetence and corruption that is often pervasive in many developing countries. It is clear that most refugees or displaced persons would prefer to return to their homelands, but the policies of most developed countries do not reflect this priority. Instead, the consequences of displacement are seen primarily as an immigration problem, where effective policy responses are highly circumscribed.

The general question that must thus be confronted is why policy-making in democratic societies appears to exhibit this persistent and pervasive bias towards "back-ending," rather than "front-ending," the formulation of policy responses to this critically important range of problems. This is an issue which, along with others, I will take up in the concluding chapter of this book.

CHAPTER TEN

Autonomy and Welfare

The Invisible Hand

Adam Smith, in famous passages in *The Wealth of Nations*, published more than two hundred years ago, wrote:

> It is not from the benevolence of the butcher, the brewer, or the baker that we expect our dinner, but from their regard to their own interest. We address ourselves, not to their humanity, but to their self-love; and never talk to them of their own necessities, but of their advantages . . . Every individual is continually exerting himself to find out the most advantageous employment for whatever capital he can command. It is his own advantage, indeed, and not that of the society, which he has in view. But the study of his own advantage, naturally, or rather necessarily, leads him to prefer that employment which is most advantageous to society.
>
> He is in this . . . led by an invisible hand to promote an end which was no part of his intention. Nor is it always the worse for society that it was no part of it. By pursuing his own interest, he frequently promotes that of society more effectually than when he really intends to promote it.[1]

On this view, the public interest, in terms of resource allocation, economic growth, and income distribution, is furthered as a mere by-product of countless, self-serving individual decisions to engage in trade or exchange.[2] The community has no need to forge any collective consensus as to its common economic goals or values. The legal counterpart to this view of the market is the Will or Autonomy Theory of Contract Law, where obligations by individuals to one another arise out of voluntarily assumed, self-imposed obligations reflecting convergent intentions of the contracting parties. This dual claim on behalf of the private ordering paradigm—that it simultaneously promotes individual freedom (autonomy) and social welfare—is an extremely strong claim that is rarely and seldom plausibly made about alternative modes of economic organization. A major objective of this book has been to evaluate the strength of this claim, which, if true, would provide a formidable, if not decisive, normative justification for private ordering over other forms of resource allocation in many contexts. This dual claim is reflected in the title of Milton Friedman's well-known book *Capitalism and Freedom,* though in a passage from the book, Friedman provides an indication that the claim is not a simple one and raises some serious complexities that require close evaluation: "The possibility of co-ordination through voluntary co-operation rests on the elementary—yet frequently denied—proposition that both parties to an economic transaction benefit from it, *provided the transaction is bilaterally voluntary and informed.*"[3]

A large part of this book has been devoted to exploring when transactions can be regarded as bilaterally voluntary and informed, in terms of either the freedom and autonomy claims made on behalf of the private ordering paradigm or the welfare claims made on its behalf. An important part of this enterprise has been to assess whether autonomy and welfare norms indeed converge in the conditions that they imply for voluntary and informed transactions. On various central normative issues pertaining to the concept of freedom of contract, I have concluded that the claim of convergence between autonomy and welfare values is much more tenuous than proponents of the private ordering paradigm have conventionally been prepared to acknowledge. In this concluding chapter, I will draw together the strands of the analysis developed in previous chapters as they bear on this general convergence claim made on behalf of the private ordering paradigm.

Autonomy Values

To determine whether autonomy values are promoted by the private ordering paradigm, a series of complex issues have been identified in preceding chapters. Difficult questions arise as to when a transaction can be regarded as voluntary or, conversely, coerced. It has proven difficult to construct an autonomy-based theory of coercion without first constructing a moral baseline (or set of rights) for the party choosing to accept a proposal under constrained circumstances, against which the proposal can be evaluated. Similarly, difficulties arise in determining when a contracting party has sufficient information about the contract subject matter or future course of events affecting the value of the contract subject matter for a conclusion to be sustained that the choices in question were autonomous. Although contracting choices made with false information or in the absence of highly material information may, at one level, be regarded as non-autonomous, at another level the decision to forgo opportunities to acquire further information may itself be an autonomous choice. Thus, it is not obvious how complete a contracting party's information set should be for his choices to be regarded as autonomous. Even where complete information is available to a contracting party, but that party lacks the capacity to rationally evaluate the information set available to him as a result of cognitive deficiencies or limitations of one kind or another, it may often be reasonable to conclude that choices made under such circumstances are not autonomous. But again, where the line should be drawn is far from clear.

Beyond the problem of cognitive deficiencies or limitations, it has been argued that many individual choices reflect adaptive preferences that are at variance with the kinds of choices such individuals would make in the absence of social, economic, legal, or other influences that have shaped these preferences. This argument is potentially subversive of traditional autonomy values which, in emphasizing the value of self-determination or self-government, take individual preferences as given.

Yet again, it can be argued that a rich conception of individual autonomy entails not only a negative theory of liberty—that is, freedom from external constraints on the individual right of self-determination—but also a positive theory of liberty, which holds that an autonomous ability to choose one's own conception of the good life entails access to economic opportunities and resources that makes non-demeaning, self-fulfilling life choices a realistic possibility.[4] This latter conception of individual autonomy—as a form of egalitarian liberalism—has a number of implications for the law of contracts. For example, with respect to the question of coercion, it might be argued that deliberate exploitation by one party of another party's lack of choices to exact returns that exceed those normally realizable in a more competitive environment should be viewed as suspect. More generally, such a theory can be invoked to justify the adoption of contract doctrines or regimes designed to redistribute resources and thus effectuate a conception of distributive justice.

In the case of externalities, we have seen that autonomy values yield an unclear set of implications when the choices or activities of contracting parties impact on the interests or welfare of third parties, leading to claims by the latter that their autonomy has been infringed by these contractual choices or activities. To prevent the concept of externalities running wild and justifying objections to contractual activities by third parties simply on the grounds that they take exception to, or are offended by, these activities (for whatever reason), it is difficult to avoid either some form of balancing test (of the kind proposed by Feinberg),[5] which entails a kind of cost-benefit analysis not dissimilar from that implied by a utilitarian perspective, or a positive theory of liberty—egalitarian liberalism—which attaches special moral significance to third-party impacts where these entail the reinforcement or perpetuation of historical inequalities of position or status (as in the case of some feminist critiques of pornography and some justifications for anti-discrimination laws). In short, autonomy values, without extensive further explication, do not readily yield a set of clear, normative implications for what kind of legal constraints should be imposed on the private ordering process.

Welfare Values

I have embraced under this rubric all the major classes of normative theories bearing on the private ordering process that are end-state or consequentialist in their orientation. These theories include efficiency theories, in particular concepts of Pareto efficiency and Kaldor-Hicks efficiency, related utilitarian theories, theories of distributive justice, and communitarian theories. The strongest welfare claim that can be made on behalf of the private ordering paradigm is from the perspective of Pareto efficiency. Here, the claim is that if two parties are to be observed entering into a contract, one should normally presume that they would not have done so unless they felt that the contract was likely to make them better off. However, as the quote from Friedman implies, such a welfare inference can be confidently drawn only if the parties enter into the exchange relationship voluntarily and with complete information about the contract subject matter. Within a Paretian framework, the issue of voluntariness is particularly problematic, because in a wide range of settings where we may well wish to conclude that autonomy values have been violated, the transactions in questions appear to make both parties better off in their own terms, given the limited contract opportunity set available to them. But then we appear to be making inferences of voluntariness from judgements about welfare effects, rather than the converse, which is what the welfare claim on behalf of the private order paradigm centrally rests on. The Paretian framework runs into similar difficulties with respect to imperfect information. Here, *ex ante* and *ex post* Paretian perspectives are likely to lead to very different welfare inferences. From an *ex ante* perspective, if both parties to a contract at the time of entering into the agreement feel that it will make them better off, then the fact that one or both of them are subsequently disappointed following the revelation of new information about the contract subject matter should be irrelevant. However, from an *ex post* perspective, if one or both parties, subsequent to entering into a contract, find that the contract has made them worse off relative to their pre-interaction status, we would end up excusing most contract breaches. This is what I refer to as the "Paretian dilemma," the resolution of which, within an efficiency framework, tends to force the analysis into a Kaldor-Hicks efficiency framework. Further difficulties confront the Paretian perspective with respect to externalities. It is possible to argue that if anybody out there objects to a particular transaction, or class of transaction, for whatever reason, the transaction or transactions cannot be Pareto superior, in the sense of making some better off and nobody worse off.[6] This would suggest that almost no transactions are likely to meet the literal Paretian test. Again, a resolution of this dilemma is likely to force the analyst, within an efficiency perspective, into the Kaldor-Hicks efficiency framework, where some balancing of costs and benefits with respect to the interests of the contracting parties and those of third parties is undertaken, much as appears to be entailed in Feinberg's balancing test designed to resolve conflicting autonomy claims with respect to externalities.

If one moves from a Paretian efficiency framework to a Kaldor-Hicks efficiency framework, with its predominantly utilitarian orientation, to better address these dilemmas raised by the Paretian framework, a new set of difficulties has to be confronted. In designing a set of legal rules to structure and constrain the contracting process in order to promote Kaldor-Hicks efficiency, social welfare, or average utility, the strong welfare claim made on behalf of the private ordering process has been largely abandoned. That is, the argument that we can more confidently infer positive welfare effects from voluntary and informed transactions or exchanges between individuals than from collective resource allocation decisions or regimes to which all affected parties have not unanimously consented is not central to Kaldor-Hicks efficiency, social welfare, or utilitarian judgements.[7] Indeed, if we are so confident about our ability to make these judgements within this framework, then the circumspection evinced by most neo-classical economists about our ability to make welfare judgements about public ordering decisions or regimes generally loses a good deal of its persuasiveness.[8]

The Kaldor-Hicks efficiency perspective can be invoked both to constrain the contracting process and to facilitate it. With respect to constraints on the contracting process, I have shown that the question of what contracts or promises, or classes of contracts or classes of promise should be enforced and subject to what legal strictures, when evaluated from a Kaldor-Hicks efficiency or social welfare perspective, typically yields a highly speculative and inconclusive set of implications. With respect to facilitating the contracting process, Kaldor-Hicks efficiency or social welfare considerations are often invoked to justify particular background legal rules or regimes in cases of incomplete contracts, where the parties have not explicitly assigned particular benefits, burdens, or risks. Here again, whether one attempts to divine what the particular parties to a given contract might have agreed to had they focussed their attention on the particular issue, starting from the premise that they would rationally have chosen *ex ante* the joint welfare maximizing rule, or whether one attempts instead to aggregate welfare effects over large numbers of transactions and contracting parties in designing broad, categoric legal rules, the welfare implications of alternative legal rules or regimes are typically inconclusive. Nevertheless, in the case of incomplete contracts, it is not obvious that the legal system has any alternative but to make its best estimates of welfare-enhancing specific or generic background rules, always leaving open to the parties the option of exercising their right of self-determination by contracting out of these background rules in the event that they find them mutually uncongenial.

However, it must be acknowledged that the implications of Kaldor-Hicks efficiency or social welfare considerations in fashioning legal rules to constrain the contracting process, or to facilitate it in the case of incomplete contracts, largely rest on some notion of *hypothetical* and not *actual* consent, in that it is hypothesized that the particular parties to a specific transaction would have chosen a given legal rule had they addressed their minds to the matter at issue, or that large aggregations of contracting parties would consent to a particular legal regime suggested by efficiency or welfare analysis if they were to be consulted *ex ante* before their stakes in particular transactions *ex post* had become clear. But the normative force of any theory of hypothetical consent is substantially weaker than a normative theory of the private ordering process that rests on the actual consent of the affected parties; in this respect, it provides a dramatically different normative basis for the private ordering paradigm than classical autonomy theories, whose normative force rests centrally on notions of actual consent.

Moreover, once we are driven into the realm of designing legal rules or regimes by reference to notions of hypothetical consent, not only is it the case that the welfare implications of alternative legal regimes, even within an efficiency perspective, are often highly indeterminate, but the way is now clear for alternative legal regimes to be proposed on the basis of some theory of hypothetical consent that is not primarily based on efficiency or social welfare considerations as conventionally understood by economists. In particular, theories of distributive justice of the kind proposed by Rawls,[9] building on the Kantian categorical imperative of equal concern and respect, provide a basis on which legal rules structuring and constraining the contracting process can reasonably be proposed in terms of furthering distributive justice goals to which all or most individuals behind some veil of ignorance might hypothetically consent. Again, as with legal rules or regimes sought to be justified by reference to welfare judgements based on hypothetical consent, it is far from clear that theories of distributive justice predicated on hypothetical consent generate a very determinate set of implications for the law of contracts. Indeed, it has been persuasively argued that by making plausible modifications to the assumptions that Rawls makes about the values and objectives of individuals in the original position, the normative implications may not be substantially different from those suggested by an efficiency or utilitarian calculus.[10]

It will be obvious that there is sufficient plasticity to concepts of autonomy, efficiency, and distributive justice to allow for either sharp divergences between and among these perspectives or alternatively strong congruences.

For example, if autonomy values are interpreted as entailing theories not only of negative liberty, but also of positive liberty, autonomy values and distributive justice values may largely elide, even though conventionally autonomy values have been conceived of as deontological, and distributive justice values as consequentialist. Similarly, efficiency values, to the extent that they emphasize Paretian notions of efficiency, might not, in most contexts, sharply diverge from autonomy values; however, to the extent that Kaldor-Hicks efficiency values are substituted for Paretian efficiency values, these values become much more consequentialist and less consistent with classical autonomy values. Yet, in justifying the general claim by autonomy theorists that more individual freedom of choice is better than less, it is difficult to avoid ultimately being driven to a consequentialist rationale, probably with utilitarian (or welfare) connotations.[11] Indeed, in some cases, individual welfare considerations may justify limitations on individual freedom of choice, even in the absence of coercion or imperfect information—for example, to solve Prisoner's Dilemma and Tragedy of the Commons (collective action) problems, as outlined in Chapter 1, or adverse selection or signalling problems, as outlined in Chapter 5. Yet again, if one assumes significant degrees of risk aversion among most members of the population and makes welfare judgements based on this premise in choosing among alternative legal regimes for constraining or structuring the contracting process, these welfare judgements may not be strikingly different from those implied by the Rawlsian distributive justice perspective, or an autonomy perspective that emphasizes positive as well as negative theories of liberty.

This plasticity in the central elements of all these competing normative frameworks might suggest or induce a high degree of nihilism on the part of analysts of the private ordering paradigm and, perhaps as a corollary, lead to the conclusion that any set of legal rules that is likely to be constructed for governing the private ordering process is likely to be relatively unprincipled and to reflect the personal normative whims of judges in the case of judge-made law and similar whims on the part of legislators or regulators in framing legislative or regulatory regimes for the contracting process; worse still, it may simply reflect the outcome of political factionalism and intrigue. The claim might be further made that once all law—private and public—is recognized as political, the distinction between public and private ordering largely collapses, and as a collectivity or community, we should feel free, through democratic dialogue and participation, to adopt any kind of collective reconciliation of these competing norms that may prove congenial to us as a community and to impose the resulting norms on all individual members of the community.[12] This conclusion would be highly subversive of the private ordering paradigm as we have known it. Although I acknowledge the indeterminacies implicit in all the major competing normative perspectives, I believe that a conclusion as extreme as this is unwarranted. The fact of the matter is that all the values reflected in the various normative perspectives reviewed appear to command wide-spread public support and to be legitimate in their own terms.

Both as individuals and as a community, we do not operate within a one-value view of the world. Any such view is likely to prove self-defeating. For economists to claim that they are interested only in maximizing the total value of social resources, without being concerned about how gains in the value of social resources are to be distributed and whether these gains are in fact making the lives of individuals better, and whose lives, or while ignoring the impact of economic change on the lives of individuals or on the integrity or viability of long-standing communities, reflects a highly impoverished view of the world.[13] Alternatively, theorists committed only to concepts of distributive justice, who proceed in their analysis by inviting us to assume a given stock of wealth, or a given increase in the stock of wealth, and then asking what a just distribution of that wealth might entail, are largely engaging in idle chatter as long as the wealth creation function is simply assumed. Creating wealth is a necessary pre-condition to distributing it. Similarly, communitarians who stress values of solidarity and interconnectedness and discount values of individual autonomy and freedom risk pushing this perspective to an extreme, where communitarian values become exclusionary, authoritarian, or repressive.

Although I do not pretend to be able to offer a meta-theory that weighs or ranks these various values, I believe significant progress can be made at a lower level of abstraction by identifying the institutions or instruments which are best placed, among the array of instruments and institutions available to a community, to vindicate these values. Too often, we confound debates about choices of values with debates about choices of instruments. In other words, it seems important that we try to think clearly about an appropriate institutional division of labour for vindicating these values, recognizing that they all command legitimate adherence. I realize that this exercise entails resort to "practical reasoning" or "pragmatism"[14] that has utilitarian over-tones which might be viewed as according utilitarian considerations primacy over other normative values. I do not intend this implication. It simply seems sensible to choose instruments that are likely to vindicate, rather than negate or undermine, the values that we seek to promote.

The Institutional Division of Labour

The Common Law of Contracts

The common law of contracts, as supplemented or revised by statutory law bearing on the civil rights and obligations of private parties and applied by judges, typically in two-party disputes, seems best adapted to vindicating values that are particular to the parties to a given exchange. For the most part, though not exclusively, these seem to be autonomy values, that is, the particular choices and preferences of the parties involved.[15] Because of the much more generic judgements typically involved in Kaldor-Hicks efficiency considerations or distributive justice considerations, and the polycentric nature of these kinds of considerations,[16] courts in private contractual disputes do not seem as well equipped as institutions to play a dominant role in vindicating these latter values. This said, however, autonomy values are far from self-defining. Nevertheless, courts, typically faced with a decision of whether to enforce a particular contract or not, or on what terms, are not well placed to vindicate positive theories of liberty, which entail providing greater access to economic opportunities and resources for disadvantaged individuals or classes of individuals. The courts also do not seem well-equipped, in the context of two-party contract disputes, to make generic judgements about historical or social processes that may have led to adaptive preferences on the part of individuals or classes of individuals in the community. Nevertheless, in some contexts, such as the coercion context (one example being the tug and the foundering ship), any serviceable concept of autonomy probably requires some sensitivity to concerns about exploitation of situational inequalities. But what distinguishes these cases from other forms of inequalities is precisely that they are situational and not systemic. Systemic inequalities of the kind exemplified in the non-monopolized necessity cases are not well suited to judicial redress in two-party contract disputes, in part because the courts are unlikely to have complete information of the full manifestations of the phenomenon of which the particular case is alleged to be representative, and in part because the courts do not possess the appropriate remedial instruments to ameliorate significantly the phenomenon in question, and indeed may even exacerbate it. Moreover, singling out the particular contracting party or class of contracting party to bear a disproportionate share of the burden of some larger community commitment to distributive justice values, simply by virtue of the relative fortuity of their interaction with victims of inequality, itself offends a sense of justice. Similarly, structural as opposed to situational monopolies raise complex efficiency and distributive considerations that courts in two-party litigation do not seem well equipped to address.

In other cases, autonomy values and welfare values may sharply conflict. For example, in the asymmetric information cases, welfare considerations may suggest that buyers should not have to disclose superior information they possess (whether deliberately or casually acquired) to sellers, although autonomy values might suggest that sellers' decisions in these cases are not fully voluntary, in the absence of highly material information about the value of the contract subject matter. This is a difficult tension in values for courts in two-party contract disputes to resolve. However, even if it is resolved in favour of welfare values, this still leaves open to the seller the ability to negotiate for a clause in the contract that permits her to rescind the contract in the event of non-disclosure by the buyer; thus ultimate weight is assigned to the autonomous choices of the parties. Similar tensions arise in the case of incomplete contracts, for example, with respect to symmetric information imperfections or remedies for contract breach, where the legal system has no alternative but to construct a set of background rules for the parties. Here, the essential choice is either to design rules that are particularized to given parties and transactions (tailored default rules) or to adopt more generic or categoric rules that are applicable to broad classes of transactions (untailored default rules).[17] In designing either set of rules, it is impossible to avoid invoking general welfare considerations or some notion of distributive justice, either of which would be predicated on some theory of hypothetical consent. From an efficiency perspective, welfare judgements should probably take into account transaction costs, error costs, and uncertainty costs, which might well argue for the adoption of general or categoric, albeit crude, background rules, which would always recognize the right of particular contracting parties to contract away from these rules if their particular circumstances render this mutually beneficial; thus again, autonomy values would ultimately be vindicated. Similar tensions among competing values also arise with respect to externalities. However, in two-party disputes, invocation of externality effects as a reason for not enforcing a contract is sensibly confined to cases where a relatively tangible harm to third-party interests is entailed. To ask courts in such contexts to evaluate the validity of third-party claims—typically of a generic and diffuse nature, about personal offense or profound offense at the activities of the contracting parties, or about reinforcement or perpetuation of systemic inequalities—let alone to do anything effective about these, seems well beyond any sensible mandate that might be conferred on courts in contract cases.

Contract Regulation

In a range of contexts, the same values that parties might seek to vindicate in the courts in case-by-case adjudication will be more effectively dealt with generically through various forms of regulation. In other words, in these contexts one is dealing not with transaction-specific forms of contracting failure but with market failure.[18] This will presumably be true of some forms of coercion, though beyond the autonomy values implicated here, some forms of systemic coercion involve structural monopolies that inflict welfare losses on consumers who are priced out of the market and are therefore no longer engaging in contractual relationships with the monopolist. In such cases, regulation is concerned not only with autonomy values but with welfare values, and as in antitrust law or rate of return regulation, an appropriately systemic perspective can be adopted in fashioning relevant remedies. Similarly, in many markets, information failure may be so endemic that case-by-case sniping in contract litigation is much less effective than various forms of regulation. Also, many forms of externalities have such pervasive and diffuse third-party effects that relying on the civil litigation process is much less effective than relying on pre-emptive regulation. As in the case of externalities, some contexts may present co-ordination and collective action problems. For example, with respect to labour markets, many of the legal constraints commonly advocated, including workplace safety laws, minimum job security, plant closing laws, maximum hours, grievance mechanisms, worker-management consultation or co-determination mechanisms, may be consistent with a well-functioning market, in that they address effectively collective action problems facing individual workers who seek to negotiate over policies that are essentially indivisible, at least at the plant level.[19] Thus, these various rationales for contract regulation add up to a substantial agenda for collective action to correct for market failures. Although regulatory performance in many of these areas in the past has often been disappointing,[20] notable successes have also been registered and margins for enhancing regulatory performance (rather than wholesale retrenchment) seem extensive—in part by harnessing more effectively economic incentives in the realization of regulatory objectives.[21]

An important issue is whether the regulatory agenda should be even more ambitious and not limited to redressing problems of monopoly, information failures, externalities, and collective action and coordination problems. For those who take the view that adaptive preferences are a pervasive and serious problem, extensive forms of contract regulation would on that account be justified. I am deeply sceptical of, and troubled by, this rationale for contract regulation. It has no natural or inherent limits if one accepts that most preferences are socially shaped or constructed, and at the limit it is a license for tyranny or authoritarianism. Although accepting that many individuals' preferences are likely to have been shaped by their historical and social circumstances, often in the face of heavily constrained alternatives, I believe that a relevant policy response would be to ensure that possibilities and opportunities are created (by state action, where necessary) to which such individuals have access and among which they can more freely choose.[22] For similar reasons, I am deeply troubled by proposals that the concept of externalities be given so expansive a definition as to include notions of personal offense or profound offense, even if widely held, in order to permit majoritarian imposition of collective conceptions of the good life on individuals who do not share them. This form of legal moralism or moral majoritarianism is deeply antithetical to autonomy values that underlie the private ordering paradigm, and it reveals the dangers of welfare, utilitarian, or communitarian judgements on these issues. Even egalitarian liberal justifications for regulating externalities, for example, in the case of pornography, on the grounds that the externalities entailed (even when violence is not explicitly sanctified) reinforce or perpetuate historical inequalities through negative attitudinal changes, on closer examination reveal startling implications for the potential range of government regulation of private contracting activity, while holding out relatively tenuous prospects, in themselves, for ameliorating the inequalities that motivate them. Legal sanctions against invidious forms of discrimination and some form of statistical discrimination seem clearly warranted because of the harm entailed. But though the urgency of redressing the consequence of racial discrimination may warrant the temporary enactment of mandatory affirmative action programmes, the normative dilemmas that surround them and the empirical uncertainties regarding their probable impacts militate against assigning such programmes a central, long-term policy role in this context. Thus, a high degree of caution seems warranted in assigning a major role to contract regulation on egalitarian liberal grounds. Again, state action designed to expand the possibilities and opportunities available to historically disadvantaged groups would seem much more responsive to these concerns.

Yet again, outside the monopoly context, I am deeply sceptical of assigning a major role to contract regulation in the service of distributive justice goals. As noted above, in the context of judicial adjudication of two-party disputes, contract regulation designed to redistribute wealth in competitive markets is likely to be counter-productive, in terms of its impact on its intended beneficiaries, as well as singling out some sub-set of the population to bear the burden of society's distributive justice values, by virtue of the relative fortuity of who they do business with. In this context, notions of inequality of bargaining power are often crudely invoked to justify such forms of regulation. For example, where sellers or employers are much larger than the customers or employees with whom they deal, it is often assumed that this disproportion in resources will lead to unfairness in the distribution of the gains from exchange. However, this view overlooks the fact that large suppliers and employers are competing *not with their customers or employees,* but with other large suppliers or employers for customers or employees. Here, strength and size are pitted against strength and size, and customers and employees are the potential beneficiaries. Minimum wage laws are an example of contract regulation typically motivated by this concern over inequality of bargaining power, but are often imposed on some of the most competitive and marginal industries in the economy. Although some employees benefit from the higher wages mandated, other employees or potential employees typically confront reduced job opportunities, so that the welfare effects are at best ambiguous and, in many cases, negative from the point of view of employees themselves as a class.[23] As suggested in Chapter 1, similar arguments can be made about other forms of contract regulation, such as agricultural marketing boards or supply management schemes and rent controls. In the case of anti-discrimination laws, mandatory affirmative action programmes motivated by general distributive justice considerations may end up disadvantaging less well endowed members of the dominant group and advantaging only a relatively small number of the better-endowed members of the historically subordinate group, while excluding altogether disadvantaged members of non-targetted groups.

The Unfinished Normative Agenda

With the courts attempting to vindicate autonomy values and, to a lesser extent, welfare values, in two-party contract adjudications, and the state, through contract regulation, attempting to vindicate both autonomy and welfare values when confronted with more systemic market failures, what values are left unvindicated by these responses to contracting and market failures? The most obvious normative value left unvindicated is distributive justice. As noted above, this can readily be given an autonomy basis by invoking positive notions of liberty—that the right of self-determination or self-government becomes meaningful only if individuals have access to some base-line level of economic opportunities and resources that make autonomous, non-demeaning, self-fulfilling choices among alternative life plans feasible. Distributive justice theories also tend to be consequentialist in that they reject the outcomes of private ordering processes as necessarily reflecting any defensible concept of desert. Economists who concern themselves with issues of distributive justice generally reflect a predilection for invoking the tax and transfer system to redistribute resources from the well-endowed to the poorly endowed. However, this prescription, cast at this level of abstraction, is not especially helpful. It says little about the magnitude of the transfers that are required to vindicate distributive justice values, the potential claimants, or the form which the transfers might take. However, two further predilections of many economists should be noted. First, many take the view that transfers should typically be in cash rather than in kind, because cash transfers are more respectful of the autonomy of the recipient and less paternalistic or patronizing than in-kind transfers. Unfortunately perhaps, many donors (tax payers) are likely to take the view that the extent of the transfers which they are prepared to underwrite is at least partly contingent on how the transfers are spent—in particular, many will seek some assurance that the resources being transferred are being expended on needs which the donors feel are worthy, and in the absence of such an assurance, they are unlikely to commit themselves to such generous transfer programmes. Here, once again, a tension arises between autonomy values and welfare values.

Second, in evaluating the design of tax and transfer programmes, whether in cash or in kind, economists tend to be preoccupied with incentive effects, both on the supply side in terms of whether increased tax burdens are likely to attenuate work incentive effects, and on the receiving end, by similar concerns over work incentive and related effects commonly characterized as moral hazard problems. This conjunction of a bias towards cash rather than in-kind transfers and a preoccupation with moral hazard problems often leads to an extremely austere view of the role of the state in vindicating distributive justice goals. For example, in Charles Murray's destructive critique of the U.S. social welfare system, *Losing Ground*,[24] the author argues that many social welfare programmes, in attempting to alleviate economic necessity, simply reinforce the dependencies and patterns of behaviour to which they purport to be responsive. Providing financial assistance to families with dependent children simply encourages more teenage girls to become pregnant, or family breakups to occur, or single parents to remain on welfare rather than attempting to acquire marketable job skills. In turn, Milton Friedman has argued against a plethora of tailored social welfare programmes and in favour of a general, non-categoric minimum guaranteed income, in part because of the greater administrative efficiencies realizable in a non-categorical programme, and in part because of his predilection for cash rather than in-kind transfers.[25] However, presumably reflecting his concern for moral hazard problems, he proposed, for a family of four with no other income, a negative income tax (minimum guaranteed income) of $3,600 (in 1978 dollars), which would be forfeited at a tax-back rate of 50 percent if outside income was earned and would phase out at an income level of $7,200 (the value of all social benefits then apparently available to such a family in the United States).[26] It is impossible to believe that this level of support could provide meaningful, non-demeaning, autonomous life choices for most families qualifying for these benefits.

The concept of a non-categorical minimum guaranteed income has also attracted support from the political left,[27] largely because it appears to avoid the horizontal inequities of a categorical approach that provides different levels of benefits to recipients depending on the source or cause of their misfortune that has led to economic necessity: economic necessity is economic necessity whatever its cause. However, it is far from clear that a categorical approach can or should be avoided.[28] In a minimum guaranteed income programme that is cast broadly and non-categorically so as to avoid inquiries into fault or into the cause of a claimant's income deficiency, the circumstances that induced the deficiency will vary widely, as will the future prospects for self-sustaining economic activity. Establishing a single benefits schedule for all beneficiaries under a universal income security scheme will involve an unavoidable tendency for the community to adopt an arbitrary average or mean needs profile that will fit very poorly with many individual cases.

One group of claimants may be totally and permanently disabled in the sense of being unemployable in any significant way forever or for the foreseeable future. Another group of claimants may be first-time job searchers or temporarily unemployed workers who have realistic prospects of future employment. For the first group, benefits should ideally be set high enough to provide for a meaningful, non-demeaning, autonomous life, in recognition of the fact that income-generating prospects are next to zero. But if benefits are set at this level—which would almost certainly need to be significantly more generous than our existing melange of social welfare programs—these benefits will spill over to the second group, whose financial disability is potentially temporary. The only way to curtail these spill-over effects is to provide that on the securing of gainful employment, income therefrom will substitute for benefits and the beneficiaries will cease to qualify for benefits. But this will involve an implicit tax (or "tax-back") rate on outside income of 100 percent, which creates severe work disincentive effects for those whose personal qualifications and abilities make gainful employment a realistic expectation. Mitigation of these work disincentive effects in the second group of beneficiaries is likely to entail one of three responses. First, a much more gentle tax-back rate on the surrender of benefits can be adopted as outside income is earned—this will, however, entail the receipt of benefits by the second group of beneficiaries at total income levels (benefits plus outside income) well above those considered appropriate to ensure adequate means of support. Second, one is driven to a general scaling down of the benefit schedule for both groups and to the adoption of less severe tax-back rates on outside income, so as to bias the labour-leisure trade-off for the second group of beneficiaries more strongly towards working. But this creates a serious equity problem: the target group, who cannot realistically be expected to secure employment, is now receiving insufficient financial support. Third, one could provide higher levels of benefits and high tax-back rates as outside income is earned and rely primarily on somewhat subjective and arbitrary administrative judgements in individual cases as to when benefits are appropriate and when they should be denied because of income-earning potential.[29]

Even if the case for a categorical approach is accepted, it still does not follow that the transfers in question for a category of recipient should take the form of cash rather than other forms of assistance. Providing cash or, in other cases, vouchers (if the case for in-kind transfers is sometimes accepted) such as food stamps or, more debatable, school vouchers, has its virtues in terms of expanding the range of choices open to recipients and also in some cases of avoiding the inefficiencies of monopoly public provision. However, in other cases subsidies on the supply side of the goods and services needed may not only serve distributive justice goals better by ensuring more coordinated provision of services, but also communitarian goals by creating the possibility of subsidizing community groups, including groups of the recipients themselves, to assume a significant degree of control over the institutions that are responsible for delivering the goods or services in question. For example, Lisbeth Schorr, in her recent inspiring book *Within Our Reach*,[30] describes a whole range of concrete initiatives, many communally based, beyond general economic growth-promoting policies and an adequate general social welfare net, that we might collectively undertake or underwrite to improve the life prospects of children at disproportionate risk. She draws heavily on actual programmes that have been successfully implemented in particular communities in the past, for example, with respect to family planning, pre-natal care, more effective child health services and family support services, high-quality day-care and pre-school education, and elementary schools that are more responsive to the needs of high-risk children and families. Robert Howse in turn describes possibilities for reorienting the delivery of social welfare programmes.[31] He suggests that delivery of programmes to aid a particular target group might in many contexts be contracted out to the members of the group in question, say, disabled persons, single mothers, and so forth. The government could grant directly, for instance, to women's self-help groups the funding necessary to run shelters for battered women, with minimal direct bureaucratic control of the provision of care. In this way, the dependent or supplicant position of the beneficiary group can be mitigated or reversed. Such an approach also may lead to the creation of new organizations (in response to opportunities to deliver the services) that become important structures for mutual support and interdependence, providing an alternative or at least a counter-balance to dependency on transfers from strangers (the impersonal welfare state), manipulation by professional therapists, or dependency on traditional structures (church, family, private charity), each of which can impede the path to personal autonomy. In other words, though collective underwriting of the costs of social programmes is necessary, it does not follow that in every case they need to be publicly delivered. Much more imagination than has been evident in the past in the design of social welfare programmes is needed in promoting a rich mix of public, private, and community organizations for the delivery of social services. By pursuing these possibilities we have serious potential for realizing more fully both distributive justice and communitarian goals by creating the intermediate and overlapping communities of interest that Feinberg describes,[32] or the "communities of memory" that Bellah and his associates describe in their recent study of American society, *Habits of the Heart*.[33]

But the role of the state in promoting these goals goes even further. As my associates and I have argued in our study of the transition costs associated with changing international trade patterns, there is much unrealized potential in designing domestic adjustment assistance programmes that will ease the cost of transition for displaced workers.[34] These programmes would be sensitive to both distributive justice and communitarian values, while avoiding the negative welfare consequences of seeking to vindicate these values through protectionist policies that generate costs grossly disproportionate to the benefits. Beyond the need for collective commitment to adjustment assistance programmes that address not only trade-induced dislocations but other substantial causes of job dislocation, the core commitment of governments to the public education system from day-care, pre-school, through elementary and secondary school to tertiary education and vocational and apprenticeship programmes is in serious need of re-evaluation. In Ontario at present, about 30 percent of high school students fail to graduate. In many large U.S. cities the drop-out rate is as high as 50 percent, and the resources devoted to public education—in significant part financed by local property taxes—vary dramatically from one community to another.[35] In an increasingly competitive international economy, the availability of low-skilled, well-paid jobs in North America is sharply diminishing. Young people without advanced job skills and the capacity to learn new skills throughout their working lives in the face of rapidly changing economic circumstances face sharply constrained future career prospects and declining real incomes.[36] Even classical liberals such as Adam Smith[37] and John Stuart Mill[38] were strong advocates of the need for high quality, widely accessible, and to some extent collectively underwritten education systems. Again, as Smith and Mill stressed, collective underwriting of some of the costs of education is not necessarily synonymous with public delivery in all contexts. In many cases, contracting out either to the private sector or to community groups or the use of voucher systems may be the most effective form of delivery, as well as an empowering tool for providing individual citizens with opportunities to participate in shaping their own destinies.

The unifying element in many of the foregoing possibilities for reorienting and reinvigorating the delivery of social services is a commitment by the community through the state to investments in the development of human capital. The case for such a commitment derives from all the major normative values that have animated this book: the realization of truly autonomous choices among alternative life plans in large part depends upon the possession of significant human capital; the material prosperity and international competitiveness of mature industrial economies increasingly depend upon it; distributive justice goals can often be vindicated only through facilitating the acquisition of such capital; and communitarian values can be promoted by increasing the opportunities for individuals both to leave communities in which they might otherwise be trapped and their personal growth stifled and to join and participate in other communities of interest, which will increasingly revolve around the various processes relating to the acquisition and deployment of human capital both on the job and in leisure activities.[39]

In focussing on the central role that the state must play in promoting the development of human capital, many of the political labels, ideologies, and shibboleths of the past seem increasingly irrelevant. From the perspective of the political left, much greater recognition is needed that so-called progressives cannot exclusively pre-occupy themselves with issues of redistribution. The obvious truth is that social policies of the kind that the state should be underwriting can be realistically contemplated only in relatively prosperous societies. The left cannot continue, as it often has in the past, to eschew any interest in the wealth creation function. Indeed, many policies espoused by the left in North America and elsewhere have in the past been antithetical to the wealth creation function and have indeed reflected an extreme form of economic conservatism, wherein the economic status quo must be maintained at all costs. This view has been hostile to trade liberalization, privatization of inefficient public enterprises, contracting out of government services, deregulation of inherently competitive industries, avoidance or termination of subsidies to non-self-sustaining industries, or containing costs and enhancing the efficiency of delivery systems in major social programmes such as health care. The left also should see itself as having a central stake in the adoption of sensible macroeconomic policies and recognize the implications of huge budget deficits, high interest rates, and overvalued exchange rates for the wealth creation prospects of its economy and the maintenance or adoption of social and educational programmes that can promote the various values canvassed in this book.

In turn, the political right, and many economists, can no longer justify adopting the view that any policy issue beyond that of wealth creation is "just a distributional issue," in which they have no direct stake or expertise; or alternatively allow themselves to become paralysed by real or imagined moral hazard problems[40] in the design of policies and programmes intended to alleviate the consequences of poverty or racial discrimination; or to mitigate the cost of transitions encountered by individuals or whole communities caught in the midst of economic upheavals in their personal or collective existences. Economists should see public expenditures on social programmes designed to promote the development of human capital as social investments with major public goods aspects which would be sub-optimally supplied if left to the private sector, as well as sub-optimally demanded because of inequalities on the demand side; they should also realize that such investments could potentially yield high social and economic returns. This view of the role of the state in promoting the development of human capital largely obliterates the boundary between the domains of economic and social policy-making.

A persistent view from the right has been that expenditures on many social programmes, but particularly social welfare programmes, are a drain on the economic system, and the myth is perpetuated that recipients of most of these forms of assistance are the lazy and the work-shy who are leeching off the system. The statistics belie this perception. For example, as of December 1990, in Ontario 42 percent of all beneficiaries of the social welfare system were children. In terms of the recipients of social welfare payments (single individuals or whole families), over 23 percent were persons with disabilities; 29 percent were sole support parents (mostly women); almost 25 percent were unemployed persons; about 7 percent suffered ill-health; and the remainder depended on social assistance for a variety of other reasons. For most people, social assistance is a temporary income support programme to be relied on at a time of crisis in their lives. For example, about 56 percent of people receiving general welfare assistance in Ontario stay three months or less on the programme. Only a small proportion of recipients—about 5 percent—stay on assistance for more than two years. Moreover, with respect to criticisms of the U.S. social welfare system by commentators such as Charles Murray, there is no evidence that in states where AFDC payments are more generous, more children are born outside marriage. Also, spending on AFDC, in real terms, fell by nearly one-fifth between 1975 and 1989—the period that saw the biggest growth in illegitimate births.[41] This, of course, is to argue not that major improvements in social welfare programme design are not possible or desirable,[42] but rather that it is an unwarranted exercise in cynicism to assume that we can never make things better.

One of the unfortunate by-products of the virtues of specialization in the economy at large that Adam Smith so eloquently preached in *The Wealth of Nations* and so dramatically defied in the eclectic sweep of his own intellectual interests has been a radical disconnection among the major normative perspectives reviewed in this book, with a refusal on the part of proponents of each to recognize the legitimacy in particular contexts of the other perspectives, as well as a failure to recognize substantial points of convergence that could be realized through appropriate choices of institutions or instruments. In the striking phrase of U.S. economic historian and economic philosopher Donald McCloskey, "It is time to reunify some pieces of the conversation of humankind."[43]

In focussing as directly as I do on the role of the state in promoting the development of human capital, and creating a richer menu of life possibilities for a broader cross-section of the community, particularly those who have been the victims of historical inequalities and disadvantage as well as individuals facing more particular forces of misfortune, I believe that this strategy has vastly more potential than succumbing to the temptation of utilizing contract regulation for objectives to which it is ill-adapted, such as correcting adaptive preferences or vindicating distributive justice values. It is particularly tempting for lawyers to exaggerate the potential of the law (as it is conventionally understood) for vindicating all kinds of values. It is even in their self-interest to propagate this perception. Designing or redesigning social or educational programmes conventionally falls outside the domain of expertise of lawyers, but the fact that this is so should neither excuse lawyers for encouraging the dissipation of precious political and economic capital in promoting regulatory or other policies that are likely to have few positive impacts on their proclaimed goals—and in many cases are likely to prove counter-productive—nor should it excuse lawyers engaged in public policy-making roles or public policy analysis from acquiring the relevant forms of expertise in other governing instruments. Of course, lawyers are not the only, or even the principal, culprits in distorting the choice of institutions and instruments for vindicating widely held and legitimate normative values. The predilection for regulatory responses to all manner of perceived social ills is often attractive to both political representatives and large groups of voters, in that the social costs entailed are largely off-budget, do not require the raising of tax revenues, and appear to impose costs on relatively small and often somewhat unromantic sub-sets of the population. It is politically tempting to single out as the target for regulation ghetto merchants, slumlords, door-to-door peddlers, loan-sharks, drug dealers, pimps, johns, pornographers, and surrogacy agencies in an attempt to project onto them much larger social dysfunctions of which they are merely symptomatic. Ease of formulation and painlessness of execution (especially for the proponents) should not be the criteria by which policy responses to these larger social dysfunctions are chosen.

In arguing for a new convergence between economic and social policy-making around the role of the state in promoting the development of human capital, I recognize that these political biases have to be defied. I also recognize that the costs of the social programmes that are called for will largely be borne by average citizens. Another enduring myth espoused by the political left is that the rich in many cases do not pay their fair share of taxes and that new social programmes can be financed by increasing taxes on the wealthy. Although it may well be true that in many cases the wealthy do not pay their fair share of taxes, anybody with a passing acquaintance with public finance theory and underlying demographic statistics knows that if the income of the rich was taxed away completely, this would provide trivial sources of additional revenue to support new or enhanced social programmes. Equally, increasing taxes on large and wealthy corporations entails another fiscal illusion. Corporations do not exist except in the minds of lawyers. In real life, they are aggregations of individuals: shareholders, creditors, suppliers, employees, and customers, who, to one degree or another, bear all corporate taxes. The vast proportion of the revenue-raising capacity of most developed industrialized economies lies with middle-class citizens. Thus, just as ghetto merchants, slumlords, and so on have proved easy, although irrelevant, targets in ameliorating conditions of inequality or poverty in the marketplace, it is also time that the myth that most of us can escape being part of the solution was finally buried.

The question that must now be addressed is whether a better politics is possible in terms of better aligning institutional competence and institutional responsibilities in vindicating the major normative values canvassed in this book.

The Visible Hand: The Dangers of Government Failure

In capitalist democracies, individual citizens function within economic and political systems with very different properties. In the words of Arthur Okun: "The anatomy of the American economy contrasts sharply with the egalitarian structure of its polity."[44] On the one hand, a market economy differentiates in the returns to unequal natural endowments, unequal economic opportunities, and unequal effort; on the other hand, the political system is ostensibly premised on equal political entitlements and equal access to justice. The pursuit of efficiency in a market economy necessarily creates (and, for incentive reasons, requires) inequalities, whereas the exercise of political entitlements is likely to tend in the opposite direction.

Despite these tensions between our economic and political systems, the fact remains that no genuine democracy has existed in recent times outside a capitalist economy, and few durable and successful capitalist economies have existed outside democratic polities.[45] This suggests that viable compromises between the inequalities of the economic system and the equalities of the political system are attainable.

Here the economist's view of what incentives shape the behaviour of political agents (as compared with economic agents) needs fuller specification (often referred to as the "public choice theory" of politics). The economic origins of formal government are often, in a public choice framework, traced to the inefficiencies inherent in unstable property rights in a stateless world. In such a world, the classic "Prisoner's Dilemma" problem is seen as pervasive, representing a situation where individuals perceive gains from non-cooperative behaviour, even though if everybody behaves non-cooperatively, all end up worse off. Thus, in this world, rather than grow my own food, I am tempted to steal it from my neighbour. He, in view of this threat, will face incentives to divert part of his resources and energies to non-productive defensive measures against my depredations or, if these are too ineffective or costly, abandon growing food and perhaps plan to steal food from me or others. I, then, in the face of such threats, will be tempted to curtail my food production further or to take costly and non-productive defensive measures. Clearly, it would be in our mutual interests to agree to behave cooperatively rather than uncooperatively, to respect each other's property rights, and perhaps to engage in voluntary exchanges of these entitlements where gains from scale and specialization make this mutually advantageous. But such cooperative accords must be enforceable. In small, static, homogeneous societies, such as primitive tribes or clans, social conventions and pressures may prove adequate to this task. But as societies become more numerous, more mobile, more heterogeneous, more impersonal, the effectiveness of these conventions is likely to become attenuated, and individuals will probably need to turn to an agreed-upon third party to define and protect their property rights and to enforce voluntary non-simultaneous exchanges of entitlements.[46] Thus, the apparatus of the formal state begins to emerge (according to this theory, for sound economic reasons).

The State, of course, requires a constitution which defines the rules by which it is induced to act, even with respect to its minimal role of defining and protecting property rights and facilitating their voluntary exchange. To play this role, the State requires authority and legitimacy. It is unlikely that all individuals will agree to the appointment of a non-accountable, non-removable dictator, a move which subjects their property rights and perhaps physical integrity to the risk of capricious, coercive, or malicious encroachment. Thus, typically, some form of representative and accountable decision-making process emerges, where individual citizens vote for their political agents; hence results at least the partial compatibility between capitalism and democracy. Next the constitution must define the voting rules for individual citizens as well as the voting rules for the political assembly in which their representatives make decisions on their behalf. Here the complications begin.[47] A rule of unanimity requiring that all individual citizens must agree on some collective course of action is unworkable, even though in theory it replicates the virtues of private voluntary exchanges by ensuring that only courses of action are taken that make everybody feel better off. This rule does not work, partly because of the transaction costs entailed in securing unanimous consent in larger communities, even if all members act in good faith, and partly because such a rule creates incentives for strategic, non-cooperative behaviour where individuals find it personally advantageous to withhold their consent to some proposed course of action in order to extort for themselves a disproportionate share of the gains from such an action. Each individual under a unanimity rule faces such incentives, and thus the Prisoner's Dilemma problem reappears in another form. Similar difficulties arise if a more relaxed voting rule obtains for individual citizens but a rule of unanimity applies to their representatives.

There will be compelling reasons to adopt less exacting voting rules to mitigate these problems. These rules will probably apply both to individual citizens and to their representatives, in the form, for example, of simple majority voting rules at both levels. These appear to reduce both transaction (decision) costs and hold-out problems. But now a different order of problems arises. Whereas with unanimous voting rules, the concern was that minorities might act strategically to exploit majorities, now the concern becomes that majorities will act strategically to exploit minorities, and that the newly created State will not confine its activities to the initial definition of property rights (although this exercise itself is problematic under such a rule), to their subsequent protection, and to the facilitation of voluntary exchanges thereof. Instead, it will rearrange entitlements on an ongoing basis in whatever way any majority or minimum winning coalition of voters or their representatives at any point in time find to be in their own interests. The behavioural assumption made by economists (public choice theorists) in this context is that political decision-making should be modelled as an implicit market in which voters or interest groups demand policies which they consider will maximize their utility, and that politicians will choose to supply those demands which will maximize their utility, which is assumed to equate with their prospects of election or re-election. Bureaucrats and regulators in turn will seek to maximize personal pay, power, and prestige, and perhaps future employment prospects in the private sector. Thus, individual utility maximizing behaviour will dominate the process of collective decision-making, much as economics assumes it does in voluntary, arms-length, explicit market exchanges. On this view, policy outcomes are the result not of the disinterested pursuit of some notion of the public or national interest, but of an intricate web of implicit, self-interested exchanges among voters, interest groups, politicians, bureaucrats, regulators, and the media (although it should be noted that similar ambiguities surround the concept of "self-interest" in this context as pertain to it in the explicit exchange context, as discussed in Chapter 2). While pluralist theorists (mostly political scientists)[48] have argued in the past that competition among interest groups and political parties may lead to a natural equilibrium where all interests are reconciled by appropriate political compromises and trade-offs (an "invisible hand" theory of politics), economists point out that democratic politics entail a much higher potential for coercion than the voluntary exchange process; that political competition on the supply side often takes the form of a duopoly, with parties offering highly aggregated policy platforms and engaging in "full-line forcing" of voters; that short electoral time-frames bias policy offerings towards those with significant or concentrated short-run benefits for some and deferred or thinly-spread but perhaps more substantial costs for others; and that the information and transaction costs and collective action (free-rider) problems facing widely dispersed interest groups relative to concentrated interest groups will exacerbate this tendency.

In this process, the Prisoner's Dilemma problem emerges once more where incentives for non-cooperative or coercive behaviour between some groups of the polity and others may overwhelm the virtues of cooperative outcomes. "Rent-seeking," as it has come to be called in the contemporary economic literature, is a direct analogue to theft in the stateless society to which the evolution of a formal state was sought as an answer, and the economic implications are similar. This is the fundamental dilemma for capitalism and democracy. One cannot exist without the other: capitalism requires democracy because any other political system potentially offers less stable protection of property rights; democracy seems to flourish most strongly in some form of market economy because its stress on individual civil liberties seems to require a substantial measure of respect for private property rights.[49] For example, exclusive state ownership of the press and other instrumentalities of individual expression may make the preferences of the populace subject to gross manipulation by the incumbent political party. Moreover, entitlements to homes, apartments, and jobs that are subject to arbitrary conferment or confiscation also seriously compromise individual liberties. Yet the two systems represent constant threats to each other: capitalism threatens to overwhelm equality of political entitlements and influence with inequalities of wealth that may imply disproportionate political influence; democracy threatens capitalism because of the tendency to destabilize private property rights through the exercise of political influence by constantly shifting distributional coalitions of voters and interest groups.[50]

The economist's view of the political process is in many respects a depressing one.[51] It suggests that one should have little confidence in the state's ability to confine the domain of its collective decision-making to protecting private property rights and facilitating their transfer, correcting for contracting and market failures, and vindicating normatively defensible distributive justice, communitarian, or other goals. As we have seen in Chapter 9, with respect to domestic anti-discrimination policies, international trade policy, and immigration policy, these concerns are not without foundation. We thus seem left with two very unattractive dilemmas, one normative, the other positive: as a matter of normative theory we are unlikely to settle soon on a meta-theory that ranks and resolves conflicts in values produced by established normative theories. If we attempt to minimize the severity of this problem by placing more emphasis on choice of policy instruments to maximize the domain of normative convergence, we find ourselves confronted with a positive dilemma wherein the functioning of the political system is likely to systematically distort the choice of policy instruments in the pursuit of agreed policy goals. Is there any reason to hope that a better politics is achievable?

The Marketplace for Ideas

While not denying the importance of self-interest in the political process, Steven Kelman,[52] in a recent, important book, demonstrates that the economist's (public choice) view of the political process dramatically underestimates the role of what he calls "Public Spirit," or "Civic Virtue," or simply non-self-interested ideas in the political process (perhaps this reflects, in part, the ambiguities surrounding the concept of self-interest). He invokes many examples to substantiate this view, such as the enactment of extensive consumer protection and environmental legislation in the 1960s and early 1970s in the United States and many other countries over the protestations and resistance of concentrated and entrenched interests, and deregulation, privatization, and tax reform in the late 1970s and 1980s in the United States and many other countries, again over the protestations of many powerful and deeply entrenched interests. Indeed, the so-called paradox of voting itself[53]—why do so many citizens choose to vote in national elections at some cost to themselves, and with minimal prospects of influencing the outcome?—suggests a powerful notion of Civic Virtue at work. Thus, politics, to an important extent, is as much about what are thought to be good ideas as what are thought to be salient political interests. In other words, persuasion has important currency in the political process, in a reciprocal sense: voters and interest groups may persuade politicians, bureaucrats, and regulators of the virtues of a position or idea; similarly, political leaders, bureaucrats, or regulators may persuade interests groups and voters of the wisdom of an idea. Just as in private markets, where I have conceded that most preferences are not innate, it is equally true that preferences are not fixed and immutable in the political process. It is an odd irony that economists, who stress the dynamic qualities of private markets and the forces of innovation and new entry in breaking down entrenched market positions (the "perennial gale of creative destruction," in Joseph Schumpeter's famous words),[54] are inclined to view the political process in such static terms and the role for policy innovations and policy entrepreneurs as so limited.

Remembering McCloskey's call for reunifying the pieces of the conversation of humankind and thinking more concretely about how such a conversation about policy innovations might be enhanced, I am drawn to three broad strategies.

Constitutional Review

With the adoption by Canada of a Charter of Rights in recent years, it, like other countries such as the United States with much longer constitutional traditions of this kind, now provides a forum where reasoned argument, facts, and persuasion are the primary currency of debate in evaluating whether existing or proposed collective policies are violative of fundamental individual rights and freedoms. Although in the Canadian Charter a kind of utilitarian over-ride is permitted under s. 1, the Supreme Court of Canada appears to have interpreted this as requiring governments to demonstrate that they have adopted policies, in the service of some legitimate collective goal, that are least restrictive, given alternative policies available to serve the same ends, of constitutionally guaranteed individual rights.[55] The adoption of the Charter significantly elevates the role of reasoned argument and principled justification in our collective decision-making processes and provides an important check on illegitimate majoritarian encroachment on individual rights and freedoms. However, as Michael Sandel points out,[56] any rights-based constitutional philosophy is likely to be biased towards preventing improper actions by government and provides few guarantees of affirmative government action where it is legitimately justified, say, for distributive justice or communitarian reasons, and where individual rights are not in jeopardy. Here, we need to turn to other institutional reform possibilities to encourage appropriate government action, rather than to discourage inappropriate government action.

Institutional Reform

As my colleagues and I have shown, for example, in the international trade policy field, consumer interests are systematically discounted in the policy-making process because of various institutional features of that process. These features accentuate information and participation asymmetries between producer and consumer interests; the mandates of the decision-making agencies often explicitly disenfranchise from consideration legitimate interests such as those of domestic consumers; and a number of trade policy instruments in common vogue evade formal justificatory processes altogether. In addition, decision-making agencies are often confronted with a choice for or against trade protection, and they do not have at their disposal a range of other policy instruments that could vindicate legitimate distributive justice and communitarian concerns at much lower cost to domestic consumers, again, as in the constitutional review context, applying a least restrictive means test. I am sure that our observations about the international trade policy-making process apply to countless other areas of collective decision-making. More generally, electoral reforms that reduce the power of incumbency and wealth and enhance access to the political process for representatives of constituencies or perspectives hitherto marginalized in the process are likely to create a more vigorous and diverse political marketplace for ideas.

The dilemma to be confronted in proposing institutional reforms of these kinds is that identified by James Buchanan:[57] why would a biased polity agree to institutional reforms that are designed to reduce the gains to the currently dominant interests in the process? Buchanan's reply entails drawing a distinction between what he calls "constitutional" law-making and day-to-day politics. In the case of the former, fundamental and system-wide values of transparency, accountability, and participation are invoked—values that, abstracting from particular policy contexts, are highly valued by a very broad cross-section of the polity. Constitutional reforms that seek to enhance these values across a wide range of policy settings hold out some prospect of attracting the necessary popular support and suppressing the particular special interests that might benefit from the rejection of such values in specific policy contexts. Again, as with constitutional review, the common thread with institutional reforms that emphasize transparency, accountability, and participation is that typically these reforms elevate the role played by reasoned argument and principled justification in the policy-making process.

The Role of the Academy

As noted above, I believe that the disciplines which represent the major normative perspectives on policy-making in Western industrialised societies cannot continue to ignore one another. All civilized societies will wish to see vindicated, to a greater or lesser extent, all the major normative values canvassed in this book. One-value views of the world are inherently counterproductive. Attempting to reconcile tensions among these values, and choosing or designing instruments or institutions most appropriate to the values sought to be vindicated, is a task that no policy-oriented discipline can avoid confronting. In this context, intellectual specialization, whatever its benefits, has exacted serious costs. Adam Smith should be followed by example rather than precept in this respect.

But beyond "reunifying the pieces of the conversation of humankind," scholars need to take more seriously the proposition that many individual preferences are socially constructed and are amenable to revision. Too many scholars view themselves either as writing to each other (typically within narrow parochial enclaves) or, when not writing to each other, as advising the Prince rather than the public. Scholars need to view the constituencies for their ideas in much broader terms.

. . .

Ultimately, then, my exploration of the limits of freedom of contract suggests two broad strategies that require much greater collective attention in the future: First, we need to be much more alert to the possibilities of adopting public policies that *broaden* (rather than restrict) access to market opportunities for members of the community who either historically as classes, or as individuals through more specific sources of misfortune or disadvantage, would otherwise be denied these opportunities. Correspondingly, we should waste less time and energy on policies designed to restrict the domain of the market by limiting even further the contract opportunity set of such individuals, meagre as this may sometimes be at present. Second, in identifying policies which may indeed enhance access to rewarding and fulfilling market opportunities for those otherwise likely to be denied such access, we must also contemplate a set of strategies that broaden and deepen the marketplace for ideas in our collective decision-making processes. In order to minimize the risks of demagoguery or simply ill-conceived ideas or policy errors—to pursue effectively a strategy (in Alan Blinder's words)[58] of "hard heads but soft hearts"—the marketplace for ideas is the one market where we cannot afford to countenance anything less than a fierce, talented, and sophisticated state of competition. Thus, the quality and accessibility of a society's educational system (broadly defined) is of primary importance to both objectives. If we can successfully advance these two complementary market-broadening strategies—in both economic and intellectual markets— then we will have given greater substance to the observation of John Maynard Keynes that in the long-run ideas matter more than special interests in our collective policy-making processes[59] and to that of James Buchanan that history need not be "a random walk in socio-political space."[60] We will also have ensured that the market is widely accepted as an engine, not an enemy, of social as well as economic progress.

Notes · Index of Cases · General Index

Notes

1. The Private Ordering Paradigm and Its Critics

1. Francis Fukuyama, "The End of History?" (Summer 1989) *The National Interest* 3; see also Francis Fukuyama, *The End of History and the Last Man* (1991).
2. Robert Heilbroner, *The Making of Economic Society* (1975).
3. See Freidrich Hayek, *Individualism and Economic Order*, 77–78 (1948); Randy Barnett, "The Sound of Silence: Default Rules and Contractual Consent," 78 *Virginia Law Review* 821, 829–859 (1992).
4. See Mancur Olson, *Beyond the Measuring Rod of Money* (forthcoming).
5. See Arthur M. Okun, *Equality and Efficiency: The Big Trade off* (1975).
6. See, e.g., Reuven Brenner, "The Long Road from Serfdom and How to Shorten It," 17 *Canadian Business Law Journal* 195 (1991).
7. See Richard Posner, *Economic Analysis of Law*, 3–28 (4th ed., 1992); C. G. Veljanovski, *The New Law and Economics*, chap. 3 (1982).
8. See Gordon Tullock, "The Transitional Gains Trap," 6 *Bell Journal of Economics* 671 (1975).
9. For an excellent exposition and critique of alternative conceptions of efficiency, see Jules Coleman, *Markets, Morals, and the Law*, chap. 4 (1988).
10. Milton Friedman, *Capitalism and Freedom*, 13 (1962).
11. John Stuart Mill, *On Liberty* (1859).
12. Freidrich Hayek, *The Road to Serfdom* (1944).
13. Friedman, *Capitalism and Freedom*.
14. Robert Nozick, *Anarchy, State, and Utopia* (1974).
15. Charles Fried, *Contract as Promise* (1981).
16. Ibid., 132.
17. See, e.g., John Rawls, *A Theory of Justice* (1971).
18. For a discussion, see Joel Feinberg, *Harmless Wrongdoing*, chap. 29A (1988).
19. See, e.g., Hayek, *Road to Serfdom*; Friedman, *Capitalism and Freedom*; Nozick, *Anarchy, State, and Utopia*.
20. See Brenner, "The Long Road."
21. On the economic role of property rights, see generally Posner, *Economic Analy-*

sis of Law, chap. 3; Robert Cooter and Thomas Ulen, *Law and Economics,* chap. 4 (1988). For a critique of efficiency arguments for private property, see Duncan Kennedy and Frank Michelman, "Are Property and Contract Efficient?" 8 *Hofstra Law Review* 711 (1980).

22. See R. D. Luce and Howard Raiffa, *Games and Decisions,* 94–97 (1957); Robert Axelrod, *The Evolution of Cooperation,* 7–11 (1984).

23. See Dennis Mueller, *Public Choice II,* chap. 2 (1989); Cooter and Ulen, *Law and Economics,* chap. 4.

24. Mueller, *Public Choice II,* 13–15.

25. See Garett Hardin, "The Tragedy of the Commons," 162 *Science* 1243 (1968).

26. See, e.g., Michael Jensen and William Meckling, "Theory of the Firm: Managerial Behaviour, Agency Costs, and Ownership Structure," 3 *Journal of Financial Economics* 305 (1976); Eugene Fama, "Agency Problems and the Theory of the Firm," 88 *Journal of Political Economy* 288 (1980).

27. See Mueller, *Public Choice II,* chap. 4.

28. Elinor Ostrom, *Governing the Commons,* chap. 3 (1990); Robert Ellickson, *Order without Law* (1991).

29. Mueller, *Public Choice II;* Michael Trebilcock, Douglas Hartle, Donald Dewees, and Robert Prichard, Economic Council of Canada, *The Choice of Governing Instrument* (1982).

30. See Anthony T. Kronman and Richard A. Posner, *The Economics of Contract Law,* chap. 1 (1979); for a critique of efficiency arguments for freedom of contract, see Kennedy and Michelman, "Are Property and Contract Efficient?"

31. See Anthony Kronman, "Contract Law and the State of Nature," 1 *Journal of Law, Economics, and Organization* 5 (1985).

32. See Jules Coleman, "A Bargaining Theory Approach to Default Provisions and Disclosure Rules in Contract Law," 12 *Harvard Journal of Law and Public Policy* 639 (1989).

33. See Richard Craswell, "Efficiency and Rational Bargaining in Contractual Settings," 15 *Harvard Journal of Law and Public Policy* (forthcoming); see also, for a statement and critique of this approach, Ian Ayres and Robert Gertner, "Filling Gaps in Incomplete Contracts: An Economic Theory of Default Rules," 99 *Yale Law Journal* 87 (1989).

34. See, e.g., Michael Sandel, *Liberalism and the Limits of Justice* (1982); Alastair MacIntyre, *After Virtue* (1989); Charles Taylor, *Philosophy and the Human Sciences, Philosophical Papers 2,* especially "Atomism," 190 (1986); Robert N. Bellah et al., *The Good Society* (1991).

35. Adam Smith, *The Wealth of Nations,* 13 (1937).

36. Karl Polanyi, *The Great Transformation* (1944); see also Patrick Atiyah, *The Rise and Fall of Freedom of Contract,* chaps. 3 and 4 (1979).

37. Richard Posner, "A Theory of Primitive Society, with Special Reference to Law," 23 *Journal of Law and Economics* 1 (1980).

38. F. A. Hayek, "History and Politics," in Hayek, *Capitalism and the Historians,* 16–21 (1954).

39. See, e.g., Michael Walzer, *Spheres of Justice* (1983); Alan Fox, *Beyond Contract* (1974); Margaret Jane Radin, "Market Inalienability," 100 *Harvard Law Review* 1849 (1987); James Boyd White, "Economics and Law: Two Cultures

in Tension," 54 *Tennessee Law Review* 161 (1987); Jay Feinberg, "Critical Approaches to Contract Law," 30 *UCLA Law Review* 829 (1983); Robert Gordon, "Macauley, McNeil, and the Discovery of Solidarity and Power in Contract Law," *Wisconsin Law Review* 565 (1985); David Beatty, "Labour Is Not a Commodity," in *Studies in Contract Law* (John Swan and Barry Reiter, eds., 1980).

40. See Jules L. Coleman, "Market Contractarianism," in *Markets, Morals, and the Law,* 243–276 (1988).
41. See, e.g., C. B. McPherson, *Democratic Theory,* especially "Elegant Tombstones: A Note on Friedman's Freedom," 143–156 (1973).
42. See, e.g., Guido Calabresi, "The Pointlessness of Pareto: Carrying Coase Further," 100 *Yale Law Journal* 1211 (1991).
43. See, e.g., Amartya Sen, *On Ethics and Economics* (1987); Ronald Dworkin, "Is Wealth a Value?" and "Why Efficiency?" in Dworkin, *A Matter of Principle,* chaps. 12 and 13 (1986); Calabresi, "Pointlessness of Pareto"; Will Kymlicka, *Contemporary Political Philosophy: An Introduction* (1990).
44. Rawls, *A Theory of Justice.*
45. Anthony Kronman, "Contract Law and Distributive Justice," 89 *Yale Law Review* 472 (1980).
46. See, e.g., Cass Sunstein, "Disrupting Voluntary Transactions," in *Markets and Justice* (J. R. Pennock and J. W. Chapman, eds., 1989).
47. See, e.g., Sandel, *Liberalism and Liberal Justice;* Bellah et al., *The Good Society.*
48. For a discussion, see, e.g., Isaiah Berlin, "Two Concepts of Liberty," in Berlin, *Four Essays on Liberty* (1969).

2. Commodification

1. Kenneth Arrow, "Gifts and Exchanges," 1 *Philosophy and Public Affairs* 342 (1972).
2. See Michael Walzer, *Spheres of Justice,* 100–103 (1983). There may be other objections to privatizing public functions. See, for example, debates over plea bargaining: Robert Scott and William Stuntz, "Plea Bargaining as Contract," 101 *Yale Law Journal* 1909 (1992); ensuing comments by Frank Easterbrook and Stephen Schulhofer; and rejoinder by Robert Scott and William Stuntz.
3. John Stuart Mill, *On Liberty,* chap. 5, para. 11 (1956), discussed in Chapter 7.
4. Margaret Jane Radin, "Market Inalienability," 100 *Harvard Law Review* 1849 (1989).
5. See also James Boyd White, "Economics and Law: Two Cultures in Tension," 54 *Tennessee Law Review* 161 (1987); Jay Feinman, "Critical Approaches to Contract Law," 30 *UCLA Law Review* 829 (1983).
6. For a somewhat analogous argument, see Fred Hirsch, *Social Limits to Growth* (1978), especially chap. 6.
7. See Patrick Devlin, *The Enforcement of Morals* (1965).
8. Radin, "Market Inalienability," 1909.
9. Margaret Jane Radin, "Residential Rent Control," 15 *Philosophy and Public*

Affairs 350 (1986). For an ensuing exchange, see Timothy Brennan, 17 *Philosophy and Public Affairs* 66 (1988); and Margaret Jane Radin, 17 *Philosophy and Public Affairs* 80 (1988). For employment contracts see David Beatty, "Labour Is Not a Commodity," in *Studies in Contract Law* (John Swan and Barry Reiter, eds., 1980).

10. See Scott Altman, "(Com)modifying Experience," 65 *Southern California Law Review* 293 (1991).

11. Richard Titmuss, *The Gift Relationship: From Human Blood to Social Policy* (1970).

12. Arrow, "Gifts and Exchanges."

13. See Susan Rose-Ackerman, "Inalienability and the Theory of Property Rights," 85 *Columbia Law Review* 931, 947 (1985).

14. Eric Mack, "Dominoes and the Fear of Commodification," in *Markets and Justice,* 198 (J. R. Pennock and J. W. Chapman, eds., 1989).

15. For an insightful discussion of the ambiguities inherent in the notion of self-interest, see Amartya Sen, *On Ethics and Economics* (1987).

16. David Gauthier, *Morals by Agreement,* 84 (1987).

17. The discussion of this example is largely derived from Guido Calabresi and Philip Bobbit, *Tragic Choices* (1978).

18. Ibid.

19. Richard Posner, *The Economics of Justice* (1981).

20. Kenneth Arrow, *Social Choice and Individual Values* (rev. ed., 1963).

21. See Dennis Mueller, *Public Choice II,* chap. 20 (1989).

22. For an extended critique of communitarianism, see Stephen Macedo, *Liberal Virtues* (1990).

23. Henry Hansmann, "The Economics and Ethics of Markets for Human Organs," 14 *Journal of Health Politics, Policy, and the Law* 57 (1989).

24. Manitoba Law Reform Commission, "Report on the Human Tissue Act," 3 (1986).

25. Lloyd R. Cohen, "Increasing the Supply of Transplant Organs: The Virtues of a Futures Market," 58 *George Washington Law Review* 1, 5 (1989); see also Hansmann, "Markets for Human Organs," 60.

26. Manitoba Law Reform Commission, "Human Tissue Report," 24.

27. Hansmann, "Markets for Human Organs," 60; James F. Childress, "Ethical Criteria for Procuring and Distributing Organs for Transplantation," 14 *Journal of Health Politics, Policy, and the Law* 87, 91 (1989).

28. Manitoba Law Reform Commission, "Human Tissue Report," 24.

29. Cohen, "Transplant Organs: Futures Market," 8; Manitoba Law Reform Commission, "Human Tissue Report," 25.

30. William N. Gerson, "Refining the Law of Organ Donation: Lessons from the French Law of Presumed Consent," 19 *New York University Journal of International Law and Politics* 1013, 1027 (1987); Cohen, "Transplant Organs: Futures Market," 19.

31. Australian Law Reform Commission, "Human Tissue Transplants," Report no. 7 (1977).

32. The Manitoba Reform Commission, "Human Tissue Report," 111.

33. Ibid., 110.
34. Ibid.
35. Bernard Dickens, "Morals and Markets in Transplantable Organs," *Transplantation/Implantation Today* 29 (1990).
36. Ibid., 28; quoting from Lori Andrews, "My Body, My Property," 16(5) *Hastings Center Report* 28, 32 (1986).
37. Hansmann, "Markets for Human Organs," 73.
38. Ibid.
39. Ibid., 74.
40. Peter H. Schuck, "Government Funding for Organ Transplants," 14 *Journal of Health Politics, Policy, and the Law* 169, 172 (1989).
41. Ibid., 171.
42. Ibid., 173.
43. Ibid.
44. Ibid., 181.
45. Ibid.
46. Cohen, "Transplant Organs: Futures Market," 1, 33.
47. Ibid., 2.
48. Ibid., 28.
49. Hansmann, "Markets for Human Organs," 63.
50. Ibid., 65.
51. Ibid., 70.
52. Ibid., 67.
53. Arthur R. Bauer, "Bioethical and Legal Issues in Fetal Organ and Tissue Transplantation," 26 *Houston Law Review* 955, 957 (1989).
54. Debra H. Berger, "The Infant with Anencephaly: Moral and Legal Dilemmas," 5 *Issues in Law and Medicine*, 67, 68 (1989).
55. Bauer, "Fetal Organ and Tissue Transplantations," 973.
56. Ibid., 971. (These are federal regulations adopted from the recommendations of the National Commission for the Protection of Human Subjects of Biomedical and Behavioural Research, formed immediately after the Roe v. Wade decision in 1973.)
57. Berger, "The Infant with Anencephaly," 70.
58. Bauer, "Fetal Organ and Tissue Transplantations," 981.
59. Anencephalic babies are born with only a small fragment of a brain and often with little or no skull covering. They die within hours or days. The organs of these babies, however, are healthy. See Berger, "The Infant with Anencephaly," 69.
60. Ibid., 80.
61. Ibid., 79.
62. John A. Robertson, "Fetal Tissue Transplants," 66 *Washington University Law Quarterly* 443, 465 (1988).
63. Ibid., 452.
64. Ibid., 453.
65. Ibid., 454.
66. Bauer, "Fetal Organ and Tissue Transplantations," 989.

67. Nicolas P. Terry, "Politics and Privacy: Refining the Ethical and Legal Issues in Fetal Tissue Transplantation," 66 *Washington University Law Quarterly* 523, 529 (1988); see also Robertson, "Fetal Tissue Transplants," 455.
68. Histocompatibility is the compatibility between the grafted tissue and the recipient.
69. Robertson, "Fetal Tissue Transplants," 456.
70. Terry, "Politics and Privacy: Fetal Tissue Transplantation," 527–528.
71. Ibid., 528.
72. Bauer, "Fetal Organ and Tissue Transplantations," 1003–1004.
73. Radin, "Market Inalienability," 1849, 1884 (1987).
74. Ibid., 1872–1873.
75. Ibid., 1881.
76. Ibid., 1912–1913.
77. Ibid., 1922.
78. Nancy Erbe, "Prostitutes: Victims of Men's Exploitation and Abuse," 2 *Law and Inequality Journal* 609 (1984).
79. Carole Pateman, *The Sexual Contract*, 194 (1988).
80. Catharine A. MacKinnon, *Toward a Feminist Theory of the State*, 243 (1989).
81. Ibid., 131.
82. Ibid., 130.
83. Jody Freeman, "The Feminist Debate over Prostitution Reforms: Prostitutes' Rights Groups, Radical Feminists, and the (Im)possibility of Consent," 5 *Berkeley Women's Law Journal* 75, 78 (1990).
84. Canadian Criminal Code, R.S.C., chap. C-46, sec. 213(1) (1985) (Can).
85. Ibid., secs. 212(1)(a–i).
86. Ibid., sec. 210(1).
87. Ibid., secs. 212(1)(j) and 212(2).
88. Ibid., sec. 213.
89. Priscilla Alexander, "Prostitution: A Difficult Issue for Feminists," in *Sex Work: Writings by Women in the Sex Industry,* 189–190 (Priscilla Alexander and Frédérique Delacoste, eds., 1987).
90. Ibid., 197. Forty percent of the prostitutes on the street are women of colour. Scibelli reports that a black woman is twenty-two times as likely as a white woman to be arrested for prostitution: Pasqua Scibelli, "Empowering Prostitutes: A Proposal for International Legal Reform," 10 *Harvard Women's Law Journal* 117, 120 (1987).
91. Ministry of Supply and Services Canada, "Report of the Special Committee on Pornography and Prostitution: Pornography and Prostitution in Canada," vol. 2 (Chair: Paul Fraser, 1985). Hereafter cited as "The Fraser Report."
92. For various estimates, see Alexander, "Prostitution: Difficult Issue for Feminists," 188; Christopher Bagley and Kathleen King, *Child Sexual Abuse: The Search for Healing* 118 (1990); Belinda M. M. Cheney, "Prostitution—A Feminist Jurisprudential Perspective," 18 *Victoria University of Wellington Law Review* 239, 243 (1988); Judith Enew, *The Sexual Exploitation of Children,* 94 (1986); Jean Goodwin, *Sexual Abuse: Incest Victims and Their Families,* 4 (1982); Patricia Beezley Mrazek and C. Henry Kempe, *Sexually Abused Children and Their Families,* 230 (1981); "The Fraser Report," 352.

93. Bagley and King, in *Child Sexual Abuse,* 59–69, cite eleven studies from Britain, Canada, and the United States, reporting varying percentages of adult women who experienced some form of sexual abuse as children. The inconsistency can be attributed to the diverse populations used in each study, the formulation of the questions, the various definitions of sexual abuse which were employed, and the size of each sample.

94. Alexander, "Prostitution: Difficult Issue for Feminists," 200.

95. Richard Symanski, *The Immoral Landscape: Female Prostitution in Western Societies,* 62 (1981).

96. Cheney, "Prostitution—A Feminist Perspective," 243.

97. Moira Griffin, "Wives, Hookers, and the Law," 10 *Student Lawyer* 18, 20 (1982).

98. Belinda Cooper, "Prostitution: A Feminist Analysis," 11(2) *Women's Rights Law Reporter* 99, 112 (1989); see also Alexander and Delacoste, for anecdotes by prostitutes about "the life."

99. Freeman, "Feminist Debate over Prostitution Reforms," 90.

100. Cheney, "Prostitution—A Feminist Perspective," 253.

101. Ibid., 243.

102. Arlene Carmen and Howard Moody, *Working Women: The Subterranean World of Street Prostitution,* 16 (1985).

103. Scibelli, "Empowering Prostitutes," 132.

104. Alexander, "Prostitution: Difficult Issue for Feminists," 206.

105. Freeman, "Feminist Debate over Prostitution Reforms," 82.

106. "The Fraser Report," Recommendation 55 at 534.

107. Ibid., Recommendation 56 at 536 and Recommendations 59 and 60 at 543.

108. Ibid., Recommendation 57 at 538 and Recommendation 61 at 546.

109. Ibid., 683.

110. Ibid., 360.

111. In the famous English case of Pearce v. Brooks (1866) *Law Reports* 1, ex. 213, a right of action was denied in analogous circumstances and presumably would have been denied if the parties' roles had been reversed.

112. Griffin, "Wives, Hookers, and the Law."

113. Pateman, *The Sexual Contract,* 122.

114. Ibid.

115. Ibid., 124.

116. This section (separation agreements) and the next (surrogacy) are derived from Michael Trebilcock and Rosemin Keshvani, "The Role of Private Ordering in Family Law: A Law and Economics Perspective," 41 *University of Toronto Law Journal* 533 (1991).

117. See Nitya Duclos, "Breaking the Dependency Circle: *The Family Law Act* Reconsidered," 45 *University of Toronto Faculty of Law Review* 1, 4 (1987).

118. Law Reform Commission of Canada, "Report on Family Law," 3 (1976).

119. Ibid., 35.

120. Family Law Act, S.O. chap. 4, sec. 5(1) (1986) (Can).

121. Ibid., secs. 33(8) and (9); see also Divorce Act, R.S.C. chap. 4, sec. 15(7)(d) (1986) (Can.).

122. Pelech v. Pelech 7 R.F.L. (3d) 225 (S.C.C. 1987).

123. See Robert Mnookin and Lewis Kornhauser, "Bargaining in the Shadow of the Law: The Case of Divorce," 88 *Yale Law Journal* 1015 (1979).
124. Ibid.
125. Katherine Baker, "Contracting for Security: Paying Married Women What They've Earned," 55 *University of Chicago Law Review* 1193 (1988); the data cited is from Lenore Weitzman, *The Divorce Revolution* (1985).
126. Martha Minow, "Learning to Live with the Dilemma of Difference," 48 *Law and Contemporary Problems* 157 (1985); Martha Minow, *Making All the Difference* (1990).
127. See, e.g., Pelech; however, for a recent retrenchment by the Court from this position, see Moge v. Moge (S.C.C. December 1992), as yet unreported.
128. See, e.g., Brenda Cossman, "A Matter of Difference: Domestic Contracts and Gender Inequality," 28 *Osgoode Hall Law Journal* 303 (1990).
129. Duclos, "Breaking the Dependency Circle," 28–32.
130. See, e.g., Neil Komesar, "Toward a General Theory of Personal Injury Loss," 3 *Journal of Legal Studies* 457 (1974).
131. Baker, "Paying Married Women," 1225–1226.
132. See Lloyd Cohen, "Marriage, Divorce, and Quasi-Rents; Or I Gave Him the Best Years of My Life," 16 *Journal of Legal Studies* 267 (1987).
133. See June Carbone and Margaret Brinig, "Rethinking Marriage: Feminist Ideology, Economic Change, and Divorce Reform," 65 *Tulane Law Review* 953 (1991).
134. See Ira Ellman, "The Theory of Alimony," 77 *California Law Review* 3 (1989); Stephen Sugarman, "Dividing Financial Interests on Divorce," in *Divorce Reform at the Cross-Roads* (Stephen Sugarman and Herman Hill Kay, eds., 1990).
135. In Re Baby M, 109 N.J. 396, 537 A. ed. 1227 (S.C. New Jersey 1988).
136. In the United States every year there is an excess of 13,130 children in need of homes. The majority of these children are non-white and have special needs. See *The World Almanac and Book of Facts—1990* at 843 (1990). Although infertile couples should not be made to bear the burden of creating homes for these children, it might be argued that the recent attention paid to surrogate motherhood should remind fertile and infertile couples alike to give more thought to the welfare of these needy children.
137. *Baby M,* 1235.
138. For sympathetic views of the advantages of surrogacy, see Carmel Shalev, *Birth Power: The Case for Surrogacy* (1989); Lori Andrews, *Between Strangers* (1989); and Amy Overvold, *Surrogate Parenting* (1988).
139. For an overview of potential conflicts with the traditional conception of family, see Martha Field, *Surrogate Motherhood,* 33–45 (1988).
140. See Sacred Congregation for the Doctrine of the Faith, *Instruction on Respect of Human Life in Its Origin and the Dignity of Procreation,* 39 (1987).
141. Arguments which derive purpose or telos from "nature" are often oppressive and should be viewed with caution. Consider the Social Darwinist justification for racial supremacy or slavery. Similarly, consider Aristotle's defence of slavery and the natural inferiority of women (see Aristotle, *Politics, Book I,* chaps.

2–7); the classic model and methodology of "natural law" comes from Aristotle, who posited that man's correct nature and telos could be determined through rational reflection on the essential nature of the person (see Aristotle, *Posterior Analytics, Book II,* chap. 5).

142. See generally F. E. Olsen, "The Family and the Market: A Study of Ideology and Legal Reform," 96 *Harvard Law Review* 1497 (1983); Constance Backhouse, "Pure Patriarchy: Nineteenth-Century Canadian Marriage," 31 *McGill Law Journal* 265 (1986); Shalev, *Birth Power,* 21–36; G. Greer, *The Female Eunuch,* 198–238 (1971); Simone de Beauvoir, *The Second Sex* (1949).

143. See Shalev, *Birth Power,* 22, where she supports the argument that "adultery" is related not to the fact of sexual intercourse, but to the husband's right to "certainty of paternity," citing Orford v. Orford 49 O.L.R. 15, 23 (Ont. C.A. 1921), in which a married woman who conceived through artificial insemination was found to have committed adultery, thereby forfeiting her right to alimony.

144. See Catharine MacKinnon, "Feminism, Marxism, Method, and the State: Toward a Feminist Jurisprudence," 8 *Signs* 635 (1982).

145. See, e.g., Phyllis Chesler, *Sacred Bond* (1988); Radin, "Market Inalienability," 1849; Elizabeth Kane, *Birth Mother* (1988); Thomas Shannon, *Surrogate Motherhood* (1988); E. S. Anderson, "Is Women's Labor a Commodity?" 19 *Philosophy and Public Affairs* 71 (1990).

146. Anderson, "Women's Labour," 72–73.

147. See, e.g., Gena Corea, *The Mother Machine: Reproductive Technologies from Artificial Insemination to Artificial Womb* (1985).

148. See Field, *Surrogate Motherhood,* 26–29.

149. See Radin, "Market Inalienability."

150. Ibid.

151. See Richard Arneson, "Commodification and Commercial Surrogacy," 21 *Philosophy and Public Affairs* 132 (1992).

152. See Susan Sherwin, "Feminist Ethics and In Vitro Fertilization," supplementary volume 13 *Canadian Journal of Philosophy* 265, 299 (1987), where it is argued that surrogacy in practice would amount to exploitation of poor, under-educated, and emotionally unstable women; see also Debra Satz, "Markets in Women's Reproductive Labour," 21 *Philosophy and Public Affairs* 107 (1992). For a critique of this view, see Alan Wertheimer, "Two Questions about Surrogacy and Exploitation," 21 *Philosophy and Public Affairs* 211 (1992).

153. Shalev, *Birth Power,* 164; for a Marxist argument to similar effect, see Jane Ollengburger and John Hamlin, "All Birthing Should Be Paid Labour," in *On the Problem of Surrogate Parenthood* (H. Richardson, ed., 1987).

154. For a feminist argument that such freedom should be recognized, see Lori Andrews, "Surrogate Motherhood: The Challenge for Feminists," 16 *Law Medicine and Health Care* 72 (1988).

155. See Peter Schuck, "Some Reflections on the *Baby M* Case," 76 *Georgetown Law Journal* 1793, 1795 (1988).

156. United Kingdom Department of Health and Social Security, "Report of the Committee of Inquiry into Human Fertilization and Embryology," Cmnd 9314

in Sessional Papers at 46–47 (Chair: Dame Mary Warnock, July 1984); see also J. R. S. Prichard, "A Market for Babies?" 34 *University of Toronto Law Journal* 341 (1984).

157. Eric Mack, "Dominoes and the Fear of Commodification," in *Markets and Justice,* 217 (J. W. Chapman and J. R. Pennock, eds., 1989), emphasis added.

158. For studies on the empirical question of "bonding," see "Reports of Phyllis R. Silverman" (Professor of Social Work in Health Care, Massachusetts General Hospital Institute of Health Professionals) for use in the *Baby M* litigation, October 23, 1986, which finds that birth mothers greatly underestimate the degree of grief they will feel from giving up the child—95 percent of them felt it was worse than they had ever imagined; see also Leverett Millen and Samuel Roll, "Solomon's Mothers: A Special Case of Pathological Bereavement," 55 *American Journal of Orthopsychiatry* 2 (1985), in which it was found that birth mothers experience anguish as much as twenty years later; see also Vicki C. Jackson, "*Baby M* and The Question of Surrogate Parenthood," 76 *Georgetown Law Journal* 1811, 1821 (1988), in which she cites numerous studies establishing that many birth mothers severely underestimate the emotional trauma resulting from giving up the child; see also Kane, *Birth Mother,* but compare Schuck, "Reflections on Baby M," 1799 (Schuck argues that "[t]he risk of subsequent regret is the price we pay for our commitment to personal autonomy and responsibility in the face of uncertainty").

159. Field, in *Surrogate Motherhood,* 27, maintains that "to portray surrogacy contracts as representing meaningful choice and informed consent . . . reveals an idealized perspective and a failure to take account of realities"; see, however, Schuck, "Reflections on Baby M," 1800 (Schuck argues that "a choice is not morally unacceptable simply because it is constrained or even because some choosers are more constrained than others . . . constraint is what makes choices problematic—and thus morally relevant—in the first place").

160. See Louis Michael Seidman, "*Baby M* and The Problem of Unstable Preferences," 76 *Georgetown Law Journal* 1829, 1933 (1988), where he suggests that if we are serious about controlling externalities, surrogate parenting may not be an appropriate place to start. Taken to its logical conclusion, the regulatory approach may well mandate the establishment of administrative agencies to oversee child bearing and child rearing questions generally; see also Judith Areen, "*Baby M* Reconsidered," 76 *Georgetown Law Journal* 1741, 1758 (1988), where she suggests that because a child conceived through surrogacy is produced precisely for the purpose of being adopted, this may create a set of relationships fraught with peril—specifically, the child may view herself as a commodity; see also Radin, "Market Inalienability," where she argues that allowing for the commodification of children would inevitably alter our perception and valuation of them; see also B. K. Rothman, *The Tentative Pregnancy,* 28 (1986), in which she suggests that reproductive technologies, including surrogate motherhood, are the first step towards a "developing ideology [in which] we are learning to see our children as products, the products of conception"; see also Anderson, "Women's Labour."

161. Radin, "Market Inalienability."

162. See Ontario Law Reform Commission "Report on Human Artificial Reproduction," 232 (1985).
163. See Field, *Surrogate Motherhood,* 139, for an argument that precise rules determining custody are to be preferred, in the case of surrogacy, to avoid the negative effects on the child; and see also, *Baby M,* 1247, where C. J. Wilentz suggests that the real failure with surrogacy contracts is that "a child, instead of starting off its life with as much peace and security as possible, finds itself immediately in a tug-of-war between contending mother and father"; compare Marsha Garrison, "Surrogate Parenting: What Should Legislatures Do?" 22 *Family Law Quarterly* 149, 157 (1988). Garrison argues against the need for a clear rule on the custody question, suggesting surrogacy be treated no differently from other forms of custody disputes.
164. See Ontario Law Reform Commission, "Report on Human Artificial Reproduction," 236–261 (1985).
165. Field, *Surrogate Motherhood,* 151–152.
166. See Richard A. Posner, *Sex and Reason,* 422–423 (1992).
167. Ronald Coase, "The Problem of Social Costs," 3 *Journal of Law and Economics* 1 (1960).
168. Field, *Surrogate Motherhood.*
169. Ibid., 97–109.
170. Daigle v. Tremblay (1989) 2 S.C.R. 530 (S.C.C. Can.).
171. This position parallels the present laws governing AID, in which the biological father does not possess legal rights with respect to the child.
172. See, e.g., Wanda Wiegers, "Economic Analysis of Law and Private Ordering: A Feminist Critique," 42 *University of Toronto Law Journal* 170 (1992).

3. Externalities

1. See Guido Calabresi, "The Pointlessness of Pareto: Carrying Coase Further," 100 *Yale Law Journal* 1211 (1951).
2. Carl J. Dahlman, "The Problem of Externality," 22 *Journal of Law and Economics* 141 (1979).
3. J. M. Buchanan and W. C. Stubblebine, "Externality," 29 *Economica* 37 (1962).
4. Dahlman, "The Problem of Externality," 155–156.
5. Ronald Coase, "The Problem of Social Cost," 11 *Journal of Law and Economics* 1 (1960).
6. Harold Demsetz, "Information and Efficiency: Another Viewpoint," 12 *Journal of Law and Economics* 55 (1969).
7. E. J. Mishan, "The Effect of Externality on Individual Choice," 73 *International Review of Law and Economics* 97 (1981); see also E. J. Mishan, "The Post-War Literature on Externalities: An Interpretive Essay," 9 *Journal of Economic Literature* 1 (1971).
8. Guido Calabresi and A. Douglas Melamed, "Property Rules, Liability Rules, and Inalienability: One View of the Cathedral," 85 *Harvard Law Review* 1089 (1972).

9. John Stuart Mill, *On Liberty,* chap. 1, para. 9 (1859).

10. See John Gray, *Liberalism,* 53, 54 (1986).

11. Joel Feinberg, *Harm to Others* (1984); *Offense to Others* (1986); *Harm to Self* (1986); *Harmless Wrongdoing* (1988).

12. Feinberg, *Harm to Others,* 12.

13. Feinberg, *Offense to Others,* 1.

14. Mill, *On Liberty,* chap. 6, para. 12.

15. Feinberg, *Offense to Others,* 10–13.

16. Ibid., chap. 8.

17. Ibid., chap. 9.

18. Feinberg, *Harmless Wrongdoing,* chaps. 28, 29, 30.

19. Patrick Devlin, *The Enforcement of Morals* (1965).

20. H. L. A. Hart, "Immorality and Treason," in *Morality and the Law,* 54 (Richard A. Wasserstrom, ed., 1971); more generally, H. L. A. Hart, *Law, Liberty, and Morality* (1963).

21. See Jeremy Waldron, "Mill and the Value of Moral Distress," 25 *Political Studies* 410 (1987); Anthony Ellis, "Offense and the Liberal Conception of Law," 13 *Philosophy and Public Affairs* 3 (1984); Ronald Dworkin, "Do We Have a Right to Pornography?" in Dworkin, *A Matter of Principle,* chap. 17 (1985).

22. R. v. Butler 134 N.R. 81 (S.C.C. 1992) (Can.).

23. See Pierre Schlag, "An Appreciative Comment on *Coase's Problem of Social Cost: A View from the Left,*" (1986) *Wisconsin Law Review* 919; Duncan Kennedy, "Cost-Benefit Analysis of Entitlement Problems: A Critique," 33 *Stanford Law Review* 387 (1981).

24. Feinberg, *Offense to Others,* chap. 11.

25. United States Attorney General's Commission on Pornography (1986).

26. See, e.g., Edward Donnerstein and Daniel Linz, *The Question of Pornography* (1987); H. B. McKay and D. J. Dolff, "The Impact of Pornography: An Analysis of Research and Summary Findings," Background Study to the Report of the Special Committee on Pornography and Prostitution in Canada (1986); Richard Posner, *Sex and Reason,* 366–371 (1992).

27. *Butler,* 1.

28. See Robin West, "Taking Preferences Seriously," 64 *Tulane Law Review* 659 (1990) (on the Georgia anti-sodomy statute).

29. *Butler,* 141.

30. See McKay and Dolff, "The Impact of Pornography."

31. Catharine MacKinnon, *Feminism Unmodified: Discourses on Life and Law,* 140 (1987).

32. Andrea Dworkin, *Pornography: Men Possessing Women* (1989).

33. Caryn Jacobs, "Patterns of Violence: A Feminist Perspective on the Regulation of Pornography," 7 *Harvard Women's Law Journal* 41 (1986).

34. Catharine MacKinnon, *Toward a Feminist Theory of the State,* 204 (1989).

35. Ibid.

36. Ibid., 205.

37. MacKinnon, *Feminism Unmodified,* 140.

38. Jacobs, "Patterns of Violence," 45.

39. MacKinnon, *Feminism Unmodified*, 193.
40. Dworkin, *Pornography: Men Possessing Women*, 2.
41. Ibid., 13.
42. Cass Sunstein, "Pornography and the First Amendment," 4 *Duke Law Journal* 589, 597 (1986).
43. Ibid., 603–604.
44. Ibid., 601; Deana Pollard, "Regulating Violent Pornography," 43 *Vanderbilt Law Journal* 130 (1990).
45. MacKinnon, *Toward A Feminist Theory*, 207.
46. Ibid., 208.
47. See also Ruth Colker, "Pornography and Privacy: Towards the Development of a Group-Based Theory for Sex-Based Intrusions of Privacy," 1 *Law and Inequality Journal* 198 (1983).
48. Christina Spaulding, "Anti-Pornography Laws as a Claim for Equal Respect: Feminism, Liberalism, and Community," 4 *Berkeley Women's Law Journal* 128, 136 (1989).
49. Ibid., 161.
50. Ibid., 142.
51. Ibid., 143.
52. See Jacobs, *"Patterns of Violence,"* 17; Alice Walker, "Coming Apart," in *Take Back the Night* (Laura Lederer, ed., 1980); Luisah Teish, "A Quiet Subversion," in Lederer, *Take Back the Night*.
53. Charlotte Burch, "Lesbianism and Erotica in Pornographic America," in Lederer, *Take Back the Night*.
54. David Dyzenhaus, "Liberalism, Pornography, and the Rule of Law," in *Canadian Perspectives on Legal Theory* (Richard F. Devlin, ed., 1991); see also Kathleen Mahoney, "The Limits of Liberalism," in Devlin, *Canadian Perspectives;* see more generally, David Dyzenhaus, "Liberalism, Autonomy, and Neutrality," 42 *University of Toronto Law Journal* 354 (1992).
55. See also Rae Langton, "Whose Right? Dworkin, Women, and Pornographers," 19 *Philosophy and Public Affairs* 311 (1990).
56. David Dyzenhaus, "John Stuart Mill and the Harm of Pornography" (University of Toronto Law School, 1991).
57. Marianna Valverde and Lorna Weir, "Thrills, Chills, and the Lesbian Threat, or the Media, the State, and Women's Sexuality," in *Women Against Censorship* (Vanda Burstyn, ed., 1985).
58. See MacKinnon, *Feminism Unmodified*, 177.
59. Such an ordinance was struck down as unconstitutional in American Booksellers Assn. v. Hudnut 771 F. 2d. 323 (7th Circ. 1985).
60. See Feinberg, *Harm to Self*, 22.
61. See André Raynault and Jean-Pierre Vidal, "Smokers' Burden on Society: Myth and Reality in Canada," 18 *Canadian Public Policy* 300 (1992).
62. Calabresi and Melamed, "One View of the Cathedral."
63. See Chet Mitchell, "Regulative Drug Taxes and Tax Rates: Politics, Efficiency, or Justice," Law and Economics Workshop Paper, University of Toronto Law School (September 26, 1990).

64. Reference re ss. 193 and 195 1(1)(c) of the Criminal Code 1 S.C.R. 1123 (S.C.C. Can.), "The Prostitution Reference."
65. R. v. Keegstra 1990 3 S.C.R. 697 (S.C.C. Can.).
66. However, in a later case, Zundel v. R. (1992) 2 S.C.R. 731, a majority of the Supreme Court of Canada struck down provisions in the Canadian Criminal Code (p. 181) that made it a criminal offense for anyone wilfully to spread news that he knows is false, and causes or is likely to cause injury or mischief to a public interest, on the grounds that these violated constitutional guarantees of freedom of expression (sec. 2(b)) and were not justified under sec. 1. The accused had been charged under sec. 181 for disseminating anti-semitic literature alleging that the Holocaust was a myth.
67. David Dyzenhaus, "Regulating Free Speech" (University of Toronto Law School, 1991).

4. Coercion

1. Thomas Scanlon, "Liberty, Contract, and Contribution," in *Markets and Morals,* 43 (Gerald Dworkin, Gordon Bermant, and Peter Brown, eds., 1977).
2. See C. B. McPherson, "Elegant Tombstones," in McPherson, *Democratic Theory: Essays in Retrieval,* 143 (1973).
3. Alan Wertheimer, *Coercion,* 10 (1987).
4. Robert Nozick, "Coercion," in *Philosophy, Science, and Method* (Sidney Morgenbesser et al., eds., 1969).
5. Charles Fried, *Contract as Promise,* chap. 7 (1981).
6. Joel Feinberg, *Harm to Self,* chaps. 23 and 24 (1986).
7. Wertheimer, *Coercion,* 450.
8. Ibid., 207.
9. Nozick, "Coercion," 450.
10. Fried, *Contract as Promise,* 96, 97.
11. Ibid., 98, 99.
12. David Zimmerman, "Coercive Wage Offers," 10 *Philosophy and Public Affairs* 121, 122 (1981).
13. See Wertheimer, *Coercion,* Part Two, and Feinberg, *Harm to Self* for reviews of these debates and citations to the extensive literature.
14. For an excellent review of these debates, see James Boyle, "A Theory of Law and Information," in Boyle, *Critical Legal Studies* (forthcoming); see also James Lindgren, "Unravelling the Paradox of Blackmail," 84 *Columbia Law Review* 670 (1984); James Lindgren, "Blackmail: On Waste, Morals, and Ronald Coase," 36 *UCLA Law Review* 597 (1989); Lindgren, "In Defense of Keeping Blackmail a Crime," 20 *Loyola of Los Angeles Law Review* 35 (1986); Richard Epstein, "Blackmail Inc.," 50 *University of Chicago Law Review* 553 (1983); Ronald Coase, "Blackmail," 74 *Virginia Law Review* 665 (1988); Walter Black and David Gordon, "Blackmail, Extortion, and Free Speech," 19 *Loyola of Los Angeles Law Review* 37 (1985).
15. Peter Benson, "Abstract Right and the Possibility of a Nondistributive Conception of Contract: Hegel and Contemporary Contract Theory," 10 *Cardozo Law Review* 1077 (1989).

16. James Gordley, "Equality in Exchange," 69 *California Law Review* 1587 (1981).

17. The tenability of a distinction between substantive and procedural fairness is critically examined by Arthur Leff in his widely cited article "Unconscionability and the Code: The Emperor's New Clause," 115 *University of Pennsylvania Law Review* 485 (1967).

18. Anthony Kronman, "Contract Law and Distributive Justice," 89 *Yale Law Journal* 472 (1980).

19. Benson, "Hegel and Contemporary Contract Theory," 1119–1146.

20. Frank Buckley, "Three Theories of Substantive Fairness," 19 *Hofstra Law Review* 33 (1990).

21. Randy Barnett, "A Consent Theory of Contract," 86 *Columbia Law Review* 269, 280–281 (1986).

22. The issue of actual or hypothetical consent presents a distinctive set of problems in arguably incomplete contracts; see Chapter 5, "Asymmetric Information Imperfections."

23. See Timothy J. Brennan, "Voluntary Exchange and Economic Claims," 7 *Research in the History of Economic Thought and Methodology* 105, 121 (1990).

24. See Jules Coleman, *Markets, Morals, and the Law,* chap. 4 (1988), and Richard Craswell, "Efficiency and Rational Bargaining in Contractual Settings," 15 *Harvard Journal of Law and Public Policy* 805 (1992).

25. See Richard Epstein, "Unconscionability: A Critical Reappraisal," 18 *Journal of Law and Economics* 243, 296 (1975).

26. Feinberg, *Harm to Self,* 246, 248. Feinberg takes the position that where A merely exploits but does not create B's vulnerability, B's consent is not invalidated.

27. Fried, *Contract as Promise,* 109–110.

28. See William Landes and Richard Posner, "Salvors, Finders, Good Samaritans, and Other Rescuers: An Economic Study of Law and Altruism," 7 *Journal of Legal Studies* 82 (1978).

29. Alaska Packers Assn. v. Domenico 117 F. 99 (9th Circ. 1902).

30. See more generally Varouj Aivazian, Michael J. Trebilcock, and Michael Penny, "The Law of Contract Modifications: The Uncertain Quest for a Bench-Mark of Enforceability," 22 *Osgoode Hall Law Journal* 173 (1984); Richard Posner, "Gratuitous Promises in Economics and Law," 6 *Journal of Legal Studies* 411 (1977).

31. See Robert Nozick, *Anarchy, State, and Utopia,* 180 (1974).

32. F. A. Hayek, *The Constitution of Liberty,* 135–136 (1980), discussed by Harold Demsetz, "The Meaning of Freedom," in Demsetz, *Ownership, Control, and the Firm* (1988).

33. Fried, *Contract as Promise,* 95.

34. Hayek, *The Constitution of Liberty.*

35. Landes and Posner, "Salvors, Finders, Good Samaritans."

36. Post v. Jones 60 U.S. 150 (1856).

37. See Grant Gilmore and Charles Black, *The Law of Admiralty,* chap. 8 (2nd. ed., 1975); Landes and Posner, "Salvors, Finders, Good Samaritans."

38. Daniel Kahneman, Jack Knetsch, and Richard Thaler, "Fairness as a Constraint

on Profit-Seeking: Entitlements in the Market," 76 *American Economic Review* 728, 729 (1986).

39. Wertheimer, *Coercion*, 10, 225, 229.
40. Fried, *Contract as Promise*, 104.
41. See Henningsen v. Bloomfield Motors, Inc., 32 N.J. 358, 161 A. (2a) 69 (1960).
42. See Alan Schwartz, "Unconscionability and Imperfect Information: A Research Agenda," 19 *Canadian Business Law Journal* 437, 454–455 (1991).
43. See Gordon Tullock, "The Welfare Costs of Tariffs, Monopolies, and Theft," 5 *Western Economics Journal* 224 (1987); Richard Posner, "The Social Costs of Monopoly and Regulation," 83 *Journal of Political Economy* 807 (1975).
44. Kahneman, Knetsch, and Thaler, "Entitlements in the Market," 729, 730.
45. See Lon Fuller, "The Form and Limits of Adjudication," 92 *Harvard Law Review* 352 (1978).
46. Mitchell Polinsky and Steven Shavell, "The Optimal Trade-Off between the Probability and Magnitude of Fines," 69 *American Economic Review* 880 (1979).
47. Fried, *Contract as Promise*, 104.
48. McPherson, "Elegant Tombstones."
49. Milton Friedman, *Capitalism and Freedom* (1962).
50. Ibid., 13.
51. Margaret Jane Radin, "Market Inalienability," 100 *Harvard Law Review* 1849 (1989); see also Chapter 2, "Commodification."
52. See generally Richard Craswell, "Passing on the Costs of Legal Rules: Efficiency and Distribution in Buyer-Seller Relationships," 43 *Stanford Law Review* 361 (1991).
53. Kronman, "Contract Law and Distributive Justice"; see also to the same effect Mark Kelman, *A Guide to Critical Legal Studies*, 176–185 (1987); Duncan Kennedy, "Distributive and Paternalist Motives in Contract and Tort Law, with Special Reference to Compulsory Terms and Unequal Bargaining Power," 41 *Maryland Law Review* 563 (1982); Bruce Ackerman, "Regulating Slum Housing Markets on Behalf of the Poor: Of Housing Codes, Housing Subsidies, and Income Redistribution," 80 *Yale Law Journal* 1093 (1971); Duncan Kennedy, "The Effect of the Warranty of Habitability on Low-Income Housing: 'Milking' and Class Violence," 15 *Florida State University Law Review* 485 (1987).
54. John Rawls, *A Theory of Justice* (1971).

5. Asymmetric Information Imperfections

1. Milton Friedman, *Capitalism and Freedom*, 13 (1962).
2. Kim Lane Scheppele, *Legal Secrets: Equality and Efficiency in the Common Law*, 25 (1988).
3. See George J. Stigler, "The Economics of Information," 69 *Journal of Political Economy* 213 (1961).
4. Anthony Kronman, "Contract Law and Distributive Justice," 89 *Yale Law Journal* 472, 498 (1980).
5. Charles Fried, *Contract as Promise*, 9–12 (1981).
6. See Richard Craswell, "Interpreting Deceptive Advertising," 65 *Boston Uni-*

versity Law Review 657 (1985); Craswell, "Regulating Deceptive Advertising," 64 *Southern California Law Review* 549 (1991).

7. See William Bishop, "Negligent Misrepresentation through Economists' Eyes," 96 *Law Quarterly Review* 360 (1980).

8. See Ernest Weinrib, "Understanding Tort Law," 23 *Valparaiso University Law Review* 485 (1989).

9. For a review of legal doctrine in the common law, see Stephen Waddams, "Pre-Contractual Duties of Disclosure," in *Essays for Patrick Atiyah* (Peter Cane and Jane Stapleton, eds., 1991); for a review of legal doctrine in civil law systems, see Pierre Legrand, "Information in Formation of Contracts: A Civilian Perspective," 19 *Canadian Business Law Journal* 318 (1991).

10. Anthony Kronman, "Mistake, Disclosure, Information, and the Law of Contracts," 7 *Journal of Legal Studies* 1 (1979).

11. Fried, *Contract as Promise*, 58–67.

12. Kronman, "Contract and Distributive Justice."

13. Scheppele, *Legal Secrets.*

14. Laidlaw v. Organ 15 U.S. (2 Wheat.) 178 (1817).

15. Strong v. Repide 213 U.S. 419, 29 S.Ct. 521 (1909).

16. Dyke v. Zaiser 80 Cal. App. 2d. 639, 182 P.2d. 344 (1947).

17. Jappe v. Mandt 130 Cal. App. 2d. 426, 278 P.2d. 940 (1955).

18. Fuller v. DePaul University 12 N.E. 2d. 213 (1938).

19. Simmons v. Evans S.W. 2d. 295 (1947).

20. See John Harsanyi, "Can the Maximin Principle Serve as the Basis for Morality? A Critique of John Rawls' Theory," 69 *American Political Science Review* 594 (1974).

21. George Akerlof, "The Market for Lemons: Quality Uncertainty and the Market Mechanism," 84 *Quarterly Journal of Economics* 488 (1970).

22. See Kronman, "Mistake, Disclosure, Information."

23. See Robert Cooter and Thomas Ulen, *Law and Economics,* 259–261 (1988); Jules Coleman, Douglas Heckathorn, and Steven Maser, "A Bargaining Theory Approach to Default Provisions and Disclosure Rules in Contract Law," 12 *Harvard Journal of Law and Public Policy* 639, 691–697 (1989); Steven Shavell, "Acquisition and Disclosure of Information Prior to Economic Exchange," Harvard Law School Law and Economics Discussion Paper no. 91 (April 1991).

24. See, e.g., Daniel Kahneman, Jack Knetsch, and Richard Thaler, "The Endowment Effect, Loss Aversion, and Status Quo Bias," 5 *Journal of Economic Perspectives* 193 (1991); Kahneman, Knetsch, and Thaler, "Experimental Tests of the Endowment Effect and the Coase Theorem," 98 *Journal of Political Economy* 1325 (1990); Knetsch, "The Endowment Effect and Evidence of Non-Reversible Indifference Curves," 79 *American Economic Review* 1277 (1989).

25. Andrew Kull, "Unilateral Mistake: The Baseball Card Case," 70 *Washington University Quarterly* 57 (1992).

26. James Gordley, "Equality in Exchange," 69 *California Law Review* 1583 (1981); more generally, Gordley, *The Philosophical Origins of Contract Doctrine* (1992).

27. C. B. McPherson, "Elegant Tombstones," in McPherson, *Democratic Theory: Essays in Retrieval,* 143 (1973).

28. Melvin Eisenberg, "The Bargain Principle and Its Limits," 95 *Harvard Law Review* 741 (1982).

29. Lloyds Bank Ltd. v. Bundy (1975) 1 Q.B. 326.

30. See Don Dewees and Michael J. Trebilcock, "Judicial Control of Standard Form Contracts," in *An Economic Approach to Law,* chap. 4 (Paul Burrows and Cento Veljanovsky, eds., 1981).

31. See, e.g., Friedrich Kessler, "Contracts of Adhesion: Some Thoughts about Freedom of Contract," 43 *Columbia Law Review* 629 (1943); Todd D. Rakoff, "Contracts of Adhesion: An Essay in Reconstruction," 96 *Harvard Law Review* 1173 (1983); David Slawson, "Standard Form Contracts and Democratic Control of Law-Making Power," 86 *Harvard Law Review* 529 (1971).

32. Michael J. Trebilcock, "The Doctrine of Inequality of Bargaining Power: Post-Benthamite Economics in the House of Lords," 26 *University of Toronto Law Journal* 359 (1976); Trebilcock, "An Economic Approach to the Doctrine of Unconscionability," in *Studies in Contract Law* (Barry Reiter and John Swan, eds., 1980), 379; Dewees and Trebilcock, "Standard Form Contracts."

33. See also Alan Schwartz and Louis Wilde, "Intervening in Markets on the Basis of Imperfect Information: A Legal and Economic Analysis," 127 *University of Pennsylvania Law Review* 630 (1979).

34. See Avery Katz, "The Strategic Structure of Offer and Acceptance: Game Theory and the Law of Contract Formation," 89 *Michigan Law Review* 215, 287 (1990).

35. Buckley suggests that in some such cases, courts may be more efficient "screeners" of contract terms than some "consumers"; see Frank Buckley, "Three Theories of Substantive Fairness," 19 *Hofstra Law Review* 33 (1990). Craswell is more sceptical of the ability of the courts to select terms superior to those selected by sellers; see Richard Craswell, "Property Rules and Liability Rules in Unconscionability and Related Doctrines," 60 *University of Chicago Law Review* 1 (1993).

36. In other words, the problem is one of market failure, not transaction-specific contracting failure. See Arthur Allen Leff, "Contract as a Thing," 19 *American University Law Review* 131 (1970); and Alan Schwartz, "Unconscionability and Imperfect Information: A Research Agenda," 19 *Canadian Business Law Journal* 437 (1991).

37. Richard Craswell, "Contract Law, Default Rules, and the Philosophy of Promising," 88 *Michigan Law Review* 489 (1989).

38. Randy Barnett, "The Sound of Silence: Default Rules and Contractual Consent," 78 *Virginia Law Review* 821 (1992).

39. Ibid., 906.

40. David Charny, "Hypothetical Bargains: The Normative Structure of Contract Interpretation," 89 *Michigan Law Review* 1815 (1991).

41. Ian Ayres and Robert Gertner, "Filling Gaps in Incomplete Contracts: An Economic Theory of Default Rules," 99 *Yale Law Journal* 87 (1989).

42. Hadley v. Baxendale 156 E.R. 145 (1854).

43. Jason Johnston, "Strategic Bargaining and the Economic Theory of Contract Default Rules," 100 *Yale Law Journal* 615 (1990).

44. Ian Ayres and Robert Gertner, "Strategic Contractual Inefficiency and the Optimal Choice of Legal Rules," 100 *Yale Law Journal* 720 (1992).

45. For an accessible account of basic elements of game theory, and a balanced assessment of its insights and limitations, see David Kreps, *Game Theory and Economic Modelling* (1990); see also Kreps, *A Course in Microeconomic Theory,* Part 3 (1990).

46. Samuel Rea, "Arm-Breaking, Consumer Credit, and Personal Bankruptcy," 22 *Economic Inquiry* 188 (1984).

47. Philippe Aghion and Benjamin Hermalin, "Legal Restrictions on Private Contracts Can Enhance Efficiency," 6 *Journal of Law, Economics, and Organization* 381 (1990).

48. See George Akerlof, Murray Rothchild, and Joseph Stiglitz, "Equilibrium in Competitive Insurance Markets: An Essay on the Economics of Imperfect Information," 90 *Quarterly Journal of Economics* 629 (1976); C. Wilson, "A Model of Insurance Markets with Incomplete Information," 16 *Journal of Economic Theory* 167 (1977).

49. Samuel Rea, Ontario Economic Council, *Disability Insurance and Public Policy,* 36 (1981).

50. William Bishop, "Is He Married? Marriage as Information," 34 *University of Toronto Law Journal* 245 (1984).

51. See Ayres and Gertner, "Filling Gaps in Incomplete Contracts," 91.

52. See Charles Lindblom, "The Science of 'Muddling Through,'" 19 *Public Administrative Review* 79 (1959).

6. Symmetric Information Imperfections

1. George Triantis, "Contractual Allocations of Unknown Risks: A Critique of the Doctrine of Commercial Impracticability," 42 *University of Toronto Law Journal* 450 (1992).

2. Douglas Baird, "Self-Interest and Cooperation in Long-term Contracts," 19 *Journal of Legal Studies* 583, 591 (1990).

3. Clayton Gillette, "Commercial Rationality and the Duty to Adjust Long-Term Contracts," 69 *Minnesota Law Review* 522, 534–536 (1985).

4. Baird, "Self-Interest and Cooperation in Contracts," 596.

5. See Richard Craswell, "Contract Law, Default Rules, and the Philosophy of Promising," 88 *Michigan Law Review* 489 (1989); Randy Barnett, "The Sound of Silence: Default Rules and Contractual Consent," 78 *Virginia Law Review* 821 (1992); David Charny, "Hypothetical Bargains: The Normative Structure of Contract Interpretation," 89 *Michigan Law Review* 1815 (1991); see also Chapter 5, "Asymmetric Information Imperfections."

6. Charles Fried, *Contract as Promise,* 60–61 (1981).

7. Richard Posner and Andrew Rosenfield, "Impossibility and Related Doctrines in Contract Law: An Economic Analysis," 6 *Journal of Legal Studies* 83 (1977).

8. Ibid., 90–92.
9. Varouj Aivazian, Michael J. Trebilcock, and Michael Penny, "The Law of Contract Modifications: The Uncertain Quest for a Bench-Mark of Enforceability," 22 *Osgoode Hall Law Journal* 173 (1984).
10. Michael Trebilcock, "The Role of Insurance Considerations in the Choice of Efficient Civil Liability Rules," 4 *Journal of Law, Economics, and Organization* 243 (1988).
11. Transatlantic Financing Corp. v. United States 363 F. 2d. 312 (D.C. Cir. 1966).
12. Posner and Rosenfield, "Impossibility: An Economic Analysis," 104.
13. Ibid., 104–105.
14. Ibid., 106.
15. For a similar analysis, see Alan Sykes, "The Doctrine of Commercial Impracticability in a Second-Best World," 19 *Journal of Legal Studies* 43, 88–91 (1990).
16. Paul Joskow, "Commercial Impossibility, the Uranium Market, and the Westinghouse Case," 6 *Journal of Legal Studies* 119 (1977).
17. Anthony Kronman and Richard Posner, *The Economics of Contract Law,* 153 (1979).
18. Florida Power and Light Co. v. Westinghouse Electric Corp. 826 F. 2d. 239 (4th Circ. 1987).
19. Sykes, "Commercial Impracticability in a Second-Best World," 77–79.
20. Taylor v. Caldwell 3 Best and South (K.B.) 826 (1863).
21. Sykes, "Commercial Impracticability in a Second-Best World," 85.
22. See Sykes, "Commercial Impracticability in a Second-Best World"; Baird, "Self-Interest and Cooperation in Contracts"; Robert Scott, "A Relational Theory of Default Rules for Commercial Contracts," 19 *Journal of Legal Studies* 597 (1990).
23. See Triantis, "Unknown Risks and Doctrine of Commercial Impracticability"; Baird, "Self-Interest in a Second-Best World"; Scott, "Default Rules for Commercial Contracts." Michelle White also argues that all cases involving unperformed contracts should be treated as breach cases attracting damages, but that the damages should be varied depending on the relative degrees of risk aversion of the parties; see Michelle White, "Contract Breach and Contract Discharge Due to Impossibility: A Unified Theory," 17 *Journal of Legal Studies* 353 (1988). However, this approach, by requiring determinations of relative degrees of risk aversion on a case-by-case basis, would seem to raise many of the same operational problems as that of Posner and Rosenfield.
24. See Paul Joskow, "Vertical Integration and Long-term Contracts: The Case of Coal-burning Electric Generating Plants," 1 *Yale Journal of Law, Economics, and Organization* 33 (1985); Victor Goldberg, "Price Adjustments in Long-term Contracts," (1985) *Wisconsin Law Review* 527; Oliver Williamson, "Assessing Contract," 1 *Yale Journal of Law, Economics, and Organization* 177 (1985); Alan Schwartz, "Relational Contracts in the Courts: An Analysis of Incomplete Contracts and Judicial Strategies," 21 *Journal of Legal Studies* 271 (1992).
25. Clayton Gillette, "Commercial Relationships and the Selection of Default Rules for Remote Risks," 19 *Journal of Legal Studies* 535 (1990).

26. Scott, "Default Rules for Commercial Contracts," 616.
27. See Aivazian, Trebilcock, and Penny, "The Law of Contract Modifications"; Timothy Muris, "Opportunistic Behaviour and the Law of Contracts," 65 *University of Minnesota Law Review* 521 (1981).
28. See Alaska Packers Assn. v. Domenico 117 F.99 (9th Circ. 1902).
29. Oliver E. Williamson, *Markets and Hierarchies,* 29 (1975).
30. See King v. Duluth, Missabe, and Northern Rly Co. 61 Minn. 482, 63 N.W. 7105 (1985), holding such a modification to be unenforceable.
31. See Linz v. Schuck 106 Md. 220, 67 A. 286 (1907), holding a modification in these circumstances to be enforceable.
32. Sherwood v. Walker 66 Mich. 568, 33 N.W. 919 (Mich. S.C. 1887).
33. For a game theory analysis of Sherwood v. Walker and other cases of mistake, see Ian Ayres and Eric Rasmussen, "Mutual and Unilateral Mistake in Contract Law," Stanford Law School Working Paper in Law and Economics, no. 95 (June 1992).
34. Ian R. Macneil, "Contracts: Adjustment of Long-Term Economic Relations under Classical, Neoclassical, and Relational Contract Law," 72 *Northwestern University Law Review* 854, 905 (1977–1978).
35. See Richard Craswell, "Contract Law, Default Rules, and the Philosophy of Promising," 88 *Michigan Law Review* 489 (1989).
36. Fried, *Contract as Promise,* 69–74.
37. Ibid., 71. Other proponents of some form of loss-sharing principle include White, "Contract Breach and Discharge Due to Impossibility"; Harrison, "A Case for Loss Sharing," 56 *Southern California Law Review* 573 (1983); Robert Hillman, "Court Adjustment of Long-Term Contracts: An Analysis under Modern Contract Law," 1 *Duke Law Journal* (1987); Leon Trakman, "Winner Take Some: Loss Sharing and Commercial Impracticability," 69 *Minnesota Law Review* 471 (1985); Richard Speidel, "Court-Imposed Price Adjustments under Long-Term Supply Contracts," 76 *Northwestern Law Review* 369 (1981).
38. See Ian R. Macneil, "Efficient Breach of Contract: Circles in the Sky," 68 *Virginia Law Review* 947 (1982); Daniel Friedman, "The Efficient Breach Fallacy," 18 *Journal of Legal Studies* 1 (1989).
39. See Robert Cooter and Thomas Ulen, *Law and Economics,* 289–292 (1988).
40. Robert W. Gordon, "Macaulay, Macneil, and the Discovery of Solidarity and Power in Contract Law" (1985) *Wisconsin Law Review* 565, 578.
41. See Triantis, "Unknown Risks and Doctrine of Commercial Impracticability," 46, 47; Thomas Jackson, "The Fresh Start Policy in Bankruptcy Law," 98 *Harvard Law Review* 1393 (1985).
42. See also Michael Walzer, *Spheres of Justice* (1983).
43. Fried, *Contract as Promise,* 73.
44. Ibid., 69–74.
45. A point brilliantly demonstrated by Craswell, "Contract Law, Default Rules."
46. Aluminum Co. of America v. Essex Group, Inc., 499 F. Supp. 53 (W.D. Pa 1980).
47. Andrew Kull, "Mistake, Frustration, and the Windfall Principle of Contract Remedies," 43 *Hastings Law Journal* 1 (1991).

48. See White, "Contract Breach and Discharge Due to Impossibility."

49. See Daniel Kahneman, Jack Knetsch, and Richard Thaler, "Experimental Tests of the Endowment Effect and the Coase Theorem," 98 *Journal of Political Economy* 1325 (1990); Knetsch, "The Endowment Effect and Evidence of Non-Reversible Indifference Curves," 79 *American Economic Review* 1277 (1989).

7. Paternalism

1. John Stuart Mill, *On Liberty,* 13 (1956).

2. Joel Feinberg, *Harm to Self,* 113 (1986).

3. Ibid., 58–62.

4. Margaret Jane Radin, "Market Inalienability," 100 *Harvard Law Review* 1849 (1989).

5. Ibid., 12.

6. Gerald Dworkin, "Paternalism," in *Morality and the Law* (Richard A. Wassenstrom, ed., 1971).

7. Feinberg, *Harm to Self,* 317.

8. Anthony Kronman, "Paternalism and the Law of Contracts," 93 *Yale Law Journal* 763 (1983).

9. See Rochelle Spergel, "Paternalism and Contract: A Critique of Anthony Kronman," 10 *Cardozo Law Review* 593 (1988).

10. For critical analysis of the war on drugs, see Bruce K. Alexander, *Peaceful Measures: Canada's Way out of the War on Drugs* (1990); Chester N. Mitchell, *The Drug Solution: Regulating Drugs according to Principles of Efficiency, Justice, and Democracy* (1990).

11. Feinberg, *Harm to Self,* 116.

12. Dworkin, "Paternalism," 124.

13. See Alan Schwartz, "Views of Addiction and the Duty to Warn," 75 *Virginia Law Review* 509 (1989).

14. Gerald Dworkin, "Paternalism: Some Second Thoughts," in *Paternalism* (Rolf Sartorius, ed., 1982).

15. Feinberg, *Harm to Self,* 22, 140, 131.

16. Ibid., 134.

17. Cass R. Sunstein, "Legal Interference with Private Preferences," 53 *University of Chicago Law Review* 1129 (1986); Sunstein, "Disrupting Voluntary Transactions," in *Markets and Justice* (John W. Chapman and J. Roland Pennock, eds., 1989); Sunstein, "Preferences and Politics," 20 *Philosophy and Public Affairs* 3 (1991).

18. See also Dworkin, "Paternalism," 119 (1971).

19. See Jon Elster, *Ulysses and the Sirens* (1976).

20. John Kenneth Galbraith, *The Affluent Society* (1958).

21. Friedrich A. Hayek, "The Non Sequitur of the 'Dependence Effect'" (1961), excerpted in *Microeconomics: Selected Readings,* 3–6 (Edwin Mansfield, ed., 1982).

22. Michael J. Sandel, *Liberalism and the Limits of Justice* (1982).

23. Alasdair MacIntyre, *After Virtue* (1981).

24. Charles Taylor, *Philosophy and the Human Sciences: Philosophical Papers 2* (1986), especially "Atomism" at 190; Taylor, *Sources of the Self* (1989); Taylor, *The Malaise of Modernity* (1991); see also Mary Ann Glendon, *Rights Talk: The Impoverishment of Political Discourse* (1991); Amitai Etzioni, *The Moral Dimension* (1988); Robert N. Bellah et al., *Habits of the Heart* (1985); Robert N. Bellah et al., *The Good Society* (1991).

25. Joel Feinberg, *Harmless Wrongdoing,* chap. 29A (1988).

26. However, for liberal arguments for a more active role on the part of the state in protecting minority cultural values, see Will Kymlicka, *Liberalism, Community, and Culture* (1989).

27. Sunstein, "Disrupting Voluntary Transactions."

28. See Jon Elster, *Sour Grapes* (1983).

29. See, e.g., Daniel Kahneman, Jack L. Knetsch, and Richard Thaler, "The Endowment Effect, Loss Aversion, and Status Quo Bias," 5 *Journal of Economic Perspectives* 193 (1991); Knetsch, "The Endowment Effect and Evidence of Nonreversible Indifference Curves," 79 *American Economic Review* 1277 (1989); Kahneman, Knetsch, and Thaler, "Experimental Tests of the Endowment Effect and the Coase Theorem," 98 *Journal of Political Economy* 1425 (1990).

30. Sunstein, "Legal Interference with Private Preferences," 1170.

31. Sunstein, "Disrupting Voluntary Transactions," 275.

32. Eric Mack, "Dominoes and the Fear of Commodification," in Chapman and Pennock, *Markets and Justice.*

33. Duncan Kennedy, "Distributive and Paternalistic Motives in Contract and Tort Law with Special Reference to Compulsory Terms and Unequal Bargaining Power," 41 *Maryland Law Review* 563 (1982).

34. Robin West, "Taking Preferences Seriously," 64 *Tulane Law Review* 659 (1990).

35. Kennedy, "Distributive and Paternalistic Motives in Contract and Tort Law," 649.

36. West, "Taking Preferences Seriously," 665.

37. Ibid., 680.

38. See further Robin West, "Authority, Autonomy, and Choice: The Role of Consent in the Moral and Political Views of Franz Kafka and Richard Posner," 99 *Harvard Law Review* 384 (1985); and ensuing colloquy, Richard Posner, 99 *Harvard Law Review* 1431 (1986), and Robin West, 99 *Harvard Law Review* 1449 (1986).

39. West, "Taking Preferences Seriously," 671.

40. See, e.g., Margaret Jane Radin, "Market Inalienability," 100 *Harvard Law Review* 1849 (1989).

41. West, "Taking Preferences Seriously," 678.

42. Sandel, *Liberalism and Limits of Justice.*

43. Radin, "Market Inalienability."

44. Irving Kristol, "Pornography, Obscenity, and the Case for Censorship," *New York Times Magazine* (March 28, 1971), reprinted in *Philosophy of Law* (Joel Feinberg and Hyman Gross, eds., 2nd. ed., 1980).

45. See also Sunstein, "Preferences and Politics."

46. James Q. Wilson, "Against Legalization of Drugs," 89 *Commentary* 21 (1990).
47. Ibid., 24, 26.
48. Mill, *On Liberty*, chap. 5, para. 11.
49. See Richard J. Arneson, "Mill versus Paternalism," 90 *Ethics* 471 (1980); Feinberg, *Harm to Self*, 77; John Kleinig, *Paternalism* (1984); Anthony T. Kronman and Richard A. Posner, *The Economics of Contract Law*, 256–260 (1979).
50. Feinberg, *Harm to Self*, 79.
51. See Michael J. Trebilcock, *The Common Law of Restraint of Trade*, chaps. 1, 2, and 3 (1986).
52. See also Dan Brock, "Paternalism and Promoting the Good," in Sartorius, *Paternalism*.
53. Milton Friedman, *Capitalism and Freedom*, 33, 34 (1962).
54. Kennedy, "Distributive and Paternalistic Motives in Contract and Tort Law."

8. Consideration

1. Milton Friedman, *Capitalism and Freedom*, 13 (1962); emphasis added.
2. For recent reviews, see Richard Craswell, "Contract Law, Default Rules, and the Philosophy of Promising," 88 *Michigan Law Review* 489 (1989); Randy Barnett, "A Consent Theory of Contract," 86 *Columbia Law Review* 259 (1986); Frank Buckley, "Paradox Lost," 72 *Minnesota Law Review* 775 (1988); Peter Benson, "Abstract Right and the Possibility of a Nondistributive Conception of Contract: Hegel and Contemporary Contract Theory," 10 *Cardozo Law Review* 1077 (1989).
3. Charles Fried, *Contract as Promise*, 7–8 (1981); see also Andrew Kull, "Reconsidering Gratuitous Promises," 21 *Journal of Legal Studies* 39 (1992); David Gauthier, *Morals by Agreement*, chap. 6 (1987).
4. Craswell, "Contract Law, Default Rules," 505–508.
5. Buckley, "Paradox Lost," 816.
6. Craswell, "Contract Law, Default Rules," 508.
7. Buckley, "Paradox Lost," 816, 824.
8. Barnett, "A Consent Theory of Contract," 272–273.
9. See Charles Goetz and Robert Scott, "Enforcing Promises: An Examination of the Basis of Contract," 89 *Yale Law Journal* 1216 (1980).
10. Both difficulties are noted by Barnett, "A Consent Theory of Contract."
11. Fried, *Contract as Promise*, 17.
12. Craswell, "Contract Law, Default Rules," 518.
13. See A. Mitchell Polinsky, *An Introduction to Law and Economics*, chaps. 5 and 8 (2nd ed., 1988); Robert Cooter and Thomas Ulen, *Law and Economics*, 288–325 (1988).
14. Lon Fuller and William Perdue, "The Reliance Interest in Contract Damages," 46 *Yale Law Journal* 52, 373 (1936); for a recent review, see Todd D. Rakoff, "Fuller and Perdue's *The Reliance Interest as a Work of Legal Scholarship*" (1991) *Wisconsin Law Review* 203.
15. Goetz and Scott, "Enforcing Promises: The Basis of Contract."
16. Ibid., 1285.

17. James Gordley, "Equality in Exchange," 69 *California Law Review* 1583 (1981).
18. See Melvin Eisenberg, "The Bargain Principle and Its Limits," 95 *Harvard Law Review* 741 (1982).
19. See Varouj Aivazian, Michael J. Trebilcock, and Michael Penny, "The Law of Contract Modifications: The Uncertain Quest for a Bench-Mark of Enforceability," 22 *Osgoode Hall Law Journal* 173 (1984).
20. Central London Property Trust Ltd. v. High Trees House Ltd. (1947) K.B. 130.
21. Ibid., 134.
22. See Timothy Muris, "Opportunistic Behavior and the Law of Contracts," 65 *University of Minnesota Law Review* 521 (1981).
23. Lon Fuller, "Consideration and Form," 41 *Columbia Law Review* 799 (1941).
24. Melvin Eisenberg, "The Principles of Consideration," 67 *Cornell Law Review* 646, 660 (1982).
25. Ibid., 661.
26. Melvin Eisenberg, "Donative Promises," 47 *University of Chicago Law Review* 1 (1979).
27. Steven Shavell, "An Economic Analysis of Altruism and Deferred Gifts," *Journal of Legal Studies* 401 (1991).
28. Goetz and Scott, "Enforcing Promises: The Basis of Contract."
29. Dalhousie College v. Boutilier Estate (1934) S.C.R. 642 (S.C.C. Can.).
30. Richard Posner, "Gratuitous Promises in Economics and Law," 6 *Journal of Legal Studies* 412–413 (1977).
31. See also Shavell, "Altruism and Deferred Gifts," 402.
32. Eisenberg, "The Principles of Consideration," 640.
33. Goetz and Scott, "Enforcing Promises: The Basis of Contract."
34. Balfour v. Balfour (1919) 2 K.B. 571 (Eng. C.A.).
35. Ibid., 578–579.
36. Merritt v. Merritt (1970) 2 All E.R. 760 (Eng. C.A.).
37. Ibid., 762.
38. Goetz and Scott, "Enforcing Promises: The Basis of Contract," 1304.
39. Jones v. Padavatton (1989) 2 All E.R. 616 (Eng. C.A.).
40. Hamer v. Sidway (1891) 27 N.E. 256 (Ct. Appeals of N.Y.); the facts of this case turn out to be somewhat more complicated than conventionally stated: see Douglas Baird, "Reconstructing Contracts," University of Chicago Law School Law and Economics Working Paper no. 11, 2nd series (1992).
41. Ibid., 257.
42. Eisenberg, "Donative Promises," 27.
43. Ibid., 29.
44. Barnett, "A Consent Theory of Contract," 314–315.
45. Timothy Muris, "Subjective Values in Contract Law," Law and Economics Center, University of Miami LEC Working Paper no. 8 (1981).
46. Samuel Williston, *Contracts,* s. 112 (1968).
47. Fried, *Contract as Promise,* 32.
48. See Edwin Patterson, "An Apology for Consideration," 58 *Columbia Law Review* 929 (1958).
49. Ibid., 35.

50. Kull, "Reconsidering Gratuitous Promises."
51. See Jay Feinman, "Critical Approaches to Contract Law," 30 *UCLA Law Review* 837 (1983).
52. Goetz and Scott, "Enforcing Promises: The Basis of Contract," 1274.
53. Ibid., 1312.
54. See also P. S. Atiyah, "Consideration," in *Essays on Contract*, 240–243 (1986); John Swan, "Consideration and the Reason for Enforcing Contracts," in *Studies in Contract Law* (John Swan and Barry Reiter, eds., 1980).
55. Fried, *Contract as Promise*, 39.
56. Eisenberg, "The Bargain Principle," 665.
57. See David Cohen and Jack Knetsch, "Judicial Choices and Disparities between Measures of Economic Values," *Osgoode Hall Law Journal* (forthcoming).

9. Discrimination

1. See Robert Howse, J. R. S. Prichard, and Michael J. Trebilcock, "Smaller or Smarter Government?" 40 *University of Toronto Law Journal* 498 (1990).
2. See Michael J. Trebilcock, M. A. Chandler, and Robert Howse, *Trade and Transitions*, 3 (1990).
3. See *The Economist*, 17 (March 3, 1990), 17 (March 30th, 1991).
4. See Leroy Clark, "Comment," 79 *Georgetown Law Journal* 1695, 1701 (1991); see generally, Andrew Hecker, *Two Nations: Black and White, Separate, Hostile, Unequal* (1992).
5. Brown v. Board of Education of Topeka 347 U.S. 483 (1954).
6. See, e.g., Richard A. Epstein, *Forbidden Grounds: The Case against Employer Discrimination Laws* (1992); Jennifer Roback, "Southern Labour Law and the Jim Crow Era: Exploitative or Competitive?" 51 *University of Chicago Law Review* 1161 (1984).
7. See Ian Ayres, "Fair Driving: Gender and Race Discrimination in Retail Car Negotiations," 104 *Harvard Law Review* 817 (1991).
8. Robert Nozick, *Anarchy, State, and Utopia* (1974).
9. Epstein, *Forbidden Grounds*, 3, 505; for searching critiques of Epstein's thesis, see J. Hoult Verkerke, "Free to Search," 105 *Harvard Law Review* 2080 (1992), and George Rutherglen, "Abolition in a Different Voice," 78 *Virginia Law Review* 1463 (1992).
10. Christie v. York Corporation (1940) 1 C.L.R 81 (S.C.C. Can.).
11. Ibid., 82.
12. Ibid., 81.
13. See George Sher, "Ancient Wrongs and Modern Rights," 10 *Philosophy and Public Affairs* 3 (1980).
14. John Gardner, "Liberals and Unlawful Discrimination," 9 *Oxford Journal of Legal Studies* 1, 3 (1989).
15. See John Gray, *Liberalism,* chap. 9 (1986).
16. Ronald Dworkin, "Reverse Discrimination," in Dworkin, *Taking Rights Seriously* (1977).

17. See G. A. Akerlof, *An Economic Theorist's Book of Tales* (1984); Cass Sunstein, *After the Rights Revolution* (1990); Jon Elster, *Sour Grapes* (1983).

18. See Mary Becker, "Needed in the Nineties: Improved Individual and Structural Remedies for Racial and Sexual Disadvantages in Employment," 79 *Georgetown Law Journal* 1659 (1991).

19. Economic Council of Canada, *Economic and Social Impacts of Immigration*, chap. 9 (1991).

20. For a colloquy on the efficiency implications of anti-discrimination laws, see John Donahue, "Is Title VII Efficient?" 134 *University of Pennsylvania Law Review* 1411 (1986); Richard Posner, "The Efficiency and Efficacy of Title VII," 136 *University of Pennsylvania Law Review* 513 (1987); John Donahue, "Further Thoughts on Employment Discrimination: A Reply to Judge Posner," 136 *University of Pennsylvania Law Review* 523 (1987); Richard Posner, "An Economic Analysis of Sex Discrimination Laws," 56 *University of Chicago Law Review* 1311 (1989); John Donahue, "Prohibiting Sex Discrimination in the Workplace: An Economic Perspective," 56 *University of Chicago Law Review* 1337 (1989); see more generally Epstein, *Forbidden Grounds*, chap. 2.

21. See Gary Becker, *The Economics of Discrimination* (1957).

22. This argument derives from Gary Becker, ibid.

23. See Posner, "Sex Discrimination Laws."

24. Donahue, "Is Title VII Efficient?"

25. John Donahue and James Heckman, "Continuous Versus Episodic Change: The Impact of Civil Rights Policy on the Economic Status of Blacks," University of Toronto Law and Economics Workshop Paper (October 9, 1991); see also Donahue and Heckman, "Re-evaluating Federal Civil Rights Policy," 79 *Georgetown Law Journal* 1713 (1991), and Heckman and J. Hoult Verkerke, "Racial Disparity and Employment Discrimination Law: An Economic Perspective," 8 *Yale Law and Policy Review* 276 (1990).

26. Donahue and Heckman, "Continuous vs. Episodic Change," 35.

27. J. G. MacIntosh, "Employment Discrimination: An Economic Perspective," 19 *Ottawa Law Review* 275 (1987).

28. Epstein,, *Forbidden Grounds*, chap. 2.

29. See Michael J. Trebilcock, *The Common Law of Restraint of Trade*, chap. 2 (1986).

30. Epstein, *Forbidden Grounds*, chap. 3.

31. See Janet Landa, "A Theory of the Ethnically Homogeneous Middleman Group: An Institutional Alternative to Contract Law," 10 *Journal of Legal Studies* 349 (1981); Janet Landa and Jack Carr, "The Economics of Symbols, Clan Names, and Religion," 12 *Journal of Legal Studies* 135 (1983); Lisa Bernstein, "Opting Out of the Legal System: Extralegal Contractual Relations in the Diamond Industry," 21 *Journal of Legal Studies* 115 (1992).

32. Plessy v. Ferguson, 163 U.S. 537 (1896).

33. See Gardner, "Unlawful Discrimination," 9.

34. J. M. Buchanan, "Fairness, Hope, and Justice," in *New Directions in Economic Justice* (Roger Shurski, ed., 1983). My discussion here draws on Sheila Eastman, "Affirmative Action in a Law and Economics Perspective," Canadian Law and Economics Association Paper (September 21, 1991).

35. Ibid., 74.
36. Ibid., 70.
37. John Rawls, "A Theory of Justice" (1971).
38. Michel Rosenfeld, *Affirmative Action and Justice* (1981).
39. Ibid., chap. 5.
40. Gardner, "Liberals and Unlawful Discrimination," 9.
41. Ibid., 16.
42. Ibid., 8.
43. Joseph Raz, *The Morality of Freedom* (1986).
44. Gardner, "Liberals and Unlawful Discrimination," 11.
45. For a useful review of the U.S. Supreme Court case-law on affirmative action programmes, see Rosenfeld, *Affirmative Action*, 167–215.
46. See, e.g., I. M. Young, *Justice and the Politics of Difference*, 200 (1990).
47. See, e.g., Ronald Dworkin, "Bakke's Case: Are Quotas Unfair?" in Dworkin, *A Matter of Principle*, 299 (1985).
48. For a review of arguments on both sides of the utility ledger, see Kent Greenawalt, *Discrimination and Reverse Discrimination*, 63–68 (1983).
49. See Michael H. Gottesman, "Twelve Topics to Consider before Opting for Racial Quotas," 79 *Georgetown Law Journal* 1737 (1991).
50. Rosenfeld, *Affirmative Action*, chap. 10.
51. See David Strauss, "The Myth of Colorblindness," *Supreme Court Review* 99 (1986).
52. See Becker, "Needed in the Nineties."
53. Donahue and Heckman, "Continuous vs. Episodic Change."
54. This is also broadly the position that Epstein takes with respect to private sector employees, although he would make such programmes totally voluntary and unconstrained by legal norms; see Epstein, *Forbidden Grounds*, chap. 20.
55. As proposed by David Strauss, "The Law and Economics of Racial Discrimination in Employment: The Case for Numerical Standards," 79 *Georgetown Law Journal* 1619 (1991).
56. See comments on Strauss (ibid.) by Gottesman, "Twelve Topics"; Mary Becker, "Needed in the Nineties"; and Jerry Mashaw, "Implementing Quotas," 70 *Georgetown Law Journal* 1769 (1991).
57. See also Gottesman, "Twelve Topics."
58. See Donald E. Lively, "Affirmative Action and Marketplace Freedom: A Constitutional Intersection of Equality and Liberty," 16 *Journal of Contemporary Law* 1 (1990).
59. Rights of the University of California v. Bakke, 438 U.S. 265 (1978).
60. For a review of the case-law, see Rosenfeld, *Affirmative Action*, 167–215.
61. See also Becker, "Needed in the Nineties."
62. *The Economist*, 18 (March 3, 1990).
63. On the relationship between exit and voice as disciplining mechanisms in markets and politics, see Albert Hirschman, *Exit, Voice, and Loyalty* (1970).
64. See Stephen L. Carter, *Reflections of an Affirmative Action Baby* (1991).
65. *The Economist*, 21 (March 30, 1991).
66. *The Economist*, 12 (March 30, 1991).

67. See Richard G. Harris, *Trade, Industrial Policy, and International Competition* (1985), vol. 13 (research paper for the Royal Commission on the Economic Union and Development Prospects for Canada 1986).

68. David Ricardo, *Principles of Political Economy* (1817).

69. Paul A. Samuelson and Anthony D. Scott, *Economics*, 807 (1980).

70. See, e.g., Peter B. Kenen, *The International Economy*, chap. 11 (2nd. ed., 1989).

71. For a review of the genesis and central features of the GATT, see Olivier Long, *Law and Its Limitations in the GATT Multilateral Trade System* (1987); John Jackson, *The World Trading System*, chap. 2 (1991).

72. Economic Council of Canada, *Managing Adjustment*, 1 (1988).

73. See Michael J. Trebilcock, "On the Virtues of Dreaming Big and Thinking Small," 8 *Boston University International Law Journal* 291 (1990).

74. The data are from Michael J. Trebilcock, "The Case for Free Trade," 14 *Canadian Business Law Journal* 387 (1988).

75. George Grant, *Lament for a Nation: The Defeat of Canadian Nationalism* (1967).

76. Ibid.

77. See Jagdish Bhagwati, *Protectionism*, chap. 3 (1988); Bhagwati, *The World Trading System at Risk* (1991); Trebilcock, Chandler, and Howse, *Trade and Transitions*, chap. 2.

78. Gary Hufbauer and Joanna Shelton-Erb, *Subsidies in International Trade*, 16 (1984).

79. Alan Rugman, "U.S. Protectionism and Canadian Trade Policy," 22 *Journal of World Trade Law* 363 (1986).

80. Commonwealth Secretariat, *Protectionism: Threat to International Order— The Impact in Developing Countries* (1982).

81. Ibid.

82. John Whalley, "The North-South Debate and the Terms of Trade: An Applied Equilibrium Approach," 66 *Review of Economics and Statistics* 224, 231–232 (1984).

83. See Jagdish Bhagwati, "Fair Trade, Reciprocity, and Harmonization: The New Challenge to Theory and Policy of Fair Trade," in Alan Deardorff and Robert Stern, eds., *Analytical and Negotiating Issues in the Global Trading System* (forthcoming); Robert Hudec, "Mirror, Mirror, on the Wall: The Concept of Fairness in United States Foreign Trade Policy," 1990 Proceedings of the Canadian Council on International Law 88.

84. Robert W. Crandall, "Import Quotas and the Automobile Industry: The Costs of Protectionism," 2(4) *Brookings Review* 8 (1984).

85. Economic Council of Canada, *Managing Adjustment: Policies for Trade Sensitive Industries*, 61, 70, 76 (1988).

86. Michael J. Trebilcock, "The Politics of Positive Sum," in *Ottawa and the Provinces: The Distribution of Money and Power* (T. J. Courchene, D. W. Conklin, and G. C. A. Cook, eds., 1985); and Michael J. Trebilcock and John Quinn, "Compensation, Transition Costs, and Regulatory Change," 32 *University of Toronto Law Journal* 117 (1982).

87. Mancur Olson, "Beyond the Measuring Rod of Money: The Unification of Economics and the Other Social Sciences," Law and Economics Workshop, University of Toronto Faculty of Law (November 20, 1985).

88. John Rawls, *A Theory of Justice* (1971).

89. Joseph Carens, "Aliens and Citizens: The Case for Open Borders," 49(2) *The Review of Politics* 251 (1987).

90. Peter Singer, *Practical Ethics* (1979).

91. Henry Shue, *Basic Rights: Subsistence, Affluence, and U.S. Foreign Policy* (1980).

92. See, e.g., Michael Sandel, *Liberalism and the Limits of Justice* (1982).

93. Ibid., 146.

94. Olson, "Beyond the Measuring Rod."

95. Robert Reich, *The Power of Public Ideas* (1988).

96. Carens, "Aliens and Citizens," 252.

97. Joseph Carens, "Migration and Morality: A Liberal Egalitarian Perspective," paper delivered at the Ethikon Institute Conference in Mont Saint Michel, France (September 23, 1989).

98. Carens, "Aliens and Citizens," 263.

99. Peter H. Schuck, "The Transformation of Immigration Law," 84 *Columbia Law Review* 1, 6 (1984).

100. Michael Walzer, *Spheres of Justice*, chap. 2 (1983).

101. Ibid., 61–62.

102. Robert L. Heilbroner, *The Worldly Philosophers—The Lives, Times, and Ideas of the Great Economic Thinkers*, 76 (5th ed., 1980).

103. See, e.g., Julian L. Simon, *The Economic Consequences of Immigration*, 329–335 (1989); George J. Borjas, *Friends or Strangers: The Impact of Immigrants on the U.S. Economy*, 225–227 (1990).

104. See *The Economist*, 18 (March 3, 1990).

105. Walzer, *Spheres of Justice*, 51.

106. Ibid., 4.

107. Ibid.

108. Carens, "Migration and Morality."

109. Ibid.

110. Ibid., 21.

111. Ibid.

112. Ibid.

113. Walzer, *Spheres of Justice*, 46.

114. See Simon, *Economic Consequences of Immigration*; Borjas, *Friends or Strangers*; Economic Council of Canada, *Economic and Social Impacts of Immigration* (1991).

115. Bob Hamilton and John Whalley, "Efficiency and Distributional Implications of Global Restrictions on Labour: Calculations and Policy Implications," 14 *Journal of Development Economics* 61 (1984).

116. See Simon, *Economic Consequences of Immigration*, chap. 14.

117. Carens, "Aliens and Citizens," 268.

118. Walzer, *Spheres of Justice*, 60.

119. Audrey Macklin, "The History of Asian Immigration," 69 (University of Toronto Law School, 1987).
120. *The Colonist,* 2 (April 13, 1884).
121. House of Commons Debates, Official Report (Ottawa: Queen's Printer, 1922) at 1555.
122. Ibid., 1555–1556.
123. Irving Abella and Harold Troper, *None is too Many: Canada and the Jews of Europe, 1933–1948* (1982).
124. See Arthur Schlesinger, *The Disuniting of America: Reflections on a Multicultural Society,* 10, 11 (1992).
125. See Carter, *Affirmative Action Baby.*
126. See for a historical perspective, Gerald A. Dirks, *Canada's Refugee Policy* (1977).

10. Autonomy and Welfare

1. Adam Smith, *The Wealth of Nations,* 14, 421, 423 (1937).
2. Charles E. Lindblom, *Politics and Markets: The World's Political Economic Systems,* 8 (1977).
3. Milton Friedman, *Capitalism and Freedom,* 13 (rev. ed., 1952).
4. See Ronald Dworkin, "What is Equality? Part 2: Equality of Resources," 10 *Philosophy and Public Affairs* 283 (1981); Will Kymlicka, *Contemporary Political Philosophy: An Introduction* (1990).
5. Joel Feinberg, *Offense to Others,* chap. 8 (1986).
6. See Guido Calabresi, "The Pointlessness of Pareto: Carrying Coase Further," 100 *Yale Law Journal* 1211 (1991).
7. See Richard Craswell, "Efficiency and Rational Bargaining in Contractual Settings," 15 *Harvard Journal of Law and Public Policy* 805 (1992).
8. See Randy Barnett, "A Consent Theory of Contract," 86 *Columbia Law Review* 269, 280, 281 (1986); Timothy J. Brennan, "Voluntary Exchange and Economic Claims," 7 *Research in the History of Economic Thought and Methodology* 105 (1990).
9. John Rawls, *A Theory of Justice* (1971).
10. See, e.g., John Harsanyi, "Can the Maximin Principle Serve as the Basis for Morality?: A Critique of John Rawls' Theory," 69 *American Political Science Review* 594 (1975).
11. See Frank Buckley, "Paradox Lost," 72 *Minnesota Law Review* 775 (1988).
12. See generally Peter Gabel and Jay Feinman, "Contract Law as Ideology," in *The Politics of Law: A Progressive Critique* (David Kairys, ed., 1982); Clare Dalton, "An Essay in the Deconstruction of Contract Doctrine," 94 *Yale Law Journal* 997 (1985).
13. See Amartya Sen, *On Ethics and Economics* (1987); Amitai Etzioni, *The Moral Dimension: Toward a New Economics* (1988).
14. See Richard Posner, *The Problems of Jurisprudence,* chap. 15 (1990).
15. For an ambitious recent attempt at reconciling autonomy and welfare values

in the law of contracts, see Alan Brudner, "Reconstructing Contracts," 43 *University of Toronto Law Journal* 1 (1993).

16. Lon Fuller, "The Form and Limits of Adjudication," 92 *Harvard Law Review* 352 (1978).

17. See Ian Ayres and Eric Gertner, "Filling Gaps in Incomplete Contracts: An Economic Theory of Default," 98 *Yale Law Journal* 87 (1989); David Charny, "Hypothetical Bargains: The Normative Structure of Contract Interpretation," 89 *Michigan Law Review* 1815 (1991).

18. See Arthur Allan Leff, "Contract as a Thing," 19 *American University Law Review* 131 (1970); Alan Schwartz, "Unconscionability and Imperfect Information," 19 *Canadian Business Law Journal* 437 (1991).

19. See Paul Weiler, *Governing the Workplace* (1990).

20. See Don Dewees and Michael J. Trebilcock, "The Efficacy of the Tort System and Its Alternatives: A Review of the Empirical Evidence," 30 *Osgoode Hall Law Journal* 57 (1992); Cass Sunstein, *After the Rights Revolution: Reconceiving the Regulatory State,* chap. 3 (1990).

21. See, e.g., Robert Howse, Robert Prichard, and Michael J. Trebilcock, "Smaller or Smarter Government?" 40 *University of Toronto Law Journal* 428 (1990); R. Howse, "Retrenchment, Reform, or Revolution? The Shift to Incentives and the Future of the Regulatory State," *Alberta Law Review* (forthcoming); Sunstein, *After the Rights Revolution.*

22. See, e.g., Kymlicka, *Contemporary Political Philosophy.*

23. See J. M. Cousineau, David Tessier, and François Vaillancourt, "The Impact of the Ontario Minimum Wage on the Unemployment of Women and the Young," Institute for Policy Analysis, University of Toronto (June 1991).

24. Charles Murray, *Losing Ground: American Social Policy, 1950–1980* (1984).

25. Friedman, *Capitalism and Freedom,* chap. 12.

26. Milton and Rose Friedman, *Free to Choose,* 121, 122 (1980).

27. See the discussion in Morley Gunderson, *Economics of Poverty and Income Distribution,* chap. 12 (1983).

28. See Michael J. Trebilcock, "Incentive Issues in the Design of No-Fault Compensation Systems," 39 *University of Toronto Law Journal* 19, 42–45 (1989).

29. The nature of the trade-offs entailed between target efficiency, work incentives, and administrative costs is well reviewed in Burton Weisbrod, "Collective Action and the Distribution of Income: A Conceptual Approach," in *Public Expenditures and Policy Analysis* (Robert Haverman and Julius Margolis, eds., 1970); and in Gunderson, *Economics of Poverty,* chaps. 9 and 10.

30. Lisbeth Schorr, *Within Our Reach: Breaking the Cycle of Dependency* (1989).

31. Robert Howse, "Retrenchment, Reform, or Revolution."

32. Joel Feinberg, *Harmless Wrongdoing,* chap. 29A (1988).

33. Robert N. Bellah, Richard Madsen, William M. Sullivan, Ann Swidler, and Steven M. Tipton, *Habits of the Heart* (1985).

34. Michael J. Trebilcock, Marsha Chandler, and Robert Howse, *Trade and Transitions* (1990).

35. See Jonathan Kozol, *Savage Inequalities* (1991).

36. See Robert Reich, *The Work of Nations* (1991).

37. Adam Smith, *Wealth of Nations,* 740.

38. John Stuart Mill, *Principles of Political Economy,* 950 (1965).
39. See Weiler, *Governing the Workplace;* David Beatty, *Putting the Charter to Work,* chap. 1 (1987).
40. See Murray, *Losing Ground;* Louis Kaplow, "An Economic Analysis of Legal Transitions," 99 *Harvard Law Review* 509 (1988).
41. Christopher Jencks, *Rethinking Social Policy: Race, Poverty, and the Underclass,* 82 (1992).
42. For such a set of proposals, see Ibid., chap. 6.
43. Donald McCloskey, *If You're So Smart: The Narrative of Economic Experience,* 162 (1990).
44. Arthur Okun, *Equality and Efficiency: The Big Trade-off,* 32 (1975).
45. Lindblom, *Politics and Markets,* 116.
46. Dennis Mueller, *Public Choice II,* chap. 2 (1989).
47. Ibid., Part II.
48. See, e.g., Robert Dahl, *A Preface to Democratic Theory* (1956).
49. See John Gray, *Liberalism,* chap. 8 (1986).
50. See Dan Usher, *The Economic Prerequisite to Democracy* (1981).
51. For a critical evaluation of the implications of public choice theory for the legal system, see Daniel Farber and Philip Frickey, *Law and Public Choice* (1991); Jerry Mashaw, "The Economics of Politics and the Understanding of Public Law," 65 *Chicago-Kent Law Review* 123 (1990); Daniel Farber, "Democracy and Disgust: Reflections on Public Choice," 65 *Chicago-Kent Law Review* 161 (1990).
52. Steven Kelman, *Making Public Policy: A Hopeful View of American Government* (1987); see also Mashaw, "Economics of Politics"; Farber, "Democracy and Disgust."
53. Mueller, *"Public Choice II,"* chap. 18.
54. Joseph Schumpeter, *Capitalism, Socialism, and Democracy,* 87 (1975).
55. David Beatty, *Talking Heads and the Supremes* (1990).
56. Michael Sandel, "The Political Theory of the Procedural Republic," in *The Power of Public Ideas,* 109 (Robert B. Reich, ed., 1988).
57. James Buchanan, *The Limits of Liberty: Between Anarchy and Leviathan,* chap. 10 (1975).
58. Alan Blinder, *Hard Heads, Soft Hearts: Tough-Minded Economics for a Just Society* (1987).
59. John Maynard Keynes, *The General Theory of Employment, Interest, and Money,* 383–384 (1936).
60. Buchanan, *Limits of Liberty,* 167.

Index of Cases

General Index

Abortion, 37–38, 51, 55
Adaptive preferences. *See* Preferences, adaptive
Admiralty law, 89
Adoption, 25, 26, 49, 54, 55, 56
Affirmative action, 189, 190, 197, 201, 203, 204, 206–207, 209–211, 239
Agency cost problems, 15, 115
Aghion, P., and B. Hermalin, 124–125
Agriculture, 5–6
Aivazian, V., M. Trebilcock, and M. Penny, 137
Alienation, 24
Allocation of resources: comparison of methods, 30–33, 231–232
Altruism, 3, 27–29, 34, 35, 36, 107, 183
Antitrust laws, 92, 95–96, 101
Arrow, K., 23, 27, 32
Autonomy, 7–9, 18–22; and marriage, 43, 45, 50; and surrogacy, 51; and commodification, 56–57; and externalities, 58, 75, 77; and legal moralism, 64, 68–69; and pornography, 72–73; and coercion, 79, 81; and tort law, 105; and default rules, 121; and sharing principle, 143; and paternalism, 147–150; and consideration, 164–166, 167, 168, 184; and discrimination, 192–195, 203–204, 206, 208; and consistency with private ordering, 242–244. *See also* Private ordering, critiques of
Ayers, I., and R. Gertner, 122–124

"Back-end" vs. "front-end" policies, 239–240
Baker, K., 44–47
Barnett, R., 84, 121, 165–166, 176, 181, 184
Base-line, moral. *See* Moral base-line
Bench-marks: in hiring, 209
Benson, P., 81, 83, 85, 86, 88, 91, 93, 99
Buchanan, James, 200–201, 205, 267, 268
Buckley, F., 83, 86, 88, 99, 165

Calabresi, G., 30–33, 60
Carens, J., 228–229, 233, 234, 235, 236
Cartel. *See* Monopolies
Censorship. *See* Freedom of expression
Charny, D., 121
Charter of Rights and Freedoms, Canadian, 68, 76, 266
Child custody, 43, 54
Child support, 43
Choice, constraints on. *See* Coercion; Information failure
Civic virtue, 265
Civil Rights Act (1964), 198
Coase, R., 54, 60
Coercion, 78–101; separation agreements, 44; surrogacy, 51, 52, 54; life-threatening risks, 84–87; non-life-threatening risks, 87–90; sexual favours, 90–91; monopolies, 91–97; necessity, 97–101
Cognitive deficiencies: and paternalism, 147, 150–151, 163; and unconscionability, 118–119